D1571208

PAUL D. SANSONE, O.F.M.

HOMOSEXUALITY IN GREEK MYTH

BERNARD SERGENT

Homosexuality in Greek Myth

Translated by
Arthur Goldhammer
With a Preface by
Georges Dumézil

Beacon Press   Boston

This publication was made possible in part by a grant from the French
Ministry of Culture.

Beacon Press
25 Beacon Street
Boston, Massachusetts 02108

Beacon Press books are published under the auspices
of the Unitarian Universalist Association
of Congregations in North America.

92   91   90   89   88   87   86   8   7   6   5   4   3   2   1

Library of Congress Cataloging in Publication Data
Sergent, Bernard.
   Homosexuality in Greek myth.

   Translation of: L'homosexualité dans la mythologie
grecque.
   Bibliography: p.
   Includes index.
   1. Homosexuality—Mythology.   2. Homosexuality—
Religious aspects.   3. Mythology, Greek.   4. Greece—
Religion.   I. Title.
BL795.H6S4713   1986   292'.178357662   85-73369
ISBN 0-8070-5700-2

Text design by Chris L. Smith

CONTENTS

PREFACE

by Georges Dumézil

Three quarters of a century ago, Bethe boldly violated an unavowed but effective taboo of classical philology by publishing, in the *Rheinisches Museum*, a justly famous article entitled "Die dorische Knabenliebe, ihre Ethic, ihre Idee" ("The Dorian Love of Boys, Its Ethic, Its Idea"). Yet as recently as 1916, at the Sorbonne, one of the subtlest connoisseurs of modern as well as ancient Greece, the illustrious Delphist Emile Bourguet, was explaining to graduate students Plato's *Symposium;* when he came to the scene that Victor Cousin had nobly entitled "Socrates refusing the presents of Alcibiades," he warned us "above all not to imagine things." Imagine? It was enough to read. Around the same time, one of the no less illustrious Croiset brothers, in a note to his *Démocratie athénienne*, warned the reader that what went on around the Parthenon in the fifth century B.C. had nothing to do with the odious counterfeit practiced today. Over the past half century the breach first opened by Bethe has widened. The bibliography has become, if anything, overburdened.

Croiset, if we leave aside his value judgment, was not entirely wrong—not, at any rate, if we turn our attention from Athens, already quite modern in this respect, and look instead, as Bethe did, at the Dorians of Crete and Laconia. There, the love, or at least sexual usage, of young boys was construed as a necessary social institution, which served a useful purpose and as such was the object of a justificatory ideology. As Bernard Sergent states below,

> With respect to the relationship between homosexuality and heterosexuality, Greece and Austronesia are patently similar, in contrast to societies such as our own, informed by Christian tradition. In these non-Christian societies, homosexuality is not the distinguishing trait of a minority group in one way or another marginal to the larger society but rather a normal alternative to heterosexuality. The same

men are first eromenoi, then erastai* or husbands or both. The homosexual relationship is a game in which anyone may take part, or at least any member of the dominant male group, and it is precisely the best and most powerful individuals in the society who do take part.

This is the point of departure for Bernard Sergent's book. Extending the work of Atsuhiko Yoshida on "Cretan lovers' gifts"—the three gifts that the erastes must give his eromenos when the former as it were returns the young man to circulation—Sergent points out the extent to which, on the Dorian island and in the Peloponnesus, this practice was informed by the same Indo-European trifunctional framework that shaped the political constitution. He does not, of course, conclude from this that the practice was, in its known form, inherited directly from the Indo-Europeans but simply that it is quite old, since the trifunctional framework soon ceased, throughout Greek territory, to operate as an ideological straitjacket. In Greek terms it was prehistoric. This finding enables him to state, in its full amplitude, the problem suggested by the title: To what extent do the large number of pederastic myths that we find (or suspect to have existed in earlier times) throughout Greece bear traces of an ideology that, as a living institution, is attested only among the last of the northern invaders of Greece, the Dorians? In large part, Sergent tells us, these are myths of *initiation*, involving the same key elements as the Dorian mechanisms: abduction and disappearance of the eromenos and life in the wilderness or at least away from society (with an important role assigned to hunting) in service of the erastes, resulting in a change in the status of the eromenos, either through entry into adult society or passage, in a figurative sense, into the other world, the world of the gods.

What remains to be determined in each case is the relation between each such myth and the well-known institutions that survived among the Dorians. At first sight there are three possibilities. A particular story may be a local myth corresponding to some little-known practice, where what little we do know conforms in some important respect to the Dorian model. Or it may be a purely mythical survival: The myth, after having served as the etiological foundation of some authentic practice, may have survived while the practice itself disappeared or changed form.

*These terms are defined at the beginning of Chapter 1.

Or, finally, the story may be pure literature, of relatively recent date, composed in free imitation of a tale of one of the first two types. Bernard Sergent gives reasons to believe that the first type is more abundantly represented than is generally allowed and that, given the state of our documentation, the second occurs far more frequently than the third down to Alexandrian times.

Readers thus have at their disposal not only the raw data but also brilliant applications of interpretive methods whose reliability and relevance for the analysis of each case or group of cases they may judge for themselves. As with any study based on analogies, debate is likely. It is to be hoped that anyone who wishes to challenge the author's conclusions will not lose sight of either the light that is here shed on the subject *as a whole* or the *internal consistency* of each and every demonstration. For example, the interpretation, following the general model, of the myth of Phorbas as the term-by-term inversion of a primitive myth is appealing by virtue of its simplicity and power. Many complex cases, such as that of Hylas, are here subsumed under a unifying principle that explains the successive phases of an evolving tradition.

I have so far mentioned only once the key word of this book. It bears repeating: *initiation*, that is, a ritual assuring a felicitous transition from a more "tender" age group to an older, more virile one, with help from, but also for the pleasure of, members of the latter group. Relations among adults form another subject, on which Bernard Sergent touches only slightly: in practice, for example, the Theban battalion, and, in epic, Achilles and Patroclus. To the latter pair he devotes a most sensible and tactful discussion, emphasizing one point that historians of literature and morals too often forget: the unwillingness of certain literary genres, particularly the epic, to state explicitly that which, present implicitly, gives the material its full meaning.

Are homosexuality and the love of boys properly studied in a comparative Indo-European context? This book places the question on the agenda. Both existed in the archaic Indo-European world outside Greece, but were the *forms* sufficiently typical or "improbable" that one may legitimately speak of a common heritage? As André Gide said of more elementary games, "such things are reinvented." Is it correct to speak of an "enigmatic Indo-European rite: paederasty," as Jan Bremmer does? That remains to be proven. It would be appropriate, if only it were possible, to broaden the comparison to include Cro-Magnon societies. Or Paraustralopithecine ones—for it all goes back to the freeing of the forelegs and the proliferation of neurons.

INTRODUCTION

In the state of civilization attained by the various Indo-European peoples by the time the earliest historical documents concerning them appear, the institutions comprising the rite of initiation, or ceremonies and often trials through which a particular segment of society passes from one status to another (a rite common to all "primitive" peoples), had vanished. Initiation was, except for a few special cases, no longer a living and fully meaningful institution. Yet we find traces of it, still quite clear, in the very earliest historical records of the Germans and Hellenes, and stylized or reinterpreted initiatory rituals are unmistakably attested in both classical Greece and historic India.[1]

Moreover, a fairly large number of Indo-European myths and a no less impressive number of institutions and cultural phenomena are readily interpreted as products of initiatory rites and myths.

Thus it is beyond doubt that in a certain state of civilization, roughly that which preceded the adoption of writing (I say roughly because many peoples in the Indo-European family rejected writing even after their cultures had reached a quite advanced stage: for example, the Gauls, the ancient Indians, and the Lacedaemonians), initiation, typically and essentially in the form of the promotion from adolescent to adult status, was universal in the Indo-European family of peoples, which stretched from the Atlantic to the Ganges, just as it has been found to be widespread more recently in a majority of peoples in many different parts of the world.[2]

Ethnographic work over the past century has demonstrated the frequency of an initiatory institution at variance with currently dominant western norms: the existence of a socially obligatory homosexual relationship between the master, or initiator, and the candidates to be initiated.

In our culture it is commonly thought that heterosexual behavior is normal and characteristic of the majority of people and that homosexual behavior is abnormal and characteristic only of a minority. In the worst case, the behavior of the minority is subject to moral censure. At best, the minority is acknowledged to have a right to behave differently from the majority. Midway between these is the medical view, which treats the minority as a case study in psychological deviance. Except in special circumstances (for instance, in wartime, when soldiers are obliged to reside together in barracks), it is commonly assumed that homosexuality and heterosexuality are strict alternatives, between which each individual must choose. Freud, for example, indicated that after a period of hesitation and indeterminacy in the choice of sexual object at puberty, nearly every individual chooses once and for all to be either heterosexual or homosexual (Freud does admit some exceptions to this rule, however, and he specifically allows for repression of the individual's true choice of object).[3] This restrictive definition of normal sexual behavior has had a profound effect on attitudes, so that, for example, a group like bisexuals, which is not easily classified according to this definition, is a priori placed with the deviant minority simply because its behavior includes homosexuality.[4]

What troubles many contemporary observers about the ancient customs I am discussing is the absence of a sharp division between normal and abnormal behavior; radically different notions are apparently confounded. As we shall see presently, many peoples do not distinguish between "homo" and "hetero" in sexual attraction or behavior. An individual's attraction to one sex in no way excludes her or his attraction to the other sex. Hence one of the central images of western culture, that of virility, is stunningly contradicted. Rather than identify virility with exclusively heterosexual behavior, as our own culture does (to such a degree that every male homosexual is ipso facto labeled effeminate), other cultures define social superiority—the superiority of the warrior, the leader, the shaman—in terms of homosexual behavior toward youths who will ultimately come to share their mentors' superior status.

This fundamental behavioral and psychosocial difference cannot be explained in terms of an opposition between Europeans and "savages" of other continents. Not only did the ancient Greeks take a different view of the relationship between homosexuality and heterosexuality, but there are, in fact, reasons to believe that homosexuality was a widespread and institutionalized practice, specifically related to initiatory rituals, among a number of protohistorical Indo-European peoples. I shall give two striking examples of this. One is a text by Strabo based on the Greek historian Ephorus, which concerns Cretan society in the fourth century

B.C. The other is a note by the Roman historian Ammianus Marcellinus concerning the Taifali, a Germanic people of the Gothic family, who followed in the footsteps of the Goths in the fourth century A.D. These two texts will serve as a foundation in reality for the analyses of various Greek myths which I shall give subsequently. In commenting on these texts I shall try to bring out the pedagogical, probative, and initiatory values of these institutions. The similarity between the two cases, which will, I think, become apparent, strongly suggests that the Cretan and Germanic institutions are based on a common, prehistoric tradition; since the peoples involved are, linguistically speaking, cousins, I shall therefore speak of an Indo-European institution.

This hypothesis can be strengthened, examined, and made more precise in two ways. One might attempt, first of all, to make an exhaustive study of sources bearing on the question, drawn from the various Indo-European peoples, and to push the investigation as far back as the limits of history will allow. Such an approach soon runs into difficulty, however; the abundance of the sources varies considerably from nation to nation. Sources are prodigious, even overwhelming, for the Greeks, but defective, incomplete, even altogether absent for other peoples. The second method of engaging the hypothesis is to explore a culture in which homosexuality is well attested and accepted as such in the local system of values, to see what role it plays in the most archaic system of representation. The hope is that this will provide not only familiarity with the institution's prehistory but also some sense of its connotations, correlations, and subtleties. Quite obviously, only Greece, with its prodigious mythology, can provide adequate documentation for such a study; only Greece satisfies the dual prerequisites of having known, accepted, and exalted pedagogical pederasty and of having discussed the subject, openly and without shame, in its myths. For this reason the second approach must precede the first: Armed with a diversity of examples and a wealth of symbolism drawn from the study of Greek myth, we may then embark upon comparative study of what remains of the institutions of related peoples.

At this stage of the investigation, I had best be cautious. I shall not state here to what extent this institution, with roots in the most ancient Hellenic past, deserves to be numbered among the structural features of the prehistoric Indo-European civilization that preceded the diaspora of various peoples who spoke languages of the Indo-European group. Much light has been cast on this civilization by several recent works.[5] Here my task is to lay as solid as possible a foundation for venturing such an opinion. I shall first attempt to establish the nature of the institution by examining the texts of Strabo and Ammianus and by comparing the evidence these contain with the customs of other peoples. Only then will I proceed to explore the astonishingly rich but treacherous terrain of myth. Study of institutionalized pederasty among other Indo-European peoples must be deferred to a subsequent work.

I
Foundations

ONE

The Cretans of Ephorus
and the Taifali
of Ammianus Marcellinus

器

In his description of Crete, Strabo of Amaseia, a writer who lived in the first century B.C., made extensive use of a lost work of Ephorus, a historian, geographer, and ethnographer of the fourth century B.C. The passage that touches on our present subject occurs in Strabo's *Geography* (X.4.21(483)).

They

have a unique custom in regard to erotic conventions. They do not win the objects of their love (erōmenoi) by persuasion but rather by abduction. (1) The lover apprises the friends and family of the youth three or more days beforehand that he is planning to abduct him. For them to hide the boy or not permit him to proceed along the ordained path is extremely shameful, since in effect they are publicly admitting that the boy is unworthy to get such a lover. When the parties come together, provided the abductor is an equal or a superior in rank or other circumstances to the youth, the boy's friends and family put on a merely token display of resistance and pursuit after the abductor, thus fulfilling what convention requires, after which they happily allow him to take the youth away. But in the opposite case, where the abductor is not a person of suitable rank, they take the youth from him. The limit of the pursuit is the point when the youth is led into the Andreium of the abductor. The most desirable youths, according to Cretan conventions, are not the exceptionally handsome ones but rather those who are distinguished for manly courage and orderly behavior. The lover gives the youth presents and takes him away to some place in the surrounding countryside that he chooses. The persons present at the abduction accompany them and spend two months feasting and hunting together (for it is not permitted to detain the boy longer), after which they come down again to the city.

The youth is sent home with presents, which consist of a military outfit, an ox, and a goblet (these are the gifts prescribed by convention), and besides these many other very costly gifts—so costly that the friends contribute each his share in order to diminish the expense. The youth sacrifices the ox to Zeus and gives a feast for those who came down with him from the mountains. He then declares, concerning his relationship with the lover, whether it took place with his consent or not; the convention encourages this in order that, if any violence is used against him in the abduction, he may restore his honor and break off the relationship.

For those who are handsome and have illustrious ancestors not to have lovers is disgraceful, since their rejection would be attributed to their bad character. The *parastathentes* ("standers-by")—for this is the term they use for those who are abducted—enjoy certain honors: at choral dances and at races they have the most honored places; they are permitted to wear the outfit presented to them by their lovers, which distinguishes them from other persons; and not only at that time, but in mature age, they appear in a distinctive dress, by which each individual is known to be *kleinos* ("famous"); *kleinos* is their equivalent term for *erōmenos*, and *philētor* ("befriender") for *erastēs*.

Here the word *lover* has been used to translate the Greek *erastēs*, which refers to the active partner in a sexual relationship, that is, the husband in a heterosexual couple and the person who plays the male role in a homosexual couple. In the latter case, the antonym of erastēs is *erō-menos*, the past participle of the verb *eramai*, "to desire sexually," in the passive form. Henceforth I shall use the terms *erastēs* (plural erastai) and *erōmenos* (plural erōmenoi) as though they were English words, to refer to the two roles in the initiatory homosexual relationship.

Ammianus Marcellinus, a Roman soldier and later a historian, was Greek by birth (he was born at Antioch, the great center of Hellenism in Syria) and lived in the second half of the fourth century. He wrote a history of the Roman Empire covering the years from 96 to 378 A.D. Only a part of this has survived, but he is our best historical source for the period that coincided with his own lifetime. Ammianus provides miscellaneous information about various Germanic peoples of the Gothic family, neighbors of the empire who, in the period he wrote about, became its invaders. In speaking of one particular people, the Taifali, he tells us about a custom that he describes as scandalous, doubtless anticipating the reaction of his audience and readers in high Roman society.

The Taifali had settled between the Carpathians and the Black Sea during the time when the Gothic peoples moved into the Ukraine (around 150–230 A.D.). Later, at the time of the Hun onslaught in 375, they were forced back toward the Danube and Roman territory. It was then that the imperial soldiers came to know this tribe. The Romans clashed with the Taifali on several occasions inside Roman borders and finally overcame them, sending scattered remnants fleeing toward Italy. Ammianus then writes (*Rerum Gestarum*, XXXI.9.5):

> We have learned that these Taifali were a shameful folk, so sunken in a life of shame and obscenity that in their country the boys are coupled with the men in a union of unmentionable lust, to consume the flower of their youth in the polluted intercourse of those paramours. We may add that, if any grown person alone catches a boar or kills a huge bear, he is purified thereby from the shame of unchastity [*incesti*].

It is obvious that both Strabo and Ammianus are referring to initiatory procedures. In the case of the Cretans, the activity is stylized and formalized; in the case of the Taifali, it is still a living tradition. Comparison of the two accounts, which undeniably illuminate one another, will bring this out more clearly.

Before beginning such comparison, however, it is important to demonstrate that the two texts are entirely independent. For if one is merely an indirect reflection of the other, the comparison no longer makes sense, except perhaps for philologists.

Numerous authors, from the Victorian period onward, have attempted to minimize the importance of the passage from Ammianus. For example, before taking up the problem of homosexuality among the peoples of northern Europe in his masterful study of Greek astrology, A. Bouché-Leclercq proposed the following argument: Aristotle was the first to attribute homosexual practices to the Celts.[2] His doing so was an instance of what we would call "projection": Greece laid its own vices upon the barbarians. All the writers who seem to confirm this account in fact derive from Aristotle.[3] Among them, Ptolemy extended the calumny by applying it to all the peoples of the north. It followed that it was true of the Germans: Sextus Empiricus repeated the charge against them, based on hearsay. Finally, Bouché-Leclercq argues, this reputation for wickedness came to be embodied in practices attributed to the Taifali and Heruli and other obscure peoples.[4]

If this argument is correct, then obviously Ammianus's text is purely literary and ultimately derives from homosexual practices of the Greeks themselves, including the Cretan ritual Strabo describes; in other words, the two texts are not independent.

But Bouché-Leclercq's analysis does not withstand serious scrutiny. To see that Aristotle's assertion does not account for all the subsequent texts one has only to consult them; moreover, there is a Welsh tradition that corroborates the data.[5] Hence the notion that homosexuality was common among the Celts cannot be simply a Greek "projection." Although there is less information concerning the Germans, the way Bouché-Leclercq deals with Ammianus's text is inadmissible: The Taifali are indeed an obscure people—obscure to us, precisely because Ammianus and his comrades did away with them. But to Roman soldiers in the period 375–78 they were a very important and well-known group that operated independently of the Goths (unlike the Skires, Bastarnae, Ruges, Heruli, and Alans, who joined with contingents of Ostrogoths and Visigoths) and therefore had to be dealt with specially. In the Balkans in 376–77 there was a Taifale "problem" just as there was a quite similar Goth "problem." Ammianus Marcellinus could not have said whatever he pleased about these people, for among his listeners in the Roman salons there must have been officers capable of confirming or refuting his assertions. Finally, the custom that he reports is too specific, too "barbarous" (non-Greek), too little Roman, to be taken as a mere borrowing from the general remarks made by Ptolemy and Sextus Empiricus. It looks back beyond Aristotle to the Cretan custom, not as an imitation of that custom but as another embodiment of the same underlying theme, initiation.

The parallelism is in fact astonishing. In both cases we have a relationship between two persons. One is a young man, the *puber*, as Ammianus calls the young Taifale, or *pais*, as Strabo calls the young Cretan (literally "child," but the term was commonly used to refer to an adolescent, the erōmenos,[6] and that is the case here). The affair is ended, moreover, with the gift of a warrior's gear, which implies that the *pais* is no longer a "child" as we would use the term. The fact that he has companions of his own age capable of offering physical opposition to his abductor corroborates this interpretation. Strabo refers to the other party as an erastēs, a term with a strict meaning in Greek: It always denotes a mature man, old enough at least to have a beard, whereas the erōmenos is by definition beardless.[7] The erastēs is a man capable of entering into marriage; Strabo's text pushes quite far the analogy between marriage and the Cretan initiatory ritual. It has long been noted that abduction, here so formalized, is also mentioned in Spartan legislation as a means of acquiring a spouse (obviously no one will doubt that in historic Sparta this was also a highly formalized procedure).[8] Later, the feasts, the gifts and countergifts, and especially the considerable quantity of goods that the erastēs must gather together to give to his erōmenos are all reminiscent of a universal, and certainly a Greek, typology of marriage. *Mas*, says Ammianus, literally "male." Here, opposed to *puber* (obviously also a male) rather than to *femina*, the word surely means "mature male," adult, as the translators and commentators have understood it. Taken absolutely, the word generally did mean just that; when Ovid wished to speak of "young boys," he used the expression *teneri mares*.

The relationship between the two men is pedagogical. This is not clearly stated by either author, but I will show that this was indeed the case. In any event, there is a clear suggestion of a pedagogical relationship: The crucial activity for the Cretans as well as the Taifali is hunting. According to Strabo, the erastēs leaves the city with his erōmenos, accompanied by "the persons present at the abduction," namely the young abductee's comrades and friends, who can only be other adolescents of his "age group." This is consistent with Dorian and Greek tradition,[9] and apart from these boys the young Cretan aristocrat would have been under the protection not of "friends" but of "kin." Thus an adult man leads a troop of young men into the hills and mountains, into the uncultivated regions *eskhatiē* that served as boundaries between cities. For two months they feast and hunt; indeed, they eat what they hunt, for they did not take with them sufficient provisions to last two months. Their hunting is therefore successful, and on its success depends the group's "survival." That the erastēs, the only adult male present, plays a crucial role as leader, organizer, and instructor is beyond doubt. This pedagogical element is not obvious in Ammianus's text, but here, too, the crucial point is that the hunt is "successful," only now success is defined not in terms of meeting daily needs but rather as the completion of the young man's testing and his promotion to the status of adult warrior. Though Ammianus is silent on this point, it is easy to imagine, with the aid of the Cretan parallel and others that will be mentioned in due course, that the Taifale *puber* is able to kill a bear or capture a boar because the *mas* with whom he engaged in the "shameful" relations to which Ammianus alludes has also taught him what he needs to know in order to carry off such an exploit.

The pedagogical relationship is complemented by a sexual one. Ammianus's horrified vocabulary shows this clearly, as does Strabo's use of the common terms *erastēs* and *erōmenos*.

Where and when did these sexual and educational activities take place? Ephorus, Strabo's source, is explicit: during the two months of hunting outside the city. By analogy with African initiatory customs, and following the lead of Henri Jeanmaire, I will say the events transpired during the phase of testing "in the bush." The place and duration are typical of an initiation. It is in connection with a liminal experience, outside society, that the initiator in many primitive communities conveys to the candidates knowledge of life, of practical techniques, and of tribal traditions. Greek accounts, as in Plato, for example, show homosexual couples engaged in training activities, similar to initiations; these couples are in many ways unlike the Cretan couple of erastēs and erōmenos but in their own way stable. Ammianus describes a different kind of initiation procedure, one that has no fixed and limited duration but involves a sexual relationship that begins with the puberty of the erōmenos and may continue indefinitely into adult life, so long as the hunting trial has not been completed. Thus we have two initiatory models, both of which may be quite old, for various traditions indicate the coexistence of both traditions among both Greeks and Germans. In one case the exploit that qualifies a man as an adult warrior is real, not staged, and the situation that creates inferiority is of indefinite duration. This type of trial exists among many primitive peoples. In the other case, in fact more common, the initiation is ritualized. The trials may be staged or even completely eliminated. And it is the candidates' age that determines their promotion to the status of adult citizen. In historical Greek cities we find many traces of this second procedure, but in their myths and certain of their customs we also find survivals of the first.

Except for this difference of method, the places and times are the same in the two customs under consideration. Both involve adolescents who are led, in each case at a different pace, to the end of childhood, which is to say, to the threshold of adulthood. It is during this institutionalized period of initiation that pedagogical and homosexual relations occur. As for the site of initiation, if we assume, as I have above, that the adult Taifale serves as hunting instructor for his erōmenos, then like his Cretan counterpart he must have taken his companion "into the bush," into the vast forests of northern Europe, such as the Hercynian forest, which often served as boundaries between the Germanic tribes.[10] Even in the final trial, it is doubtful that the young hunter really chased the boar or confronted the bear alone. The most celebrated Scandinavian text concerning initiation (and like the Goths the Taifali were surely natives of

Scandinavia), which deals with the young and timid Höttr's being taught to hunt by Bödhvar,[11] emphasizes the fact that Bödhvar, the king, and various warriors are present as spectators at Höttr's exploit. To sum up, then, the Cretan erōmenos went into the bush for a fixed period of two months, during which his erastēs taught him to hunt and meanwhile slept with his pupil. By contrast, we can only assume that among the Germans the master spent a longer, discontinuous period with his disciple, frequently taking him hunting and using him as a lover (which he may also have done between hunting expeditions) until the day of the final trial.

Finally, the end of the testing phase is clearly indicated in both accounts, and in both cases it results in the promotion of the youth to the status of socially responsible adult.

The Cretan erōmenos, who could not fail to win glory as a hunter in the eyes of his master and comrades, received three institutionalized gifts; I shall have more to say later on about the symbolic and historical importance of these gifts.[12] Besides those gifts legally defined as an essential part of the ritual, there was an imposing array of other presents, since, as Ephorus (Strabo) tells us, the friends of the erastēs—adults this time, members of his own age cohort—contributed to help him out; these were, as the text makes clear, aristocrats, the cream of Cretan society. This gift giving, a kind of potlatch, confirms and adds to the importance of the moment. The erōmenos then participates in an essential ritual: He sacrifices an ox—the largest of the potential victims—to Zeus, the most important of the gods. One wonders if this sacrifice was not the equivalent, inverted and urbanized, of the hunting trial that Ammianus reports was used by the Taifali.[13] In any case it was in itself a "trial" for a young man just finishing adolescence. There is, however, another proof of the promotion to adult status: Among the three institutionalized gifts was a soldier's gear. The hunt, symbolically homologous to sacrifice, was also homologous, in terms of continuity, to war; the manhunt was the logical extension of the hunt for the wild beast.[14] This was not simply a matter of technical skills or courage: in a society such as the Greek, structurally organized for war, the adult warrior and the citizen were one and the same.[15]

As much can be said, evidently, of the Taifali. Ammianus's account, much less specific than Ephorus's genuinely ethnographic work, does not yield the same kind of explicit symbolism. But what little it does tell us is perfectly clear: The hunting exploit concludes the phase of sexual subjection. It takes place, says the historian, when the *pubes* has become *adultus*: that is, biologically mature, fully grown, but not socially or civically adult. Physically, the *adultus* is capable of performing the exploit, and this capability alone determines when he is ready to accede to a higher social status. Ammianus does not specify the nature of this status, but it undoubtedly meant equality with the *mares*, the adult males or warriors previously distinguished from the *puberes*. Numerous Greek texts corroborate these facts: The erōmenos ceased to be an erōmenos when his beard began to grow,[16] or in other words with the appearance of the biological sign of transition from the state of *pubes* to that of *adultus*, which here also implies transition from the state of erōmenos to that of erastēs. We are not told whether the young Taifale's heroic hunt is celebrated with a feast, a sacrifice, or gifts; some German parallels suggest that certain of these elements were present, but leave that aside. The essential thing, the passage from one social state to another by dint of an initiatory exploit, Ammianus deigned to "add" in his concluding remarks.

That the hunt led in both cases to completion of the initiation, that is, to accession to adult status, can in any case be interpreted in two ways. On the one hand a symbolic act demonstrates that the youth is capable of rivaling adults in physical strength, and in this respect it is significant that in one case the initiation ends with the capture or slaying of the largest wild mammals, while in the other case it ends with the sacrifice, or slaying, of the largest domestic mammal. On the other hand, Ephorus's account tells us that the young Cretans, led by their erastēs/ initiator, actually spent two months hunting and thus proved that they were capable of providing their own subsistence, which would obviously be their duty as adults. A similar concern underlies the Taifali hunting exploit; for anyone physically strong enough and skilled enough to capture the largest edible wild animal in Europe, and to kill the most feared carnivore, is a fortiori capable of dealing with lesser game.

Thus the parallelism of the two customs is clear in a variety of respects. At the same time, the archaism of the themes underlying these rituals is also evident. In both cases the notion that hunting was the basis of the food supply was anachronistic: the Germans of Ammianus's time lived by agriculture and breeding, with hunting serving only as a supplement.[17] As in certain analogous Greek and Celtic traditions, boar-hunting had no economic value.[18] As for the Cretans, it was actually quite a gamble to try to feed even a small group of men on what game they could capture in the island's already largely deforested hills. In both instances we are looking at survivals, conscious survivals to be sure, of an economic and ecological state no longer prevailing when the texts were written.

There are also other proofs that these notions were quite old, indeed rooted in the prehistory of Europe.

TWO
The Antiquity of the
Cretan Traditions
卍

Ammianus's account of the Taifali is too laconic and our knowledge of the Germans prior to the great invasions is too superficial to shed much light on the antiquity of the ritual he describes. At most, other Germanic initiatory rituals confirm that peoples closely related to the Taifali were not unfamiliar with the notions of a change of life and trial by heroic exploit.[1]

Matters stand rather differently in Greece. There, the universality of initiatory homosexuality, which I examine in the next few chapters, suggests that the phenomenon was fairly ancient. More than that, Ephorus's text directly evokes the earliest Indo-European history.

THREE GIFTS . . .

The erastēs, we are told, gives to the erōmenos at the end of his "sojourn in the bush" three gifts "prescribed by convention": a soldier's gear, an ox, and a goblet. The term here translated as "drinking cup" appears in Strabo's text as *potērion*—strictly speaking, a "vessel for drinking," more generally, a "cup." In Herodotus, the Egyptians, "the most scrupulously religious of all men," drink from *potēria* of bronze, which they clean thoroughly every day (II. 37); Maeandros, fleeing Samos, arrives in Sparta and there displays his treasures, in particular, *potēria* of gold and silver (III. 148); in one French translation of Herodotus (by P.-E. Legrand) the first occurrence of *potērion* is translated as "goblet" (*gobelet*), the second as "vessel" (*vase*).[2] Larcher, however, translates consistently as "cup." In the New Testament *potērion* refers to the eucharistic chalice.[3] Note that whatever the object is, goblet or cup, in all these examples it is precious or of religious value.

We are indebted to the Greek scholar Athenaeus of Naucratis, writing in the early third century A.D., for further details concerning the Cretan *potērion*: he tells us that *chonnos* is the word "used by the people of

Gortyn for a kind of cup (*potērion*), similar to a *thericleios* and made of bronze; it is given to the boy who has been abducted by an erastēs, according to Hermonax."[4]

Athenaeus's encyclopedic work on all aspects of nourishment, the *Deipnosophists*, was composed entirely of citations from earlier works. Hermonax was an Alexandrian, probably of the Hellenistic period. Thus here is a source, slightly later than Ephorus but completely independent of him, which magisterially confirms one detail of his account. As for the *thericleios*, Athenaeus explains elsewhere that it is a kind of *kylix*, or especially deep cup with a raised foot and sides that apparently curved inward. It is named after Thericles, the Corinthian potter said to have created it.[5]

In a recent brief but careful study of pederasty, the Dutch scholar Jan Bremmer sought to determine the specific meaning of each of the three gifts. The cup played a part, first of all, in several significant Greek rituals. In Athens for example, it figured in the great festival of the phratries, the Apaturia, during which *ephēboi* (ephebes) or new citizens were inscribed on the rolls of the demes. As Louis Gernet has written, "this integration was the modern and routinized form of the rites of adolescence, which in prehistoric times must have involved actual initiation; moreover, one of those rites was perpetuated," namely, the shearing of the hair of the ephebes. The mythical model for this rite was provided by Theseus, the heroic founder of the Athenian initiatory rites, at the end of a journey from Troezen to Athens that was filled with tests of his prowess as warrior and hunter.[6] Now, as Gernet goes on to say, the festival of Apaturia "requires the ministry of those referred to as *oinoptai* ('wine pourers'), who are responsible for the performance of various duties, especially the supervision of the offerings of wine during the first day of the feast. For this meeting of the phratries was synonymous with carousing, and those gathered at the feast consumed the sacrificial beasts and the wine contributed by the fathers of the newly admitted youths. The contribution of wine was known as the *oinistēria*; the same word denoted a libation that the ephebes offered to Heracles at another hair-shearing ceremony accompanied by drinking, whose cost they bore."[7]

Without belaboring the point, I might note the archaism of the components of the Apaturia: the phratries, for example, for which the festival in question was the principal ritual, preserved the Indo-European term *phrater* (in Greek, "member of a clan" and not "brother"), whereas other words of this type had disappeared from Greek. Similarly, another initiatory rite, the consecration of a lock of hair, is equally remarkable for its archaism.

In this use of drinking cups Gernet sees "the trace of those compulsory occasions of generosity that are the ancestors of 'liturgies' and here mark the promotion of a group of young men." It is important to say why this is so. In Hellenic culture, the drinking of wine was essentially a symbolic act: It defined a "man," in the narrow sense of the word. Women and children did not drink wine, and the barbarians differed from the Hellenes in that they either did not drink wine or did so as savages, that is, without mixing it with water. The manner of consumption was also important: Wine was not drunk alone but with others, in a civic and ritual encounter known as the symposium, or banquet. The participants in the banquet were the citizens of the city. In a number of places women were not allowed to participate,[8] nor were children and adolescents (which for our purposes is the important point). Aelian even tells us that everyone under the age of 35 was excluded.[9]

It follows that the gift of a cup conferred the right to participate in the banquet. Just as the soldier's gear created the soldier, that is, the adult warrior, and the ox created the adult male capable of offering a sacrifice, so did the cup authorize its recipient to take his place at the symposium, the civic festival of the society's males.

In Rome and Greece young men of good family could attend banquets, but only in the role of cupbearers.[10] In the *Odyssey* the young son of Menelaus serves as cupbearer in his house.[11] In Athens Euripides was a cupbearer in his youth, as was Sappho's brother in Lesbos.[12] In the Poseidonia of Ephesus, young boys who bore the cult title of *tauroi* poured the wine.[13] The cupbearers of Alexander[14] and Pyrrhus of Epirus[15] were also young nobles. All had a celebrated mythical prototype: Ganymede, the Trojan prince and erōmenos of Zeus, cupbearer of the gods.[16] Following Bremmer, I emphasize the differences of status: The fathers or erastai, men of high birth, citizens, recline and hold out their cups; it is they who drink. The sons, no less illustrious by birth, are standing; they serve and do not drink.

In an admirable and celebrated study of libation in ancient Scandinavia, Cahen has noticed a correlation, in several legends, between initiatory episodes and the fact of drinking.[17] The ritual consumption of an alcoholic beverage was therefore taken as a sign of accession to adulthood well before the Greeks discovered wine. This was one meaning of the cup offered to the young Cretan; another will be indicated presently.

The gift of military gear can obviously be interpreted as representing a promotion in civic status. Bremmer therefore sought to interpret the meaning of the ox, the last of the three gifts, by examining Greek myths involving combat between a hero and a bull. Such combat is indubitably an initiatory trial: One of Heracles's first labors is to capture, by himself and nowhere other than in Crete, a fearsome bull.[18] Theseus, model of the Athenian ephebes, captures a miraculous bull at Marathon and sacrifices it to Delphic Apollo before leaving for Crete to battle the Minotaur. Both myths probably contain Minoan influences. No doubt it was for this reason that Arthur Evans, the excavator of Cnossus, put forward the bold hypothesis, repeated, oddly enough, by R. F. Willetts, that the Cretan ritual described by Ephorus reflected the ancient organization of groups of youths who served the Minoan king.[19] The problem is that there is no proof that the Cretan bullfights had the character of an initiation or trial or that the animals involved were sacrificed. The idea of sacrificing the bull appears to have been Greek rather than Minoan: Theseus is an Athenian hero, Heracles an Argive hero, and in an Aetolian myth that I shall examine, the hero Phylius, after completing three trials, sacrifices two bulls that he has captured for the young man with whom he is in love.[20] Bremmer also makes comparisons with the many instances of bull sacrifice in continental ephebic rituals. In Attica the Theseus myth was the basis of a rite in which the ephebes led a bull to the altar and sacrificed it; several inscriptions allude to this rite. The ephebes of Tanagra in Boeotia also sacrificed an ox. There are traces of similar rituals in other places.[21]

I differ with Bremmer, however, on the following grounds: An ox is not exactly the same thing as a bull, and the generality of ox sacrifice must be significant, as is the discordance, in Attica, between the founding myth (the capture and sacrifice of a bull) and the ritual (sacrifice of an ox). This recalls certain Roman facts. Jupiter, the sovereign god, received only castrated victims as sacrifices. By contrast, Mars, the warrior god, and Janus, the god of beginnings, received only intact male victims. An exact parallel to this distinction can be found in Vedic India: One of the specific victims of sacrifices to the sovereign gods Mitra and Varuna was a sterile cow, in contrast to the pregnant cow offered to Aditi, mother of the gods, and to the Maruts, or divine "plebs." After analyzing these data, Georges Dumézil proposed the following interpretation, based on ancient Indian commentaries: "The sovereign gods' aversion to the sacrifice of intact males symbolically expresses the fact that their actions, their services, are not of the order of engendering; they do not procreate, they create, and they create more than they would procreate."[22] The sacrifice of an ox to Zeus, quite common in ancient Greece, very likely reflects this attitude, which the first Greeks must have shared with the ancestors of the Latins and Aryans. But the myth is also influential in other ways: It links the sacrifice of a bovid to the theme of a probative trial; and, since there is very little merit in capturing and killing an ox, it restores, ideally, the intact animal. Rather than embarking here on an exhaustive study of the subject, I shall limit myself to the simple remark that in three major festivals celebrating Zeus as defender of a city—Athens (the Dipoleia, for Zeus Polieus), Cos (also for Zeus Polieus), and Magnesia on the Maeander (for Zeus Sosipolis)—oxen were sacrificed to the god. And Willetts, who rightly alludes to the Cretan ritual, emphasizes the correlations between these festivals and the ephebic ritual.[23]

In Athens, for example, the Dipolia were immediately followed by the Disoteria, which, like the former, linked Zeus and Athena; the Disoteria, however, involved a procession of ephebes, who also participated in a boat race.[24] Accordingly, the gift of an ox to the erōmenos enabled him to take part in a major civic ritual. In fact, the young man sacrificed the animal and staged a banquet, at which he also made use of the cup (it, too, received as a gift) for drinking wine. The three gifts mark the promotion of the young Cretan to the rank of citizen; one makes him a warrior, another gives him the right to participate in the banquet, a typical civic festival, and the third gives him the right to make sacrifices.

That is not all, however. The fact that the gifts are precisely three in number, as "prescribed by convention," opens further horizons.

. . . AND THREE FUNCTIONS

The cup, in particular, has another meaning in Greek symbolism, and this meaning will orient the discussion of the overall sense of the three gifts. In an article published in 1965, the Japanese scholar Atsuhiko Yoshida studied the role of the cup in the myths of the Greeks and other Indo-European peoples.[25] The famous story of the tripod of the seven sages is well known: The object, found in the sea by the inhabitants of Cos or one of the Ionian cities, was, according to an inscription on it or a Delphic oracle, supposed to be given "to the wisest" of the Greeks. The first to receive it was Thales of Miletus, but he then gave it to another wise man, who did the same, and so on until it came into the hands of the seventh and last sage (the list varies). In certain versions of the story, the object involved is a cup rather than a tripod, and since we know that Delphi appropriated the story and modified it to its own advantage, there is reason to believe that the cup version is older than the tripod version. Yoshida then calls attention to an astonishing parallel.

> The Narte epic of the modern Caucasians, which can certainly be traced back to a Scythian tradition,[26] in fact mentions a large magical cup that has the virtue of bringing out the best in the hero: This *Narty-amongä* [the cup] in fact betakes itself during banquets to the lips of the Narte who can boast of the most brilliant exploits.[27]

In both cases, clearly, the cup moves from one location to another in order to single out excellence.

This calls to mind another, authentically Scythian, tradition, which helps to shed further light on the Cretan custom. According to Herodotus, the first man to live in Scythia, Targitaos, had three sons, Lipoxais, Arpoxais, and, the youngest, Colaxais. In their time a number of golden objects fell from the sky: a plow, a yoke, an ax, and a cup. The eldest of the sons of Targitaos went toward them to gather them up, but as he did so the metal caught fire. Then Arpoxais tried his hand and met with the same misfortune. Finally, Colaxais tried to pick up the objects, and this time the gold did not burn. His brothers immediately ceded the kingship to him, without further ado.[28] The predestined sovereign thus took possession of the symbols of kingship, which became the royal treasure and objects of an annual feast.[29]

But why these four objects? Their significance has now been clearly elucidated. Following Arthur Christensen,[30] Georges Dumézil has shown[31] "that these four objects, which cannot be separated and which are preserved by the supreme ruler of the Scythians, symbolize the 'three functions' that formed one of the main frameworks of the thought of the Indo-Iranians, who are in this instance the faithful repositories of an Indo-European tradition: The cup is the instrument of the cult and of feasts, the ax is an arm of war, and the plow and the yoke evoke agriculture; furthermore, Emile Benveniste[32] has given a philological reason for regarding the 'plow and yoke' as a single object."[33]

This interpretation is confirmed by a story told by Quintus Curtius, which has the advantage of being independent of Herodotus and of originating with Scythians other than those whose traditions Herodotus collected. Herodotus's subjects lived west of the Caspian, while the

Scythians on whom Quintus Curtius relied lived to the east. They give the following account to Alexander, who wishes them to submit to his rule:

> Know that we have received as a gift an ox-yoke, a plow, a lance, an arrow, a cup. We use these with our friends and against our enemies. To our friends we give the fruits of the earth that the labor of the oxen gives us; and with them, we use the cup to offer the gods libations of wine; as for our enemies, we attack them from afar with the arrow, and at short range with the lance.[34]

Thus in both lists four objects correspond to three notions—agricultural production, war, religion—and these three notions correspond exactly to the "three functions" of the ancient Indo-European theology, well known since the celebrated work of Georges Dumézil: namely, kingship and religion (first function), physical strength and in particular warfare (second function), and productivity, prosperity, and health (third function).

The significance of the cup for the Scythians, together with some less clear-cut data concerning the Celts,[35] supports Yoshida's interpretation (in 1964) of the three gifts given by the Cretan erastēs. He pointed out the cultural significance of the cup; in addition, "the ox, an agricultural and comestible animal . . . was closely connected, for the Indo-Europeans and others, with the mysteries of fertility,[36] and often occupied the third position in trifunctional schemes.[37] [Similarly, in the text of Quintus Curtius] the ox is manifestly associated with the agricultural and nutritive function and the cup with the sacerdotal office. Since the warrior's gear is obviously associated with the second function, the three gifts in question clearly evoke the three functions of the Indo-European system."[38]

On the whole, Greek religious concepts do not obey the rules that governed ancient Indo-European theology.[39] In numerous instances, however, it is easy to discover survivals of the trifunctional ideology in religion, mythology, and literature.[40] It then becomes clear that, apart from a few noteworthy exceptions (certain texts of Plato, for example), these occurrences of trifunctionality stem from the oldest religious sources in Greece, frequently with Mycenaean roots.[41] Hence Crete was not an oddity in the Greek world, and Yoshida's analysis gains support from other instances in which Indo-European trifunctionality was used outside Crete.

Yoshida, who has made large contributions to the search for these occurrences in ancient Greece, reports a tradition in which the cup again seems to signify the first function. According to the Hellenistic poet Lycophron, Menelaus, having gone astray on his *nostos*, or return from Troy, approached the temple of Athena Sculatria in southern Iapygia, a famous sanctuary located between Cape Iapygia (today Santa Maria di Leuca) and Otranto.[42] There he made three offerings: a shield, Helen's slippers, and a crater (wind bowl).[43] Since Helen was above all for women what Aphrodite was for goddesses, a symbol of love, it is likely that this is a set of trifunctional gifts.[44]

In this connection, it is worth noting that, according to Strabo, this sanctuary of Athena was found among the Sallentines, and that "these Sallentines are said to have come from Crete as colonists."[45] Is the correspondence with the three Cretan gifts precise? There is reason to think not. Even if the assuredly ancient tradition that Cretans settled in southern Italy has some historical basis,[46] it is clear that this sanctuary of Athena, Greek or Hellenized, was a creation of the Greek colonizers of the first millennium B.C. In this particular region, that most probably means it was a creation of the Tarentines.[47] Tarentum was a colony of Sparta,[48] and at Sparta, or more precisely at nearby Therapnae, there was a cult of Helen, in which the Indo-European trifunctional theology is attested in the myth of Helen's three marriages.[49] Thus the tradition reported by Lycophron seems to have been authentically ancient, having actually originated with the sanctuary of Athena created by the Tarentines, no doubt shortly after their settlement in Italy. This bolsters Yoshida's interpretation, not only here but also in the case of the three Cretan gifts.

It is true that a tradition reported by Pliny holds that Helen gave a cup as an offering in the temple of Athena of Lindus (at Rhodes), and that this cup, far from evoking the first function, was exactly proportioned to the breast of Menelaus's spouse.[50] In trifunctional terms, it therefore belongs entirely to the realm of the third function, being both a gift of Helen and a symbol of femininity. But this tradition, late and unique of its kind, smacks of a belated literary development and is countered by all other occurrences of the cup as a symbolic object. Another cup occurs in the prophecy that Lycophron attributes to Alexandra (Cassandra), a gift from Medea to the god Triton: It became the symbol of the sovereignty of a Libyan tribe, the Asbustai.[51]

Another cross-check confirms the interpretation of the cup as a symbol of the "first function." Earlier, following Yoshida, we compared the cup (or tripod) of the seven Greek sages with the Osset cup, the *Narty-amonga*. The Greek cup was a sign of intellectual value, but no tradition relates it to the trifunctional schema. Not so of the *Narty-amonga*. The Nartes, the paradigmatic heroes of the Ossets, are divided into three "families," a division that has been recognized, ever since the earliest studies of Indo-European trifunctionality, as an exemplary application of trifunctional theology. From the abundant mythological material first revealed to the West and studied by Georges Dumézil, I extract the briefest characterization, due to the Osset folklorist D. A. Tuganov: "The Boratae were rich in livestock, the Alaegatae were strong in intelligence, the Aexsaertaegkatae were valiant and strong in their men."[52]

Dumézil has shown the original structural character of this division of the three qualities among different factions of the Ossets (clearest, in point of fact, among the northern Ossets) as well as its roots in Scythian history, where, as noted earlier, trifunctionality is well attested.[53]

Now in this classification, where the Boratae clearly correspond to the third function, the Alaegatae to the first, and the Aexsaertaegkatae to the second, it would appear, a priori, that the *Narty-amonga* should be associated with the Aexsaertaegkatae, since it serves to designate the heroes who perform great physical exploits, that is, the valiant. Yet it is the Alaegatae, the representatives of the first function, who possess the miraculous vessel, and it is they who stage the banquet at which the heroes distinguish themselves.

> Each family [*narte*] and each individual stages [banquets] according to the rules, possibly inviting another family to join in. The "receptions" of the Alaegatae are something else again: their house is the meeting place of all the Nartes, and it does not seem to be up to them whether these meetings do or do not take place: their principal role is to organize the *kuvd*. In these meetings, each table has its chairman, as in real life, and these chairmanships are given to the most important guests. But the Alaegatae retain the leading role. For example, it is they who decide when the magic vessel, which is in their safekeeping, should be brought in, and it is they who establish the conditions surrounding the "challenge competition" that takes place during the rounds of drinking.[54]

Hence it is probable that the Greek myth of the cup of the seven sages, the *Narty-amonga* with its Scythian antecedents, and their Celtic equivalents represent a very ancient Indo-European symbolism. A cultural object, the cup can be "loaned" to the warriors but must not on that account leave the sphere of sovereignty. This confirms the archaism of the Cretan tradition studied here.

Finally, the point that clinches the authentic structural character of the Cretan tradition and precludes viewing it as a random coincidence is that trifunctionality also informs (though Yoshida did not notice this) the fundamental theme of choice of the erōmenos in the Cretan tradition. Strabo writes: "The most desirable youths, according to Cretan conventions, are not the exceptionally handsome ones but rather those who are distinguished for manly courage and orderly behavior." In other words, the erōmenos is chosen on the basis of criteria typical of the first and second functions, and by exclusion of what is characteristic of the third. If doubt remains on this point, we have only to refer to Plato. At the end of book III of the *Republic*, the philosopher introduces typical trifunctional criteria of classification, which then inform the rest of the work.[55] He begins with a theory of musical rhythms, whose elaboration must obey the following rules: "We must not pursue complexity nor great variety in the basic movements, but must observe what are the rhythms of a life that is orderly and brave."[56] The rest of the work shows that variety and complexity are associated with the third function; that is why democracy corresponds to the power of the third social class.[57] Thus music must conform to the rules of an "orderly and brave" life—the first and second functions—while excluding the characteristics of the third function.[58]

More than that, it is, according to Strabo, still citing Ephorus, the Cretan constitution itself that is organized around trifunctionality.

With respect to the form of government, which Ephorus has described at large, it will be sufficient to give a cursory account of the principal parts. The law-giver, says Ephorus, seems to lay down as the foundation of his constitution, the greatest good that states can enjoy, namely, liberty; for it is this alone which makes the goods which a man possesses his own; in a state of slavery they belong to the rulers rather than to the ruled. The liberty which men enjoy must be guarded. Social harmony occurs when the dissensions that arise from greed and luxury are eliminated; for when all lead a well-balanced and simple life, no one has cause for envy or arrogance or hatred against those who are like him. To that end, the law orders that boys join what the Cretans call *agelai* and that adults take their meals together in *andreiai*, so that the poorest, maintained at public expense, can share the same fare as the rich. And to foster courage rather than cowardice they are raised from childhood with weapons and in harsh conditions, so that children learn not to be afraid of heat or cold or steep and rocky paths or of the blows they receive in exercises in the gymasium or in orderly battles. They also practice wielding the bow and dancing in armor as first demonstrated by the Couretes and later by Pyrrhichus, organizer of the dance which bears the name pyrrhic in his memory, so that even their games contribute to training them for war.[59]

In other words, the constituents, in order to achieve their ideal of liberty, employed three different means: two positive (concord between citizens and military education) and one negative (elimination of greed and of the taste for luxury through egalitarianism of economic opportunity and education).

There is a clear analogy between the "correctness" required of the eromenos, the "harmony" (or orderliness) invoked by Plato, and the "concord" sanctioned by Cretan law: All pertain to the first function, one of whose two main gods was, in ancient India, Mitra, the god of "contract," of proper understanding between the members of a society.[60]

CRETAN PEDERASTY

We do not know where Ephorus obtained his information about Crete. In his day the island contained a large number of independent and diverse cities. They could not all have had archaic institutions similar to those he describes. Strabo refers mainly to Cnossus, Gortyn, and Lyctus.[61] This poses a problem, which is grave only for those who wish it to be so. The most famous inscription that Crete has delivered up is the text of the Laws of Gortyn. This was written in the fifth century B.C., but it is generally acknowledged that its contents must date from the sixth or seventh century. Here we find no trace of Ephorus's Cretan institutions—there is no use of trifunctionality and nothing about homosexuality. In fact, abduction was prohibited in Gortyn just as it was in Athens, and no distinction was made in this respect between men and women; violators were subject to fine.[62] Some writers have been quick to conclude from this that Ephorus's report is a fabrication, in which observations of rare, isolated Cretan practices are combined with speculations, common at this time, about the ideal constitution.[63]

Too much evidence weighs in the balance against this view, however. First, the Gortyn text, which deals only with certain specific subjects, such as marriage, slavery and serfdom, public morality, and damages caused by animals, and which does not touch on most of the issues, the great constitutional and educational principles, raised by Ephorus, pertains only to the city of Gortyn. Ephorus's testimony is highly consistent (as I shall show in a moment) and clearly based on observations of one particular city (Cnossus, Lyctus, or some other); it would not be generalizable were it not for coincidences and recurrences observed in any number of other cities.

Second, concerning Gortyn in particular, Athenaeus of Naucratis, in a text already cited, gives that city's name for the cup that was given to a young man who had been abducted by an erastēs.[64] His source, the (Hellenistic?) historian Hermonax, is independent of Ephorus. This proves that the Laws of Gortyn are not a complete compendium, and Ephorus was justified in generalizing to this city what he may have learned somewhere else.

Third, trifunctionality structures the whole range of reported institutions: the obligatory gifts and criteria for selection of the erōmenos on the one hand, and on the other hand the constitutional principles and perhaps also the dangers to be averted by promoting civic concord, namely, "envy, arrogance, and hatred."[65] Such consistency cannot be a matter of chance: Rather, a set of basic principles must have been applied to a specific domain. However, even though the Laws of Gortyn can explain the criteria for selection of the erōmenos, as well as the exclusion of the sign of the third function, they cannot explain the three gifts, whose trifunctional character emerges from external comparison with other Greek and Indo-European examples. Hence the constitutional principles and the related yet distinct gifts together point to the dim past and plunge us into Indo-European prehistory. Ephorus's Cretan constitution must be authentic. On the whole, there is reason to believe that it was the theorists of the fourth century who took their inspiration from the Cretan institutions, and not Ephorus who foisted his ideas on Crete.[66]

The fourth point in favor of Ephorus's veracity is that homosexuality, though absent from the laws of Gortyn, is attested in Crete by other sources, which seem to suggest, with Ephorus, that it was quite common there.

Consider, to begin with, Plato, who has the Athenian in the *Laws* say
to his two interlocutors, the Cretan Clinias and the Spartan Megillus:

> For example, these physical exercises and common meals you speak
> of, though in many ways beneficial to a city, provide dangerous
> openings for faction . . . and, in particular, this practice seems to have
> corrupted the ancient and natural rule in the matter of sexual plea-
> sures common both to mankind and to animals, and the blame for
> these corruptions may be charged, in the first instance, on your two
> cities and such others as are most devoted to physical exercises.
> Whether these matters are to be discussed in play or in earnest, we
> must not forget that this pleasure seems by nature to have been
> granted to male and female natures when conjoined for procreation;
> the pleasure of males with males, or females with females, is against
> nature and a bold deed second to none, caused by a helpless rush to
> pleasure. And all of us charge the Cretans with inventing the tale of
> Ganymede; since they were convinced that their legislation came
> from Zeus, they went on to tell this story against him that they might
> follow his example and enjoy the fruits of this pleasure too.[67]

Later on, "Crete as a whole and Lacedaemon [Sparta]" are accused of
having, "in regard to sex," habits "totally contrary to" those commended by Plato.[68] In neither place does either Clinias or his Lacedaemonian companion raise the slightest protest.

A short time later, the historian Timaeus and Heraclides Ponticus
agreed that homosexuality originated in Crete.[69] Aristotle maintained
that the purpose of homosexuality was to avoid overpopulation in
Crete.[70] This is a doubtful hypothesis, at least as regards the origin of the
practice, but it does suggest that pederasty was common on the island.

Verse of an indeterminate era, written in the style of Anacreon (a
celebrated author of the sixth century B.C., of whose work only a few
fragments have survived), purports to locate the poet's innumerable
loves, homosexual and heterosexual, in various parts of the Greek and
non-Greek world. Among his encounters were several "in Crete, where
rites are held in the cities under the peristyles to celebrate the young
Erōs,"[71] an obvious allusion to the pederastic rites mentioned by Ephorus but based on a slightly different representation of the events; the
source seems to be original.

The Greeks, particularly in later periods, were fond of recounting
series of more or less exemplary stories taking pederasty as their central

theme. I shall cite several of these. One is situated in Crete. Strabo
writes:

> Leucocomas and Euxynthetus his erastēs, whom Theophrastus men-
> tions in his discourse of Love, were natives of Leben [a small town in
> southern Crete that served as a port to Gortyn]. One of the tasks
> enjoined Euxynthetus by Leucocomas was this, according to
> Theophrastus, to bring him his dog from Prasus.[72]

This dog is an animal about which nothing else is known but which we
must assume was especially ferocious. The historian Conon, of whose
work only fragments have survived, nevertheless fills in the rest of the
story. In his version Leucocomas's erastēs is named Promachus and both
are from Cnossus.

> Since Promachus did not get what he was after, he gave the last of the
> trophies that he had brought back [a splendid helmet] to another
> handsome boy, in the presence of Leucocomas; unable to control his
> jealousy, the latter killed himself with his sword.[73]

Beneath the Hellenistic veneer—evident in the romantic aspect of the
story, the allusion to the boy's beauty (in direct contradiction to the
explicitly stated values of the ancient Cretans), and the supposedly
amorous motives of the erastēs—a fundamental feature of aristocratic
pederasty can be perceived: It was a serious dishonor for a young man not
to find a lover. Strabo indicates that this was so in Crete, and an
abundant literature confirms it for the rest of Greece.[74] As Bethe has
observed, the disdain implicit in such rejection was catastrophic. It
meant that the adolescent unable to find an erastēs worthy of his rank
would be deprived of the educator whose *aretē*, or excellence, was to have
shaped his own. Only death could erase such an insult.

Finally, the Byzantine lexicographer Hesychius, author of a veritable
treasure trove of glosses, defined the expression "in the Cretan manner"
as "to use *paidika*."[75] *Paidika* was a term often used in place of erōmenos.
Hesychius collected a whole series of similar words,[76] for the most part
from Attic comedy.[77] Clearly, then, male homosexuality was sufficiently
widespread in Crete in the fourth and fifth centuries B.C. to have given
rise to an Athenian expression—though to be sure homosexuality was
not rare in Athens at the time, either.

Homosexuality must have taken different forms in different Cretan cities. Since the form described by Ephorus was particularly archaic, it was not unreasonable for him to assume that the form he observed in Cnossus, Lyctus, or elsewhere was the most general form and that other practices involving adult-adolescent relations, common throughout Greece, were derivative.

The fifth argument in favor of the truth of Ephorus's account is this: If the abduction of the erōmenos represented a violation of the Laws of Gortyn, it nevertheless recalls another institution, Dorian rather than Cretan—the abduction of the fiancée, mention of which can be found in the earliest Spartan legislation.[78]

Anyone the least familiar with Lacedaemonian institutions cannot fail to be struck by their close resemblance to certain of the institutions described by Ephorus. Military education, troops of young people, "men's houses" (Cretan *andreia*, Spartan *pheiditia*) are all found in Sparta, along with homosexuality, exclusion of beauty as a criterion for choosing the erōmenos, and legislation based on trifunctionality (I shall come back to this).

The ancients, from Herodotus on, often remarked upon and called attention to the similarities between the institutions of Sparta and Crete (oddly enough treating Crete, as Ephorus does, as a whole, ignoring its division into several cities). They discussed the question of who influenced whom: Had the Cretans, some of whom were natives of Laconia, adopted Laconian laws, or had Lycurgus, Sparta's legendary lawgiver, borrowed the institutions of the Cretans?[79] Without going into detail, one may assume first a common cultural source, which might be called Dorian or, more broadly perhaps, Achaean; later there were probably real relations and a reciprocal influence, extending throughout the archaic period: the Gortynian Thaletas settled in Sparta and revived music there; the Cnossian (or Phaestian) Epimenides stayed in Sparta; while in the sixth century B.C. Crete and Laconia together turned their backs on the outside world, rejecting foreign influences and artistic works, a development in which Sparta seems to have played the leading role and served as model.[80]

Now, in Sparta, legislation of the trifunctional type belongs to the most ancient discernible institutional stratum: the Rhetrai, or laws attributed to Lycurgus, which Lucien Gerschel was able to interpret in 1946 in light of the discovery of trifunctionality. Let the reader judge: Plutarch, in his *Life of Lycurgus*, first sets forth three positive laws (the *politeumata*) and three negative laws (the *rhetrai* proper). The *politeumata* concern the institution of the senate (political organization, hence the first function), the egalitarian division of land (economic organization, hence the third function), and the obligation to participate in the *syssitia* (or common meals of adult citizens, sometimes translated "mess companies," hence connected with military organization, that is, the second function). The three *rhetrai* were the prohibition on writing the laws (legislative level, or first function), the prohibition of luxury (an economic law, or third function), and finally the prohibition on making war repeatedly against the same enemy, to guard against the enemy's becoming inured to warfare (a precept of military training, hence pertinent to the second function). The list is strict, and in both series the order followed is the same: one, three, two.[81]

It may seem surprising that one must look to so late an author as Plutarch (circa 100 A.D.) for a trifunctional account (that is, an explanation in terms of archaic structure) of the Spartan constitution. But this is only natural: Plutarch is the first author whose works have survived to have specifically studied Sparta.[82] Earlier allusions (in Herodotus, Aristotle, and Plato, among others) do not provide an exhaustive account of the ancient legislation attributed to Lycurgus.[83] Some of these allusions, which constitute a kind of summary of that legislation, accord well enough with what Plutarch says to allow us to affirm the antiquity of their source.[84]

Thus like the Cretan laws reported by Ephorus, ancient Lacedaemonian legislation was organized in accordance with the trifunctional scheme. But the resemblance does not end there. The historian Diodorus of Sicily, after Herodotus, reports the Delphic oracle that Lycurgus is supposed to have received when he asked the god about the best legislation that he could give to Sparta. After an introduction in which Lycurgus himself is said to be "rather like a god" (this is the text of the oracle, according to Herodotus and Diodorus), we come to a statement of major themes:

Two paths there be which farthest parted are,
One leading on to freedom's honored house,
The other to the house of slavery which
All mortals shun. Progress is made on the first path
By manly courage and sweet social harmony;
And on this way I charge you lead the file;

The latter is the path of loathsome strife
And weak delusion. This the way which thou
Must guard against most carefully.

The sum and substance of the oracle was that the greatest attention
should be devoted to concord and manly spirit, (and not to money-
making, for)

Covetousness, and it alone, will work
The ruin of Sparta.[85]

The coincidence with the "Cretan constitution" is total: The desired
goal in both cases is liberty, the positive means are similarly civic
concord (first function) and courage (second function), and the negative
means is prohibition of economic activity (third function).

The homology is such that it is difficult to see here the manifestation
of a common heritage, a "Dorian" or other source. One has to think
instead of a direct influence of one country on the other, practically a
collaboration. But the two must have started from quite similar places.
Trifunctionality was widely used in both Crete and Laconia. But it was
used in two different ways. At times, the first two functions were
opposed to the third, as was the case in India as well as in the works of
Plato.[86] At other times, all three were placed on the same plane (in Crete
the three institutional gifts and probably also certain lists of divinities;
in Sparta Helen's three husbands, Menelaus's three gifts, the Ambulioi
gods of the Spartan agora, and probably the three Lacedaemonian
Heras).[87] This suggests that Cretans and Spartans alike had known and
used trifunctionality since prehistoric times. Consider, in particular, the
two sets of three gifts, those given by the Cretan erastēs to his erōmenos
and those given by Menelaus to Athena Sculatria, a tradition that can be
traced, as we saw earlier, through Tarentum back to the cult of Helen at
Therapnae. These two lists, at once quite similar (the cup and military
objects are common to both) and quite different (the relation of Helen's
slippers to an ox is certainly not direct!), and set in quite dissimilar
contexts (a tradition of sanctuaries and an initiatory ritual[88]), cannot
derive one from the other. What we have here is not a borrowing of Crete
from Sparta or Sparta from Crete, but surely a common symbolic
heritage.

If, however, the legislation discussed above is a straightforward
borrowing by one country from the other, that borrowing itself sends us

back to an earlier period: the Rhetrai probably date from the early seventh century B.C., perhaps as early as the eighth century.[89] This was, according to tradition, precisely the period of closest contact between Sparta and Crete. It is inconceivable that the borrowing took place after 550, when Sparta and the Cretan cities turned in upon themselves and the Lacedaemonian constitution changed profoundly with the strengthening of the ephors, or magistrates, and other related phenomena.[90] Thus Ephorus's text is based on a seventh-century tradition at the latest. Since it seems archaic compared with the Gortyn laws, which do in fact date from the seventh century, it is clear that, whatever point of view one takes, these institutions derive from a very remote past.

Finally, it is worth mentioning a source that may provide direct evidence of homosexual practices in Crete in the seventh century B.C., an engraved bronze plaque that Boardman says dates from the seventh century. It shows a man carrying a bow meeting and grasping the forearms of a young hunter who is carrying a wild goat on his shoulders. Both men wear short tunics, in such a way that the younger man's genitals are visible.[91] There are two possible interpretations of the scene: It depicts either a dispute, the start of a fight, or else a mature adult courting a younger man. The age difference, expressed through the representation of hair, the way the older man grasps the youth's arms, and the patent sexual reference argue in favor of the second interpretation.[92] The slain goat corroborates this, in that it makes the plaque almost an interpretation of Ephorus's story: The erōmenos, already grown up, is capable of hunting alone, and the motif—a hunting exploit by a young man, instructed by an older man who enjoys sexual rights over him—gives full expression to the spirit of the Cretan initiation rite.

To sum up: Ephorus, in the fourth century B.C., describes a ritual of a very archaic type, which he says is widely practiced in Crete. But his is not an eyewitness account and may reflect fashionable theories. The only surviving example of early Cretan legislation, the Laws of Gortyn, does not confirm his assertions. Still, several contemporary texts provide partial cross-checks of what Ephorus says, for they attest to the importance of homosexual practices in Crete in the fourth century. This does not show that the ritual was widespread, but it does confirm one of its features. Pederasty of this kind was in fact an ancient and traditional Cretan practice. Classical authors state as much, and a seventh-century source seems to confirm them. Moreover, initiatory homosexuality in Crete occurred in an institutional context dominated by the trifunctional theory. If it first developed under Laconian influence, it must be dated from the period of intense relations between Crete and Lacedaemonia, that is, the seventh century at the latest. If not, it represents a primitive Indo-European heritage. In fact, the singular applications of functional tripartition in Crete and Laconia suggest that the two countries were independently influenced by very early institutions, rituals, and cults organized along trifunctional lines. This remote influence may have been Dorian, since there are good reasons to think that the Dorians came to Crete from the Peloponnesus in the twelfth century B.C.[93] Such a heritage does not preclude, indeed it facilitates, later influences and borrowings.

A final indication of Ephorus's basis in fact is that the weight of trifunctionality in the Dorian institutions, together with the archaism of the Cretan ritual, sends us back to a much earlier period, to the primitive Indo-European era, to prehistoric, Neolithic times. No dating is possible here. But the purpose of this book will be, in part, to check the value of this induction.

It cannot be directly cross-checked. Documentation of rituals other than funerals is spotty for any culture lacking written records, as I pointed out in the case of the Germans. Ancient Indo-European institutions must therefore be explored indirectly, essentially by means of comparative linguistics: Emile Benveniste has given a masterful demonstration of the method in his *Vocabulaire des institutions indo-européennes*. However, the realm of sexual practice is par excellence the realm of taboo; we have numerous examples of linguistic taboos in the Indo-European family.[94] Consider, for example, the concept of the menstruating woman: *galmuda* in ancient Celtic, *malinī* in Sanskrit. That specific words exist in these ancient languages to express a very ancient concern suggests that the words refer to a prehistoric sexual taboo. But these words are not related, and their respective etymologies are unknown.[95] We suspect the existence of a primitive concept, possibly common to all the Indo-European peoples, but because this concept was sexual in nature the ways of expressing it changed rapidly.

The same can be said of the problem that concerns us here. None of the words in the several Indo-European languages for "pederast," "erastēs," or "erōmenos" seems "Indo-European" in the sense that a common root can be traced across linguistic boundaries. From this it does not follow that homosexuality was unknown to our Neolithic or Bronze Age ancestors, but merely that the words that may have denoted shared sexual notions quickly became obsolete or were subject to some linguistic taboo. Accordingly, we shall take a different approach and resort to mythological anamnesis, as it were, to further our research. As the foregoing discussion will have made clear, Ephorus's text has started us on our way. Other milestones mark the route.

Jan Bremmer has pointed to the term *harpagē*, abduction, which Strabo uses systematically. Bremmer rightly suggests that this was a technical term in Cretan and Greek, for we find the same word used in the same sense—meaning abduction of an erōmenos—in the myths of Chrysippus and Ganymede.[96] It is also used by Plutarch to denote the Lacedaemonian mode of marriage (by abduction).[97] And we shall see how, in Chalcis, in Euboea, the abduction of the handsome Ganymede by Zeus was said to have occurred in the place known as Harpagion.[98]

According to Strabo, the *harpagē* takes place with varying degrees of ritualized complicity by the young man's friends (*philoi*), to whom the erastēs announces his plans "three or more days" beforehand. With knowledge of the age structure of Cretan society, it is not difficult to identify these friends. The same author has already mentioned that, in an earlier stage, little boys sit on the ground in the *andreia* and eat in the company of adult males. At this point they are in the charge of a *paidonomos*. Then,

> as they grow older they are formed into *agelai* or troops of youths. It is the most illustrious and powerful of the youths who form the agelai, each individual assembling together as many as he can collect. The ruler of the troop is generally the father of the youth who has assembled them together, and has the power of taking them to hunt and to exercise themselves in running, and of punishing the disobedient. They are maintained at the public charge. On certain set days troop encounters troop, marching in time to the sound of the pipe and lyre, as is their custom in actual war.[99]

Immediately after this, Strabo discusses "amorous relations" among the Cretans, and the correlation is evident. It is easy to see in these "most illustrious and powerful" boys the erōmenoi who will soon be promoted to Kleinoi, or "glorious ones," and in the children of their age cohort, whom they have recruited, the "friends" who protect them at the time of the abduction and who, after the return from the "sojourn in the bush," participate in the sacrificial meal, thus enjoying, at the same time as their leader and thanks to his virtue, the advantages of a higher social status.

Strabo continues:

All the Cretans who are selected at the same time from the *agele* of
youths are compelled to marry at once. They do not, however, take
the young women whom they have married immediately to their
homes, until they [i.e., the wives] are qualified to administer household affairs.

Strabo does not tell us how one leaves the *agelē*, but on this point there
can be no doubt: The pederastic ritual in which the chosen one, the
leader of the *agelē*, participates, results in the promotion to the status of
citizen of all the *agelē* members. At that point the group dissolves, for its
educational role is over. Here we discover a further feature of the Cretan
initiation rite: not only does it make the young man a warrior, a
banqueter, and a sacrificer, but it makes him eligible for, indeed obliges
him to enter into, marriage.

All of this can also be found, implicitly or explicitly, in the Lacedaemonian institutions. And we shall see presently how myths from
throughout Greece confirm the idea that in the ordinary course of events
marriage follows the relationship with the erastēs.

The *harpagē* ends with the arrival at the erastēs' *andreia*. Literally, the
word means "men's house." Institutions of this type are found in certain
Melanesian and African cultures and in some South American tribes.
Comparisons have often been made between these institutions and the
Greek *andreia*.[100] According to Aristotle, the Laconians once called the
common meals "not *pheiditia* but *andreia*, like the Cretans, which proves
that this institution came from Crete."[101] But Aristotle is wrong. The
evidence he cites proves only that the Laconians changed the name of the
thing, for reasons of military history. The Andreion, a specific place in
Sparta near the Hyacinthian Way,[102] could not follow the army into the
field; mobile substitutes were used instead, the so-called *syssitia* or
pheiditia, which eventually lent their names to the institution. By
contrast, Crete maintained both the institution, which was common in
Greece, and the ancient name.[103]

The "men's house" was not a typical feature of Indo-European cultures, but in Irish medieval literature we find mention of warriors'
meeting places, institutionalized banquet halls.[104]

Conservative in the use of certain words, the Cretans were innovators
when it came to the designation of the participants in the initiation
ritual: *philētor* and *parastatēs* are limpid words in Greek, compared with

the rather archaic terms, of obscure etymology, used in Sparta and elsewhere to characterize the same roles. The Cretans no doubt allowed these primitive designations to fade into obscurity. *Philētor* is of course "he who loves," using the agent suffix -*tor*/-*ter*, originally Indo-European and much used in Greek. *Parastatēs* means "he who stands beside." The word makes sense, since the two lovers lived side by side for two months. But erastēs and erōmenos lived together for only a short while and not exactly in public, so that it seems surprising that the word caught on, unless there was some more compelling reason for its use. And such a reason is available. The historian Sosicrates, cited by Athenaeus, reveals that in Sparta and Crete sacrifice was made to Eros before every battle, in Crete in the presence of the best and handsomest citizens.[105] The passage alluded to occurs in a discussion of homosexual Eros, and Sosicrates' assertion is not ambiguous: Warriors still young enough to be erōmenoi participated in or observed the battle. Sosicrates interprets this fact in terms appropriate to a much later period (for example, he alludes to the "beauty" of the young men), which Ephorus's Cretans would have rejected. No matter: The presence of erōmenoi at the battle directly evokes the Theban institution of the Sacred Battalion, composed of homosexual couples, or, better, the Theban army, from which this battalion was drawn. Prior to the reform that led to the formation of this battalion, homosexual couples were dispersed throughout the army, and the power of emulation, which drove each pair of lovers to outdo themselves, was not yet concentrated in a unique force.[106] The comparison suggests that Ephorus's account is not quite complete: After the "sojourn in the bush," the relationship between the erastēs and the erōmenos was periodically revived at significant moments in the life of the city—war, common meals, positions in the assembly, and so on. Accordingly, the erōmenos, or former erōmenos, was indeed the *parastatēs* of the erastēs.

As a countergift to the several gifts of the erastēs with which the period of initiation ended, the erōmenos invited his erastēs to a meal, at which the featured dish was naturally the meat of the sacrificial ox. The companions of the erastēs, who had accompanied the young man home, participated in this meal. A similar custom has survived among contemporary Germans: Recipients of a doctorate offer a dinner to their teacher and others who assisted them in their work. The comparison would be empty if the origins of this custom, attested since the early Middle Ages, were not lost in the night of time. Once again, an initiation ritual of ancient Greece finds its most specific parallel in a Germanic country. We have met similar instances previously, and there are others. [107] But in the Greek context it is not so much the trial as its result, social integration, that stands out. The young man has just made a sacrifice. Now he must take part in a banquet where for the first time he will drink wine mixed with water in a cup to be filled by someone else, no doubt a younger man. Present are his peers and the companions of his erastes; the elite of the city welcome him into their ranks. [108]

The Cretans' "sojourn in the bush" lasted two months, a common duration for initiatory retreats. Here are a few ethnographic comparisons, chosen at random from my reading. Among the Pitjentara of central Australia, novices withdraw into the bush for one or two months. [109] And among the Bali of northeastern Zaire, initiation takes place in a "bush school," and for two months novices wear garments made of leaves and are whipped to produce scars that will signify their accession to adult status. [110] Among the Dogons, the initiation retreat lasts three months. [111] In Greece itself, a two-month period is mentioned in the account of a curious trial that may well represent the memory of some initiatory probation; Theocritus alludes to this at length in his poem on the Thalusia, and the scholiast makes these indications explicit, citing a mythographer, Lycus of Rhegium. Here is the story: Comatas, goat-herd and poet, stole some goats from the herd that he was supposed to be tending for sacrifice to the Muses. His master learns of this, has him seized, and locks him up in a trunk, asking Comatas whether the goddesses whom he so honored would help him out in this situation. But "the snub-nosed bees, attracted from the meadow by the fragrant cedar, fed him with their tender flowers, because the Muse had smeared his mouth with a creamy nectar," and in this way he spent two summer months, fed with honey, and emerged victorious from his ordeal. [112]

The final result of initiation is the integration of the young man into the group of full-fledged adults. Henri Jeanmaire wished to say more: aware that the former *parastatēs* bore a title, that of Kleinoi, "the glorious ones," and wore special clothing, he assumed that they formed a sort of "order," or *Männerbund*, similar to orders known to exist among other peoples, including some Indo-European ones, and of which traces can be found in Greek mythology. [113] But there is no evidence to sustain this interpretation: the Kleinoi are simply members of the highest Cretan aristocracy. [114] No doubt their meetings did exclude men of lower social rank, but for the moment there is no reason to believe that they met privately or even secretly, united by a private symbol and cult.

Two points remain to be clarified. First, the age of the erastēs: In Greece as in other cultures he was himself often a recently initiated young man.[115] A story told by both Plutarch and Aelian, and set by the latter in Crete, depicts an erastēs who in the midst of combat falls flat on his face. He begs his enemy to allow him to turn around before finishing him off, so that his erōmenos will not see him die of a wound in the back.[116] Aelian uses the word *neanias*, young man, to refer to this warrior. It is a pity that we cannot be certain that the detail is in fact ancient.

Finally, the mode of pederastic coitus is a pertinent item of information, since the type of relation with the erōmenos determined the manner in which he was "feminized." As Bremmer has pointed out, initiatory homosexual coitus was normally anal, as is implicit in Bethe's thesis concerning the intrinsic spiritual value of sperm in Greece. The only known allusion to the question in the case of Crete is a fragment of a poem by Rhianus, who lived in the third century B.C. and was born in Bene, a small town in west central Crete. In this fragment the poet seems to praise a young boy's posterior.[117]

This concludes our survey of what is known about initiatory homosexuality in Crete. The information given here will prove useful in our discussion of the less trustworthy indications to be gleaned from Greek myths with homosexual content. But first, before using this preliminary research as the basis of further discussion, I want to bolster the results obtained so far by comparison with ethnographic data, based on observation of homosexual initiation customs still practiced today and of extinct practices documented by contemporary ethnographers before the cultures in which they occurred were buried beneath ideological and material fallout from our own civilization. This comparison will help to clarify what the early Indo-European initiatory custom may have— indeed what it must have—been like. It will make vivid and vital what would otherwise have to be pieced together from surviving traces of a vanished prehistoric world.

THREE
Pederasty and Initiation:
Ethnographic Parallels
🔂

It is almost always true that pedagogical relationships ultimately take on a sexual dimension. There is, in particular, abundant evidence of homosexual relations between priests or shamans and their disciples.[1] In this respect, the relationship between erastai and erōmenoi among the Cretans and Taifali is merely a special case of a very general phenomenon. But pederasty as an aspect of the initiation of a soldier and hunter is, geographically speaking, a much more limited phenomenon. Here the purpose of the pedagogical relationship is also different. It is not to train specialists, in some sense marginal to society, but rather to form "citizens," adult warriors, members of a group that does not define itself as distinct from the rest of society by virtue of its specialty (warriors or priests for instance) but that is, quite simply, "society" itself: the society of male adults. This martial pederasty thus accompanies a strengthening of the male influence within the larger society, such that the group of adult males occupies the whole of "civic" space, defines itself as society par excellence, and relegates other social groups to a marginal position.

Accordingly, this type of initiation is not universal. Oddly, it appears to be common in one specific region of the world, southwestern Oceania: in Australia and especially Melanesia. Most of the examples that I shall give come from this part of the world.

Serge Moscovici, in a book whose interpretation of initiatory homosexuality I shall touch upon in a moment,[2] writes that in Australia "initiation lasts two or more years, during which [the young man] is placed under the guardianship of an older man, such as his sister's husband, who teaches him hunting and other skills peculiar to males. The initiator benefits from this relationship, for he has the right to claim the product of the neophyte's hunting and gathering. The relationship that develops between the two men is in obvious ways analogous to that between the guardian and his spouse, the young man's sister." Initiation is marked by an important ceremony, for the purpose of circumcision and in some cases subincision:[3] "Among the Nambuti of [northwest central] Australia, the operation is carried out by the boy's future father-in-law, assisted by two or three of the mother's brothers. The ceremony is called *ulkuteta* (with the mouth), which signifies adoption. It establishes a lasting bond between the boy and the circumciser, who also performs the subcision; they communicate in an esoteric idiom and engage in homosexual relations in which the boy plays the role of the woman. At the proper age the boy accedes to full adult status and takes as his bride the daughter of his circumciser."[4]

The Great Namba were the most important tribe of the northern peninsula of the island of Malekula in the New Hebrides. Among them, according to the ethnographer A. B. Deacon, homosexuality was a veritable institution, linked to initiation. Here the essential step was circumcision. When the time for circumcision arrived, the father of the young man set out to find a tutor, a *dubut* or *nembtaremb*, who was well paid with hogs for his services and who enjoyed sexual relations with the novice, the *bau* or *mugh vel*. Homosexual practices were so common, says Deacon, that every chief had several erōmenoi, and it was said that some men preferred these relations to those they had with their wives. Here a belt of bark had the same significance as military gear in Crete: Until a young man had the right to wear such a belt, he could not have an erōmenos. Instead he served as the erōmenos of some adult.[5]

The relationship thus began some time before the circumcision ceremony. Erastai and erōmenoi each wore distinctive insignia.[6] Homosexual coitus took place standing up (as was generally also the case in Greece).[7] The erōmenos, or *mugh vel*, referred to his erastēs as *nilagh sen*. The latter term was in fact that used by a man to refer to his sister's husband, but as Deacon notes, its use here is ironic, for the marriage rules of the Namba made it impossible for a man to have pederastic relations with his wife's brother.

The relationship between the erastēs and the erōmenos was very close and almost as exclusive as marriage. The erastēs had exclusive sexual rights over his erōmenos, and if the latter had relations with another man his tutor was furious. The tutor could, however, "sell" his rights to another man; immediately after the sexual act, the other man gave the boy ribbons, feathers, or other items of decoration, and the erōmenos then passed these on to his erastēs. This "sale" was for a short period of time only.

The bond between tutor and novice was not only sexual, however. The boy accompanied his erastēs everywhere and worked in his garden

(which explains why chiefs had several erōmenoi), and if one member of
the couple died during the period of their relationship, the other went
into deep mourning.

There were rules governing the choice of an erōmenos. Ineligible were
all boys of the erastēs' own lineage (but not necessarily of the same clan),
sons of sisters, and boys to whom the erastēs was related by marriage.
Violation of these taboos was not punished by death as in the case of
incest, but the pair that committed the sin were required to kill a hog
and exchange it.

In some cases the *dubut*, or tutor chosen by the father, was not the
same person as the *nilagh sen*—for example, when the latter had previously established a relationship with the adolescent. But once the
agreement for circumcision was made, the *dubut* enjoyed exclusive sexual
rights over the boy. He then assumed the position of the boy's "husband" and jealously protected him from other men, including other
dubut of the village. During the thirty-day period of seclusion that was
part of the circumcision ritual, the *dubut* was not allowed to have
relations with any other young man. Between the day of circumcision
and the time the wound healed sexual relations were suspended, and the
dubut served simply as guardian of the young initiate, taking care of all of
his needs. Pederastic relations resumed some time later and continued
until the bark belt had been acquired.

The Malekulians maintain that these homosexual practices make the
novice's phallus stronger and larger and that growth of the penis ends on
the day the initiate dons the bark belt.[8]

Deacon offers the further observation that female homosexuality is
also known among the Great Namba.[9]

Initiatory sexuality is quite common in New Guinea among the
Papuan peoples. A. E. Jensen, in his study of circumcision rituals, cites
the example of the Marind-anim, an important tribe inhabiting the
banks of the Gulf of Huon in the western part of the large island. During
initiation young men reside in the men's house. There each boy has for
sponsor a man, generally married, next to whom he lies during the
night. The boy is available for sexual relations of any kind. More
generally, during religious festivals, heterosexual relations are suspended and replaced by free homosexuality.[10] This affects not only
conjugal relations but also relations between erastai and erōmenoi, for at
other times there is jealousy and rivalry among the tutors.[11]

F. E. Williams has found that such practices are common west of the
Fly River, which rises in central New Guinea and empties into the Gulf

of Papuasia. According to Dr. G. Landtman, the Masingara who reside near the mouth of the river Fly believe that sodomy stimulates growth among boys and is sanctioned by myth.[12] Among the Keraki, who live along the Fly, novices undergoing initiation must make themselves available for nocturnal intercourse with older youths from the tribe's other moiety. "The young initiates continue to play the passive role in sodomy for about a year," and "youths view this as a kind of lesson. None of them makes the slightest objection."[13]

This period ends with what is, by our standards, an atrocious ceremony: the ingestion of quicklime. Each of the young initiates is held between the knees of a slightly older man, with the initiate's head bent backward and his mouth open. An officiant takes the lime in a leaf and pours it into each boy's open mouth. The novice surges forward with pain and runs to spit out the lime and vomit in the bushes; he returns a short while later, his mouth and throat swollen with blisters. The purpose of this ritual, we are told, is to neutralize the effects of homosexual intercourse, but in fact, according to Williams, it is designed to keep the young men from becoming pregnant! For belief in the reality of this danger is well attested: Williams himself collected the names of at least five men who were said to have been pregnant. One had died shortly before the ethnographer joined the Keraki. Had he given birth, this would have revealed the secret of sodomy to women—a great shame for the men!

The young man is then promoted to adult status, either immediately following the end of his homosexual period or a short while later. He receives a number of gifts: a phallic symbol (or "phallocrypt," his second, for he has already received another during initiation), a *sair* belt, a set of arrows, a *paj* collar made of a pig's tail, bracelets, leg rings, and a small bag. With the receipt of the second "phallocrypt" the passive pederastic role comes to an end, and the young man can now assume the active role. The initiation is over, and the promotion to adult status culminates in marriage.[14]

Sodomy is also practiced during initiation among the Bugilai of eastern New Guinea.[15] In addition, homosexual relations are known to exist among the Iatmul of northern New Guinea and other tribes inhabiting the banks of the Gulf of Papuasia. These will be discussed further.[16]

Jensen notes that the Alfuru of western Seram, an island situated just west of New Guinea, have a culture similar in many ways to Melanesian tribes, even though they speak an Indonesian language. In the tribes of the Patasiva group there is a society known as the Kakihan. In order to become a member one must be initiated, but all young men of the tribe are obliged to join. Here we find, as in Melanesia, all the following elements combined: a sojourn in the bush, mystical death of the novices, rebirth, and a radical break between initiates and their mothers, who are shown bloody lances as proof that their sons have been killed. The novice has two sponsors; he is led blindfolded to the House of the Kakihan. There he remains in seclusion, during which time he is tattooed. Then, according to Wirz, he learns to play the flute and to use a rhombus-shaped object for frightening women and becomes acquainted with dietary taboos and pederastic practices.[17]

Similar to the Kakihan, which all males must join, are other, more selective societies found in the same region. Here again we find the same initiatory rites. In northern Bougainville (in the Solomons, east of New Guinea) there is an important ceremony involving ritual masks. Young men are chosen to participate in this ceremony. They are first isolated from the tribe and live in the forest until their hair has grown to a certain length. Then, according to Parkinson, the men in charge have sexual relations with them. This is followed by an initiation ritual. This group of young men represents a sort of social elite, symbolic of the society as a whole. During the ceremony they are given new names, as is often the case in initiation rituals to indicate a change of status.[18] That this goes along with seclusion, a sojourn in the bush, and passive homosexual relations accords with the interpretation of the ceremony as a rite of initiation.[19]

Until the beginning of this century there existed in the Gazelle Peninsula in northern New Britain (in the Bismarck Archipelago, between the Solomons and New Guinea) a society known as the Marawot or Ingiet. Its function is not clear (though it had to do with medicine and magic, among other things), but like certain Polynesian societies it enjoyed considerable prestige. Members joined in early childhood. Novices took part in very complicated dances.[20] During initiation, which again involved a change of name, "an older member of the society undressed and covered himself with lime from head to foot. In his hand he held the end of a mat, the other end of which he gave to one of the novices. They alternately pulled and did battle until the old man fell on the novice and the act was executed. Each novice was obliged, one by one, to submit to the same procedure. Pederasty," says Van Gennep, "was not regarded as a vice by the Melanesians but as an enjoyable act."[21]

Among the medieval Japanese, as different from the ancient Greeks

and Germans as from the Melanesians and New Guineans, we find traces
of a similar notion. Martial homosexuality may have been of prehistoric
origin or it may have been introduced into Japan by Buddhist monks
who arrived around 600 A.D.; in any case there is evidence that it became
increasingly common among samurai after 1200. Samurai apparently
considered love between men, associated with courage and martial
exploits, to be more virile than heterosexual love. Each warrior chose a
young lover worthy of the honor and taught him the martial arts. The
relationship between them was one of brotherly emulation, for which we
find close parallels in Greece. Here again, erōmenoi became the focus of
rivalries, which were resolved by dueling.[22]

I hope that this brief review of homosexual initiation rituals will
suffice. Examples exist in other societies, but the point, I think, has been
made. That institutionalized pederasty had both a pedagogical and a
probative character is explicitly stated by all the authorities.

It is surprising to see how closely these rituals resemble the ones with
which I began this discussion. Note that it is the older man who assumes
the active sexual role and the younger who plays the passive role, so that
the Greek terms *erastēs* and *erōmenos* apply perfectly. This pattern occurs
everywhere.[23] Also universal is the fact that the relationship between the
erastēs and the eromenos ends as soon as the initiation of the latter is
complete and he accedes to the status of adult. Marriage generally
ensues, and we shall find traces of this equivalence in Greece. Among the
Great Namba, erastai and erōmenoi bear characteristic markings; similarly, in Crete, the eminent Kleinoi distinguish themselves, according
to Ephorus, by wearing a special costume—and there is every reason to
believe that the erastai are themselves former erōmenoi, that is, all are
Cleinoi.

Among both the Australians and the Keraki of the river Fly there is a
homology between matrimonial rules and the rules governing the choice
of erastēs: the sexual relationship, homo- or hetero-, establishes a
connection between two families. With the Great Namba, on the other
hand, one type of relationship excludes the other: the tutor cannot be of
the same family as his charge by either blood or marriage. But this is
tantamount to an extension of the incest taboo, and the principle
involved is similar to that just mentioned: Erastēs and erōmenos must
belong to distinct family groups. In Greece we find evidence of identical
rules.

Whatever the young Australian hunts and gathers goes to his tutor;

the young Malekulian works for his tutor, either as a farmer or a sexual object. We are reminded of the Cretan bronze mentioned earlier: the young man is carrying a wild goat, the older man grabs him by the arms. If we are correct in assuming that this plaque provides the earliest evidence for the Cretan initiation ritual,[24] then we may suspect that what we are seeing here is the young man bringing the fruits of his "labor," the product of the hunt, to his erastēs.

Since the three gifts offered by the Cretan erastēs are trifunctional, it is of course impossible to find an exact parallel in the western Pacific. We do find that gifts are given to end the initiation, however: the bark belt among the Great Namba, the embellishments, arms, and phallic symbol among the Keraki.

Throughout the region there is evidence of a sojourn in the bush or in the forest, which is also commonly found in African initiations. Equivalent practices are found in Crete and probably among the Taifali. Above all, we have the men's houses, often located either in the center of the village or on the periphery and closed to women. These house the symbols of the adult male community. Again, the closest parallel is with Greece, with its *andreia*, literally "men's houses." The paradox of an institution common to ancient Greece and the south Asian archipelagos has long been noted.[25]

Note, too, that the duration of initiation may vary from a year or more to a relatively brief period of isolation. We find the same contrast between Taifali and Cretans, and the thirty days' seclusion of the Great Namba is of the same order of magnitude as the two months of the Cretan Kleinoi.

Other precise parallels with ancient Greece include the exclusiveness of the homosexual couple, rivalries between adult males, jealousy, strong emotional ties leading to violent despair in case of death or to virile brotherhood as among the Great Namba, the Marind-anim, and the Japanese samurai.

There are also equivalents, finally, for the learning of complicated dances and flute playing. Tattooing may have been practiced in early periods in connection with initiation, as the example of neighboring Thrace suggests.[26] As for the humorous aspect of homosexual practices, which Van Gennep reports for Melanesia, Attic pottery is surely the most convincing evidence that this was also known in Greece.

With respect to the relationship between homosexuality and heterosexuality, Greece and Austronesia are patently similar, in contrast to societies such as our own, informed by Christian tradition. In these non-Christian societies, homosexuality is not the distinguishing trait of a minority group in one way or another marginal to the larger society but rather a normal alternative to heterosexuality. The same men are first erōmenoi, then erastai or husbands or both. The homosexual relationship is a game in which anyone may take part, or at least any member of the dominant male group, and it is precisely the best and most powerful individuals in the society who do take part. In Greece and in the South Seas we observe identical phenomena: Chiefs surround themselves with a number of erōmenoi,[27] and some men take such a liking to pederasty that they neglect their wives.[28] It would be presumptuous to assume that the latter were "real" homosexuals in the current western sense of the term. Unless we wish to foist upon societies different from our own concepts shaped by the ambience of twentieth-century civilization (as Georges Devereux does, unfortunately, in a well-known article[29]), we cannot say that similar phenomena are identical when the social norms in terms of which they are defined are different. Specifically, western homosexuals define themselves in opposition to society; no ruling system of values underlies or supports their behavior, the motives for which are essentially psychological.[30] The Greek or Melanesian who favored homosexual relations over heterosexual ones was not defining himself in opposition to the fundamental values of his society. He was merely exaggerating one of those values. Rather than attempt to realize his predilection in a hostile environment, he took advantage of his environment to follow a penchant that society suggested to him and authorized. The motives for his behavior may have been purely sensual, or they may have been symbolic—elitism, need for virile brotherhood, prestige. Rarely if ever were they psychological.

In all the cases we have looked at thus far, the initiation procedure is the key. In Australia, Melanesia, New Guinea, ancient Crete, and among the Tailfali, the pattern is always passive homosexuality in adolescence, followed by initiation, followed by active homosexuality as an adult. Deacon observed that the homosexuality of the Great Namba was intrinsically related to initiation.[31] Other reports confirm this, and Ephorus's text proves it in the case of Crete. I therefore propose the following inductive argument: If Austronesian homosexuality resembles Greek homosexuality; if this Austronesian homosexuality is based on an initiation procedure; and if the Cretan example shows that homosexual relations of an initiatory and quite archaic kind were clearly practiced in

Greece, then does it not follow that Greek homosexuality in general originated with initiatory institutions that vanished before history began?

This is the question that we shall pursue in the following chapters.

But first, even though this work is not concerned with initiatory homosexuality in general (the study of which would require a different approach from the one taken here), I want to examine the nature of pederastic initiation and the reasons for its recurrence. For the way in which one frames the problem sets the terms of debate.

FOUR

The Meaning
of Initiatory Homosexuality
囧

Two main theses emerge from the various interpretations put forward to explain the social phenomenon of initiatory homosexuality.[1] One places the accent on relations between men and men, the other on relations between men and women.

The first and evidently more widespread interpretation is stated most clearly by Henri-Irénée Marrou in his remarkable book, *Histoire de l'éducation dans l'Antiquité*. If the Dorian states accorded pederasty

if not a greater place then at least a more official place . . . the reason is that Crete and Sparta saw an ossification of their institutions which left them in an archaic state; that is why they retained, well into the classical era, many aspects of the military way of life associated with their inception.

Hellenic pederasty in fact seems to me one of the clearest and most durable survivals of the feudal "middle ages." In essence it is an extension of camaraderie among warriors. Greek homosexuality was typically military. It is quite different from the initiatory and sacerdotal forms of inversion that contemporary ethnography has studied in a number of "primitive" peoples from various parts of the world (Australia, Siberia, South America, and Bantu Africa), whose purpose is to initiate the witch doctor into a magical world of superhuman relations. It would not be difficult to find parallels to Greek love less remote from us in space and time: I am thinking, for example, of the trial of the Templars, of the scandals that erupted in 1934 in the *Hitlerjugend*, and of the customs that flourished, I am told, in the ranks of certain armies during the last war.

Friendship between men seems to me a constant feature of military societies, in which a circle composed exclusively of men tends to shut itself off from the outside world. The physical exclusion of women, their elimination from the scene in any way, always leads to an upsurge of masculine love: think of Muslim society (admittedly an

example from a quite different theological context and civilization).
The phenomenon is more pronounced in military circles, where there
is a tendency to discredit the normal love of man for woman by
exalting an ideal based on virile virtues (strength, courage, loyalty)
and by cultivating peculiarly masculine forms of pride.

The Greek city, a kind of "men's club," never forgot its martial
past. That masculine love in Greece was in fact associated with
Kriegskameradschaft is attested by numerous customs.[2]

E. Westermarck favored this interpretation, and he cited the following observation of M. Foley about the Melanesians:

Among [the New Caledonians] the greatest fraternity is not that of
the womb but that of arms. This is especially true in the village of
Poepo. It is true that the brotherhood of arms is complicated by
pederasty.[3]

This interpretation is appealing. It does not, however, account for all
the facts, particularly when one considers Greek and New Caledonian
homosexuality in relation to the broader context already discussed.
Furthermore, it seems to me to be based on a historical misunderstanding. To be clear: But for rare exceptions, societies with "men's houses"
are not homologous to barracks societies or religious orders. The constit-
uent social groups are not the same, and therefore the causal relations
cannot be identical. It is of course undeniable that the ancient Greeks,
the Melanesians, and the Papuans are or were warriors. But war did
not—at any rate not in Greece, in that early period, the "feudal 'middle
ages'" in which Marrou situates the origins of Greek homosexuality
—produce groups of professional "soldiers" living together without
women for long periods of time. Melanesian, Papuan, and ancient Greek
warriors were generally married men who lived with or close to their
wives.[4] The occupants of the men's houses were either adolescents (who
were, in the examples considered here, including the Greek example,
sexual objects, means of gratification for older men, and not the root
cause of homosexual behavior) or adult men, none of whom lived
permanently in the men's residence. In those exceptional cases where the
men's house really was the long-term residence of a group of men, as for
example among the Bororo of South America, pederastic habits do
indeed develop within the group, but these have nothing in common
with what we know about the virile fraternity of homosexual couples in

ancient Greece and, unlike Greek and Austronesian pederasty, exhibit no initiatory aspect.[5]

In all the societies in question, moreover, war is not war as we conceive of it: It is ritualized, probative, does not aim at extermination of the enemy, and only rarely seeks conquest. Among both the Papuans and the early Greeks[6] combat ends with the first death. We are a far cry indeed from the Templars, the *Hitlerjugend*, and modern armies. Muslim homosexuality, for its part, is the product of a developed urban society utterly unlike the society of archaic Greece. It also presupposes a division between male and female; women are excluded from many functions and often confined. Undeniable antecedents of such practices may be found in classical Greece, but as the result of a social evolution that reduced the status of women in the city. This evolution seems to have occurred, moreover, in the late archaic period—at the very end of the "feudal 'middle ages'" invoked by Marrou, indeed, in crucial respects, even later.

Finally and relatedly, if the Cretans were assuredly warriors, as were, in other ways, the Nambuti, the Great Namba, the Keraki, and others, it is clear that war in itself plays no role whatsoever in initiations in which homosexuality plays a part. The point of these initiation rituals is to form the adult citizen, among whose roles, or faculties, is that of warrior, as is shown by the military atmosphere and symbolism associated with the initiation rite. But the term *warrior* does not exhaust the social definition of the initiates: They are not soldiers.

In fact, in most Greek cities, and in most Austronesian tribes, the isolation of men was not carried far enough to cause homosexual behavior by imposing sexual isolation and purely masculine values; rather, isolation and homosexuality had a common root, namely, the need for initiation. This was the primary need, at least in the Austronesian societies, and the primacy accorded to the homosexual relationship, bolstered by the exaltation of masculinity, was secondary. As for Greece, one of the purposes of this book is to prove that this was also the case there.

Hence we must look to the initiation symbolism itself to discover the meaning of the rite. This is the approach followed in the second of the two interpretations I mentioned at the start of this chapter.

The young men who undergo the initiation ordeal, who die a symbolic death and are born again, acquire a new being different from the one they have shed. They become "men," in the full sense of the word (biological and civic). It is this change of being that is signified by the change of name, the bodily mutilations, and other common practices. Accordingly, prior to the initiation, the adolescent is necessarily, "by definition," a "non-man," that is, he is supposed to be wanting in masculine nature. Now, the best way to encode this notion is to conceive of the uninitiated male in femine terms, too classify him with the women.

This interpretation, proposed some time ago by J. Winthuis, for example, is well expressed by Serge Moscovici.

> During childhood and prior to initiation, the young adolescent is identified, and probably identifies himself, with a female, namely, his sister or his mother. It is with this in mind that he approaches the ceremony. "To a certain extent," writes Gregory Bateson, speaking of the Iatmul, "expecially during the first phases of initiation, they [the initiates] play the role of women."[7] Because they symbolize the other sex, neophytes are bullied and mistreated, and the initiators who make them manipulate their penes refer to them as "women." The vocabulary used on such occasions points toward an analogy between, on the one hand, relations between men and women and, on the other hand, relations between initiators and initiated. It seems almost as though the purpose of the ritual is partly to make vivid and real the antagonism between the sexes and partly to demonstrate the ineluctable outcome, by exorcising the feminine portion enclosed within the masculine. It teaches a law of society by ensuring the defeat of the one and the triumph of the other, by humiliating the child of the woman in order to glorify the child of the man, so as to preserve the purity of the members of a group that now contains only true men.[8]

In this spirit and on this basis virile fraternity (which is emphasized by proponents of the first interpretation) is able to flourish. It depends upon and reinforces the opposition of the sexes, further increasing the significance of the social encoding. Hence the second interpretation encompasses the first, but not vice versa.

> The battle of the sexes shapes not only heterosexuality but also homosexuality. In primate societies, homosexuality is a positive solution to the problem of intergenerational tension. The young male, the subordinate, seeks and obtains the protection of the adult or superior through ceremonies in which the youth adopts a feminine posture and is the object of symbolic or real sexual assault. Masculine congregations[9] must live, overtly, in a homosexual climate made

necessary by their inability to reproduce. Resumption of cohabitation with females occurs as soon as the opportunity arises.

In human societies the initiation of boys bestows new significance on homosexual behavior by dissimulating or sublimating it, not so much in the eyes of men as in the eyes of women. The atmosphere of an initiation is one of rupture, struggle, passage. The child is faced with a choice, or, rather, a choice is imposed upon him between two groups of relations, two loyalties, two ways of life. One of the outcomes was probably homosexual masculinity. This ideal state, involving complete identification with male society, adherence to strict, secret contracts, and conspiracy against women, assumes a complete suspension of communication with the other sex. Any contact with the impure or inferior is avoided; regret and guilt are cast aside; and men live among their equals. The masculine world closes in upon itself. It avoids dependence, shuns conflict, and circumvents not only the incest taboo but also the reasons for which that taboo was instituted. [10]

Some contrasts bear emphasizing: Animal homosexuality—a recent discovery of ethnology that forcefully refutes any attempt to argue from the (mythical) innocence of animals to the (impossible) innocence of humans—has been found to exist in several ape species among groups of young males left isolated when a few dominant males appropriate all available females. [11] This homosexuality is strikingly reminiscent, in origin and purpose, of homosexuality among modern soldiers and monks. Quite different from these forms of homosexuality is initiatory homosexuality, which occupies a *central place* in society, since it is practiced either by all adult males or by a small but dominant aristocratic group. The difference is based on a difference of direction. Homosexuality in groups of male primates, like that imputed by Marrou to soldiers and monks (strange bedfellows!), originates with a lack: It occurs when males are left to their own devices, alone with other males. Initiatory homosexuality results not from a lack but from a rejection; the men have their women before their eyes, and the purpose of the initiation is to establish an unbreachable gap between the feminine and the masculine.

That is why, apart from the specific problem raised by this book, the meaning of Greek homosexuality has universal human value. It is clear that those authors who argue that Greek homosexuality was an archaic local phenomenon, including Marrou, whose views on the subject have been cited, Devereux, for whom the Greeks exemplify regression to an infantile stage of "polymorphous perversity," and Dover, Bethe, and others still to be discussed, see it as an "accident," a "vice," a historic misfortune, which can only be explained by an exceptional set of circumstances. I take a different line. If, as is suggested by abundant evidence (some of it already examined, some still to come), Greek homosexuality was the continuation of very ancient, very primitive Indo-European practices, similar to practices found elsewhere around the globe, then it is not (or is no longer) an accident. It is the local variant of the social interpretation of sexuality. For just as men in different cultures speak different languages and marry in different ways, so, too, do they choose different ways of defining and experiencing their sexuality. As we have recently been reminded by André Langaney,[12] among others, in addition to the gender that is genetically determined by our chromosomes (XX, XY), there is another, physiological gender determined by the varying amounts of male and female hormones present in every individual. And there is also a social gender, in which the distinctions are much sharper because they are based on a binary code, which in each society determines the social roles of "man" and "woman." Socially we are all assigned to one sex or the other, and this assignment establishes the structural rules that shape our sexuality. The ancient Greeks were not biologically different from us, nor are the present-day Papuans. What was different was the rule, the social rule, that defined what Greeks took to be "normal." This difference takes us back to the oldest of human concerns: Our way of dealing with sexual attraction is certainly no more "normal" than theirs.

This, as we shall see, is the message of the Greek myths.

I I
Poseidon and
the Royal Founders

Greek mythology contains a number of important stories of pederasty. It is not hard to demonstrate that each of these originates in a particular region, and often it is clear that the myth in question is the myth of origin of homosexuality in a specific province or city. These are the grounding myths of a type of social behavior.

Now, these myths provide a strong argument in favor of my thesis, for nearly all are stories of initiation.

Since we know that Greek myths preserve the memory of many vanished institutions,[1] and in particular of initiation rituals,[2] it is reasonable to assume that myths in which initiatory homosexuality occurs represent an ancient form of Greek homosexuality. To put it another way, it is reasonable to assume that the Cretan ritual described by Ephorus is nothing other than a remarkable survival, in historical Greece, of an institution that was once much more widespread, and hence that initiatory homosexuality was in fact the prehistoric antecedent of the homosexuality of the classical era.

It is in fact noteworthy that in societies in which the typical form of pederasty is no longer initiatory, such as Elis or Thebes, the myths that introduce the "first homosexual" characteristically make him the hero of an initiatory tale.[3] This could hardly be a matter of chance, and it seems reasonable to suppose that the Eleans and Thebans knew what they were saying.

This interpretation immediately runs up against a serious obstacle, however, which has given rise to several views different from my own. The founding myths in question are known to us exclusively through fairly late sources; none is mentioned explicitly in the earliest Greek literary works, the Homeric poems and Hesiodic writings.

On this negative finding rests the view of Bethe, that Greek pederasty originated in a particular place—namely, in the area occupied by the Dorians—and subsequently spread, after the time of Homer and

Hesiod, to the rest of Greece.[4] It also underlies the view of K. J. Dover and Georges Devereux, that pederasty is an invention of the seventh century B.C. explicable in terms of changes in the "social psychology" of Greece at that time.[5] And finally, it is the cornerstone of Marrou's contention that pederasty was a consequence of military life in the Greek "feudal 'middle ages.'"[6]

I shall later examine the basis for all of these assertions: the supposed absence of homosexuality in Homer.[6] Here I want to consider only the founding myths themselves. Note, first, a situation that is highly paradoxical if one does not accept the prehistoric origin of Greek homosexuality: How can it be, if all the founding myths of homosexuality are from a late epoch, that all or almost all of them involve initiations, when other, similar tales are certainly very ancient? Conceptually, these myths are based on notions no longer current in historical Greece. By what miracle did these founding myths acquire precisely the form that one finds replicated in the rituals of the Cretans, the Taifali—and the Austronesians?

In any case, the works of Homer and Hesiod are not textbooks in religious history.[7] The authors dwell upon a few selected myths. They mention many others, but without recounting them in detail, and obviously are silent about still others. The argument *ex silentio* is not admissible, however. The genealogies in the Hesiodic *Catalogues* inevitably omit pederastic relations. This does not mean that other tales from the same period, less suitable for poetry, perhaps, or never developed in literary form, did not mention homosexual episodes in the lives of Pelops, Hyacinthus, and Laius. We shall see presently that the brief allusion to Pelops in the *Iliad* cannot tell us anything about the underlying ritual—whether homosexual or not. And yet the whole story of Pelops, as set forth in (necessarily) later works, is based on the theme of initiation.

Finally, the antiquity of the myths we shall be looking at, like that of the Cretan ritual examined previously, is evident in many details.

FIVE
Pelops and Laius
꫞

THE SUCCESSION OF OENOMAUS

All that the Iliad says about Pelops is that he is the founder of a kingdom.

> Powerful Agamemnon
> stood up holding the scepter Hephaestus had wrought him carefully.
> Hephaestus gave it to Zeus the king, the son of Kronos,
> and Zeus in turn gave it to the courier Argeiphontes,
> and lord Hermes gave it to Pelops, driver of horses,
> and Pelops again gave it to Atreus, the shepherd of the people.
> Atreus dying left it to Thyestes of the rich flocks,
> and Thyestes left it in turn to Agamemnon to carry
> and to be lord of many islands and over all Argos.[1]

Here we divine a royal myth concerning the foundation of a dynasty. It is frustratingly opaque, and the author is so discreet that he even avoids telling us of the great conflict involved in the transfer of power from Atreus to Thyestes and Thyestes to Agamemnon—a tradition attested and subsequently developed if ever there was one.

Hesiod mentions Pelops only in his genealogies,[2] and for the first developed account we must await Pindar (in his first *Olympian Ode* for Hieron of Syracuse).

> And his fame shines
> among strong men where Lydian Pelops went to dwell,
> Pelops, whom he who clips the earth in his great strength,
> Poseidon, loved, when Klotho lifted him out
> of the clean cauldron, his shoulder gleaming ivory.
> Great marvels in truth are these, but tales
> told and overlaid with elaboration of lies
> amaze men's wits against the true word.
> Grace, who brings to fulfillment all things for men's delight,

granting honor again, many a time makes
things incredible seem true.
Days to come are the wisest witnesses.
It is better for a man to speak well of the gods; he is less to blame.
Son of Tantalus, against older men I will say
that when your father summoned the gods
to that stateliest feast at beloved Sipylus,
and gave them to eat and received in turn,
then he of the shining trident caught you up,
his heart to desire broken, and with his horses and car of gold
carried you up to the house of Zeus and his wide honor,
where Ganymede at a later time
came for the same desire in Zeus.
But when you were gone, and men from your mother looked, nor
    brought you back,
some man, a neighbor, spoke quietly for spite,
how they took you and with a knife
minced your limbs into bubbling water
and over the table divided and ate
flesh of your body, even to the last morsel.
I cannot say that any god could gorge thus; I recoil.
Many a time disaster has come to the speakers of evil.
If they who watch on Olympus have honored
any man, that man was Tantalus; but he was not able to
swallow his great fortune. . . .
Therefore, they sent his son
back to the fleeting destiny of man's race.
And when at the time of life's blossoming
the first beard came to darken his cheek,
he thought on winning a bride ready at hand,
Hippodamia, the glorious daughter of a king in Pisa.
He walked alone in the darkness of the gray sea,
invoking the lord of the heavy trident,
and he appeared clear at this feet.
He spoke: "Look you, Poseidon, if you have had any joy of my love
and the Cyprian's sweet gifts, block the brazen spear
of Oenomaus, and give me the fleeter chariot
by Elis' river, and clothe me about in strength.
Thirteen suitors he has killed now, and ever
puts aside the marriage of his daughter.
The great danger never descends upon a man without strength;
but if we are destined to die, why should one sit

to no purpose in darkness and find a nameless old age
without any part of glory his own? So my way
lies this hazard; yours to accomplish the end."
He spoke, with words not wide of the mark.
The god, increasing his fame, gave him
a golden chariot and horses never weary with wings.
Breaking the strength of Oenomaus, he took the maiden and brought
    her to bed.
She bore him six sons, lords of the people, blazing in valor.
Now he lies at the Alpheus
crossing, mixed with the mighty dead.
His tomb is thronged about at the altar where many strangers pass;
    but the glory
of Pelops looks afar from Olympia
in the courses where speed is matched with speed
and a man's force harsh at the height.[3]

That is the myth. It is a founding myth in two respects: First, it is
among the myths of origin of the Olympic Games, and that is indeed the
role it plays here, in the first *Olympian Ode* of the great Theban poet;
second, it fills in a "gap" in the *Iliad*, in the sense that it reveals the
origin of several royal dynasties—the six sons that the poet accords the
founder—including the Mycenaean dynasty. According to tradition,
the name *Peloponnesus* comes from the fact that the dynasties that descended from Pelops reigned over the greater part of the territory so
called. This is only approximately true, and the real explanation of the
toponymy must be sought elsewhere. I leave this question aside.

Pindar, then, sets forth the founding myth of a great kingdom. The
point of the tale is accession to the status of king. The tradition was that
before Pelops there was a first king, whose only function seems to have
been to provide the son of Tantalus with an opportunity to take his place.
For Oenomaus was the ruler of Pisa, which in early times dominated the
entire valley of the lower Alpheus—all Pisatis—and was probably located close to Olympia.[4] The victory of Pelops coincided with the death
of Oenomaus, because the king fell from his chariot during the race,
because Pelops killed him, or because Zeus struck him with a
thunderbolt.[5] Pelops's marriage to Hippodamia gave him the Pisan
throne.

But this marriage was the climax of a series of events that can easily be
interpreted as an initiation. The race with Oenomaus is a trial that

demonstrates the superiority of the victor—a difficult trial, since thirteen pretenders had failed and paid with their lives for their defeat. Tradition suggested a number of ways in which young Pelops might have beaten Oenomaus. Pindar says that Poseidon gave him a chariot drawn by winged steeds. Others claimed that he bribed Oenomaus's charioteer, Myrtilus.[6] It makes no difference which version we accept. For the ancients, divine assistance complemented heroic action; it did not preclude such action. As for the use of a ruse, and a "technical" ruse at that (Myrtilus is supposed to have removed the linchpin from his master's chariot wheel and to have replaced it with wax), the Greeks took a positive view of such cunning trickery.[7] Instruction in ruses was an essential part of the training of the Hippeis, the Spartan military elite,[8] and Spartan education was of course shot through with the symbolism of initiation.[9]

Successful completion of the trial was supposed to open the way to marriage and royalty. This was the logical conclusion of the initiation, proof that training had been successful and that the hero was ready to enter a new stage of life. Before this came a preparatory phase, in which the neophyte, isolated from the community, received the education that would make a man of him (and, in Pelops's case, a king). It was during this time that he experienced the first rites of passage. In ethnographic terms there must have been at this point a sojourn in the bush or a retreat to the "men's house." In almost all initiation ceremonies the passage to a new stage of life is encoded in terms of life and death. Specifically, the neophyte dies a mystical death and is then resurrected in a new, and superior, state.

This is in fact what Pindar recounts. Pelops's legendary "life" begins with his disappearance. It is also worth noting that for all intents and purposes his life ends with his accession to the throne, except that sometime thereafter he fathers several children. Pelops, like Heracles, Perseus, and the Argonauts, exists only as the symbol of an initiation. Now, there are two "explanations" for his disappearance. The first, which Pindar mentions only to reject it at once as incompatible with the purity of the gods, is that Tantalus, Pelops's father and friend of the gods, invites the gods to his home and, to test their knowledge, offers them his son to eat. The gods are supposed to know what they have been served. Only one god—Demeter, Ares, or Thetis, depending on the version—distracted or preoccupied, actually consumes a portion. When Zeus, who is needless to say not duped, restores Pelops to life, he is missing a shoulder, so a new one is made for him, of ivory.[10] Pindar in

any case contradicts the vulgate—not of his own time but as it is known
to us from late mythographers. The "strong" version of the myth is that
the guests, that is, the gods, shared the flesh of Pelops and ate it. Pelops,
dismembered, actually entered the stomachs of the gods. The ivory
shoulder then requires explanation, but Pindar does not mention any. In
any case, he rejects this version of the story: "I cannot understand how a
god could gorge thus; I recoil."

I am far from sharing his opinion. The tradition he rejects seems much
too authentically ancient. The caldron of death and resurrection is an
important motif in Greek mythology, and the whole story accords well
with the most common initiatory symbolism. Often it is explained—to
mothers, children, and ethnographers—that the neophytes are taken to
a place were they are snatched by demons, torn apart, and devoured.
They are obviously reborn some time later, but by then they are no
longer the same. According to Apollodorus, the resurrected Pelops was
handsomer and more resplendent than before.[11]

The second explanation, which Pindar proposes because to his way of
thinking it saves the dignity of the gods, is that Pelops has been
abducted by Poseidon, who is in love with him. Poseidon takes him to
the abode of the gods, where Zeus himself brought Ganymede—in other
words, to the gods' *andreia*. The pederastic content is clear: Pindar
speaks of the god's sexual desire (*himeros*) for Pelops. And Poseidon is
indeed the hero's "tutor," as that word is usually construed in initiatory
contexts: It is he who provides Pelops with the chariot that enables him
to win the victory.

This raises the following question: Is this second version of the myth a
pure figment of Pindar's imagination?

The work of the great poet is marked throughout by a homosexual
sensibility,[12] and it is not impossible that he altered the myth to suit his
own conceptions. What is more, his very words suggest that he is
proposing his own interpretation, which he claims as his own without
invoking any other authority.

However, when he rejects the story of Tantalus's cannibalistic feast a
few lines later, and is therefore forced to find other reasons for Tantalus's
being subjected to infernal tortures, the explanation that he proposes—
the theft of ambrosia and nectar—derives from the earliest Greek
tradition.[13] Thus Pindar was not obliged to create a new version of the
myth out of whole cloth: Every myth, every legend, existed in several
versions, especially in oral tradition, and each author could choose
among them.

Now, pederasty was, according to the ancients, quite widespread in Elis. Pindar had no need to invent what could have (and must have) existed in tales told by people in the Olympian region.

Last but not least, the resemblance between Pindar's story and the one told by Ephorus a century later about Cretan initiation rites is too strong to be explained away as a mere coincidence. The same point has been made by J.-P. Vernant, who links the two versions and does not hesitate to situate the origin of this great myth in Mycenaean times.

This tale of qualification for kingship places the trial of the chariot under the patronage of Poseidon, the old horse-god, who at this stage of Mycenaean civilization appears no longer in pastoral guise but as a warlike and aristocratic chariot driver. It is in fact the altar of Poseidon at Corinth (a Poseidon Hippius and Damaeus) which is chosen to mark the end of the race, and it is there that the victor is consecrated. Pelops, moreover, is closely associated with Poseidon in his legend. When the young man is reborn after the initiatory trial in which he is dismembered and cooked in his father's cauldron, he is immediately "abducted" by Poseidon. The god makes him his "page," in conformity with an archaic practice that survived in the warrior societies of Crete and that Strabo, citing Ephorus, has preserved for posterity.[14]

It may be, of course, that Pindar knew of Cretan or other, similar customs by hearsay and borrowed their central idea to justify the temporary disappearance of the hero in the myth of Pelops. But while this assumption would partially explain the coincidence, there is still one element not accounted for: By what miracle could the poet have made just the right substitution, replacing a segment of the initiatory myth—the dismemberment—with its exact symbolic equivalent? For the sequence of events (disappearance, trial, marriage) no longer corresponded to a real fifth-century B.C. institution or ritual, so that not even Pindar himself could have read an initiatory tale as we are able to do with the aid of comparative ethnography. Moreover, Cretan homosexuality itself was initiatory only by comparison with parallel customs that gave it meaning, while the extreme ritualism of the procedure described by Ephorus and the absence of a closing trial would have prevented the drawing of any parallel with the sequence of events in the Pelops myth.

A more logical interpretation is that the myth and the Cretan ritual share a common origin: a prehistoric Greek institution.

It is true that, since the work of the nineteenth-century German

philological school (whose merits as to textual criticism and the comparative dating of sources are undeniable), mythological research has become accustomed, when faced with a number of variants of a tale, to
seeking first "the oldest" and then "the original" version. Philologically,
the method is sound; it avoids folly by carefully dating and locating texts
and their allusions. Mythologically, it is, as scholars have gradually
come to appreciate, unacceptable. Whenever myths and legends are
gathered in a particular region, their variety is the first fact that must be
taken into account. That is one reason why it is wrong to declare the
chronologically oldest known version of a myth to be the original
version, for if some author gives a different version a century later, that
does not necessarily mean that he has distorted the original, but only
that he has independently picked up some other variant from some other
source, which there is no reason a priori to assume any less ancient than
the first. This is especially true in a country like Greece, where the use of
writing grew slowly from very early times down to the Hellenistic
period, changing form and content as it spread, and the professional
collectors of traditions (such as Apollodorus of Athens, Diodorus of
Sicily, Plutarch, and Pausanias, to mention only the most famous) came
not at the beginning but at the end of this development. Last but not
least, modern students of mythology have found that variation is not the
random consequence of history but a structural property of myth itself.
As the myth passes from one ethnic group to another, or from one
preoccupation to another, we find changes in its code or in the order and
value of the elements that make up the code.[15]

Far from being contradictory, as Pindar suggests for circumstantial
reasons and modern scholars have been all too ready to believe, the
"cauldron version" and the "abduction version" of the Pelops myth both
signify initiatory seclusion. One version uses the very essence of the
symbolism (the mystical death and resurrection) while the other merely
uses its form (Poseidon is the master and erastēs of Pelops). If, on the
other hand, the two myths must be linked, then it is clear that one
version encompasses the other. The developed sequence would then be,
in effect, as follows: abduction of Pelops is equal to symbolic death;
sojourn in the *andreia* is equal to education and homosexuality; exit from
the *andreia* is equal to resurrection.

Compare the two myths with respect to Pelops's victory in the chariot
race with Oenomaus. In one versoin he wins because of Poseidon's gift of
a winged chariot; in the other Myrtilus's removal of a linchpin from
Oenomaus's chariot gives Pelops the victory. This has been called a

contradiction: Either Pelops won with miraculous assistance from a god, or else he caused his adversary to lose with technical help from a man. Either form of assistance renders the other superfluous. Yet the ancients saw no contradiction in this. Sophocles says the Atridae have experienced misfortune "since Myrtilus was hurled from his golden car to an ocean bed."[16] It is clear that Myrtilus is mentioned because of the role he is supposed to have played in the race and because of the ensuing conflict with Pelops, while if Pelops is equipped with a golden chariot, it can only be a divine and miraculous one! Thus Sophocles combines the two versions. Similarly, Euripides mention both the murder of Myrtilus and the winged horses.[17] And a fragment of Pherecydes (hence prior to Pindar) already appears to combine the two versions.[18] Thus the "primitive version" cannot be found, either textually, since both versions coexist in the earliest text, or logically, since the ancients themselves combined both explanations.

The oldest cult building at Olympia seems to be the famous tomb of Pelops mentioned by Pindar, the so-called Pelopion, in the heart of the Altis. German excavations have proved that this was a cenotaph (the tumulus contained no human remains) and that it must date from the eleventh century B.C. that is, from the century following the collapse of Mycenaean culture.[19] There are many signs, though no conclusive proof, that the Olympian sanctuary was already in existence in the Mycenaean era,[20] and several authors believe that Pelops was by that time already a cult figure.[21] Since the decipherment of Mycenaean writing in Linear B (a form of writing used between the fifteenth and twelfth centuries B.C.), we know that several heroes of the mythology of the first millennium B.C. already existed as such in the second millennium B.C., for they gave their names to cities in Messenia: Atreus, Achilles, Lynceus, among others.[22] It is also quite likely that Pelops, eponymous hero of the major Greek peninsula, belongs to the same "generation" of heroes. Be that as it may, the eleventh-century cenotaph allows us to date the Pelops cult from at least that period. The following parallel has not, to my knowledge, been reported: During excavations on the temple of Apollo at Delphi in 1934–35, E. Lerat discovered beneath the temple, in approximately the position where ancient texts placed the tomb of Neoptolemus, son of Achilles, a large Mycenaean *pithos* (vase), containing coal ashes and animal bones, like a funerary *pithos*, but no human bones.[23] It may date from the twelfth or thirteenth century B.C. Thus, well before the great wave of foundations of heroic cults in the eighth century,[24] we find two Greek sanctuaries, among the most celebrated of all, in which archeological evidence shows the existence of heroic cults at the end of the second millennium B.C.

According to Greek tradition, the Olympic Games are also an innovation of the eighth century, and what we know today of the considerable revolution—economic, social, political, artistic, religious, and literary[25]—that occurred in Greece at that time tends to confirm the authenticity of this tradition. But the sanctuary, without its temples, is much older, and it must be conceded that the myth of Pelops was the royal myth implied by the allusion in the *Iliad* before it became the founding myth of the games, as set forth by Pindar.

To sum up: The myth of Pelops seems extremely ancient, in terms of both its elements and its structure. The complete initiatory sequences, from seclusion of the neophyte to marriage, with mystical death, death caldron and resurrection caldron, homosexuality of tutor and pupil, and trial in the form of a race,[26] constitute a coherent, unified whole. Its meaning becomes clear when compared with the known initiatory customs of primitive peoples and the custom known to have been practiced in Crete in historical times.

Archeology brings us close to some sort of chronology. It attests that Pelops had been the object of a cult from at least the eleventh century. This is one index of antiquity, and our consideration of Laius will furnish others. As in the case of Crete, supplementary evidence suggests that we look to an early Greek source: either to the invaders of the eleventh and twelfth centuries, Dorians and Eleans, or to the Mycenaeans—if not, obviously, to an even earlier source.

THE ABDUCTION OF CHRYSIPPUS

The same events as those surrounding Pelops occur again (as is only logical) in the next generation.

Alongside the common Greek tradition that attributed to the Cretans the honor or shame of having invented pederasty, another tradition credited Laius, the legendary king of Thebes, with the same invention. But the affair is closely related to the Pelops cycle.

The practice of pederasty came into Greece from the Cretans first, according to Timaeus. But others declare that Laius initiated such love practices when he was the guest of Pelops; he became enamored of Pelops's son, Chrysippus, whom he seized and placed in his chariot, and then fled to Thebes. Yet Praxilla of Sicyon says that Chrysippus was carried off by Zeus.

This brief but valuable comment on the subject is from Athenaeus.[27] Apollodorus adds an interesting detail: At the time of Labdacus's death, Laius was only one year old, and the kingship was usurped first by Lycus and then by his nephews Amphion and Zethus. They exiled Laius to the court of Pelops. "And, while he was teaching Chrysippus, the son of Pelops, to drive a chariot, he fell in love with the young man and abducted him."[28]

This moralistic version of the tale, which blames Laius, makes one thing quite clear: Laius is to Chrysippus what Poseidon was to Pelops, at once instructor in the art of driving a chariot and erastēs. It is remarkable that the poet Praxilla replaces Laius with Zeus. Similarly, Pindar compared the abduction of Pelops by a god with the abduction of Ganymede, also by a god, namely, Zeus. The story of Chrysippus reproduces that of his father, which is to be expected assuming that initiation with pederastic relations was institutionalized in early Greek history. The two tales shed light on one another: The story of Pelops, interpreted in light of what we know about Crete, tells us that Laius must have been taking Chrysippus to his *andreia*. Now, in fact he took him to Thebes. Doesn't the abduction of Pelops by a god who takes him to the palace where Zeus also took Ganymede signify, among other things, a departure for a foreign country?

Initiation may possibly be associated with another institution that according to legend was not unknown in prehistoric Greece and that is known to have existed in a number of societies, in particular among the Celts: foster parentage, that is, the education of a child in a family related by marriage.[29] In the age of the city-state ephebes were of course taken in charge by the city, and it is impossible to imagine an adolescent from Athens or Sparta leaving his family to take military training at Argos or Thebes. But in earlier times aristocrats maintained relations with their colleagues in foreign cities in the form of institutionalized reciprocal hospitality (*proxenia*) and marriages.[30] It is hardly surprising that traces of foster parentage in Greece show a close correlation between the sending of sons from one family to another and marriages between those two families.[31] One immediately suspects that the same correlation must exist in the sphere of initiatory homosexuality, and indeed this proves to be the case. If Pelops entrusted his sons to a future king of Thebes in Boeotia, mythology also tells us that he gave the women of his *genos* (family) to Boeotians. His sister Niobe married Amphion, the Theban king who reigned during Laius's exile at Pisa;[32] and he gave his daughter Astymedusa to Oedipus, son of Laius.[33] We shall see shortly that these matrimonial relations between Boeotians and Pisatans were much closer than they may appear. For now it suffices to note that, as with the Australians and the Keraki of New Guinea, in primitive Greece the tutor (Laius) of the son (Chrysippus) was sometimes related to him by marriage (in this case as father of the son-in-law Oedipus).

Chrysippus is the unwilling hero of another myth, of his own death. There are two versions. In the moralistic one he commits suicide for shame after his abduction by Laius.[34] In the other, as the son of the nymph Axioche, he is killed by his two half-brothers (sons of Hippodamia) Atreus and Thyestes.[35] What is clear is that Chrysippus must die. Hence I propose an interpretation of the myth based on the following elements: 1) Chrysippus, like his father only more so, exists in mythology only to signify an initiation, as is shown by the initiatory homosexuality that demonstrates his relationship with Laius. If this is right, then it is probable that his death, like the earlier death of Pelops, is a mystical death, all the more so in that his name, which literally means "golden horse," directly alludes to the golden chariot that enabled his father to triumph over Oenomaus; Chrysippus is that part of Pelops which is institutionally passed on to the following generation. 2) The principal sons of Pelops are Atreus and Thyestes. It is they who succeed him, according to the *Iliad*—in Mycenae, to be sure, but that is one of the fundamental themes of the myth. The succession of Pelops, king of western Peloponnesus, takes place in the cities of eastern Peloponnesus. One would then expect that an initiatory myth would apply to the sons as it applied to the father. This is only partly true. Atreus's accession to the Mycenaean throne avoids the themes of symbolic death, trial, and homosexual education.

Chrysippus, whose myth has the elements that one would expect and that are lacking in the myths of Atreus and Thyestes (who live the life that Chrysippus should have lived after his initiation), apparently is a direct complement to them: He is educated and dies in order to be reborn as Atreus/Thyestes. Furthermore, the difference in their respective mothers (Axioche and Hippodamia, the one a nymph, the other a woman and queen) encodes the essential differences between them in still another way.

It should also be noted that, according to Hyginus, a Latin writer who often used ancient Greek mythological sources, Laius took the son of

Pelops on his chariot not to Thebes but to the Nemean Games, which is perfectly compatible with Pelop's adventure.[36] For these games took place in northeastern Peloponnesus, also the location of the sanctuary of Poseidon Isthmius, the finish line of the race between Pelops and Oenomaus. But if Pelops, having won and having thrown Myrtilus into the Myrtilian Sea north of Argolis, returned to reign in Pisa, it was in fact in the vicinity of Nemea, south of Mycenae, east of Troezene, and north of Megara, that the Pelopidae reigned.

SIX
The Taboo of the Aegidae
卐

The Aegidae were a famous family (*genos*) of Thebes. The family's traditions suggest that Laius was the founder of warrior homosexuality in that city. As we have seen, a certain version of the myth holds that he was the creator of pederasty in Greece. But we have yet to examine a crucial related issue: the date of the legend of Laius and Chrysippus. All the sources for this legend are fairly late. But we know that Euripides wrote a tragedy entitled *Chrysippus* around 411–409 B.C. The great German mythologist C. Robert assumed that all the later authors drew from this source, and that Euripides was therefore the creator of the legend.[1] However, the historian Hellanicus gave a brief résumé of the story around the same date, and this he surely would not have done had he learned of it from Attic drama.[2] Furthermore, the same story figures in two fifth-century B.C. vases from southern Italy.[3] Finally, when Herodotus, in the early fifth century, collected Theban traditions brought to Sparta by the Aegidae,[4] he learned that "the men of this clan (*genos*) were advised by an oracle to build a shrine to the Furies of Oedipus and Laius, because their children never survived. . . . The same thing happened to their descendants in Thera."[5]

The taboo on reproduction was thus common to the Aegidae of Sparta and Thera, yet it never prevented them from producing offspring. What we see here is a kind of ritual, in which each male member of the Aegidae clan was for a time forbidden to engage in sexual relations with women. Subsequently, these same males participated in some sort of cult act associated with the sanctuary of the Furies of Laius and Oedipus. Then and only then were they allowed to procreate. The founding myth of this taboo can be traced back beyond Oedipus to Laius: Aeschylus and later Euripides showed how all the misfortunes of the royal family of Thebes could be traced to Laius's failure to obey the order given him by Apollo (or by Hera, goddess of marriage!) not to have a child.[6] So it was that Laius and Oedipus both committed, against the advice of the oracle, the egregious sin of having normal sexual relations with their legitimate wives: Laius because his son would eventually kill him, as a result of which Thebes suffered incalculable ills, and Oedipus because his legitimate wife happened to be his mother.

But what was the reason for Laius's initial sin? In what respect was it a crime to have sexual relations with his wife? The taboo originally related to procreation. It was institutionalized among the Aegidae, descended from the Thebans of heroic times,[7] and it involved a ritual. We know that homosexual relations were commended by the Greeks as a means to avoid producing children.[8] And we also know that Laius's sin was linked (as early as the fifth century, hence from its inception) to his behavior with Chrysippus.[9] It follows that Laius's real original sin—a sin that, being sexual in nature and producing no children, was transformed into a prohibition of sexual relations, and hence reproduction, between the hero and his wife—was homosexuality, of which Laius was the paradigmatic founder.[10] In truth, the notion of "sin" is surely secondary: Pederasty was sufficiently official in Thebes that the relationship between Laius and Chrysippus would not have been considered monstrous. Furthermore, Aeschylus and his successors do not say that the oracle forbidding Laius to have children was a punishment. The advice is given for no apparent reason, largely as prior justification for the dramas that will follow. But there is a simple reason for this: There is a conceptual incompatibility between homosexual relations, extramarital and sterile, and heterosexual relations, conjugal and fertile.

Several authors concede that the myth of Laius was in fact of Boeotian origin.[11] The Homeric poems neglect Laius but mention the misfortunes of Oedipus.[12] The Theban cycle is at least that old. And the Aegidae, whose traditions were the same in Sparta and Thera, are even older. The common institutional and ritual principle that these traditions appear to share is that every man's life consists of two phases, one military and homosexual, the other civic and matrimonial. The colonization of Thera, which caused certain of the Aegidae to take leave of their relatives in Sparta,[13] took place in the eleventh or tenth century.[14] Thus the common tradition of the Aegidae of Sparta and Thera is very old. But the correlation between the traditions of these Aegidae and those of Thebes, collected by poets as early as the eighth century ("Homer") refer back to even earlier times. It was when the Heraclidae moved toward Peloponnesus, some say, that the Theban Aegidae met them and became their allies.[15] This legendary episode refers to events that culminated, in southern Greece, in the replacement of the Mycenaean aristocracy by a new aristocracy that spoke Dorian (which is not a derivative of Mycenaean), in all probability in the twelfth century.

This is the latest date by which there must have existed a myth naming the king of Thebes as the founder of homosexuality. But the tradition of matrimonial relations between Pisatans and Boeotians allows us to follow this thread a few centuries further back.

SEVEN

Pisatans and Boeotians

Let me remind the reader of a few relationships mentioned earlier: Niobe, daughter of Tantalus and sister of Pelops, married Amphion, king of Thebes; Astymedusa, daughter of Pelops, was given to another king of Thebes, Oedipus. These traditions are ancient: The first is Homeric,[1] and the second is attested in the *Catalogues* of Hesiod. But what value can be attributed to them? No explanation of these recurrent relations is given to us, and it might be simply a matter of poetic manipulation of secondary genealogies.

There were, in any case, other close relations between Boeotians and Pisatans. They do not become apparent, however, in and through the explicit tradition but only through mythological analysis. Having described the overt tradition, I am ready now to look at the silent one. There is, moreover, an explanation for the different character of the two: Whereas the explicit tradition speaks only of marriage, the silent tradition develops the notion that the Pisatan and Boeotian families that exchanged members between themselves are in fact identical.

In the first place, Pelops is the son of Tantalus. According to classical mythology, these men are Asiatics: Phrygians, Lydians, etc. Pelops and Tantalus are associated with Mount Sipylus, on the border between Lydia and Phrygia.[2] As usual, then, we are here dealing with projections: Tantalus and Pelops are Greek heroes whom the colonizers of the Aegean coast brought with them as part of their own traditions. In fact, it was long ago observed that Tantalus is none other than a doublet of Atlas, as is shown by their names (derived from the same root, the verb *tlao*, to carry), their homologous relationships (of titanic type) with the gods, and the myth that assigns to both the function of holding up the earth or a mountain or a rock.[3] The split between the two is very old. Their myths have evolved in quite different directions, with the result that Tantalus became one of the damned great ones, and Atlas a component part of the universe (for it is he who holds up the sky). I shall presently give a reason for accepting an approximate date of this split. But what needs to be said at once is that originally Atlas was quite certainly connected with eastern Boeotia. His progeny illustrate this. In addition to his son Hesperus and his daughters the Hesperides, who have few if any specific geographic connotations, there is another son, Hyas, and other daughters, the Pleiades and Hyades. Hyas is the eponym of a very ancient Boeotian tribe, the Hyantes, which vanished before the historical era.[4] The Pleiades were pursued through Boeotia for five years by the famous giant Orion. Orion is the putative son of Hyrieus, king of Hyria on Mount Cithaeron in eastern Boeotia. The Pleiades, according to genealogies that, though late, surely reflect ancient sources (for otherwise one would have to assume some extraordinary coincidence), are the ancestors of several heroes of eastern Boeotia. These descendants include Lycus, the very same person who seized the throne of Thebes during the childhood of Laius; his brother Nycteus and hence Nycteus's grandsons Amphion and Zethus, who banished Laius to Pisa; Hyrieus, the king of Hyria (mythology being unembarrassed by contradictions, since on the one hand the chaste Pleiades are said to have been pursued by Orion, who on the other hand turns out to be the grandson of one of them!);[5] and Eleuther, eponym of Eleutherae, a city situated not far from Hyria in the other direction from Cithaeron. Such cross-references do not deceive; they show that Atlas and his children originally had solid roots in eastern Boeotia and prove that the Peloponnesian Atlas, the grandfather of Hermes (born in Arcadia) and of Lacedaemon, eponym of Lacedaemonia, is a derivative or displacement of the Boeotian one.

Thus, not only did Pelops marry his sister to Amphion (relation of the first rank), but Amphion, like Pelops, was the descendant of a Titan, Atlas/Tantalus, whose home ground was in the region of Mount Cithaeron. Pelops and Amphion are related both by marriage and descent.

These facts immediately provide the explanation of a silent tradition, in some sense implicit or repressed. In Greece, in early times at any rate, marriage within the *genos* was proscribed. Niobe could marry only outside the Tantalidae. Hence Pelops cannot be of the same family as Amphion.

Another aspect of the silent tradition that points to the Pisatan and Boeotian families being identical is that upon arriving at Pisa, Pelops tried for the hand of Hippodamia, daughter of Oenomaus. Oenomaus's only function, as we saw earlier, was to enable Pelops to acquire a kingship; he exists in order to provide his successor, the only one who counts, with the means to prove himself. That said, it would be easy to understand if the genealogists were not much concerned with his ancestry and were content simply to make him, say, the son of a god and a local nymph. This was not precisely the case, however. His father was the god of war, Ares, or a hero with the quite martial name of Hyperochus, meaning eminent.[6] His mother was either a daughter of the river Asopus, Harpinna or Eurythoe, or one of the Pleiades, Sterope. This ancestry is entirely Boeotian. Sterope belongs to the family of Atlas, whose origins were discussed above. Harpinna/Eurythoe is the daughter of Asopus. There are several rivers by this name in Greece, but the largest one, the only one to which legends ascribe daughters with occasionally important roles in mythology, is found in eastern Boeotia and flows across the plain of Thebes at the foot of Cithaeron. Ares himself, father of a chariot driving hero and grandfather of one Hippodamia, is apparently found in Boeotia as the husband of the nymph Tilphossa, who is the mother (with Poseidon, the two gods being quite closely related in this group of legends) of the miraculous horse Areion.[7]

Paradoxically, the result of this is that not only did the Pisatan Pelops ultimately marry his sister in a *genos* that turns out to be his own, but he also married a woman, daughter of another Pisatan, whose ancestry can also be traced back to Atlas, or, if not, to a divinity of eastern Boeotia. The explicit, attested, literary mythology demolished these correlations: Pelops's father is named Tantalus; Oenomaus's father is Ares; Amphion, the grandson of Nycteus, is a descendant of Sisyphus, who married one of the Pleiades. A determination to make certain points obscure is obvious in the distinction between Tantalus and Atlas and in the divine paternity of Oenomaus. But this set of correlations is compelling. The lineages of Pelops and his father-in-law are both, so far as human ancestors are concerned, Boeotian in origin. Furthermore, there exist obscure affinities between Oenomaus and Dionysus (beginning with Oenomaus's name, which means "he who desires wine," in addition to which Dionysus, a native of Thebes, is related through the female line to Laius and Oedipus).

Still other cross-confirmations need not be examined here in any detail. For example, certain surprising religious parallels establish a connection between the lower Alpheus valley and Boeotia.[8] Finally, it is possible to show, thanks to the Mycenaean tablets discovered at Pylos in Messenia, that at the end of the thirteenth century (the tablet era) several individuals whose names have resonance in the Boeotian traditions were known in the northern part of the kingdom, and this has implications for the rest of the kingdom as well.[9] The Pylian kingdom probably extended at that time as far as the southern bank of the lower Alpheus.[10]

The onomastic coincidences, religious parallels, and implicit family relationships described above admit of only one possible explanation: a real, historical movement of population from Boeotia to Pisatis. Mythology is full of stories of movements that carry northern heroes, generally from Thessaly, into the Peloponnesus: Neleus, the founder of Pylos, comes from Iolcus in Thessaly; Salmoneus, founder of a kingdom in the region of Elis, was also a Thessalian; Melampus, who became king at Argos after a sojourn in Pylos, was also a native of Iolcus; and so forth. These traditions certainly correspond in large part to real phenomena, even if we cannot affirm the historical reality of Neleus, Salmoneus, and Melampus. There is nothing improbable about a movement from Boeotia into northwestern Peloponnesus. This has two consequences for my study: 1) Historically, relations between Pisatans and Boeotians could be traced simply to their common origin; what mythology groups together as "descendants of Atlas" or "descendants of Asopus" historically signifies a group of different *gene* without any authentic kinship among them. The interference of legendary filiations complicated the issue and necessitated denials that distorted traditions. Thus, the system of exchange between Pelopidae and Thebans is based on extremely old relations. Now, just as the traditions concerning the original "sexual sin" common to the Spartan Aegidae, the Theran Aegidae, and the Thebans led us to date those traditions from the twelfth century, so, too, in the two provinces Elis and Boeotia the memory was preserved of relations among the great families, and a homosexual relationship was placed at the origin. These parallelisms imply a very early date for these relations and for the establishment of the initiatory myth: broadly speaking, in the Mycenaean period. 2) Chronologically, in fact, it is the Mycenaean documents from Pylos that confirm the presence of an element of Boeotian origin in the region of the lower Alpheus. But these documents cannot be recent: The Phylian kingdom had recently expanded at the expense of Pisatis and had found the tablets there. To judge by the tradition (which would not have remained as important as it did had it not corresponded in some measure to reality), this Boeotian contribution coincides with the constitution of the kingdom of Pisa. I have shown elsewhere why there is good reason to think that this was indeed the case. For example, Pisatis is flanked on the north and east by two rivers of the same name: Ladon. This place name existed in Boeotia and was there associated with similar legends. The clearest interpretation of this is that the Mycenaean colonizers of Pisatis brought with them, as part of their traditions, the name of the river and bestowed it upon two important rivers in their new country.[11]

Here an important Egyptian document has a bearing on the question. Around 1380 B.C. the pharaoh Amenophis III, in preparing his funerary temple, caused the names of all the peoples who, in his opinion, were subject to Egypt to be engraved on its walls. When this temple was unearthed in 1964, it was found to contain several clearly Aegean names, among them Cnossus, Mycenae, and Messenia.[12] In a study published in 1977, I proposed reading one of these toponyms, Bi-sa-ja, as Pisaia, the word for Pisatis used by Pausanias;[13] I further showed that each term in the Egyptian list corresponded to a specific kingdom.[14] Hence Pisatis was an independent kingdom, constituted as such prior to 1380.

The Boeotians therefore established this kingdom in the sixteenth or fifteenth century, and when they did we must assume that they brought with them their traditional baggage, including Ladon, Ares and Poseidon, the golden chariot, and initiatory homosexuality, with its founding myths. Pindar was not the creator of the myth. The myths of Pelops and Laius, founders of pederasty and kings protected by a Poseidon who was god of horses, war, and the chariot, date from earliest Mycenaean times.[15]

III
Apollo and Civic Advancement

EIGHT
Hyacinthus, Narcissus, and Cyparissus

Hyacinthus, Narcissus, and Cyparissus: three characters, natives respectively of Laconia, Thespiae in southern Boeotia, and Chios, an island off the coast of Attica. Among these three there are no direct links like those between Pelops and Laius, but they do resemble one another, and there is reason to study them together.

Hyacinthus is the eponym of the great Lacedaemonian festival known as the Hyacinthia, which took place in the summer of every year at Amyclae in southern Sparta. In the most common version of the story Hyacinthus is the son of a king of Sparta, Amyclas or Oebalus. He is the youngest and handsomest of the king's sons, and a god, Apollo (or, in some versions, Zephyrus or Boreas), falls in love with him. Attic potters were fond of representing him with Zephyrus, often in recumbent intercrural coitus; almost all other instances of homosexual coitus; in Attic ceramics show the partners standing up. [1]

Apollodorus reports an original version that contrasts with other genealogies, which are generally Laconian and somewhat artificial. Hyacinthus, he says, is the son of the Thessalian Pierus and the muse Clio. Apollodorus goes on to say that Thamyris (a legendary bard of Thracian origin according to the *Iliad*[2]) fell in love with him and thus became the inventor of pederasty. [3]

Desperate after the death of Hyacinthus, Apollo is said to have caused a plant to grow out of the blood that flowed from his wounds: the *hyacinthus* (probably not the same as our hyacinth[4]), whose petals are marked with letters, either the hero's initial, Y, or Apollo's cry of lamentation, AI. [5]

Cyparissus, son of Telephus, lived on Chios and was remarkably handsome. Apollo (or, again, Zephyrus) falls in love with him. Cyparissus keeps a pet stag but one day, while hunting, accidentally kills him. Afterward he is so distraught that he begs the gods to kill him and allow him to mourn for all eternity. He dies and is transformed into the tree of sadness that bears his name, the cypress.[6]

Like Hyacinthus and Cyparissus, Narcissus is known from relatively recent literary sources, and he has suffered more than they from his adoption by poets and writers. Various allusions provide clues to his geographic roots, however. He is probably the son of Cephissus, a name borne by several rivers, the largest of which, and the only one to which children are imputed, flowed from Phocis into Lake Copais in western Boeotia. The Theban soothsayer Teiresias is involved in his legend.[7] Furthermore, we are indebted to Conon for what must be the original version of the story: Narcissus, a very handsome young man from Thespiae, wants no part of love. Another young man, Ameinias, falls in love with him, but Narcissus repeatedly spurns him. One day he even sends him an ironic gift: a sword. Ameinias then takes this sword and stabs himself in front of Narcissus's house, cursing his beloved as he dies. Shortly thereafter, Narcissus sees his reflection in a well and falls in love with himself. This unbearable contradiction is the cause of his suicide, and the Thespians dedicated a temple to love, the cause of this terrible tragedy. From the blood of Narcissus there grew a plant, the narcissus.[8]

An original version depicts Narcissus as a Euboean from Eretria. A certain Epops, or Eypo, kills him, and the story ends similarly with the growth of a plant.[9]

These three stories have an astonishing number of points in common. All three personages are homonyms for a plant. All three bear names from the same linguistic "stratum" (which Paul Kretschmer at the end of the last century dubbed pre-Hellenic), names marked by the suffixes -nthus (Hyacinthus, Corinthus, Olynthus, Cynthus at Delos, Tiryns, genitive Tirynthus, etc.) and -ssus (Cyparissus, Narcissus, Parnassus, Cnossus, Tylissus, Mount Hymettus of Attica, etc.). There are good reasons to assume these suffixes are of Anatolian origin.[10] The lover of Hyacinthus was Thamyris. In Thespiae, Narcissus's home town, there was a confraternity of thamuriddontes, who organized great musical contests.[11]

No less clear are the common points that bear on the questions we are investigating. All these heroes die young. The first meets with a violent death, Narcissus succumbs either to violent death or suicide, and Cyparissus to suicide. These deaths are homologous, and the fates of Pelops and his son, discussed in Part 2, suggest how we ought to interpret them—they are surely initiatory. In all cases there is a murder—of Pelops by his father, of Chrysippus by his brothers, etc.—which suggests that the stories of suicide are "mild" or "weak" versions. The Chians, with their more sophisticated Ionian temperaments, must have been more reluctant than the Lacedaemonians to have their heroes killed off by Apollo. Hence they shift the object of the murder: It is not Apollo or Zephyrus who kills Cyparissus but Cyparissus who kills a stag—obviously a symbolic substitute for himself, since it is the death of the stag that brings on the hero's own death. Only this change obliterates the link between Cyparissus's homosexuality and his death, a link that the two other legends keep intact.

The Boeotian legend involves an inversion: Narcissus causes the death of his erastēs by his refusal to give in to his advances. This is because in the legend as it has come down to us, Narcissus signifies something other than the foundation of virile homosexuality. Like Hippolytus in the Attic cycle,[12] he represents the adolescent rebel opposed to established institutions and civic life. He rejects love, not only homosexual love but also heterosexual, as shown by the famous story of the nymph Echo, desperately in love.[13] He is a paradigmatic asocial character. His function is to articulate what must not be done. His rejection of Ameinias, his rejection of Echo, and his love of himself are homologous: To reject the love of others is to turn inward, a cul-de-sac that can only lead to self-destruction.

We saw, however, that a more "orthodox" version of the story survives in one Euboean variant, in which another man, Epops or Eypo, kills Narcissus. Furthermore, these legends contain hidden phallic symbolism. The sword that Narcissus sends to Ameinias is not only a symbol of death, which Ameinias understands as such, but also a negation of the (homo)sexual relationship (inasmuch as Ameinias must stab himself, just as Narcissus, guilty of this death, will fall in love with himself and thereby cause his own death). The linguist von Blumenthal observed some time ago that the name of the king Oebalus, father of Hyacinthus and ancestor of the mythical kings of Sparta, makes no sense in Greek but may, like other names from Laconian legend (Hyllus, Bateia, etc.), be of Illyrian origin (since the Dorians came from Pindus,[14] it would not be surprising if they brought Illyrian elements with them). Taking account of what we know of Illyrian phonetics, the name Oebalus is reminiscent of the Aeolian participle *oipholes*, "lubricious," both words deriving from the root *oibh-*, "to swell," root of the Greek *oipho*, "to make love with," the infix -*l*- being participial.[15] It is worth noting that Pausanias situates the sanctuary of Oebalus at Sparta near a place consecrated to Poseidon Gentylius, literally, "who engenders."[16]

Of the three legends, that of Hyacinthus is the most informative. Many authors allude to it. We know the Hyacinthia from several references, though there is no sustained description of the festival. Pausanias's description of the sanctuary of Apollo at Amyclae, where the Hyacinthia were celebrated, is very suggestive. To go into all these matters in detail here is out of the question: the problems, correlations, and implications are so numerous that an entire book has been devoted to Hyacinthus[17] on top of innumerable articles, and there is still room for a fresh treatment, since Mellink is surely on the wrong track.[18] Here I shall limit myself to making a few important points.

As long ago as 1939 Henri Jeanmaire made the important observation that the festival was essentially initiatory in nature. Until then the leading thesis, still prominent in a number of works,[19] was that it was an agrarian feast. The myth of Hyacinthus is reminiscent (vaguely!) of the myths of Adonis and Osiris; his name is the name of a plant; at the Hyacinthia people ate fruits and vegetables.[20] None of this is convincing: The Hyacinthus myth is far more reminiscent of the myths of Narcissus, Cyparissus, and Pelops, which have nothing agrarian about them, than of Osiris or other oriental gods. The *hyacinthus* is a plant, but it is not cultivated, and just because a myth uses plant symbolism, or, for that matter, animal, cosmic, social, or technical symbolism, does not mean that it must be interpreted in terms of these categories. True, people used to think that myths could be classified in such terms, but that is no reason for accepting such classifications now. Finally, we know that pork was eaten at the Hyacinthia (a fact not easily reconciled with the notion that the purpose of the festival was to celebrate spring's first fruits, as proponents of the agarian thesis hold). Also eaten were broad beans, which played an important role and which Marcel Détienne has shown symbolized the "anti-nourishment" par excellence.[21] In truth, plant symbolism is pertinent to the interpretation of the Hyacinthia, but the festival was in no sense peculiarly agrarian.

The time has come to return to the myth itself. It will enable us to understand the ritual, and the ritual will help us to grasp the full significance of the myth.

HANDSOME HYACINTHUS

Hyacinthus, like Cyparissus, Narcissus, Pelops, and Chrysippus, is first of all a young ephebe remarkable for his beauty. Lucian, in his *Dialogue of the Gods*, refers to Hyacinthus as one of the handsomest men of antiquity of whom tradition had preserved the memory. The plant that grew from his blood was adduced as further proof of this: It is "the loveliest flower of all flowers."[22]

Hence it is easy to understand why Hyacinthus was loved by so many. Among those who became enamored of him were Thamyris the musician, two of the wind gods, Apollo, and the muse Erato.[23]

Again like Pelops, Chrysippus, and Laius, Hyacinthus was of royal blood. His father, in the Laconian tradition, was a king of Sparta, either Oebalus or Amyclas. In Apollodorus's version his father is Pierus, son of Magnes. Pierus and Magnes are both eponyms of peoples and countries, the first of the Pieres and Pieria, a region of southern Macedonia, separated from Thessaly by Mount Olympus, the second of the Magnetes and Magnesia, that is, the peninsula of the Pelion, in eastern Thessaly. Isidore of Seville noticed this aspect of Hyacinthus when he characterized him as *puer nobilis*.[24]

Loved by a man and three gods, Hyacinthus was the paradigm for the erōmenoi of the human generations to come. Correspondingly, his lovers are typical erastai: Apollo is the god to whom the largest number of masculine loves is attributed (as the rest of this chapter will make clear). Vanquisher of the monster who watched over the sanctuary of Delphi, he is the eternally young *kouros*, youth, in all the splendor of his virility. An accomplished initiate, he is the model, the teacher par excellence, of the adolescents of legend. As for Zephyrus, according to a tradition traceable to the Attic potters of the classical era he was a great lover of young men. Besides Hyacinthus, he also loved Cyparissus, and this was often depicted on pottery. A very late tradition has him the father of a hero in large part inspired by Hyacinthus and his images: He was named Carpus, "fruit," and was loved by Calamus, "reed," son of the river Maeander. But he drowned while competing in a swimming race with his lover, and in despair Calamus withered away on the river bank (a motif from the Narcissus story). Carpus became the "fruit of the fields," which every year die and are reborn.[25]

Spartan homosexuality is today widely recognized.[26] It comes out clearly here. By placing Hyacinthus at the very beginning of their legendary history (well before Carnus, for example, who is discussed at the start of Chapter 10), the Lacedaemonians were probably (though it is not explicitly stated) taking the relationship between Apollo and Hyacinthus as the original model of their custom. In any case, in Apollodorus's northern version of the legend, in which Hyacinthus is the son of a Macedonian, Pierus, and loved by a Thracian, Thamyris, it is Thamyris who is credited with the invention of pederasty.

The Cretan initiation included a sojourn in the bush. Among the Taifali initiation ended with a hunting exploit, and in Crete traces of something similar may survive, as was mentioned earlier, on an archaic bronze in which a young man carrying a wild goat approaches an older male. Now the sojourn in the bush, the hunt, the hunter's exploit are all called to mind by the legend of Cyparissus killing his pet stag. Ovid, though, weaves similar elements into his version of the Hyacinthus legend: Apollo, in his passion for Hyacinthus, "entirely heedless of his usual pursuit . . . refuses not to bear the nets, nor hold the dogs in leash, nor go as comrade along the rough mountain peaks of the rugged ridges."[27] This is exactly what the Cretan erastēs and erōmenos did for a period of two months. It is also exactly what was required of young Spartan males who took part in the most difficult of the military initiation procedures, the so-called Crypteia.[28]

Like the Cretan lover during the sojourn in the bush, Apollo played the role of Hyacinthus's instructor. According to Philostratus the Younger, Apollo taught him archery, music, divination, the art of the lyre, and all the exercises of the palaestra.[29] As Ileana Chirassi has observed, it is through Hyacinthus that knowledge of these things is transmitted to humanity. He is a sort of "cultural hero,"[30] but his knowledge is that of the Greek "gentleman," not that of the peasant or technician. Philostratus's story is remarkable for its archaism. No other Greek literary source mentions the lyre of Hyacinthus, but Attic potters represented him with a cithara,[31] and, in excavations of the Amyclaeon (the sanctuary of Hyacinthus and Apollo at Amyclae), a fragment of a vase was found that shows a choir of men accompanied by two lyre players,[32] along with a small seven-string bronze lyre that probably dates from the Late Helladic period.[33] The bow, by the way, with which Hyacinthus was skilled, was the weapon commonly used by the Cretans.

Hyacinthus is closely related to the Muses. One of them, Clio, is (in the northern version) his mother, and another, Erato, is his only heterosexual lover. What does this recurrent relationship mean? The Muses were originally mountain nymphs: *Mousai* is a regular contraction of *montai*. The nymphs of Mount Olympus in Pieria were called Pierides, and these were an ancient form of the Muses.[34] Pierus's relationship with one Muse and Hyacinthus's with another are metaphors for the learning of music, the art of the Muses (the *Iliad* mentions the competition between Thamyris and the Muses at Dorionin Messenia, a musical contest in which Thamyris loses his life[35]), and the sojourn of the neophyte in the wild, mountainous regions in which initiation takes place.

In comparing the death of Hyacinthus with that of Chrysippus, I proposed the hypothesis that it was mystical, symbolic, and initiatory. This hypothesis is corroborated by the facts now in our possession.

It is only in literature, in poetry, that Hyacinthus dies and gives rise to a plant. Pausanias saw something else at Amyclae. The central edifice of the city, the Amyclaeon, was the throne of Apollo, built in the sixth century by Bathycles of Magnesia. Its façade was entirely covered with reliefs, which Pausanias in large part enumerates, and which are, as we shall soon see, highly instructive. On the upper portion stood a large statue of Apollo in the archaic style, with helmet, shield, and bow.

> The base of the statue is like an altar, and they [the Spartans] say Hyacinthus is buried there, and at the festival of Hyacinthus, before they sacrifice to Apollo, they make offerings to Hyacinthus as a hero at this altar through a brazen door which is on the left of the altar. And carved upon this altar are effigies of Biris and Amphitrite and Poseidon, and Zeus and Hermes talking together, and near them Dionysus and Semele, and near Semele Ino. On this altar too are effigies of Demeter and Proserpine and Pluto, the Destinies and the Seasons. Aphrodite and Athena and Artemis; and they are carrying to heaven Hyacinthus and his sister Polyboea who they say died a virgin. Hyacinthus on this frige has a beard, but Nicias the son of Nicomedes[36] in his painting of Hyacinthus portrayed him as an ephebe, hinting at the love of Apollo for him. There is also a representation on the altar of Hercules being taken to heaven by Athena and the other gods.[37]

One could hardly be more clear, and it is difficult to understand the efforts of authors like Nilsson to demonstrate what they take to be the "agrarian" character of the Hyacinthus story.[38]

Quite obviously what is being shown here is an apotheosis; the parallel presence of Heracles proves that this is the case. And the meaning of this apotheosis is clear. Pausanias sees a contradiction between this ascent to heaven and the story of Hyacinthus's death followed by the appearance of the *hyacinthus*, and he is astonished that Hyacinthus is here shown bearded whereas elsewhere he is beardless. Even though this fact has given rise to complex historicist interpretations (according to which Spartan ideas are supposed to have changed between the sixth century, when Bathycles showed us a bearded Hyacinthus, and the fifth century, when Nicias chose to paint the same figure without a beard), there is a simpler, more consistent explanation that determines the meaning of the Hyacinthus myth. The hero is bearded as soon as he ceases to be the adolescent ephebe over whom Apollo and Zephyr quarreled. In other words, Hyacinthus's beard is to his previous lack of beard what his apotheosis is to his life as erōmenos. Or, again, the death of the hero, far from being the end of life, is a transition, a passage, from the condition of beardless, adolescent erōmenos to that of bearded adult and therefore, implicitly, erastēs.

This interpretation is reinforced by three further items of evidence. According to the poet Nonnus, in his *Dionysiaca*, the festival of Amyclae—the Hyacinthia—included the singing of a brief hymn, which apparently went as follows: "Hyacinthus with the fine head of hair, Apollo brought him back to life."[39] The song speaks of resurrection, the bas-relief by Bathycles of apotheosis. It is not too bold to say that here we have two ways of expressing the same thing. Hyacinthus's death is mystical and temporary—a first stage in his transformation. His resurrection brings him back to life in a different state, a superior mode of existence.

Furthermore, for the Spartans, the presence of a beard was not a neutral and insignificant fact: It was the trait that characterized the adult warrior. The typical aspect of the Laconian warrior is evoked numerous times by Aristophanes, Plato, and others. Bringing together such scattered references, François Ollier has shown how the Lacedaemonian warrior also sported a frightening attire, with his blood-red tunic or rude wool cloak known as a *tribōn*; he let his arms dangle at his side, sometimes holding a cudgel; his hair was long, his beard thick, his mustache shaved.[40] He bore a strong resemblance to certain trained warriors of northern Europe.[41] Now we can understand why Hyacinthus's looks changed so dramatically, and it is surprising that Brelich seems to have been the only one to notice this.[42] Hyacinthus is reborn; he undergoes apotheosis, in the form of an adult warrior.

The third and final piece of evidence supporting this interpretation is that throughout Greece the growth of the beard marked the end of the homosexual phase in which the boy served as erōmenos. Attic authors confirm this statement, which may be taken as one of the structural features that demonstrate the initiatory origins of Greek homosexuality.[43]

Pausanias the rationalist, along with many of his modern emulators, sees a contradiction between Hyacinthus's death, which gives rise to a plant, and his apotheosis/resurrection. Seen in context, however—that of an initiation, as is shown by the pedagogical and sexual relations between Hyacinthus and Apollo followed by Hyacinthus's change of state—the death of the hero followed by the appearance of the *hyacinthus* is easy to interpret. Note first that the antique tradition does not say that Hyacinthus was transformed into the *hyacinthus*; it says that Apollo caused the plant to grow from his body,[44] or that it grew from the blood that flowed from his wound.[45] This second version has a strict parallel in the Narcissus story: It is from the blood of Narcissus, which flows along the banks of the river, that narcissuses grow.[46] Hyacinthus himself will be reborn. Thus the plant does not symbolize a real, biological death but rather a mystical one: It expresses the death of his adolescence.

According to Pliny and Dioscorides, the *hyacinthus* had very interesting properties indeed. It could delay puberty, and slave traders used it when they dealt in adolescents.[47] Thus the *hyacinthus* connotes the essence of puberty. Now the myth makes sense: With the blood of the hero—and remember that Spartan military initiation and training resulted in genuine wounds, from which real blood flowed—what flows out of him is his adolescence, or more precisely the mythical principle that characterizes the adolescent state.

One possible objection to this line of argument is that the death of Hyacinthus cannot be distinguished from the deaths of Narcissus, Cyparissus, or Carpus, who are all young erōmenoi loved by gods or men, and whose names evoke the plants to which they gave rise. But the essence of mythology is of course to use polysemous signs, meaningful on more than one level. Within the set of symbols common to these various heroes, which we shall examine shortly, the *hyacinthus* stands out because of the special connotation given it by the ancients: It stands for adolescence.

The function of Polyboea, clear though it is, has been the subject of bizarre interpretations. For J. G. Frazer and Luigi Piccirelli (who followed Frazer's lead) she is the wife of Hyacinthus.[48] For many others[49] she is the hero's nurse, there being at Cnidos, a Dorian colony in Asia Minor, a cult of Artemis Hyacinthotrophos, "Nurse of Hyacinthus."[50] These hypotheses are not only useless, they are totally in contradiction with what little we know about her. Pausanias, our only source, says she is the sister of Hyacinthus and undergoes apotheosis along with him. There is no mystery here, no "error" on Pausanias's part. Spartan society was composed of men and women, the women being first the sisters and then the wives of the young men. If Hyacinthus, the paradigmatic initiate from the mythical age when the world was being organized,[51] is the model of the young Spartan citizen-warrior, then his sister is the model of the young Lacedaemonian woman.

Indeed, we know (from Plutarch in particular[52]) that initiation ceremonies for young women in Sparta were almost equal in importance to those for young men, and that both girls and women played an important role in the Hyacinthia.[53] Polyboea is here in her rightful place. It is true that the initiatory myth mentions only Hyacinthus, and nowhere is there mention of a goddess who takes care of Polyboea the way Apollo takes care of her brother. Yet it is certain that in early periods there were pedagogical relations among women quite similar to those symbolized by Hyacinthus and Apollo among men.[54] The omission is understandable, however. In part, the Hyacinthus myth symbolizes the entire Lacedaemonian initiation ceremony; it subsumes, in masculine terms, a process that was both masculine and feminine. Then, too, Sparta, like all the Greek states, whatever the Athenians may have said,[55] was a society strongly dominated by males. There as elsewhere, the class of citizens was an exclusive club of adult males. Hence the story of Hyacinthus is much more important than that of his sister. Were it not for the exuberance and concern for detail of Bathycles of Magnesia, we would know nothing about Polyboea.

The Byzantine lexicographer Hesychius did know Polyboea, however, and defined her as follows: "A divinity, identified by some with Artemis, by others with Kore." This is the text that drew the attention of some commentators to Artemis Hyacinthotrophos of Cnidos. The relationship does in fact exist, but it is of a different kind from what the commentators have supposed. Artemis is the goddess of initiations— male but above all female. In Attica Artemis Brauronia presided over the initiation of young Athenian girls;[56] in Sparta Artemis Orthia was the patron of an important phase in the initiatory process for males;[57] another Artemis presided over the choirs and dances of young Spartan girls at Caryae, on the border between Laconia and Arcadia.[58] There are still other instances. Finally, we know that Artemis was present at Amyclae in connection with the female choirs.[59]

Furthermore, Artemis was in charge of the education and upbringing of children from the moment of birth: she was *kourotrophe*, the nurse and teacher of the *kouroi*, or "boys."[60] Hyacinthus is a typical *kouros*, in the sense investigated by H. Jeanmaire in his *Couroï et Courètes*.

It is at this quite general level that Polyboea and the Hyacinthotrophos are related: Polyboea, having undergone apotheosis, is a deity.

Apotheosis has raised her to the rank of Artemis, just as it raised Hyacinthus to the rank of Apollo.[61] The Hyacinthotrophos takes charge of Hyacinthus's education, in a sense parallel with Polyboea's, just as Artemis Orthia in Sparta took charge of the education of all young people.

Polyboea is also a *kore*, literally a "young girl," because the myth of Kore is also paradigmatic: Kidnapped by the god Hades, much as the young Spartan woman is kidnapped by her husband,[62] Kore takes the name Persephone, symbolizing her change of state from virgin to married woman.

Thus as Nilsson rightly observed,[63] Polyboea represents the young women of Sparta who have reached the end of adolescence and the beginning of adulthood. She and Hyacinthus die at the same time because they belong to the same generation, undergo related initiatory trials, and must at the same time turn adult and marriageable—but not to marry each other. They merely represent an age cohort, in which the emulators of Hyacinthus will exchange their Polyboeas among themselves.

To sum up, Hyacinthus is the paradigm of Spartan youth. He expresses the idea that accession to citizenship was like ascension to paradise—a Lacedaemonian way of indicating to young people that citizenship is the absolute ideal, an ideological depiction of a relatively prosaic reality.

All of this emerges easily from the data. The interpretation of the myth as an initiation runs into no obstacles and accounts for all the elements of the story. Scholars have been troubled, however, by Pausanias's assertion that sacrifices were made to Hyacinthus as to a hero, before the sacrifices to Apollo, which were obviously sacrifices to a god. This reinforces the image of Hyacinthus's death and seems to run counter to the idea of a resurrection, even though Bathycles expressed this through the apotheosis represented on the altar itself.

But there are no inconsistencies in all this. Hyacinthus, the son of a king, is a man and can be honored only through a hero's cult; and heroic cults in Greece are always chthonian, for heroes represent dead ancestors, that is, buried men. In Olympia the Pelopion was the site of a nocturnal cult.[64]

Many scholars have drawn from this the idea that the cult of Hyacinthus was quite distinct from the cult of Apollo, the former being an invocation of chthonian powers, of the dead, primarily, it seems, for agricultural purposes.[65] This is absurd; There is nothing infernal or agrarian about the cult of Pelops, for example. We know of many a hero associated with a god and buried next to him and yet with no trace of agrarian, chthonian, or vegetal associations. In one Messenian cult, Eurytus, a typical warrior, is buried alongside the Great Goddesses at Andania (Demeter and Kore for their part have obvious agrarian over-tones, but Eurytus has none).[66] The legendary musician Linus was buried in the temple of Apollo at Argos.[67] The seer Telmessus lies beneath the temple of Apollo at Telmessus.[68] The king of Cyprus, Cinyras, is buried in the temple of Aphrodite at Paphos.[69] The Hyperborean Virgins who came to worship Apollo at Delos have their tomb inside the enclosure of Artemision.[70] A heroine, Leucophryne, is buried in the sanctuary of Artemis Leucophryne (who is also the patron of initiations)[71] at Magnesia on the Maeander.[72] Neoptolemus, another warrior hero, has his tomb in the temple of Apollo at Delphi.[73] Clement of Alexandria speaks of the tombs of Acrisius, king of Argus, in the temple of Athena on the Larissa of Argos, of Cecrops and Erechtheus beside Athena on the Acropolis of Athens, and of Immaradus (another warrior) in the Eleusinion; he also says that the Milesian hero Cleochus is buried in the Didymaeon of Miletus, as is its founder Branchus.[74]

None of these names carries agrarian connotations, except perhaps the Hyperboreans—but the divinities with which they are associated are obviously not agrarian. Yet there are warrior heroes and kings, as well as a musician, a seer, and some founding heroes. To see the agrarian or chthonian element in all this is simplistic and arbitrary and profoundly mistaken. In fact, as Enmann, from whom I have taken part of this list, observed, to say that such and such a personage is buried alongside such and such a divinity is to establish a specific relationship between them, and the nature of this relationship may vary considerably, depending on the quality of the god and of the hero.[75]

In this respect the link between Hyacinthus and Apollo is twofold: First, there is a deep equivalence between Hyacinthus and Apollo, for this god is the *kouros* par excellence, like his pupil defined by his resplendent ephebe's beauty and splendid head of hair;[76] and second, since the erastēs-erōmenos relationship is temporary, there comes a moment—that of the initiatory ceremony itself—when the erōmenos is transformed into an erastēs, whereupon Hyacinthus, and all the Spartans who resemble him, play the role that had previously been Apollo's. In short, in the domain of myth, just as Polyboea is Artemis, so, too, is Hyacinthus Apollo. Accordingly, one might even say that after his mystical death Hyacinthus is "reborn as Apollo," if the Greeks, like the Indians, believed in the absorption of one divine (or human) essence by another. The distinction between Hyacinthus and Apollo was always maintained in Sparta.[77] But south of Tarentum, a Spartan colony, there was a tomb of Apollo-Hyacinthus.[78] Here there is not the least confusion: The notion—of a hero who dies and is reborn a god—is the same as in Amyclae, only expressed in a slightly different way.

THE HYACINTHIA

As for the Hyacinthia, there is a masterful study by Henri Jeanmaire, entitled *Couroï et Courètes*, which is compatible with the interpretation proposed here of the Hyacinthus myth. There is also a study published in Brelich's *Paides e Parthenoi*. I myself hope to reconsider the problem in a fresh light, but this is not the place to do so; the present work would be considerably weighed down. I shall therefore refer to the two works cited for proof of my assertions. Here are the main points.

The festival was divided into two parts, the first sad, the second gay, extending over three days—there is some controversy about this,[79] but the proposition is supported by one of the few certain pieces of evidence to be found in the sources, a description by Athenaeus.

> Polycrates relates in his *History of Sparta* that the Spartans observe the ritual of the Hyacinthia for a period of three days, and because of the mourning which takes place for the death of Hyacinthus they neither wear crowns at the meals nor introduce wheat bread, nor do they dispense any cakes, with their accompaniments, and they abstain from singing the paean to the god, and do not introduce anything else of the sort that they do at other festivals. On the contrary, they eat with great restraint, and then depart. But in the middle of the three-day period there is held a spectacle with many features and a noteworthy concourse attended by many. Boys with tunics girt high play the lyre or sing to flute accompaniment while they run the entire gamut of the strings with the plectrum; they sing the praises of the god in anapestic rhythm and in a high pitch. Others march through the theater mounted on gaily adorned horses; full choirs of young men enter and sing some of their national songs, and dancers mingling among them go through the figures in the ancient style, accompanied by the flute and the voice of the singers. As for the girls, some are

carried in wicker carts which are sumptuously ornamented, others parade in chariots yoked to two horses, which they race, and the entire city is given over to the bustle and joy of the festival. On that day they sacrifice very many victims, and the citizens entertain at dinner all their acquaintances and their own servants as well. Not one misses the festival; on the contrary, it so happens that the city is emptied to see the spectacle.[80]

The clear distinction introduced by Polycrates is supported by the only information that Pausanias provides about the cult of Amyclae: "At the Hyacinthia, before the sacrifice of Apollo, they make offerings to Hyacinthus as a hero, at this altar, through a bronze door."[81]

The sequence of events is easy to interpret. Those who have traveled from Sparta to Amyclae are sad and austere on the first day. That night (sacrifices to heroes were always made at night in Greece), they sacrifice to Hyacinthus, because he is a hero, of course, and because he is a man and is dead, and not because he is a chthonian god or vegetable spirit or what have you. On the second day—probably around midday, to respect the division of the three days into two parts—a gay and colorful crowd, comprising the whole of Spartan society, left the city for the sanctuary. At this stage Apollo was honored and there was singing, dancing, and parades; the paean, absent the first day, dominates.

This corresponds exactly to the myth. In the first stage (as the whole poetic tradition confirms) Hyacinthus has been killed and Apollo mourns him. In the second stage (compare the sculptures of Bathycles and Nonnus's allusion to the Laconian song celebrating the resurrection of Hyacinthus by Apollo) Hyacinthus and his sister ascend to heaven, which is to say, they are resurrected on a higher plane—a legitimate reason for joy.

This structure, says Jeanmaire, is highly reminiscent of that of the Attic Theseia.[82] Initiatory symbolism underlies both.

Another author cited by Athenaeus, Polemon, collected various information about the Hyacinthia in the second century A.D. He calls the festival the Kopis ("knife"), surely after one of its phases. People slept in tents alongside the temple, he says, on branches strewn upon the ground. At this point only goats were sacrificed. The meal consisted of meat, cakes, cheese, belly, sausages, figs, broad beans, and green beans. All Lacedaemonians were allowed to attend, but for infant boys there was a special Kopis, held at the same time, which was called the Tithēnidia, during which nurses carried the infants to the temple of Artemis Korythalia on the banks of the Tiassos (the Tiasa of Pausanias) between Sparta and Amyclae.[83] The Attic comic poet Cratinus, cited by Polemon, describes old men eagerly devouring sausages hung in the public gates. Given that Xenophon mentions choruses of adult males[84] and Euripides choruses of married women,[85] it is clear that all social categories were involved—citizens, their wives, slaves, and nurses (the name of the Tithēnidia comes from *tithēnē*, "nurse")—and participants were grouped according to their age: baby boys (to the Tithenidia), boys (*paides*), young men (*neaniskoi*), adult citizens, old men, young girls (*parthenoi*), and married women.

It has been suggested—cautiously by Brelich, with certainty by Ileana Chirassi—that this classification should be interpreted as a survival of a rigorous system of age classification, which we know from other sources was once an important Spartan institution, the idea being that careless authors obscured the system's once sharp outlines.[86]

It is essential to carry this argument one step further, as Brelich does in viewing the Hyacinthia as more than an initiatory rite, indeed as a festival of universal renewal.[87] His arguments are powerful: Why include slaves and any foreigners who wished to participate if the festival involved only the promotion of new citizens? Why the annual change, on the occasion of the Hyacinthia, of the *peplos* (cloak) of Apollo, woven during the year in the sanctuary of the Leucippides at Sparta?[88] Indeed, if we were dealing simply with an initiatory passage from one state to another, we would expect the rite to include a change of clothing. But if the point was to signify global renewal (society conceiving of itself as a kind of wheel, in which each vanished generation is replaced by the newly born), then it would have been enough to restore the existing garment; the festival would then evoke a transitive cycle and not an intransitive linear passage.

Seen in this way, the festival involves more than just a contrast between mourning at the beginning, joy at the end; its purpose is to obliterate normal social relations. Several indications suggest that this was indeed the case. If, in the Hyacinthia, the Lacedaemonians intended to recover a "state of nature" characteristic of initiations, they would have slept on strewn reeds—as young Spartans did during civic and military training.[89] But the sources refer explicitly to strewn *branches*, which is not quite a return to "nature." Similarly, the sacrifice to Hyacinthus is more than a sacrifice to a hero. According to Polycrates, failure to wear a crown at a banquet or sacrifice in ancient Greece was tantamount to denying an essential aspect of the ceremony. I shall here use the term "antisacrifice"[90]—in all their great rituals, the Lacedaemonians, like other Greeks, were crowned.[91] Polycrates also tells us that people abstained from bread and cakes the first day. In Greece grains defined the human condition. Not to eat them was to suspend one's humanity. On the second day, the reception of slaves as equals and of foreigners as fellow citizens, coupled with unbridled excesses of gaiety and the sacrifice of dozens, perhaps as many as a hundred, head of cattle,[92] constituted another way of nullifying the world's normal state, complementary (or opposite) to the method used the previous day. This suggests, though we have no independent confirmation or proof, that the third day corresponded to the restoration of order.

It does not follow that Hyacinthus's death stands for anything other than the mystical death of the initiate. Nothing in the myth justifies any other hypothesis. But the initiatory death itself is simply a key element in a larger event (I say key element because it is this ritual death that creates a whole new group of citizens). This larger event is the death of society, of the whole world, followed by rebirth. Everything is the same, but a year's time has passed.

INVERSIONS

We know nothing about Cyparissus or Narcissus beyond their legends; whatever correspondences there may have been with religion or ritual have disappeared. But they resemble Hyacinthus so closely that what we have learned about him sheds light on the significance of the other two, enabling us to analyze further the meaning of these parallel legends.

The stories of Cyparissus and Narcissus seem almost like a distortion of an original version that is given to us in its exact form in the Hyacinthus myth. The Boeotian version (Narcissus) inverts the motif, denying both the homosexuality and the heterosexuality of the hero in order to make him into the model of the asocial adolescent; the Chian version (Cyparisus) preserves the original scheme but weakens it, changing the murder of a human into the killing of an animal and justifying the hero's death by depicting it as a suicide committed out of despair.

With the killing of the stag, however, the Cyparissus legend seems to preserve an archaic element that is missing from the Hyacinthus myth: the hunting exploit.

It is noteworthy, in fact, that according to the letter of the tale the death of Cyparissus is a direct consequence of the death of the animal. In terms of initiation, the sequence of events can be interpreted as follows: At the end of a sojourn in the bush with his erastēs and educator Apollo (as in the Hyacinthus myth), Cyparissus kills a large wild animal. This exploit concludes the testing phase of the initiation cycle, just as the killing of a boar or a bear does among the Taifali, and permits the hero to pass to the rank of adult citizen after his mystical death.

Note that in Greek symbolism the animals that occur in hunting exploits are primarily the stag, the boar, the lion, and the goat. Consider, for example, the reliefs on the Amyclaeon described by Pausanias: We find the legendary hunt for the boar of Calydon, Heracles' combat with the lion of Nemea, Bellerophon and the Chimaera, which is actually a goat combined with a lion and a serpent, and Admetus subduing a lion and a boar and hitching them to his chariot.[93] In connection with the Chimaera, we may recall the wild goat carried by the young man in the bronze medallion that may be the oldest Cretan evidence for the existence of a homosexual initiation rite.[94] Heracles kills a redoubtable wild boar in the mountains of Erymanthus in northern Arcadia, and in the same region he pursues a fantastic doe with golden horns and bronze feet. Actaeon, famous for having been devoured by his dogs, belongs to the same series of asocial heroes as Hippolytus and Narcissus. Passionate about hunting (like Hippolytus), Actaeon becomes obsessed, transgresses human and divine laws, and trespasses on Artemis's domain; he is transformed into a stag.

To us it is a surprising logic that equates the killing of a goat with that of a stag or lion (the European lion still existed in archaic Greece). The bear, on the other hand, is excluded from this Greek symbolism (though not from the symbolism of the Taifali). None of the ancient Greek heroes does battle with a bear. Instead, bears raise abandoned children[95] and couple with humans,[96] and humans are transformed into bears,[97] all of which tends to humanize this animal and to animalize the humans involved with it. The reason for this is that in Greece the bear, like the wolf, encodes a certain social situation, that of the initiate (the female virgins dedicated to the service of Artemis at Brauron in Attica were *arctoi*, bears[98]) or professional warrior (the Arcadians were known as Bears, sons of Arcas[99] and acorn-eaters[100]). The same thing can be expressed in different ways: Among the Taifali the man who kills a bear or a boar shows that he is as strong as these animals and worthy of being considered an adult male; in primitive Greece the man who kills, say, a boar becomes an adult worthy of comparison with a bear.

It is worth noting that the hunting exploit, which is omitted from the Hyacinthus myth, is strongly suggested in the work of Bathycles, in which we find any number of heroes killing or subduing various wild animals. It is possible that the exploit was left out of the story because there was no room for it, because it was not pertinent, but that it loomed large in the eyes of young Lacedaemonians. It would not be surprising if it had also been left out of the Narcissus story, in which even the sojourn in the bush is barely suggested (for the meaning has been altered), and yet we do find a trace of it: The disappointed lover, the nymph Echo, withdraws into a wild and lonely place, not far from where the hero, upon returning from a hunt, bends over a spring to quench his thirst and falls in love with his own reflection.[101]

Thus homosexuality, hunting, and mystical death link Hyacinthus, Cyparissus, and Narcissus. And as we have seen, their names also link them, as does what becomes of their blood or corpses. Hyacinthus's blood gives rise to the *hyacinthus*, whose meaning we have investigated; Cyparissus's body is transformed into a cypress; and Narcissus's blood becomes the narcissus. What do these allusions to plants mean?

Once again, the agrarian interpretation is to be rejected. The narcissus and the cypress are no more appropriate than the *hyacinthus* as symbols of agriculture. Rather, it is the plant world whose very variety is a rich source of symbolism.

In the first place, the cypress, an evergreen, was to the ancient peoples of the Mediterranean what the fir was to the peoples of the north: It symbolized the triumph of life over death. A durable wood, believed impervious to rot and for that reason used by the earliest sculptors,[102] cypress was a symbol of longevity. It was the antithesis of death and thus its symbol. Cypress has been planted in cemeteries since antiquity. Symbols of eternal life, cypresses surrounded the grotto in Crete where Zeus was born. According to the people of Ephesus, it was not in Delos but in their city that Leto gave birth, in a forest composed primarily of cypress.[103] Frequently, too, cypress symbolized rebirth and initiation rituals. In Cyprus, at the festivals of Adonis, speeches were made at the temple gates to tree trunks called *aoia*, probably cypress.[104] Cypress was associated with Artemis, goddess of initiations, with Aphrodite

Melainis, goddess of generation,[105] with Persephone (who symbolized the resurrection of nature and the annual cycle of plants), and with Asclepius, executed by Zeus for resuscitating a dead man and then apotheosized. Near Cnossus people worshiped Rhea, mother of the gods, in a forest of cypress,[106] and the temple of Zeus at Nemea was surrounded by the same trees. There, the murder of a child, Opheltes, by a serpent was at the origin of his cult, under the name Archemorus, and of the Nemean Games, to which, according to Hyginus, Laius took Chrysippus.[107] Similarly, the temple of Asclepius at Titane was surrounded by cypress, and a sacred cypress stood in front of the temple of Asclepius at Cos. The tree also appeared on the coins of Epidaurus.[108] In all of this there is no agrarian or even funerary symbolism, except perhaps in the use of the perennial cypress to symbolize its antithesis, death.[109]

Of the three plants the narcissus is the one whose symbolic significance comes closest to what some scholars have ascribed to all three. It connotes the exuberance of nature in springtime. According to the *Homeric Hymn to Demeter*, Hades, when he decided to abduct Kore, asked Gaea to cause a splendid narcisus to spring from the earth. Kore was then playing with the Oceanides in the midst of the Nysaean meadow, full of roses, saffron, gladiolus, lilies, violets, and *hyacinthus*. Just as she reaches out to grasp the magnificent narcissus, the earth opens and Hades emerges.[110] According to Sophocles, saffron and narcissus grew at Colonus and also in the mythical land of Nysa, where Dionysus and the nymphs who fed him were staying.[111] Narcissuses form the crowns of Demeter and Persephone, Hades, Hermes, Dionysus, and perhaps the Erinyes.[112] Hence if the blood of Narcissus gave rise to a narcissus, it was not because the hero symbolized the rebirth of nature in the spring (nothing in the various versions of the myth supports such a hypothesis) but because a plant that summed up the mystery of the plant cycle and nature's annual renewal was especially apt to signify the fact that Narcissus's death is only apparent, not real. Like a plant, the erōmenos dies, because like a plant he will be reborn, though on a qualitatively different plane.

It is also worth noting that the ancient Greeks stressed the beauty of the narcissus. When Gaea caused the miraculous plant to spring from the earth in order to seduce Kore,

the flower shone with marvelous brilliance and astonished all who

gazed upon it, immortal gods as well as mortal men. From its root
sprang a stalk with a hundred heads, and all of the vast heavens above
smiled at the fragrance from that bowl of flowers.[113]

Perhaps for the Boeotian creators of the myth Narcissus's beauty stood
out among men as the narcissus stood out among flowers.

Thus, if initiation is patent in the Hyacinthus myth, it is also subtly
apparent in the myths of Narcissus and Cyparissus and, with two rather
different modifications, can explain their origins.

It follows that each Greek region had its own founder of initiatory
homosexuality: Hyacinthus is to Sparta what Pelops is to Elis. An
obscure northern version of the myth yields the following generalization:
Thamyris, who according to Apollodorus was Narcissus's lover, was the
first Greek pederast. Narcissus, on the other hand, demonstrates behavior that is to be avoided, but it is plausible that, before the moral
system of the classical city-state took hold, he was the mythical founder
of homosexuality—prior to Laius—in the ancient Mycenaean kingdom
of Thebes.[114] In this connection it is worth nothing that Thespiae,
Narcissus's city, boasted a guild of *thamuriddontes*, musicians descended
from Thamyris. As for Cyparissus, finally, we may assume that he was to
the Chians—and possibly to the Orchomenians—what Hyacinthus was
to the Laconians.

I add the Orchomenians of Boeotia because the settlers of the Ionian
islands at the beginning of the first millennium came mainly from
Boeotia, and there are several indications that the inhabitants of Chios
actually came from Boeotia.[115] The oldest Orchomenian inscription is a
dedication by a man named Philo to a hero named Cyparissus. Little is
known about Philo; a small town between Daulis and Delphi in the
region attributed by legend to the Phlegyans, the Orchomenian warrior
class derives its name from him.[116] It is a Phlegyan, as we shall see, who
seems to have been the founder of Orchomenian warrior homosexuality.[117] It is in this context that the earliest mention of Cyparissus
occurs.

A famous Chian legend, the basis for the preeminence and privileges
of the powerful Acontiades family, was recorded by Xenomedes, a
historian of the island, and then made famous by a poem of Callimachus.
It tells of the marriage of the young Acontius, descended from the priests

of Zeus Aristaeus and Zeus Icmius, to a young Athenian woman of royal parentage, Cydippe. One of the fragments depicts Acontius pursued by his erōmenoi: "Many, who loved Acontius, threw the Sicilian *kottabos* from the bottom of the cups onto the ground."[118] This was a banquet ritual whereby, at the marriage of the erastēs, his erōmenoi marked the rupture of relations between him and them by throwing wine upon the ground. How many erōmenoi? Compare the Cretan custom in which a man of noble blood is the erastēs of an adolescent no less noble, with whose companions—the *agele*—he roams the mountains, and the Spartan custom of concluding at the age of thirty a marriage decided upon long before.[119]

This story of Acontius is not the basis of the homosexual ritual, however. It explains the importance, and doubtless the cults, of a great family; it may also have been the basis of matrimonial rituals. But there is no doubt as to the temporal priority of the mythical love affair between Cyparissus and Apollo over the human and quasi-historical loves of the ancestor Acontius. The Apollonian affair is the predecessor of the love between Acontius and his erōmenoi.

NINE
Adaptations
㗪

I have singled out Apollo's two best-known male lovers (Hyacinthus and Cyparissus) and linked them, on the basis of their distinguishing traits, to the story of Narcissus. But Apollo, the *kouros* par excellence, in classical times represented the educator, and hence the erastēs, par excellence. I shall now examine his other loves, including some highly unusual ones.

A STRANGE ERŌMENOS: KING ADMETUS

Son of Pheres, Admetus reigned over Pherae, a city in central Thessaly (today Velestino) to the northwest of Iolcus (present-day Volos). In the fourth *Pythian Ode* Pindar shows him joining his cousin Jason, among the first to take part in the quest for the Golden Fleece.[1] Apollodorus places him among those who assisted Meleager in the hunt for the Calydonian boar.[2] He had just succeeded his father when Apollo was condemned to serve him as a shepherd.

This servitude was a punishment imposed by Zeus. According to Apollodorus, Apollo's son Asclepius (mentioned earlier in connection with the cypress) busied himself restoring the dead to life. This agreeable work disturbed the order of the world. Hence Zeus struck down Asclepius with one of his thunderbolts. Furious, Apollo rained his arrows upon the Cyclopes, the artisans who fashioned Zeus's thunderbolts. The master of the gods therefore subjected him to a year's punishment as servant to a mortal. During that year Admetus's flocks grew rapidly, as each female gave birth to two offspring.[3]

Shortly thereafter, Admetus, wishing to marry, asked for the hand of Alcestis, daughter of Pelias, king of Iolcus. Pelias proposed an impressive trial: His daughter's suitor must come to him in a chariot drawn by a lion and a boar. The hero turned to Apollo, who provided him with the needed chariot. And so Admetus the king of Pherae married Alcestis. But during the marriage celebration Admetus forgot to sacrifice to Artemis (whose ambit Alcestis left in order to marry). Upon entering the marriage chamber, Admetus found it full of serpents. Once again Apollo was his savior. The god prevailed upon his sister to relent and also persuaded the Moirai, or Fates, that Admetus should be spared from death when his turn came, provided someone else agreed to take his place.[4] This is the story that Euripides so magnificently turned into tragedy in his *Alcestis*, in the year 438.

Apollo's servitude implies that the god fell in love with the young king. Callimachus has this to say in his *Hymn to Apollo*:

> We call upon Phoebus as shepherd also, ever since the day on the banks of the Amphrysus, when, burning with love for the young Admetus, he made himself guardian of the mares. Under the watchful gaze of the god, the number of livestock grew quickly, and the goats of the herd gave birth to kids.[5]

Taken literally, the story is one of initiation. Apollo's servitude and love precede the king's marriage, which involves a typical trial. Hence it seems likely that Admetus's participation in the hunt for the Calydonian boar and the Argonauts' expedition occurred earlier. This suggests that the sequence of events in the testing phase of Admetus's life was as follows: member of Jason's *agele*, member of Meleager's *agele*, homosexual loves, hunting exploit, marriage.

Yet this sequence is surely artificial, precisely because the story is not to be taken literally. As a king, the son of a king, and son-in-law of a king, Admetus would have had to be the only, or principal, hero in any trial designed to test his mettle. He might replace Jason or Meleager, but he could not be simply one of their companions, especially since the trial in which Meleager distinguishes himself, the hunt for the Calydonian boar, parallels his own trial, the capture of a boar and a lion. Evidently, it was because he hailed from Thessaly that he was very early (probably in the earliest *Argonautica* of the time of the Homeric poems, which surely postdate the *Argonautica* since they took part of their inspiration from it[6]) named as one of the constellation of heroes who accompanied Jason and who were certainly anonymous in the earliest version of the myth. Later, since many of the Argonauts joined the Calydonian boar hunt, Admetus also became the companion of Meleager. In fact, his own trial, the capture and domestication of two wild animals, surpassed his exploits in the other ordeals and sufficed to qualify him.

This trial, moreover, was a hunting exploit quite similar to those we have already encountered. Boars and lions appear commonly in Greek hunting trials. A boar occurs in the exploits of Heracles and (as we saw earlier) among the Taifali; a lion figures in the labors of Heracles and for the Taifali symbolizes, like the bear, the wild beast. The same pair of animals figures in a famous story of initiation, that of the marriage of Adrastus's daughters. Adrastus, king of Argos, has received an oracle according to which he will marry his daughters to a lion and a boar. Much later, when his two daughters are old enough to marry, two famous heroes, each exiled from his own country (Tydeus from Calydon and Polynices from Thebes), come seeking shelter in Adrastus's palace on a stormy night. Either because they fight outside the palace "like a lion and a boar" or because their shields are emblazoned with images of these animals, Adrastus recognizes the ancient oracle and gives his elder daughter Argia to Polynices, his younger daughter Deipyle to Tydeus.[7] In this beautiful myth the hunting exploit is transformed into martial symbolism. Tydeus and Polynices do not fight with animals but behave as warriors imbued with the strength of the lion and the boar. Similarly, after Heracles fights and kills the Lion of Nemea, he dons the lion's skin, thereby signifying that his strength is equal to that of the lion. This transmutation is nothing if not natural: In Greece as in Australasia, the hunting exploit confers adult status upon the adolescent, for it is but a short step from hunting animals to hunting men.

Similar use is made of the same symbol in a vase painting. Peleus, father of Achilles and educated by the Centaur Chiron, takes his child to the same teacher. The painting shows him handing the young Achilles over to the Centaur, who comes out of his cave followed by a bear, a lion, and a boar.[8] In other words, Chiron, master of wild animals, will make his pupil an accomplished warrior by teaching him how to hunt, how to subdue wild beasts. According to one well-known story, Chiron feeds Achilles nothing but lions' and boars' entrails, honey, and bears' marrow.[9] Note once again the contrast between the lion and the boar on one side and the bear on the other. Furthermore, a black-figure amphora in the Louvre represents a couple that the inscriptions describe as Kassmos and Harmonia in a chariot hitched to a lion and a boar, with Apollo accompanying, lyre in hand.[10] This is a nuptial cortège, for here Cadmus, vanquisher of the Dragon of Ares near the Theban spring, conquers Harmonia, daughter of Ares, and marries her. This reveals the "truth" about the slaying of the dragon: In the case of Admetus, the hunt for the boar of Calydon, the assistance to Jason in the quest for the Fleece, guarded by a dragon, and Admetus's own domestication of a lion and a boar are equivalent; similarly, Cadmus's killing of a dragon is expressed in this synthetic representation by showing his chariot hitched to wild beasts.[11]

To sum up, the Admetus legend bestows upon Apollo the role that falls to Poseidon in the Pelops myth. After an initiatory phase that includes homosexual relations, the god, who is also the teacher, magically provides his erōmenos, now an adult, with the means to succeed in the superhuman trial that will win him a spouse.

But things are not as simple as they seem. A series of difficulties crops up immediately. To begin with, comparison with other legends of the same type shows that the trial that results in marriage also confers royalty. Thus Pelops succeeds Oenomaus after winning the hand of Hippodamia; Cadmus, by slaying the dragon son of Ares, wins the god's daughter and becomes the founder and first king of Thebes (Harmonia is preeminently the "woman who assembles," the "guarantor of concord and social life," as F. Vian rightly observes[12]); Tydeus and Polynices, by marrying the daughters of Adrastus, become, respectively, king of Argos and eligible to capture the kingship of Thebes by force of arms; Jason's adventure culminates in his marriage to Medea, daughter of the keeper of the Golden Fleece, and his accession to the throne of Corinth, from which it came. This is not the case in the Admetus legend, however. Apollo comes to the household of a man who is already king and helps him simply to conclude a marriage—a first flaw. Furthermore, Admetus's marriage to Alcestis, daughter of Pelias, opens the way, indirectly at any rate, for Admetus to succeed his father-in-law. In the oldest text in which Admetus is mentioned, book II of the *Iliad*, the people of Pherae (Admetus's city) and Iolcus (Pelias's city) had for their leader

> the dear son of Admetus . . . Eumelus, born to Admetus by the beauty among women Alcestis, loveliest of all the daughters of Pelias.[13]

A second anomaly, strictly complementary to the first, comes from the very structure of the Apollo legend. The god is thrice exiled. The first time, after the slaying of the monstrous serpent that guarded the fortress of Delphi, he is banished for eight years to northern Thessaly, in the Tempe valley through which the Peneus flows on its way to the sea, between Ossa and Olympus.[14] The second time, because Apollo has taken part, along with Poseidon, Hera, and Athena, in a plot against Zeus, the master of the gods sends him, together with Poseidon, to serve the king of Troy, Laomedon. Depending on which version is consulted, Apollo either helps Poseidon build the walls of Troy or tends the king's flocks.[15] The third adventure, following the murder of the Cyclopes, is the exile to Admetus's household.

These three exiles are obviously homologous, and in particular the two Thessalian exiles overlap: the periods of expiation and purification— one year with Admetus, eight years at Tempe—are homologous, because the second is simply the "great year" defined by the return of the sun, moon, and visible planets to the same relative positions.[16] Thus, after the slaying of the dragon of Thebes, Ares wants to kill Cadmus, but Zeus "commutes" the punishment, and Cadmus must serve Ares for either one year or eight years, at the end of which Ares, reconciled with him, makes the hero his son-in-law.[17] The gods who perjured themselves remain for one year in a state of lethargy and then are exiled from Olympus for nine years.[18] Teiresias, having wounded a serpent, becomes a woman for seven or eight years.[19] The Arcadian lycanthrope who ate human flesh is transformed for nine years into a wolf.[20] Theseus and Orestes, murderers, respectively, of the Pallantidae and Clytemnestra, are exiled for one year.[21] Furthermore, at Delphi, where every eight years young Delphians went to Tempe in search of an olive branch to commemorate Apollo's exile, they followed a route (the Pythias) that crossed Thessaly and passed through Pherae; Admetus's seat and Tempe are on the same road and, in relation to Delphi, quite close together.[22]

There exist Indian and Greek cycles in which a person (Indra in the Indian cycle and Heracles in the Greek) has adventures that can be divided into three groups, which Georges Dumézil was able to interpret in trifunctional terms.[23] Inspired by Dumézil's interpretation, Francis Vian has proposed a similar reading of the three exiles of Apollo.[24] Trifunctionality is far from obvious in the texts, but the existence of three distinct series is beyond doubt. A series of crimes—the slaying of the Delphic serpent, the murder of the Cyclopes, the revolt against Zeus—triggers a series of exiles in the remote north (in Thessaly) or in the service of a king, or both. Note, moreover, that in the story of the servitude with Laomedon, Laomedon is not depicted as a young aspirant to royalty or marriage but rather as a sovereign master, who even takes the liberty of not paying the gods their promised wages.[25]

It follows, then, that regardless of whether the three stories derive
from one initial one or form a coherent tripartite group, the exile with
Admetus makes Apollo and not the king the young man undergoing
initiation. This was clearly understood by Vian.

> The temporary exile of the hero or murderous (or criminal) god is
> more than just expiation of a crime. It is part of a complex structure
> having to do with initiation. . . . The "passion" of the god or hero
> precedes and prepares the way for his promotion in accordance with a
> process well known from rites of adolescence. There, too, the novice
> must live for a time cut off from society. Whether he is shut up in a
> hut, obliged to serve a god, or forced to lead an animal existence in the
> wilderness, it is as if he were dead until the day when he is granted (or
> wins) the right to return to society in a new status.[26]

Thus, in the Delphic tradition, Apollo is sacrificed by the serpent and
buried under the Omphalos,[27] much as Jason, according to certain vase
paintings, is swallowed, devoured by the Dragon of the Golden Fleece in
the course of their battle.[28]

This turns the interpretation of the Admetus myth upside down.
Whether he is banished to the bush (at Tempe) or forced to serve a king,
as the erōmenoi of New Guinea and perhaps Crete were forced to serve
their erastai, it is Apollo who is the novice undergoing initiation and
who, if there is a pederastic ritual, is in the female position.

This being the case, there are two possible interpretations. Either the
homosexual relationship between Apollo and Admetus, which so far as I
know is not mentioned before Callimachus, is a poetic invention without
ritual foundations and is simply copied from widespread legends of the
Pelops type, or—and the blasphemy will scandalize many proper Hellenists—Admetus was, in a primitive version of the legend, the erastēs
of Apollo.

If one is willing to accept what it is the purpose of this book to prove,
namely, that initiation in protohistorical Greece normally involved the
sexual subjection of the novice to the teacher, then Apollo, model of the
kouroi, a *kouros* himself, and the educator par excellence, must have
undergone the full cycle of education in order to become what he is, for
example, in the Hyacinthus myth, the erastēs and teacher. The sexual
submission of god to king must have struck Greek minds as unspeakably
shocking ever since the time of the earliest written texts—the Homeric
poems are already very discreet on this score.[29] Thus it is not surprising

that we find no mention of it in literature prior to its revelation, in inverted form, in the work of a poet of the early Hellenistic era.

The reader may object that the scheme god-erastēs/man-erōmenos is coherent in a way that the scheme man-erastēs/god-erōmenos is not. This brings us to the problem of Admetus's nature. This hero is not just anyone. We saw earlier that Apollo's exile to Thessaly signifies his temporary death, which is expressed directly in the myth that shows the serpent killing the god and burying him beneath the temple at Delphi. The equivalence is even clearer in a fragment of a Hesiodic poem, of which Wilamowitz has proposed the following reading:[30] Apollo's exile could only have been to the underworld, and his release must have been secured by his mother, Leto. Other indications had already induced the German mythologists of the nineteenth century to formulate the following hypothesis, which deserves attention: Admetus, literally "the untamable," is none other than Hades, an anthropomorphization or hypostasis of the god of the underworld. Hesychius says that he was the father of the goddess Hecate, who was surely infernal.[31] The sources used by this Byzantine scholar are frequently of excellent quality, and this fact alone is highly significant. Furthermore, Admetus's mother's name was Clymene[32] or Periclymene:[33] Clymenus, "the celebrated," was a euphemism for Hades.[34] The sons of Admetus are closely associated with horses, a symbol of the underworld in Greece as in other countries.[35] One of the sons is named Hippasus,[36] and another, Eumelus, is celebrated in the *Iliad* as a chariot driver.[37] One of the epithets applied to Hades in the *Iliad* is *adamastos* "untamed," "inflexible"[38], a word quite similar to the name Admetus. In this light the Alcestis story takes on a new coloration: It is death that nourishes Hades and prolongs his existence.

Admetus is therefore not an ordinary man. It is not impossible (nor, admittedly, is it certain) that in archaic times men ascribed to the god who took a wife in the Spartan manner, by kidnapping her, the task of educating Leto's son, the young god and new Olympian, in the usual protohistorical fashion, that is, during a course of training in the bush.

NUPTIAL HYMNS

Hymenaeus is none other than the marriage chant personified. The legends about him reported by various authors of late antiquity can only be late inventions without traditional ritual underpinnings. It is interesting, however, that this mythical founder of a matrimonial ritual is repeatedly said to have engaged in homosexual love affairs and, oddly enough, is frequently described as a descendant of Admetus.

Antoninus Liberalis, following various authors including Hesiod, reports that Magnes, eponym of the Thessalian tribe known as the Magnetes, son of Argos and Perimele, herself the daughter of Admetus, had a son, Hymenaeus. Apollo saw him, fell in love, and from then on refused to leave Magnes' house. It was then, the writer adds, neatly telescoping different traditions, that Hermes stole Apollo's bullocks, which were none other than the bullocks of Admetus.[39]

As in the case of Hyacinthus, the lovers vary. According to Suidas, Hymenaeus's lover was Thamyris, the mythical bard whom Apollodorus took to be the founder of pederasty.[40] Other sources name Hesperus, the evening star, for it was at the hour that this star rose that the hymen was completed. According to Athenaeus, who reports the words of Licymnius of Chios in his *Dithyrambs*, Hymenaeus was the erōmenos of a hero named Argynnus;[41] Wilamowitz proposed correcting this to "Dionysus."

As for the hero Argynnus, Athenaeus had just told, in the immediately preceding passage, the following story: Agamemnon falls in love with Argynnus after admiring him swimming in the Cephissus. Then, in the course of swimming, in a manner not described, the young hero dies. Agamemnon buries him and establishes a temple to Aphrodite Argynnis.[42] The episode is recounted by Clement of Alexandria, who claims to have found it in a work of Phanocles, *The Loves or the Handsome Boys*, and by Stephen of Byzantium,[43] with some variants. Son of Leucon and Peisidike, Argynnus lived on the banks of lake Copais or Leuconis (into which the Cephissus flows); the amorous Agamemnon pursues him, and in order to escape he jumps into the Cephissus. The source may be ancient; Hesiod numbered Argynnus among the offspring of the Orchomenian royal family, and convergent data associated Agamemnon with water, springs, and ponds, particularly in Boeotia.[44]

So we once more encounter Argynnus/Argennos, though his presence in the affair may be nothing more (according to Wilamowitz) than a manuscript error. For now the important thing is to understand why Hymenaeus was conceived as an erōmenos, beloved of Apollo or Thamyris.

For one thing, he was of course divinely beautiful. All the authors say so, and beauty is readily understandable as an attribute of the symbol of marriage. According to Cretan values, one did not choose an adolescent because he was handsome but, according to Ephorus, because of his courage and distinction. However, in Greek culture in general, since the classical era at least, these values were not the ones that governed the choice of an erōmenos. In all the Attic literature, and in the later literature of the Hellenistic period, the essential and often the only selection criterion was physical beauty.[45]

Furthermore, by definition almost, Hymenaeus is a musician, and in the Attic representation the handsome young musician, especially the cithara player, is effeminate. In the Theban Discuroi couple consisting of Zethus and Amphion, Zethus was a crude, violent manual laborer, whereas Amphion was a delicate musician whom Hermes had taught to play the lyre. In fragments by Euripides Zethus calls his brother an effeminate man.[46] Plato says that Orpheus was unable to retrieve Eurydice from the underworld because he acted without resolve, "as is natural to a cithara player."[47] Many vase paintings show Hyacinthus being grabbed by Zephyrus as he plays the cithara.[48]

Marriage, moreover, which combines masculine and feminine, partakes of both, and this accounts for the fact that representations of Hymenaeus show certain hermaphroditic characteristics. He has long, curly hair and carries fruits (walnuts and pomegranates) and flowers (roses and marjoram), and his clothing is as much feminine as it is masculine.[49]

But in Greek tradition not all handsome young men, cithara players, and males dressed as females are said to have engaged in homosexual loves. There is something else in legends of the type that mythographers elaborated around the figure of Hymenaeus that accounts for his homosexuality.

Simply put, Hymenaeus dies at the moment of marriage. In the marriage of Dionysus and Althaea, Hymenaeus (in this version the son of Magnes) dies suddenly in the midst of chanting. In a milder version, he is the former lover of Hesperus and is chanting at the marriage of Dionysus and Ariadne when he suddenly loses his voice. Apollodorus echoes a major tradition: Hymenaeus is one of the men resuscitated by Asclepius, before Asclepius himself is struck by Zeus's thunderbolt and promoted to godhood.[50]

Hymenaeus's position as erōmenos can be understood as follows: Marriage is a rite of passage if ever there was one, and its personification, or, more precisely, the personification of one of the major matrimonial rites, adopted the symbolism of a rite of passage. In Greece, as elsewhere, marriage concludes the testing period in the lives of young men, and the rite of passage that Hymenaeus subsumes in his person is naturally an initiatory rite. Hymenaeus dies at the moment of marriage, he is reborn later on, and therefore he must previously have been the erōmenos of a god or man.

This is not ancient material. Hymenaeus was an important mythological divinity in the Hellenistic era and there is nothing to indicate that the process began earlier. Antoninus Liberalis's reference to Hesiod is misleading—Hesiod is only one of the five authors from whom he borrows his tale. Nevertheless, the case of Hymenaeus is still interesting. The authors naturally see the position of a handsome young man prior to marriage as that of an erōmenos soon to die in the nuptial ceremony only to be reborn afterward. The initiatory schema is almost intact.

Hymenaeus's ancestry is also not without interest. It varies from author to author. Some make him the son of Apollo and a Muse—Calliope, Clio, or Urania; others, the son of Dionysus and Aphrodite; still others, of Magnes and Perimele, daughter of Admetus; and yet others, of Pierus, himself the son of Magnes.

Thus tradition ascribes to Hymenaeus not only divine ancestors but also northern ones: Magnes is the eponym of a tribe and a region of Thessaly; Pierus is the eponym of Pieria, the area immediately north of Thessaly in southern Macedonia. There is a precise correlation between his human ancestry and his divine ancestry. In fact, the Muses, three of whom were said by various authors to have been his mother, are often called the Pierides, after Pieria.

We have already found northern roots in the Hyacinthus legend. According to Apollodorus, Hyacinthus was a son of Pierus and of the Muse Clio (also said to have been Hymenaeus's parent). Both heroes were loved not only by Apollo but also by the Thracian bard Thamyris. In other words, we have here a complex of legends that links together, in northern Thessaly, three lovers of Apollo: Admetus, who reigns not far from the Peneus, and two of his descendants, Hyacinthus, who is Laconian, and Hymenaeus, whose roots are in other respects generally Attic. While Hymenaeus seems to be a hero or god of relatively recent creation, he has a place in a very ancient complex of myths. A fragment of Hesiod's makes Diomede, the wife of Amyclas, the mother of Hyacinthus and of Lapithes; the Lapithae, who lived beside the Peneus, were neighbors of the Pieres, from whom they were separated by Olympus. Another fragment from the same poet states that Macedon (eponym of the Macedonians) and Magnes (eponym of the Magnetes in Thessaly) were two brothers who had chosen to live in Pieria and around

Olympus.[51] Thus a very old mythology linked not only Pieria to Thessaly but the legendary families of Laconia to those of Thessaly.

This placement of Hyacinthus and Hymenaeus therefore provides indirect proof that the association of Admetus with homosexual rituals is an ancient theme of mythology. Thus Admetus, here prior to Hyacinthus and the erōmenos, formerly erastēs, of Apollo, was no doubt in some vanished cycle of Thessalian legends the mythical founder of initiatory homosexuality.

TEN
The Prophets of Apollo
器

Apollo was the god of prophetic inspiration. The prophets of the Greek
world assumed fictional genealogies, which cast them as descendants of
either Apollo or some mortal, some primordial prophet, who had been
the pupil of the Letoidae. For example, the prophets of Olympia, the
Iamidae, were said to have descended from an eponymous ancestor,
Iamus, who had been Apollo's son and pupil. It would hardly be
surprising if in some cases the pupils of such a god, the ancestral
prophets, had been Apollo's erōmenoi as well.

It may be an ancient tradition concerning Branchus, ancestor of the
Branchidae, that is revealed to us by Conon and Lucian. The Branchidae
were the prophets associated with the principal sanctuary of Apollo in
Asia, the Didyma ("twins"), near Miletus. The story is that Branchus's
father was the mortal Smicrus. [1] Smicrus is the hero of a primary myth. A
native of Delphi (surely a late detail, since it expresses the "imperialis-
tic" attitudes of Delphi toward the other sanctuaries of Apollo), he was
"forgotten," at the age of thirteen, by his father in Miletus, where both
had gone on a journey. Found by Eritharses, a noble Milesian, he is
raised by him and, on orders of the goddess Leucothea, given Eritharses'
daughter for his bride. But Leucothea had made another request: Smicrus and his adoptive brother were supposed to tell the Milesians to
found in her honor a gymnastic competition for children. This was the
work of Branchus's father. Branchus was a very beautiful child, and one
day while tending flocks in the mountains (as Smicrus had done for
Eritharses), Apollo fell in love with him. The god gave him the gift of
prophecy, along with a garland and branch as its token and symbols. We
are told that it was the god's "kiss" that made the young man a prophet.
He then built an altar to Apollo Philesios ("friendly") and began to
prophesy. Then, suddenly, he either disappeared or died. The Milesians
built him a tomb and erected the temple of the Didyma.

This may, as I indicated, be an ancient myth, in part because the legend of Smicrus is readily interpreted as the founding myth of a Milesian ritual of testing young adolescents, in part because the motifs of the Branchus legend are archaic. The sojourn in the bush, the gifts, the qualification as a prophet, and the early death are all initiation motifs reminiscent of the earliest Hellenic sources (as well as Melanesian practices) and not at all of Greek pederasty in later periods. The cult epithet "Philesios" corroborates the antiquity of the myth and its association with ritual. This is an important point—it confirms that the alleged relations between Apollo and Admetus (for Delphi) or between the god and other prophets are not necessarily late "remakes," tailored to Hellenistic and Roman tastes, of an old mythology pure and innocent of such horrors.

These remarks cannot, however, be applied to another, similar legend, that of the love of Apollo for Helenus. Helenus, Cassandra's twin brother and like her a prophet, was the erōmenos of the god according to Prolemy Khennos.[2] Given the facts that this author of the second century A.D. was given to collecting improbable stories of pederasty,[3] that he is the only one to report this particular story, and that he could easily have made it up, inspired by other stories of Apollo's loves for his prophets and indeed for Cassandra herself, it seems unlikely that the tale is of ancient origin.

The same cannot be said of the following myth. It can be traced back to the poet Praxilla of Sicyon (fifth century B.C.), and it brings us face to face with a complex and fruitful question. Here is Praxilla's story: Carnus, or Carneus, was the son of Zeus and Europa (the Dorian form of Europē). Leto and Apollo raised him, and then the god took him to Crete. He made the youth his erōmenos and gave him the gift of prophecy.[4]

The mention of Crete is noteworthy, not only because the ritual I examined at the beginning of this book was still being practiced there in the fifth century but also because Leto was worshiped in Crete more than anywhere else in the Greek world, and in particular presided over rites of passage, marriages, and social probations.[5] She was first and foremost the protector of maternity, the paradigmatic mother, whose children were commonly called the Letoidae.

But Carnus was not specifically Cretan. Directly attested in myths, and indirectly in the Carnea festivals or the month of Carneus,[6] he was known throughout the Dorian world. Indeed, unlike Hyacinthus, who was closely associated with Amyclae and who appeared only in the colonies of Sparta, Carnus was a character in the Doric myth of origin. He was the official prophet of the Heraclidae as they moved into the Peloponnesus, but he was killed by one of them, Hippotes, prior to the crossing of the Gulf of Corinth, which murder was said to have delayed the conquest by several years.[7]

Depending on the context (by which I mean the ritual and social context) Carnus was associated with either Zeus or Apollo. Broadly speaking, his connection with Zeus was through his mythical function as guide of the army, whereas his connection with Apollo was as a prophet and patron of initiation rituals.

There are several ways to formulate a relationship between a man and a god. In one version of the myth of the Heraclidae Carnus is an "apparition" of Apollo.[8] In another he is the priest of Apollo.[9] Since the Carnea were generally a festival consecrated to Apollo, it was common to speak of Apollo Carneus.[10] In Argos, however, the festival honored Zeus.[11] Does it follow from this that the tradition reported by Praxilla is merely a random variant, an innocent way of indicating a relationship between Carnus and Apollo? No, because all the variants alluded to above have some basis. The notion of "apparition" (*phasma* in the text) or appearance, mask, is essential in the ancients' allusions to the rite.[12] Nor is the notion of priest fortuitous; the priests of Zeus and Apollo, variously characterized, played a fundamental role in the rituals associated with Carnus. Thus there are no grounds for dismissing the poet's version, particularly since what she stresses is precisely education by the god and his mother, and, further, since her version is original (nowhere else is Carnus the son of Zeus and Europa) and she lived in the sixth or early fifth century, hence prior to the common use of homosexuality to explain friendship between two characters.[13]

The myth can be localized. Praxilla is from Sicyon, a Dorian city on the Gulf of Corinth west of that city. For historical reasons Sicyonian mythology is intertwined with Theban mythology. Each city borrowed heroes from the other and developed unique, and contrasting, versions of the same myths.[14] Europa is a figure in Boeotian religion, closely associated with Demeter.[15] Outside of Crete, Sicyon was the only place in the Dorian world where Carnus could have been the son of Europa. To make him a son of Zeus, moreover, evokes the religion of Argos, whereas I mentioned the Carnea were associated with Zeus. Futhermore, the Sicyonians were Dorians of Argive origin.[16]

The nature of the Carnea varied from place to place. In Sparta they were less important than the Hyacinthia, for example, but in Cyrene they were the chief festival.[17] The initiatory aspect in which we are primarily interested must also have changed in nature as one moved from Sparta, where initiation was associated chiefly with the Hyacinthia, to cities like Argos, where the Hyacinthia were unknown, or Thera, where they were of minor importance.

We know absolutely nothing about the Sicyonian Carnea. It is of course possible to assume that the festival was quite similar to the Carnea in Argos, but we know little more about that festival than about the Sicyonian one.[18] Furthermore, the fact that the nature of the festival, one of whose chief features was its connection with Zeus, was so different in Sparta and Cyrene, the two cities for which we have any sort of documentation, precludes speculation. I shall therefore limit myself to some very general observations about the meaning of the Carnea, observations that may shed some light on the myth reported by Praxilla.

That the myth has an initiatory aspect is obvious. What is more, this aspect occupies the entire "space" of the narrative. As a child, Carnus is taken from his natural parents and raised elsewhere. Here we encounter the custom of foster parentage, which underlies certain traditions of the Pelops cycle and whose purpose is explicitly educational.[19] In early Greece as elsewhere it sometimes happens that the adoptive father, the father-in-law (who bestows a wife), and the erastēs-educator are one and the same person.[20] The myth reported by Praxilla combines the first and the third of these roles, though no allusion is made to the second. Apollo was the adoptive father, the master, and therefore, in a conception whose archaism is worthy of note, the erastēs.

The initiatory aspect also crops up elsewhere, in the best-known cults of Carnus or Carneus.

The most striking documents are the archaic inscriptions of Thera. These made it possible to locate the temple of Apollo Carneus, which was founded, according to its excavator, around 600.[21] It stood on the southeastern edge of the city, not far from the "ephebes' gymnasium." This location was certainly not accidental; wherever the documentation is adequate we find a link between Apollo Carneus and the trials of the ephebia. In Sparta his temple was next to the Dromos, where athletic trials were held.[22] In Thera inscriptions link Apollo Carneus and Hera Dromais ("of the races").[23] At Sicyon, we also know, thanks to Pausanias, that the temple of Carneus was next to that of Hera Prodromia.[24]

The ephebes' gymnasium at Thera is of considerable interest for our subject, as has been noted by several authors starting with the archaeologist F. Hiller.[25] It contains a grotto, consecrated, according to inscriptions, to Heracles and Hermes (the usual patrons of gymnasia) and covered with engraved texts of two kinds: invocations of divinites associated with initiation and education, including Apollo; and felicitations composed by erastai and addressed to their erōmenoi. Some of the more "obscene" of these inscriptions have diverted Hellenists for more than a century, but this is not the place to discuss them. I shall treat them, as Bethe and Jeanmaire have done before me, in another work.

For now suffice to say that several of the inscriptions mention the "gallantry" of the erōmenoi, such as their "gallantry" at dance. Another mentions the trial of the weights—all things that are part of normal Greek education.[26] Later, moreover, inscriptions on the Carnea speak of *agōnes*, contests.[27]

The socioreligious sequence of events is obvious. First there was a holy place, marked by a grotto, near which trials of ephebes took place. Later a temple to Apollo Carneus was built nearby. Finally, the gymnasium, a civil building, was constructed, incorporating the old holy grotto. Similar sequences can be adduced for many Greek cities. Brelich, for example, points out that the same sequence of events characterizes the sanctuary of Artemis Orthia at Sparta.

I shall not dwell further on the Carnea or the erōmenoi of Thera. It is enough to have examined the close, privileged, indeed almost exclusive relationship between Apollo Carneus and adolescent education rituals that included, in the most explicit manner, sexual elements.

The initiatory character of the Lacedaemonian Carnea was brought to light by Jeanmaire and Brelich.[28] Miltos Hatzopoulos, in a study that unfortunately has not been published, demonstrated that the Spartan Carnea were a military festival, in which citizens gathered in arms,[29] based on a series of founding myths, all martial,[30] and concerned with the difficulties of military campaigns during the hot season (the Carnea were celebrated during what corresponds to our month of August[31]), when men had to rely for food on the last plants of the summer to reach maturity: grapes, figs, and olives.[32]

According to Hesychius, the group of *agamoi*, young men not yet married, selected for the celebration of the Carnea were called Carneatai, and there were "five per . . ." (here there is a gap in the manuscript); they were responsible for preparing the festival and served for five years. In a country where celibacy was forbidden by law,[33] the term *agamoi* could only refer to a social category in the age-group hierarchy: young adults no doubt beyond the stage of the *eirēn*, the last phase of the Lacedaemonian *agōgē*.[34] The selection, "five per ?," was surely "representative." The Carneatai represented their entire age cohort; they were the most eminent, the wealthiest, for Hesychius speaks of the *leitourgia*, the families of these young men, who financed the festival. Such delegated rituals were common in Sparta as well as in Athens. In another ritual, a game with military and religious significance, fourteen young soldiers, very likely of about the same age as *agamoi* and known as *sphaireis*, played as representatives of their companions.[35]

After adolescence, age groups ceased to be annual. The Carneatai remained such for four years, which was a standard duration and does not mean that the festival was also based on a five-year cycle.[36] In Sparta the number five was associated with all sorts of magistratures, for five was the number of *ōbai*, or districts, of classical Laconia.[37] Therefore, as Hatzopoulos rightly assumes, Hesychius's manuscript must be interpreted as reading *ōba* where scholars have generally proposed reading *phylē*, "tribe."

The principal rite of the Spartan Carnea was the following: Certain young men, known as *staphylodromoi*, were selected from among the Carneatai; one man, his head covered with *stemmata*, or wreaths, ran by offering his wishes for the city's happiness; the *staphylodromoi* pursued; if they caught him, this meant that something good would befall the city.[38]

It was an honor to be a *staphylodromas*, as Spartan inscriptions make clear: "Aristandros *staphylodroms*," "Menestratos *staphylodromas*, Hippodamos priest."[39]

I will not make use of the full meaning of the elements involved in this ritual. For example, the figure covered with *stemmata* must have been a mask, an image, a representation of Carnos and/or Apollo; one text speaks of *phasma*, images.[40] It is enough to concentrate on the major points.

The Carnea were essentially a military and ephebic festival. They occurred at a point in the military season, the end of the campaign period, that coincided with a phase in the *agōgē*, a part of the life of every Spartan citizen.

The Carnea were in part a festival of civic renewal, as is shown by the wishes for a happy new year from the man covered with *stemmata*, who had to be captured so that the city might enjoy all the boons he had prophesied.[41] In this respect the Carnea resembled the Hyacinthia, and indeed this is not the only point they have in common. Both are occasions of *agōnes*, especially musical ones.[42] In both, the symbolism of death and rebirth plays an important part, thanks to Hyacinthus in the one, to Alcestis in the other. In the fifth century, in fact, the Athenian Euripides ascribed two cult sites to Alcestis in his tragedy about her, namely, Sparta and Athens.

> Much shall be sung of you by the men of music to the seven-strung mountain lyre-shell, and in poems that have no music, in Sparta when the season turns and the month Carneian comes back, and the moon rides all the night; in Athens also, the shining and rich. Such is the theme of song you left in death, for the poets.[43]

We must assume that Alcestis was celebrated during one phase of the Carnea just as Hyacinthus was celebrated in the Hyacinthia. In both stories the crucial element is a death followed by a resurrection. Note that Bathycles of Magnesia had represented on the throne at Amyclae the games organized by Acastus in honor of his father Pelias, which immediately preceded his own marriage,[44] and that the marriage of Alcestis, the daughter of Pelias, ended a period during which her husband Admetus was, according to Callimachus, the erōmenos of Apollo.

As was mentioned earlier, the initiatory aspect of the Carnea was diminished in Sparta owing to the importance of the Hyacinthia, which subsumed the central symbolism of initiatory promotion and change in the world.

But outside of Sparta, in places where the Hyacinthia were not held or were less important, it was the Carnea that assumed some of the aspects of the other festival.

In Thera once again an inscription tells us that the festival of Apollo Carneus was the occasion for the emancipation of slaves and mentions a banquet; another nearby inscription seems to speak of public banquets, *damothoinia*, to which slaves and foreigners were invited. These were surely the Carnea, and this rite corresponds directly to one of the practices associated with the Hyacinthia.[45] But it is in the Theran colony at Cyrene that we find the greatest resemblances between the two festivals. The Carnea included dances of warriors and women (the "blond Libyans" of Callimachus),[46] processions of chariots and horsemen along a sacred route,[47] and sacrifices of large numbers of bulls.[48] At the beginning of his hymn Callimachus reports the following important detail: the invocation of Apollo, "Ie Paian, Ie Paian," interrupted a time of sorrow and mourning, which may mean that a phase of ritual sadness preceded the celebration of the Carnea.[49] Shortly thereafter Callimachus mentions the god's servitude with Admetus and his love for him, on which I commented earlier. Callimachus says that the cult of Apollo Carneus came from Thera and beyond Sparta, which coincides with the opinion of the Spartans, the Therans, and the Cyreneans, as Herodotus reports in a celebrated passage.[50] While Sparta celebrated the Carnea and the even more important Hyacinthia, for Thera the only indication that the Hyacinthia were celebrated is the name of a month (Hyacinthus). There is no trace of the Hyacinthia in Cyrene. It is not unreasonable to assume that the cult of Apollo Carneus in Cyrene was a syncretism of the two Spartan rituals.

Such a syncretism, doubtless already under way in the first Dorian Thera, would not have been possible unless the two cults were largely similar. At Argos and Sicyon, which were not colonies of Sparta, there never were Hyacinthia, and Praxilla's text tells us that the initiatory aspect of the Sicyonian Carnea was of primary importance. Is it not reasonable, then, to assume that the oldest Carnea, those celebrated by the Dorian conquerors of the Peloponnesus, were primarily initiatory (as is also suggested by the oldest Theran descriptions) and that it was only in Laconia that Hyacinthus took over a symbolic function that tradition had previously ascribed to Carnus (whose name, unlike that of Hyacinthus, is Greek)?

All of this takes us once again into the remote past. It is said that Cleisthenes, the famous sixth-century Sicyonian tyrant, in fighting against the symbols of aristocratic power, replaced the names of seven kings in the official list of legendary kings of the city with the names of former priests of Carneus.[51] This suggests a hereditary priesthood, passed on from father to son (or master to disciple?), of which few examples are known in Greece. It must be assumed that the instruction of these priests included, in addition to the tradition of their succesion, the ancient history of the cult and its *hieroi logoi*, sacred words.[52]

Hence it is with a sacred subject that Praxilla's verses are concerned. And they suggest that Carneus, who was in many respects to Sicyon what Hyacinthus was to Sparta, played the role there of mythical founder of homosexuality.

ELEVEN
Katapontismoi

An obscure tradition, reported by Servius, the commentator on Virgil, holds that Apollo fell in love with one Leucatas (or Leucates), who, in order to escape from the god, jumped from the southern promontory of the island of Leucadia (or Leucas) in western Greece at the place known as "Leucadia's Leap."[1] This story is, in part at any rate, the result of a confusion between the name of the god who reigned over this cape, Apollo Leucatas,[2] and the—quite unwilling—"hero" of the principal rite of this god's cult, described by Strabo as follows:

> There upon it stands the temple of Apollo Leucatas, and the Leap, which it was thought, was a termination of love. . . . Menander then says that Sappho was the first who took the leap, but persons better acquainted with ancient accounts assert that it was Cephalus, who was in love with Pterelas, the son of Deoneus. It was also a custom of the country among the Leucadians at the annual sacrifice performed in honor of Apollo to hurl from the rock one of the condemned criminals, in order to avert evil. Various kinds of wings were attached to him, and even birds were suspended from his body, to buoy up his descent by their fluttering. Below many persons were stationed around in small fishing boats to receive and to preserve his life if possible, and to carry him beyond the boundaries of the country.[3]

Apotropē is the action of averting or warding off a danger. The man condemned to jump from Leucadia's Leap was precisely what the Hebrews termed a "scapegoat": Every year a living human being, named to represent and to take upon himself all the ills that could befall the population, was expelled from the city and driven out of the region.[4] In Greece this kind of practice was not unusual. Every year in Athens, on the first day of the Thargelia, two men, chosen from the dregs of the populace, the pharmakoi or witches, were paraded through the city, beaten, and expelled.[5]

But there was a second phase to the Thargelia, the following day, and the presence of Apollo on the summit of the cape known today as Doukato indicates that Strabo, too, focused exclusively on the initial phase of a religious festival and ignored the indispensible second phase that must have taken place in the city, at some distance from the sea. In Athens during this second phase an offering was made, to none other than Apollo, of the earth's first fruits, in the form of a *thargēlos*, or kind of biscuit, and a pot filled with seeds of all kinds[6]—for Thargelion is the month of May, and the Thargelia constituted the springtime festival. It was also on the second day of the Thargelia that the *eiresiōnē*, an olive or laurel branch garlanded with wool and embellished with fruits, cakes, and small bottles, was carried across the city. Little boys hung the *eiresiōnai* in doorways and arranged them on the threshold of Apollo's temple.[7]

In this festival we recognize an overall structure very much like that of the Hyacinthia. Indeed, the resemblances go further still. In Dorian regions the *eiresiōnē* was called a *koruthalia*. It was to Artemis Korythalia that Lacedaemonian nurses brought male babies during the Tithēnidia, which as we saw earlier took place at the same time as the Hyacinthia, of which the Tithēnidia were in the larger sense just a part.[8] Furthermore, the springtime procession of the *eiresiōnē* symbolized to Athenians the departure of Theseus.[9] Theseus was the founding hero of the rites of the Athenian ephebia and the model, the ideal type, of the initiatory hero, and, incidentally, was linked to probative homosexuality through one of his myths. Hence the tradition reported by Servius may not have been without foundation. If the Leucadian festival was, like the Hyacinthia, a great civic feast combining the expulsion of evil with renewal of the world, then it had an initiatory aspect, such that its founding hero and its god may have been, in this region of Greece, the creators of a ritual homosexuality.

What makes this even more probable is that other stories of jumping into the sea are also associated with myths of the same type. Apollo's presence apparently made the cape of Leucadia the scene of legends whose heroes in one way or another have something to do with homosexuality. If Leucatas threw himself into the water to escape from Apollo, elsewhere Cephalus does the same but for the opposite reason, namely, because he is the disappointed lover of Pterelas, king of the Taphians. Sappho, too, leapt in despair from the cliffs of Leucadia, even though Menander says that she enjoyed a heterosexual love there.[10] Originally these *katapontismoi*, leaps into the sea, were no doubt magical acts, whose

purpose was to force the beloved to recognize that a love that could drive
the lover to such extremes must be of a sacred nature. The procedure was
also used in ordeals: Gustave Glotz was right to include in his book on
ordeals in primitive Greece numerous legends involving leaps into the
ocean, intentional drownings, and dives from one of the innumerable
white rocks that dot the coastline of Greece. [11] Cephalus, before diving off
the cliffs of Leucadia, surely made another leap at Thorikos, the Attic
city of which he was, according to tradition, a native. [12] Thorikos (from
thrōskō, "jump") was built on the promontory of the same name, the
present-day Mount Velatouri. [13]

Recall Argennos/Argynnus, whose name occurred, perhaps erroneously as the result of a scribe's mistake, in the company of Hymenaeus. The Greek white rocks drew their names from the adjectives
leukos (hence Leucadia) or *argos*, "white, brilliant." Argynnus, whose
name must derive from the same root, is none other than the son of one
Leucon (and Peisidike, "justice that persuades"). He swam, moreover,
in Copais, which we are told was then called Leuconis.

Justice (*dikē, themis*), often mentioned in connection with these
aborted loves, evokes the procedures used in ordeals. The symbolism of
law is constantly intertwined with the symbolism of initiation and of
hetero- and homosexual supplication. Thus Staphylus ("grapes"),
offspring of Dionysus, had a daughter, Rhoio ("pomegranate"), whom
Apollo impregnated and then placed in a wooden chest and set adrift on
the waves. From this union came the child Anios, whom the god made
his priest at Delos. Saphylus had two other daughters, Parthenos and
Molpadia, who leapt from high cliffs into the sea and were transformed
into goddesses by Apollo. [14] Their mother was named Chrysothemis,
from *themis*, justice, and *Chryso*, "the gilded one," a common epithet of
Aphrodite. Danae, who was also placed in a chest with her child Perseus
and thrown into the sea (the theme is one of initiation), was the daughter
of one Eurydice, "ample justice," who pleaded to the gods on her
behalf. [15] Tyro, pregnant by Poseidon and mistreated by her stepmother,
saves two infants, Pelias and Neleus, by committing them to the sea in a
wooden trough. Her mother is named Alkidike. Cycnus, king of Thessaly, spurred by the calumnies of his second wife, shuts his two children
Tenes and Hemithea in a chest, and the sea carries them to the island
then known as Leucophrus, which soon took the name Tenedos; Cycnus's mother was named Scamandrodike. [16] And so on.

Thus ordeals and rites of passage exerted great influence on this cycle
of legends. It is quite possible, however, that in this series of *katapontis-*

moi heterosexual love affairs and female intervention are rooted in juridical rituals (associated with marriage, inheritance, virginity, etc.), while
allusions to homosexual love are concerned precisely with male rituals of
initiation. The story of Agamemnon and Argynnus (himself the erastēs
of Hymenaeus at a later date—possibly after his "death") suggess that
this was the case, and the allusion to Cephalus, who was, according to
tradition, a typical warrior and who defeated in battle the very Pterelas
whom Strabo depicts as the object of his desire, seems to confirm it.[17]

TWELVE
Horse Breeders
🔲

Plutarch, in his *Life of Numa*, discusses the nature of the relationship between the Roman king and the nymph Egeria and in doing so reveals two other male loves of Apollo.

> Not that it is otherwise than befitting to suppose that the gods feel towards men affection, and love, in the sense of affection, and in the form of care and solicitude for their virtue and their good dispositions. And, therefore, it was no error of those who feigned that Phorbas, Hyacinthus, and Admetus were beloved by Apollo; or that Hippolytus the Sicyonian was so much in his favor that as often as he sailed from Sicyon to Cirrha, the Pythian prophetess uttered this heroic verse, expressive of the god's attention and joy:
>
> > Now doth Hippolytus return again
> > And venture his life upon the main.[1]

Plutarch's conception of Apollo is highly sublimated,[2] and his representation of male homosexuality falls within the narrow tradition of Platonizing,[3] or more properly (as I think one may rightly say), of Platonic, ideas. Accordingly, he transforms into a deep and desexualized relationship what other strains in the tradition held to be actual pederastic relations. This is true of Hyacinthus and Admetus, and we must assume that it is also true of the two other cases, though Plutarch is the only author to report that Apollo loved these two men.

It seems clear, moreover, that the traditions on which Plutarch bases his account are authentic and ancient. For in order to reach any other conclusion we would need to know of ancient texts in which Apollo appeared in a positive, nonsexual relationship with the two mythological characters in question. This would suggest that Plutarch was merely alluding to Hellenistic reworkings of old traditions, parallel to those that made homosexual couples of Heracles and Eurystheus, Hypnos and

Endymion, and perhaps also Apollo and Admetus. But there is no tradition indicating a close relationship between Phorbas and Apollo—except as adversaries in the narrowest sense of the word. We know little about Hippolytus other than what we read in Pausanias's historical note concerning Sicyon, from which we learn that he was an ancient king of that city, from the time immediately prior to the arrival of the Heraclidae from Argos, whose only "connection" with Apollo is that he succeeded another king, Zeuxippos, who was the son of Apollo by a nymph named Syllis.[4] Hence Plutarch's account is based on traditions unknown to us, and whether or not those traditions were revised and reworked during the Hellenistic period it is interesting to determine their content and to identify the reasons why mythographers, or poets, chose to make Apollo the erastēs of these two heroes.

Phorbas is a sort of Heracles without divinity. Without any cult of his own, he did not arouse the interest of the poets, and he was divided up into a host of different heroes, all of whom shared the same name yet had distinct geographic and legendary roots. Whether Heracles is the Heracles of Argos, Thebes, Thessaly, or Sparta he remains the "same" Heracles, but the Phlegyan Phorbas was distinct from the Elian, and the Rhodian from the Lapithian Phorbas, to say nothing of still other Phorbases in Attica, Argos, Eleusis, Lesbos, Troy, and other places.

These various heroes, all of whom must derive, ultimately, from the Thessalian Phorbas, the Lapith, have certain traits in common, and it is these, rather than the individual legend of some particular Phorbas, on which I shall focus here. In fact, these traits accord perfectly with the argument I have been making.

Phorbas is a warrior hero. The epithet Lapith, and even more the epithet Phlegyan, make this clear. For if the Lapithae were a people of northern Thessaly about whom we know little other than their military involvements (though we may assume, a priori, that they were not all young men), we know much more about the Phlegyans, who, as F. Vian has shown, comprised the warrior caste of Orchomenus in the "heroic" era.[5]

This trait explains Phorbas's name. *Phorbas*, as an adjective, means "nourishing, fecund, providing fodder," from the root *pherbo*, "to cause to graze," from which "to feed," "to maintain," or (in the passive) "to graze." Since Phorbas has some connections with Demeter (of which more presently), several authors apparently saw him, against the evidence of the myths, as a demon associated with food and agriculture.[6] This makes no sense: The family of words associated with *pherbo* has to do essentially with grazing by animals and primarily horses. When the adjective *phorbas* is used with nouns other than "meadow," it usually modifies "horses,"[7] to such a degree that, as a noun, it means a horse fed out of doors.[8] A derivative term, *phorbeia*, denotes the tether used to attach a horse to a stable rack.[9] Phorbas is "equine" because horses are items of military equipment. In Elis he is the father of Aktor and the grandfather of the Molionides, heroes famed for their prowess with the chariot.[10] In Attica Phorbas taught Theseus—a military hero—to drive a chariot, and in Euripides' *Suppliants*, he is the hipparch, the cavalry leader, who defeats his Theban counterparts.[11]

Phorbas was thus a warrior, indeed an elite warrior, since a king of Elis (of a prehistoric Elis, that is, located in what was, in the classical era, western Achaea[12]) named Alektor (an enemy of Pelops who reigned to the south, in Pisatis) called upon Phorbas for reinforcements and in return for his assistance gave him half his kingdom. While the king of Elis married a daughter of Phorbas, Phorbas received the king's sister in exchange. With her he fathered two prestigious heroes, Aktor, another typical warrior, and Augeas, king of Elis, who would became famous for his vast herds.[13]

More than a leader of armies, however, Phorbas, like Heracles, was a solitary warrior of a type common in Greek legends and indeed throughout the Indo-European world.[14] In the Rhodian legends, Phorbas, said to be a native of Thessaly (but in fact brought to the island from Argos, without a doubt), is a slayer of monsters. After ridding the island of the colossal serpents that infested it, he was turned into the constellation Ophiuchus, the "serpent slayer."[15] The Phlegyan legend of Phorbas is even more interesting, for it is the only one that connects him with Apollo—and connects him with a vengeance! The myth depicts the Phlegyans as asocial bandits, enemies of gods and humans. This view probably derives from the prestige of Thebes in the remote past, for it was Thebes, the rival and vanquisher of Orchomenus, that had to combat the true Phlegyans. In any case, this Phlegyan Phorbas lived at Panopea, in Phocis, a traditional Phlegyan center, which suggests that there was a time, in the distant past, when the power of the city of Orchomenus extended far up the valley of the Cephissus, well into Phocis. From his base there Phorbas forced travelers on their way to Delphi to box with him and after defeating them had them put to death. This displeased the god of Delphi, and, disguised as a child, Apollo came to challenge Phorbas, vanquished him, and then killed him.[16]

Here Phorbas is a wicked warrior, whereas everywhere else he is viewed quite positively. We have already seen this in Rhodes. What is quite remarkable, though, is that in Attica he became an educator, an instructor: he taught Theseus to drive a chariot, and he is sometimes credited, in place of Theseus, with the invention of wrestling.[17]

The rites that I am studying in this chapter essentially involve the initiation of warriors, and homosexuality was an element in the training of a warrior. That is why Plutarch's allusion is of such great interest: it evokes the career of a Phorbas who, as a typical warrior and educator, must himself have been educated previously. As numerous traditions attest, this education often involved sexual relations with the teacher, and it is only natural that Phorbas should have been the erōmenos of the great god of male initiation.

It is possible to be more precise. In mythology it is common to invert a motif to signify its opposite. Many examples of this can be found in Greek tradition. In this connection, consider the Eleusinian Phorbas. He was a warrior, a defender of Eleusis against Erechtheus, king of Athens, and not only Erechtheus but also Phorbas and his companions Immarondas and Eumolpus were skilled charioteers.[18] Thus in Attic tradition we find both an enemy Phorbas, a chariot-driving warrior, and an Athenian Phorbas, a hipparch under Theseus and Theseus's teacher in the art of chariot driving—in other words, a good Phorbas and a bad.

Now imagine something similar in Phocis. In the myths concerning the Phlegyans the link between these warriors and Orchomenus is too close not to have corresponded to some ancient historical reality. Either the frontiers of Orchomenus in the Mycenaean period extended as far as Delphi, as I am inclined to believe, or the main road from Lebadea to Delphi, which in the classical era would become the Sacred Way, may simply have been over much of its length under the "protection" of Orchomenus. In this remote era relations between Delphi and the Phlegyans must have been conceived entirely in positive terms. Thus we discover a mythological phase in which Phorbas could well have been the pupil, the disciple, and the erōmenos of Apollo. In that case, the classical myth, the only one for which there is evidence and in which we find a rivalry between Apollo and Phorbas, must be the inversion of this primitive positive version. When we pursue this comparison in detail, the coherence of the hypothesis is strikingly apparent.

ALLEGED PRIMITIVE VERSION	KNOWN MYTH
Phorbas is an adolescent-future warrior, ally of Apollo, who is then adult.	Phorbas is an adult warrior, enemy of Apollo, who appears as a child.

Phorbas receives martial knowledge from Apollo.	Phorbas detains worshipers of Apollo using martial techniques.
They have sexual relations (conjunction).	They have violent physical relations (opposition).
The logical conclusion is the death of Phorbas, a mystical death that makes him an accomplished hero.	The conclusion is the death of Phorbas, a real death that puts an end to his military career.

It does indeed seem that Plutarch's account is based on very ancient material. This hypothesis is supported by two pieces of evidence. First, there is another positive link between Phorbas and Apollo: The first Phorbas, of Thessaly, is the son of Lapithes, who is the son of Apollo.[19] This is a clue to a state of the legend in which the Phlegyans, whose own origins lie in the land of the Lapithae, were not enemies of Delphi. Second, myths of initiatory homosexuality, many involving Apollo, abound in Orchomenian mythology. Minyas, the most famous king of Orchomenus and bearer of the epithet "the rich,"[20] was the father of one Cyparissus; he gave his daughter Clymene to Phylacus, one of whose brothers was Cephalus, the hero who jumped from Leucadia's Leap in despair over a homosexual love. Finally, Leucon, grandfather of Argynnus, the beloved of Agamemnon, was also the grandfather of Eteocles, the founding king of the cults of Orchomenus.[21]

To remove any lingering doubt about the nature of the homosexual relationship established by tradition between Apollo and Phorbas, I should like to say a word or two about the relationship between the hero and Demeter, in order to show that there is nothing in that relationship to support the interpretation of Phorbas as a "nutritional demon."

The eastern part of the territory of the Lapithae lay in what was known as the plain of Dotion. It stretched from the Peneus to lake Boibeis (now dry), which extended it southward. The Tempe pass, to which Apollo was exiled and through which flowed the Peneus, led from the plain of Dotion to the sea. This was the region from which the sovereigns of Orchomenus in Boeotia came. Pindar locates Phlegyas, eponym of the Phlegyans, at Lakereia in the Dotion plain.[22] Apollodorus makes him the son of Ares and Dotis.[23] And his brother Gyrton is the eponym of Gyrtone, a city in the northern part of the plain.[24] The founding king of Orchomenus, Andreus, was the son of the Peneus. And so on.[25]

What this suggests is a prehistoric movement from the region of the lower Peneus, from the Dotion plain, toward western Boeotia. This movement can also be seen in the diffusion of mythological themes between the two regions. The character Phorbas is one of these themes. A major cult of the Dotion plain was that of Demeter, located by Hesiod at a place near Amyrus, north of Lake Boibeis, and marked by twin peaks, whence its name, the Didymoi, or twins. Demeter there had the company and services of male heroes, presumably Erysichthon, Triopas, and Phorbas. The traditions differ somewhat as to the relationships among these three heroes; either they are brothers or else Triopas is the father of Phorbas and Erysichthon.[26]

Phorbas alone appears in the Phlegyan cycle. Without Demeter he was transported to western Boeotia and probably from there to Elis, where Phorbas is again found without Triopas, Erysichthon, and Demeter. By contrast, the entire group was at some unknown time transported to Argolis. In Argive tradition we find, first of all, a king Phorbas and his son and successor Triopas.[27] What is more, not far from Asine, in the western part of the Argive peninsula, at a place known as the Didymoi (just as in Thessaly), men worshiped Demeter, Apollo, and Poseidon.[28] This transfer of a cult from Thessaly to Argolis parallels the transfer of another, more famous cult, that of Asclepius. And just as Asclepius was subsequently transported by the people of Argolis to the Dorian islands in the southern Aegean, in particular to Cos where Hippocrates was born among the Asclepiadae, so too were Demeter and her companions taken to Rhodes and the Cnidos peninsula somewhat farther north. Cape Triopion, at the tip of this peninsula, was the site of an Apollonian cult with which Demeter and Poseidon were associated. This was the federal sanctuary of the Dorian hexapolis.[29] According to Diodorus of Sicily, the first colonizer of Rhodes was Triopas, son of Phorbas.[30] Phorbas was also Demeter's companion at Eleusis, as we have seen, but there his other companions were named Immarondas and Eumolpus.

To argue that all these characters are geniuses of agriculture because they are companions of Demeter is to engage in the worst sort of "history of religion." Their association with the goddess altogether neglects the unanimous evidence of the myths, according to which Phorbas is a warrior. Furthermore, as I have already noted, it was not uncommon in Greece for a typical warrior to be the companion of a nonwarrior goddess in her sanctuary—For example, Eurytus, the archer, at Andania, with Demeter and Kore, and Immarondas at Eleusis. One must accept the documents as they are and admit that a paradigmatic warrior was the companion of the great goddess of grain. It is then clear that the three characters, who unfortunately never appear together in our sources, can be associated with the three Indo-European functions: 1) Triopas is probably a hypostasis of the Dorian Zeus, of the Zeus Triophthalmos attested by some sources.[31] He is, moreover, the founding hero of a city or town, a characteristic of the royal function,[32] for he founded Cnidos[33] and was the first colonizer of Rhodes. 2) Phorbas was the warrior, as we have discussed. 3) Erysichthon is known from myth to have been an insatiable devourer. "Punished" by Demeter for a sacrilege, he swallowed up all the produce of his estate along with other resources obtained by his daughter Mnestra and ultimately devoured himself.[34] Because of this devouring passion he was known as Aethon, "the ardent,"[35] under which name he was transported to Argolis.[36]

Thus, like many other major Hellenic cults, the cult of Demeter was organized, from Thessaly to Triopion, in accordance with the trifunctional schema of prehistoric Indo-European origin. This, moreover, explains the nature of Phorbas: He represents the second function in relation to the goddess.[37]

Similar conclusions emerge independently from a consideration of the character of Hippolytus of Sicyon. That he is little known makes it certain that Plutarch had sources available to him that are unknown to us. Pausanias was familiar with a Hippolytus who was an ancient king, son of Rhopalos, son of Phaestus, son of Heracles. He succeeded Zeuxippos, son of Apollo and Syllis. That is all, and it is very little.

Note, however, that the legendary dynasty of Sicyon reveals a connection between Hippolytus, horses, and Apollo. Zeuxippos and Hippolytus were not father and son, but both names contain the root *hippos*, "horse.' Of the various things that a horse might symbolize in Greece, the reference here is no doubt to warfare, at least in the case of Hippolytus, who is a descendant of Heracles and whose father's name is a masculinized form of *rhopalon*, "club" (as in the club of Heracles).[38] The relationship with Apollo, though indirect, is nonetheless certain: In Pausanias's history of Sicyon, the god intervenes twice to renew the city's legendary dynasty. By Chrysorthe, daughter of the last king of the first dynasty, he has a child, Coronos, founder of a second dynasty, which ends with one Zeuxippe. Much later he is the father, as I mentioned a moment ago, of Zeuxippos.

It is not surprising to find the god intervening in this way, because in the sixth century the traditional version of the city's history was modified by order of Cleisthenes the tyrant so as to eliminate seven kings, who were replaced, as we saw earlier, by the names of priests of Apollo Carneus.

Thus in Sicyonian tradition we find positive connections between Hippolytus, war, and Apollo. To proceed further, however, we must resort to comparison. This is not difficult. As other scholars have recognized, the best known Hippolytus, the Hippolytus of Attic tradition, son of Theseus and bearer of his curse, was in fact a hero of Troezen on the northern coast of Argolis, opposite Athens.[39] Whereas there is virtually no trace of an ancient cult of Hippolytus at Athens,[40] there are numerous signs of such a cult in Troezen. In that city Pausanias was shown his house,[41] his tomb,[42] and a temple of Artemis Lycaea that he had founded.[43] Diomedes, legendary king of Argos, had founded Hippolytus's temple, where he was honored with a cult, had a priest appointed for life, and received annual sacrifices.[44] Note also that Diomedes, a typical warrior hero, founded hardly any other temples except to Athena.[45] In the Troezenian version of the myth, reported by Pausanias, Theseus, having killed his rivals the Pallantidae, went to Troezen, where he had sent his son Hippolytus to be brought up by his own grandfather, Pittheus—a good example of foster parentage.[46] He took his young wife Phaedra with him, and she fell in love with Hippolytus. We know the rest: the calumny, the curse of Theseus, the death of Hippolytus. All of this may show the retroactive influence of Euripides' *Hippolytus*, but the places indicated in the legend were located in Troezen. Not far from the stadium was the temple of Aphrodite Kataskopia, where Phaedra went to watch the young hero exercise.[47] There stood a myrtle with shredded leaves. Phaedra, in her distress, had torn them with a pin from her hairpiece. Her tomb, as well as that of Hippolytus, was located nearby.[48]

According to Louis Méridier,

> two different traditions concerning the fate of Hippolytus were widely known in Troezen. Everything pertaining to his *terrestrial* legend and death, as well as the surviving monuments of that legend, derived from popular beliefs. But the official version, which was developed in the sanctuary and which may have preserved primitive features of the legend, gave Hippolytus the rank of a god. It said nothing about the existence of his tomb, which people were still pointing out to Pausanias, and denied that he had been killed when his chariot overturned. Elevated to heaven by divine favor, he became the constellation of the Charioteer.[49]

What Pausanias says cannot be systematized in this way. The Troezenian cults tell us on the one hand that Hippolytus died and was buried and on the other hand that he did not die but went to heaven and became the Heniochus (the Auriga or Charioteer). A "contradiction" of this sort is not unusual in this type of legend; we find the same thing in Sparta in the Hyacinthus legend.

To remove all doubt on this score, note that the only rite attested in the cult of Hippolytus, but by both Euripides and Pausanias, involved having young women come prior to marriage to consecrate a lock of their hair to the hero.[50]

Are commentary and proof necessary? I think not: The rite of passage, the initiatory symbolism are patent. That Hippolytus is a warrior hero is implicit in the fact that his cult was founded by Diomedes, and like Phorbas he became a constellation. His death is an ancient part of the legend: *Hippolytus* means "freed horses," a clear allusion to the myth according to which the chariot horses, frightened by a sea monster and running wild, overturn Hippolytus's chariot and drag him along the rocks.[51] Furthermore, of the four Greek legends that explain the origin of the Charioteer constellation, three involve a hero thrown from his chariot. In one it is Phaethon, son of the sun, who imprudently tries to imitate his father by driving the chariot of the sun, threatening to set the whole world on fire, whereupon he is struck by Zeus's thunder and tossed into the river Eridanus.[52] In another it is Myrtilus, the hero who tampered with the chariot of his master Oenomaus in order to allow Pelops to win the race, who is thrown by Pelops from his chariot. Oenomaus also dies when he falls from his chariot.

Hippolytus was certainly a warrior hero in Sparta as well. Pausanias mentions a heroic monument to him there,[53] and, given the ruling ideology of Lacedaemonia, this monument was obviously not intended to celebrate the inveterate bachelor of Attic tradition. What is more, it stood next to another heroic monument, dedicated to Aulon, grandson of Melanion or of Parthenopaeus—both heroes of initiatory tales.[54]

Thus in Athens the meaning of the Hippolytus legend was altered, to judge by what it appears to have been in Troezen. In the tragedy that Euripides wrote about him, Hippolytus became a fanatic hunter, entirely absorbed in his passion and hostile to women. Surrounded by young friends—the ideal of male fraternity—he wished to remain absolutely chaste. His goddess, who presided over his hunts, was Artemis, the patron of virginity.[55]

These aspects of the legend must in part be ancient. Hunting was in
fact the basis of Greek adolescent education, and the young Troezenian
women who dedicated a lock of their hair to the hero were leaving the
sphere of Artemis to enter that of Aphrodite.[56] Thus Hippolytus presided over the initiation, the "passage," of adolescents of both sexes, just
like Hyacinthus, whose sister Polyboea is but a shadow barely mentioned in the tradition. What the Athenians did was to alter the balance
in this motif. Hippolytus, who like Narcissus was a man of Artemis,
wished to remain so—and in consequence he fell into abnormality; his
behavior became antisocial. It is worth noting that this reversal of the
myth's meaning goes along with a reversal of divine roles in Euripides'
play. The piece in fact opens with a long monologue by Aphrodite,
which announces the theme of the drama, and ends immediately after
the hero's death, with the appearance of Artemis, who tells the truth of
the story and declares what divine honors will henceforth be rendered to
her protégé.[57]

Hippolytus is also a hero of the stadium, as we know from both
Troezenian tradition and Euripides.[58] It was near the stadium, we are
told, that Phaedra and other young women of Troezen could admire,
from the temple of Aphrodite Kataskopia, the bodies of the young
athletes. Zeuxippos, who gave his name to Hippolytus's predecessor in
Sicyon, was in Attica and Argolis a stadium genius.[59] An accomplished
young man, indeed more accomplished than he should have been,
Euripides' Hippolytus played music, learned the lyre, and bred race
horses.[60] In the tradition of the priests of Hippolytus at Sicyon, moreover, Diomedes, founder of the cult, was also the founder of the Young
Pythian Games at Delphi, in honor of Apollo.[61]

Such was the original Hippolytus, Hippolytus of Troezen.

We shall assume that in nearby cities his myth was quite similar. In
Sparta, as we have seen, he was in all likelihood a military hero. Closer to
Troezen—between it and Sicyon—in Epidaurus, at the sanctuary of
Asclepius, who, according to the *Songs of Naupactus*, had revived the
hero, an ancient stele reported that Hippolytus had consecrated twenty
horses to the god.[62]

It may be taken for granted that Hippolytus was a similar figure in
Sicyonian mythology before becoming king. His association with
Apollo suggests as much, and the presence of Zeuxippos confirms it. For
Zeuxippos and Hippolytus form a couple. Both are fundamentally
associated with the stadium and chariot racing, and if the name of one

evokes "freed horses," the other evokes, in contrast, "horses held in hand." Zeuxippos is the son of Apollo, and Hippolytus, we are told, is the erōmenos. Plutarch's source may be ancient. In a city where Carnus was no doubt erōmenos of the same god, it is conceivable that a tradition anterior to Cleisthenes' reforms posited the same type of relationship between the god of the *kouroi* and a paradigmatic *kouros*.

IV
Heracles and
Apprenticeship for War

Ancient traditions tell of pederastic relations between Heracles and a whole series of partners: Eurystheus, Abderus, Iolaus, Hylas, Admetus, and Phrix or Trinx, to name a few. These traditions vary widely in value. Two of them are especially interesting. The legends concerning Iolaus and Diocles join myth and ritual in a very clear way, and both the myth and the ritual are plainly of the initiatory type. The rest are late literary composites, generally of little interest for my present purposes.

The reader unfamiliar with the subtleties of Greek mythology may well become confused by the innumerable themes that will crop up in the course of cross-checking the main points of my interpretation. Hence I shall begin by giving certain keys to the interpretation, which will, I hope, help the reader grasp the implications of particular points and appreciate the value of the various traditions.

Heracles was a pan-Hellenic hero from the time of Homer. Little is known of his origins and (pre)history, but certain points may be taken as virtually assured.

Heracles is, literally, "the glory of Hera." Human names derived from divine names other than Zeus are rare in Greek mythology. The implication here is that the relationship between goddess and hero is of fundamental importance. Indeed, Hera was said to have been Heracles' nurse (creating a paradoxical situation that certain classical authors found surprising, since some versions depict Zeus's wife as Heracles' most implacable enemy, even before his birth; she is also the mother of his divine wife, Hebe).[1]

The Hellenic pantheon, as it appears in Homer, was certainly formed in the Mycenaean era. Most of the major Greek gods are named in Linear B tablets from two Mycenaean sites, Pylos and Cnossus.[2] It was probably in the Mycenaean period that Hera was given to Zeus as a wife. The two are mentioned together for the first time in a late thirteenth-century tablet from Pylos.[3] Previously, the great god of the Indo-European heaven, of whom Zeus was the direct heir, probably had a female companion whose name was derived from his own. This was the case, for example, at Dodona in Epirus, where Zeus's wife was named Dione.[4] Hera, a divinity of unknown, perhaps non-Indo-European, origin,[5] had an ancient sanctuary in Argolis on the border between the territories of Argos and Mycenae.[6] It is quite probable that her cult originated there and subsequently spread to Greece. Indeed, this sanctuary probably existed as early as the fifteenth century,[7] whereas Mycenaean documents mention no temple of Hera at Pylos or Cnossus, for example.[8] Hera's oldest temples seem to have been subsidiaries of this one. For example, the temple that gave its name to the city of Heraea was, like the first Argive Heraeum, located on a border, in this case the border between Arcadia and Elis.[9] Furthermore, Argive legendary cycles—that of Heracles, for example, or of Perseus—treat Arcadia as an extension of Argive territory. The Heraeum of Samos is explicitly described in Greek tradition as having been founded by the priestess of Hera in Argolis.[10] Finally, the cult of Hera in Boeotia, for example, at Plataea, coincides with the expansion of the cult of Heracles which forms the subject of this section.

The character of Heracles is indeed closely associated with the Argive Hera. The cycle of the Twelve Labors of Heracles takes place entirely within the Argive sphere of influence, and all members of the hero's legendary family come from Mycenae or Tiryns. I am assuming that in early Mycenaean times the capital of the Argive plain was Tiryns, that it was not replaced as capital by Argos until the Dorian era, and, further, that the Heraeum marked the border between Tiryns and Mycenae.[11] Given that Hera delayed the birth of Alcmena and hastened that of the mother of Eurystheus, who became king of Mycenae as a result,[12] it is clear that the Argive Hera conferred royalty in the kingdoms that depended on her—a point confirmed by the myths of Io and Proetus.[13]

Hence it was probably in Argolis that Hera became the wife of Zeus, as she is, for example, in the Pylian tablet mentioned above.

Both Heracles and Hera made the journey into Boeotia at an unknown time prior to the oldest written sources. But once arrived they parted company. Hera's principle cult seems to have been at Plataea, whereas Heracles was mainly a Theban hero.

Martin P. Nilsson remarked some time ago that the cycle of Heraclean exploits, collected in a group of first ten and later twelve labors, is exclusively Argive, whereas the cycle of his birth, his marriages, and his death is Boeotian.[14] More recently, Georges Dumézil discovered[15] that Heracles' entire life, as recounted by Diodorus of Sicily in his book IV, is structured in accordance with the Indo-European trifunctional scheme.[16] On this view of the hero's life the ten or twelve labors constitute just one of three stages, and the overall structure of the life involves persons and events that Nilsson regarded as Boeotian and that we shall describe, more generally, as central Greek. I have examined these facts elsewhere and suggested that it was in Boeotia that the trifunctional conception of Heracles' life was first forged, there being nothing comparable in the traditions of purely Argive origin.[17]

Hence there were two contrasting Heracles in ancient tradition, the one derived from the other but profoundly "reworked" in the process. The life of the Argive Heracles is punctuated by ten combats with men or beasts, all monsters. His actions take place for the most part either within Argolis (the lion of Nemea, the hydra of Lerna) or in the "Thrace" of King Diomedes, which is a projection of Argolis and its old warrior hero Diomedes,[18] or in the west of Argolis (primarily Arcadia—the birds of Stymphalus, the boar of Erymanthus, the doe with brass hooves) or in Elis (the Augean stables) or in a mythical west, a projection of the previously mentioned regions (the Garden of the Hesperides, the Isle of Geryoneus).[19] This Heracles is the type of the solitary hero, a wild man living outside inhabited regions. There is no evidence that he had a wife. He is a sort of primordial hero, from the time when order was first established in the world. It is not impossible that his origins were ultimately Indo-European. That certain of his adversaries come in threes suggests that this was the case,[20] as does the existence among related peoples of similar heroes, monster-slaying warriors and asocial loners not bound by ties of matrimony.[21] The combats that reveal Heracles' physical strength are reminiscent of the several incarnations of another lonely warrior, the Iranian hero Varathragna, whose purpose is also to illustrate that hero's valor.[22] But this Heracles evidently owes nothing to the Indo-European trifunctional cycle and certainly incorporates some aspects of the Minoan and Asian Master of Animals—he is the heir of Gilgamesh, among others.[23]

This Argive Heracles lacks the social ties required by the master in an initiation ritual. The remainder of this discussion will therefore focus on the other Heracles.

This other Heracles, then, is primarily Boeotian and more precisely Theban. It was in Thebes, the mythographers tell us, that he was born, and in order to reconcile this with the traditions pertaining to the first Heracles they had to invent an exile for Amphitryon in Thebes.[24] The Boeotian Heracles is quite different from the Argive one. His adversaries are men, generally kings. He fights with some cities, such as Oechalia and Orchomenus, and lives in others, such as Thebes, Megara, and Calydon. He marries, and his marriages establish the rhythm of his life. He is no longer a solitary hero: In Thebes he commands an army and is the leader of the city's *kouroi*.[25] His adventures unfold in eastern Boeotia and the surrounding regions: Megara, Euboea, Locris, Atolia, and Thessaly. He never encounters monsters as in the Peloponnesus except for the Centaurs of Thessaly, who are accompanied by men, the Lapithae. The only important trait that the second Heracles has in common with his Argive predecessor is his military function. Neither Heracles is a king. Both are fighters, and the difference between them lies in the type of combat: One fights lonely battles on the wild outskirts of the city, in the *eskhatiē*, while the other is caught up in civil war among cities, that is, cities on the periphery of the one under attack (as a military commander Heracles stops the Orchomenians marching toward Thebes[26] and lays siege to Oechalia[27]).

This second Heracles is bound to society in many ways. He is a citizen of Thebes by birth, and he is a husband and hence a son-in-law, a brother-in-law, a father, and a father-in-law. As a leader he has disciples: among them are Iolaus and Philoctetes.

There are many good reasons to think that in very early times, in a period (the Late Helladic: sixteenth to twelfth centuries B.C.) that largely overlaps the Mycenaean, the region later known as Boeotia did not exist as such but was incorporated into a "greater Boeotia" that was divided into two kingdoms: in the west the kingdom of Orchomenus, which included all of western Boeotia, the valley of the Cephissus (which later formed the central axis of Phocis), and southern Phocis up to the region of Delphi,[28] and in the east the kingdom of Thebes, which comprised not only eastern Boeotia but also, beyond Cithaeron, the region of Eleusis[29] and perhaps even the plain of Athens,[30] as well as Megara[31] and certainly a large part of Euboea.[32]

The foregoing explains why the traditions concerning the erōmenoi of Heracles stem mainly from those parts of Boeotia under Theban dominance (including Thebes and Thespiae) and on the periphery thereof (Megara, Chalcis).

The present study is therefore concerned with this second Heracles. Obviously traits of both Heracles have been confounded in the "synthetic" poetic cycle, but, as we shall see, the monster-slaying Argive Heracles occupies but a small place in the sources used here.

THIRTEEN
Iolaus, an Exemplary Student
🔡

Plutarch—a late author, as the following remark makes clear—maintains in his *Erōticos* that Heracles' homosexual affairs were so numerous that it is impossible to list them all. A piece of evidence that carries more weight is Plutarch's report that down to his own time, since it was believed that Iolaus had been the erōmenos of Heracles, erastai went with their erōmenoi to Iolaus's tomb and swore an oath of loyalty to him.[1] Plutarch again mentions this rite in his *Life of Pelopidas*, which is based on Aristotle, and explains it by the fact that Iolaus was Heracles' squire in battle.[2]

Iolaus's "tomb" is mentioned as early as the fifth century by Pindar, who situated it near the stadium in Thebes.[3] Later, Pausanias, roughly contemporary with Plutarch, placed the hero's tomb "at Sardis," which is surely an error of transcription for "in Sardinia," based on a tradition about which I shall have more to say later on. But he also describes a heroic sanctuary in Thebes dedicated to Iolaus, which stands before the Protides gates and alongside the so-called Iolaus Gymnasium as well as a stadium and a hippodrome.[4] This is interesting in itself, but taken together the evidence concerning Iolaus has a suggestive power virtually unequaled in the present study.

1) Iolaus is the youthful assistant of Heracles in his exploits. The son of Iphicles, Heracles' "mortal" brother, Iolaus is therefore the hero's patrilateral nephew. In the literary tradition he is his companion in several adventures, a very few from the Argive cycle (the hydra of Lerna in particular) but many from the cycle of central Greece in which Heracles takes on human adversaries: the fight with Cycnus, near Iolcus, the expedition against Troy, the voyage of the Argonauts, the hunt for the Calydonian boar.[5] Artists often pictured the two together (in metopes and vase paintings), and Iolaus is shown at the hero's side in the hunt for the dog Cerberus, in the battle with the giant Antaeus, in the

Hesperides, and so on. He also accompanies him on the Oeta, when Heracles, suffering from the torture caused by the shirt of Nessus, builds a pyre and immolates himself.

Euripides in fact makes Iolaus Heracles' *parastatēs* (cf. the Cretan erōmenos) or helper and elsewhere his squire (*hypaspistēr*).[6] Now, there was in Thebes a warrior society based on homosexual friendship: the Hieros Lochos or "sacred battalion," thanks to which Epaminondas was able to defeat Sparta. This society consisted of male couples; Gorgidas, its founder, had in fact established this battalion to bring together couples previously (prior to the fourth century) dispersed throughout the Theban army.[7]

2) Iolaus, the disciple of Heracles, was a master chariot driver. When Heracles organized the Olympic Games, it was Iolaus who won the main event, the chariot race.[8] He also won the chariot race in the funeral games organized by Acastus for his father Pelias. Heracles was also present at this victory.[9] In Thebes, however, only Pindar, a Theban, mentions him as a patron of chariot races. In the first *Isthmian Ode*, dedicated to Herodotus of Thebes, victor in the chariot race, we read the following:

I will implicate him in song for Castor or Iolaus.
These two in Lacedaemon and Thebes were the mightiest charioteers
    among heroes.
In all trials of strength they won most prizes,
and their houses were made magnificent with tripods,
cauldrons, dishes of gold. The feel
of garlands given in token of victory
was theirs. That excellence is a clear shining
they had alike in the naked race and the course of warriors among
    clattering shields,
for the way of the javelin's flight thrown from their hands
and the cast of the stone discus.
There was no pentathlon then, but for each event
the end lay in itself.
And often and again, binding their brows with the clustered branched
    garlands, by Dirke's waters they appeared; and beside Eurotas,
the son of Iphicles, dweller among the breed of the Sown Men;
and among Achaeans Castor the Tyndarid of the high house at
    Therapne.[10]

Elsewhere, Pindar describes Iolaus as one of the "national glories" of Thebes, "renowned for his horsemanship."[11] "The great children of

Oeneus, at Thebes Iolaus the charioteer, have honor; Perseus at Argos; Castor's spear and Polydeuces beside the waters of the Eurotas."[12] Epharmostus of Opous in Locris won many victories, and "the tomb of Iolaus witnesses to his shining glory, as does Eleusis the sea-borne."[13]

3) Iolaus was the leader of troops of youths. Heracles was the leader of the Theban *kouroi*. After he died, Iolaus also became a troop commander. But the initiatory aspects of the concept are now more clearly emphasized.

One tradition centers on the city of Thespiae, which has already been mentioned several times as the city of Narcissus and the *thamuriddontes*. In the Boeotian cycle, Heracles' first exploit is the slaying of the lion of Mount Cithaeron (to be distinguished from one of his Peloponnesian exploits). Mount Cithaeron was under the control of Thespiae, and Thespius, eponymous king of that city, wishing to give the hero a reward, offered him his fifty daughters for one night. Heracles thus joined a sexual exploit to his feat of hunting; he impregnated all fifty girls between sunset and sunrise.

The fifty children were all boys: the Thespiadae. The eldest and the youngest girls both had twins, according to one tradition, so that the number of Thespiadae was fifty-two.

All the traditions agree that these boys embarked on a lengthy voyage. Unfortunately we know only late versions of this story, in which the primitive myth has been reinterpreted in the light of Greek colonial ventures. Pausanias and Diodorus of Sicily report that after receiving an oracle Heracles sent the Thespiadae to found a colony. He named his long-time companion Iolaus to be their leader. Pausanias repeats several times that this was the first Greek colonial expedition. According to Hyperochus, a historian whose work is known to us only through citations, the Thespiadae were the first to settle Mount Palatine.[14] More commonly they are said to have settled in Sardinia. For present purposes the origins of these traditions, which have to do with the vicissitudes of Greek history, are of little importance. The notion that the Thespiadae settled in Sardinia, for example, seems to be based solely on the name of a place or people: In eastern Sardinia there is a plain known as Iolaeion and a people known as Iolaians.[15]

The Thespiadae, then, were a group of fifty or fifty-two young men. The figure is typical of groups of young boys and girls involved in initiation procedures in Greek legends. The Argonauts numbered fifty-two, fifty of whom were oarsmen; the hunters of the boar of Calydon numbered fifty; the sons of Aegyptus, who would be killed on their

wedding day by the Danaids, and the Danaids themselves, numbered
fifty, as did the sons of Lycaon, the Arcadian "sons of the Wolf." Ilos
founded Troy after combing Anatolia in the company of fifty young men
and fifty young women. According to Statius, fifty *kouroi* commanded by
five captains were involved in the Theban ambush of the Argives. The
company of the ship that Alcinous places at the disposal of Ulysses for his
return to Ithaca includes fifty-two boys from the noblest families (and
the ship is later petrified by Poseidon as it approaches Skheria).[16] Now, in
Greek tradition the Argonauts were the heroes who first dared to venture
out upon new ocean routes. In an early, exclusively Thessalian version of
the story, the fifty warriors who formed the troop or *agele* of the leader
Jason must have been anonymous—that Heracles, Theseus, or the
Dioscuri figured among them is nothing more than a late literary
embellishment. Now we can see the nature of the Thespiadae more
clearly. A homogeneous group, all born on the same night (according to
one version, like the Partheniae, another anonymous group of fifty
warriors, the Lacedaemonian founders of Tarentum), led by Iolaus, and
pioneering colonizers, the Thespiadae are none other than the heroes of a
Boeotian version of a myth of whose Thessalian version the heroes are the
Argonauts. To be sure, in this primitive Boeotian version the adventures
of the Thespiadae do not result in the founding of a colony: The heroes
return to Thespiae and live out their days among their families.

On this point, Diodorus, who had to reconcile the Boeotian traditions
(which he knew quite well, as we saw in the discussion of his trifunctional account of Heracles' life) with their pseudohistorical colonial
complement, furnishes information of the utmost interest: Of the fifty
Thespiadae, two, he says, preferred to remain in Thebes and down to his
own time their descendants formed the object of a cult. More than that,
"seven remained in Thespiae, where they were called *dēmoukhoi*, and
where their descendants are said to have been prominent citizens until
recent times."[17] This remark sheds further light on the nature of the
affair. Like the Partheniae[18] a homogeneous and anonymous group
within the *agele*, the Thespiadae are equals after a fashion—the fashion of
Sparta, where abstract equality among citizens only partly dissimulated
the existence of a veritable aristocracy, a group of men "more equal" than
their fellows. Among other things, then, the myth of the Thespiadae
was the founding myth of the Thespian aristocracy, and very likely its
original form showed the group leaving under the direction of Iolaus and
later returning without him—for of the two unnamed Thespiadae who

Diodorus in an unusual phrase says became the object of a cult in Thebes, was not one Iolaus?

Thespiae was, as we saw earlier, the city of Narcissus and the *thamuriddontes*. But Narcissus could not have been the mythical founder of homosexuality there because he symbolizes something else, and Thamyris, who could have been, is nowhere described as a Thespian. Iolaus, the pupil of Heracles and master of the founders of the local aristocracy, is therefore a worthy candidate for this role. I am quite ready to assume that in a bygone era Narcissus was the authentic founder, like Cyparissus in Chios and Hyacinthus at Amyclae; then, with the arrival of Iolaus, imposed as a new founder by the Thebans, Narcissus was freed to assume another mythological role.

In the historical era, Thespiae was the perpetual rival of Thebes. It is hard to imagine the local aristocracy taking for its hero and for the master of its ancestors a figure from Theban mythology! The borrowing is really conceivable only prior to the era of the city-state. During the time of the Mycenaean kingdom of Thebes, the city dominated the whole of eastern Boeotia, and it was ostentation, pretension, and pride on the part of the people of Thespiae to claim for themselves a hero from the capital.

According to one tradition, the Thespiadae did not die but fell into an eternal sleep in Sardinia and were never incinerated.[19] This notion may have been associated with the Iolaian cult of the "Iolaian Father" mentioned by Diodorus, or it may be a vestige of a myth involving a mystical, initiatory death.

Several other authors suggested that the Thespiadae were joined on their expedition to the west by other men: Cadmeiones (i.e., Thebans) and Locrians according to Eustatius; Locrians according to Solinus; Cadmeiones, Locrians, and Aetolians according to a third source.[20] But the oldest and most insistent tradition says that these others were Athenians. According to Pausanias, "It was in a private capacity that the Athenians made an expedition to Sardinia with Iolaus," although they are generally linked to the Thespiadae.[21] This tradition is original and accords well with the following two facts: Several authors describe Thespius as the son of King Erechtheus of Athens,[22] while the Athenian author Euripides ascribes an important role to Iolaus, a point worthy of further attention.

In his tragedy *The Heraclidae*, staged sometime between 430 and 427, the Attic poet depicts all the sons of Heracles (by his legitimate wives; the Thespiadae are not included) pursued by the vengeful Eurystheus.

According to a tradition that goes back at least to the beginning of the fifth century, the Heraclidae ultimately sought refuge in Attica.[23] The sons of Heracles, the future conquerors of the Peloponnesus, are here only "children" (line 48) and adolescents, like Macaria, who sacrifices himself for the sake of an Athenian victory over the Argives. The leader, guide, and spokesman of this troop of women and children is old Iolaus.

There can be no doubt that the image that resurfaces here is the same one that Boeotian tradition imposed on the Heraclean cycle. Iolaus, disciple of Heracles, is the leader of an *agele* par excellence, a master in the teaching of martial arts, hunting, and sports. Here he is to the adolescent Heraclidae what he is elsewhere to the fifty Thespiadae.

At this point a most interesting theme comes into the picture. In Thebes, according to Pindar, or in Athens, as Euripides would have it, Iolaus defeats Eurystheus.[24] This presents no difficulty: A military hero and pupil of Heracles can easily vanquish a king. And Iolaus, somewhat younger than his master, is somewhat older than his sons. Pindar seems to adhere to this plain view of the matter. But other writers introduce a twist for which it would be hard to see the reason without some vestige of a tradition of death and rebirth. Specifically, either Iolaus is already dead when Eurystheus comes looking for the Heraclidae in Boeotia or he is very old (as Euripides has it). Hence he must either miraculously return to life long enough to accomplish his feat,[25] or he must persuade the gods to make him, for a moment at least, young again.[26] This episode, which at first seems pointless, cannot be meaningless, and I subscribe to the following comments of R. Roux concerning the argonautic hero Iolaus:

> Iolaus, who is mentioned as an Argonaut by Hyginus and who, like Jason, undergoes a ritual to restore his youth and is the leader of a perfectly homogeneous group of fifty youths [is] the organizer of a company of worthies [whose affinities with the Argonauts are manifest].[27]

4) Iolaus is a warrior hero. Renowned mainly as a charioteer and *agele* leader, fairly peaceful activities, Iolaus is nevertheless, as befits a Greek citizen, a warrior, especially when he is the paradigmatic hero of initiation, as in Thebes (I shall say more about this in a moment). From various sources, some of them ancient, we can reconstruct an image of the professional warrior of archaic times, such as Iolaus must have been.

As the leader of an *agele*, Iolaus was sometimes obliged to fight. We have just seen this in connection with the story of the Heraclidae, in which Iolaus covers himself with glory by halting the Mycenaean army at the gates of Thebes and killing its leader, King Eurystheus. Diodorus also tells of wars waged by the Thespiadae in Sicily, but this report may be a commonplace based on the topical events of Greek colonization.

Pindar, in any case, knows what he wants to say when he calls Iolaus a *homodamos* of the *genos* of the Spartoi. Of course the descendants of the five Spartoi born from the dragon's teeth planted by Cadmus formed the warrior caste of prehistoric Thebes. What Pindar means is that Iolaus, though born of a different family, a different *genos*, since he is of Argive origin, is nevertheless a man of the same type: All are warriors.[28]

The name of the hero reveals just how archaic this concept is. In archaic Greece, surely since the Mycenaean era, the second syllable of his name, *laus*, referred to the people in arms, in contrast to *dēmos*, the people in peacetime.[29] The root can scarcely be other than the ancient noun *ios*, "arrow, shaft," according to Chantraine "a rare and poetic word," attested in Homer and in the tragedies. We find it in very archaic compounds, and, like many other words from the Greek military lexicon, it is of Indo-European origin. The Sanskrit *isu*, and Avestan *isu*, "arrow," correspond exactly, the primitive Greek form being *isw-o* with a thematic vowel.[30] The name Iolaus therefore means "the people armed with arrows," just as the name of the semi-legendary king of Sparta Dorylaus means "the people armed with lances."

5) Iolaus is the son-in-law of Heracles. The myth of Iolaus teaches us one more thing: that we are probably looking at an ancient institution when we see Heracles abandon his first wife Megara and give her to Iolaus. The educator also gives his pupil a wife.

It is worth noting that this gift leads, in the genealogy attested since Hesiod (who, by the way, is a Boeotian poet), to a countergift in the following generation: Iolaus gives his daughter Leipephile to Phylas, son of Antiochus, son of Heracles.[31]

Note, too, Iolaus's ties to the two extremities of the ancient kingdom of Thebes to which I alluded at the beginning of this chapter, when the sovereignty of the masters of the Cadmea extended from the Saronic Gulf to Lake Copais. Thero, daughter of Iolaus's daughter, gives birth by Apollo to Chaeron, eponym of the city of Chaeronea in far eastern Boeotia, beyond Copais. Furthermore, Iolaus marries Megara, a Theban but homonymous with the city Megara, whose mother, Automedusa, is the daughter of Alcathous, the most famous legendary king of that same city. In Megara, as we shall see in a moment, we also find Diocles, who is in some sense the alter ego of Iolaus.

6) Iolaus presided over initiations in the historical era. Diodorus is quite familiar with the cults of the small town of Agyrion, in central Sicily, of which he is a native. A sanctuary there is dedicated to Iolaus, who accompanied Heracles in the quest for the oxen of Geryoneus. The hero, on orders from his master, is there honored with an annual cult, for

all the inhabitants of this city let the hair of their heads grow from their birth in honor of Iolaus, until they have obtained good omens in costly sacrifices and have rendered the god propitious. And such a holiness and majesty pervade the sacred precinct that the boys (*paides*) who fail to perform the customary rites lose their power of speech and are like dead men. But as soon as someone takes a vow that he will pay the sacrifice and vouchsafes to the god a pledge to that effect, at once, they say, those who are suffering from this malady are restored to health. Now the inhabitants, in pursuance of these rites, call the gate, at which they come into the presence of the god and offer him these sacrifices, "The Heraclean," and every year with the utmost zeal they hold games which include gymnastic contests and horse races. And since the whole populace, both free men and slaves, unite in approbation of the god, they have commanded their servants, as they do honor to him apart from the rest, to gather in bands and when they come together to hold banquets and perform sacrifices to this god.[32]

The god is none other than Heracles, whose cult Diodorus alludes to a few lines earlier. This is clearly an initiation ritual,[33] complete with symbolic death, rebirth, rite of passage (giving up the childhood haircut[34]), and sumptuous sacrifices. The themes highlighted in our study of the Hyacinthia recur here: an annual ritual involving ephebes and their promotion, which implies the existence of at least a rudimentary system of age classification up to the time of maturity; a twofold cult, devoted both to a hero, Iolaus, and to a god, Heracles, who are related in the myth through education and pederasty; major sacrifices to the god; mystical death of the novices, analogous to the death and resurrection of Iolaus; reference to a couretic divinity par excellence, Heracles; participation of the entire population with abolition of the social hierarchy; and great banquets whose abundance replenishes the human and natural resources of the city for the year to come, a sort of dip in the fountain of youth for the entire population. Beyond any doubt the feast of Iolaus was to Agyrion what the Hyacinthia were to Sparta.

Whatever the routes by which this specifically Boeotian cult, unknown to the Dorians of the Peloponnesus, arrived in Sicily, its ultimate origins certainly lay in Thebes. In enumerating the main traits of Iolaus's mythical character, I cited Pindar and Pausanias on the hero's cult in Thebes. Recall that opposite the Proitides Gates stood the tomb of Iolaus, his hērōon, which must have incorporated the tomb, the Iolaus Gymnasium, the stadium, and the hippodrome. Thus races held in Thebes took place under Iolaus's watchful eye and protection. The hero therefore presided over the gymnastic exercises and athletic training of the Theban ephebes.

The one analogy, with the ritual of Agyrion, tends to support the hypothesis that there was also an initiation ritual at Thebes in the primitive era. Civic education, carried out under the watchful eye of a paradigmatic hero of initiation, must have taken place in the archaic city in the traditional manner, with a phase of testing followed by a rite of passage.

There is further support for this hypothesis. Our reference text, that of Plutarch, mentions oaths exchanged by erastai and erōmenoi at the tomb of Iolaus. Now, this same custom, of the swearing of homosexual oaths in a consecrated place, was also practiced at Thera, at Megara with Diocles, and at Chalcis with Cleomachus; it was a rite. In its most archaic form, at Thera, prior to the moral evolution that transformed the erōmenoi into sexual objects desired and fought over by adult males,[35] the oaths were in no sense "oaths of loyalty" between erastai and erōmenoi; rather, they were declarations to the gods that the homosexual ritual had been completed. This accounts for the presence of the divinity or model hero. The erastēs and erōmenos attest that the ritual, for which the hero or god is responsible, has been carried out in all particulars.

Finally, the inscriptions in Thera suggest a more specific hypothesis: that the sexual union of master and disciple actually took place in the consecrated place, close to the gods. Bethe has deduced from early texts concerning the sacramental rites of Thebes, Megara, and Chalcis that the heroes' tombs were not only the scene of spoken rites but also of enacted rituals.[36] In fact, the location of Iolaus's tomb, on the fringes of the city near the gymnasium, is precisely that of the cavern of Thera in which the largest number of inscriptions has been found.[37] In the absence of a liaison in the bush, of which the highly civic Heracles of Theban tradition gave no inkling, this scene of education, once vacant land on the edge of town, was in fact a place to which teachers and pupils repaired for sexual purposes.

Taken together, these various items of circumstantial evidence suggest, first, that the institutions expressed in the monuments opposite the Proitides Gates of Thebes were actually the modernized, secularized, rationalized form of an ancient initiation and, further, that the myth of homosexual relations between Heracles and Iolaus, mentioned at a very late date by Plutarch, must in fact be quite old. Pindar's observations do not contradict this hypothesis, and the parallel provided by Diocles and others tends to support it.[38]

Note, finally, that although the Theban tradition ascribes the invention of homosexuality to Laius, this ascription has, according to our sources, no other impact on ritual in the historic era. Iolaus is the patron of initiation. Now, Iolaus, a native of Argos, is intrinsically associated with Heracles, who as we have seen seems to have been introduced along with Hera into Boeotia during the Mycenaean era, probably toward its end. Iolaus thus corresponds to a younger, more recent religious stratum than that with which Laius, the Cadmidae, and the Spartoi are associated.[39]

FOURTEEN
Excesses
᠊

Subsequent to the passage cited at the opening of the last chapter, Plutarch reports a second instance of Heraclean pederasty. Admetus, he says, was not only the lover of his wife Alcestis but also the beloved (erōmenos) of Heracles.[1] He then recalls that, according to other authors, Admetus was also the beloved of Apollo.

These two affairs are in some ways similar. Both have an artificial look about them. Neither fits the facts of Admetus's biography or of his relationship with Heracles. The most that can be assumed is that in some ancient version of the myth there may have been a pedagogical and sexual relationship between Apollo and Admetus, with the roles assigned by tradition reversed. In favor of this hypothesis is the antiquity of the tie between Admetus and Apollo[2] and the importance in the myth of a period in which the god serves the king, a theme that also occurs, in a slightly different form, in the story of Apollo's exile to the wilderness of the Tempe Valley. On the other hand, Heracles' involvement in the Alcestis cycle seems in no way related to the primary form of the myth. In the first work to tell the story, Hesiod's *Catalogue of Women*, and at least until the time of Apollodorus,[3] it is Persephone, goddess of the dead, who sends Alcestis back to earth without the slightest help from Heracles. Similarly, the allusions to Alcestis that one finds in the Lacedaemonian Carnea make sense only if the hero's resurrection is a mystical phenomenon or at most the work of a god acting as an agent of fate, without any unpredictable human intervention. In the current state of the question, it appears that the earliest work in which one finds the theme that gives Heracles the opportunity to intervene physically, namely, the theme of Alcestis in the grip of death (personified as Thanatos), is the first Attic *Alcestis*, a work of the poet Phrynichus from the first half of the fifth century.[4]

Thus nothing here is ancient, and most likely it is a case of Hellenistic romanticizing, as we shall see later on with Eurystheus. This interpretation of the Admetus myth may have been encouraged by its context; I have already called attention to the fact that homosexual love is a recurrent theme in this hero's entourage.

From the passage in Athenaeus concerning male homosexuality, cited earlier in connection with Argynnus and Hymenaeus, we learn that a poet by the name of Diotimus, in his *Heracleia*, made Heracles the lover of Eurystheus and said that it was to please Eurystheus that Heracles undertook his labors.[5]

This is obviously a crude reinterpretation of the Argive cycle of Heracles, and for once I shall agree with Dover and disagree with Bethe. The relationship between Heracles and Eurystheus in no way conforms to the pattern that we find in all myths involving pederasty, excepting those of most recent date: Eurystheus and Heracles are the same age; Eurystheus is even slightly older than the son of Zeus, because Hera delayed the birth of the latter so that Sthenelus's son could be born first and thus inherit the Mycenaean crown.[6] Eurystheus cannot possibly be the *paidika* of Heracles. Furthermore, Eurystheus is never the hero's companion or pupil. Encounters between the two are highly episodic, and each is active in a different sphere: One is a king who lives in his palace at Mycenae, the other a lonely warrior and hunter whose haunts are the wild mountains of the Peloponnesus. The relationship between them is surely of a quite different sort. One is a king and the son of a king, the other a warrior and the son of a warrior.[7] Such a pair in a sense duplicates the structure that Francis Vian has discovered in Theban mythology, where the royal lineage of the Cadmidae chose its mates from among the warrior lineages descended from the Spartoi: a striking parallel to the opposition between a king who is a descendant of Cadmus and a polemarch warrior descended from one of the five Spartoi.[8] That this is indeed the case in the primitive version of the legend is demonstrated by the repetition of the model: in Thebes Heracles is chief of the *kouroi* against the Orchomenians and wages war on his own, in opposition to King Creon, who prefers to surrender.[9] In the Lacedaemonian cycle of Heracles, the hero drives the usurper Hippocoon, another warrior, out of Sparta and reestablishes the legitimate king, Tyndareus.[10]

Diotimus probably lived in the early part of the Hellenistic period.[11] A common theme of that time was that of lovers subjecting themselves to trials in order to seduce their erōmenoi.[12] This is but the literary projection of real life, as pederasty (in the form of free love) became increasingly common after being freed from its primitive institutional constraints (especially in Athens), with the result that male adolescents were transformed from disciples socially obliged to submit to their masters into sexual objects courted, adored, admired, and supplicated by their would-be lovers. It is impossible to regard Diotimus's assertion as the reflection of an ancient tradition or of the influence of the "Dorian" model of pederasty.[13]

A famous legend of the third century is that of Heracles and Hylas. The story, complex and surely of late composition, is nevertheless rich in information. The following version is from Theocritus, the great bucolic poet of the early Alexandrian period:

> Not for us alone, Nicias,
> as we used to think, was Eros
> begotten, whoever of the gods
> was his father. We aren't the first
> to whom beauty seems beautiful,
> who are mortal and can't foresee
> the morrow. Even Amphitryon's
> bronze-hearted son, who withstood
> the savage lion, loved a boy—
> charming Hylas, whose hair hung down
> in curls. And like a father
> with his dear son, he taught him all the things
> which had made him a mighty man
> and famous. And he never left him,
> either at high noon, or when Dawn
> races upward with her white horses
> to Zeus's house, or when peeping chicks
> scurry toward their nest, while the mother
> perches on the smoke-stained beam
> and flaps her wings. That way the boy
> might grow the way he wanted him to,
> and yoked with him, attain
> the true measure of a man.
> And when Jason, Aison's son,
> sailed after the golden fleece,
> and all the noblest went with him,
> chosen from all the cities,
> to rich Iolkos he came too,
> the man of many labors,

son of noble Alkmena,
queen of Midea. And Hylas
went with him aboard the Argo,
the strong-thwarted ship.[14]

After reaching the Hellespont, the Argonauts land in "the land of the Kianes," that is, at the site where the city of Kios would soon be founded, on the southern shore just east of the meridian that passes through Byzantium. While the Argonauts pitch camp and prepare their meal, Hylas goes to fetch water, but as he approaches the fountain he is grabbed by its three nymphs and dragged in. Soon afterward the son of Alcmena sets out in search of him.

"Hylas!" he called
three times, as loud as he could
with his deep voice, and the boy
answered three times, but his voice
came faintly through the water.

In desperation Heracles scours the barren shore, but in vain, while the Argonauts set sail for Colchis.

A second extended account occurs in the first book of the *Argonautica* of Apollonius of Rhodes. Apollonius was a contemporary of Theocritus, and scholars disagree about which of the two stories of Hylas has priority.[15] Although Apollonius eliminates the erotic aspect of the hero's education from his version, it still contains several interesting pieces of information. The Argonauts, he says, landed "in Chian lands near Mount Arganthoneion and the mouths of the Chios." While Heracles is away, Hylas goes off to fetch water.

Meantime Hylas with a brazen pitcher went apart from the company, in quest of a sacred running spring, that he might ere his return draw for him water against suppertime, and get all else ready and in order for him at his coming. For Heracles had with his own hands brought him up in such habits from his earliest childhood, having robbed him from his father's house, goodly Theiodamas, whom he slew ruthlessly among the Dryopes, because he withstood him about a steer for plowing. . . . It chanced that lately choirs of nymphs had settled there; their care it was ever to hymn Artemis with midnight song, as many of them as dwelt there round the lovely peak. All those whose lot it is to watch o'er hilltops and mountain streams, and they who guard the woods, were all drawn up apart; but she, the nymph of the water, was just rising from her lovely spring, when she marked him near with the blush of his beauty and sweet grace upon him. For on him the full moon from heaven was shedding her light. And Cypris made the nymph's heart flutter, and scarce in her confusion could she collect herself.

She grabs him and pulls him toward her. The hero cries out, but "only one of the companions hears him, Polyphemus, son of Eilatos," who calls out and goes searching for Hylas. He warns Heracles, who searches through the night for his disciple. After various incidents the Argonauts reluctantly prepare to depart, and Apollonius comments thus:

> And so by the counsel of Zeus, the one was destined to found and build a city called after the river, namely Polyphemus, son of Eilatus, while the other returned and performed the labors of Eurystheus. Now he threatened at once to ravage the Mysian land, since they could not discover for him the fate of Hylas, either alive or dead. But they chose out the noblest sons of the people, and gave them as pledges for him, and took an oath that they would never cease from the toil of seeking him. Wherefore to this day the men of Chios ask after Hylas, the son of Theiodamas, and take care of the established town of Trachin, for there it was that Heracles did place the boys whom they sent to him from Chios to take as hostages.[16]

The legend conforms exactly to a pattern that we have encountered several times before. First there is the educational phase, involving hunting and war, designed to transform a boy into a man. As long as he remains a *pais* (boy), Hylas, whose beauty is apparently matched only by that of Hyacinthus (there is an allusion in both cases to their handsome heads of hair), is the erōmenos of his educator.

Homosexuality is surely an essential theme of the myth, and this cannot have been solely an invention of Theocritus. There are allusions to homosexuality in the work of most of the authors who treated the Hylas story, including Euphorion, Socrates of Argos, Phanocles, Simylus, and Cephalion, a historian of the Chios region.[17] The homosexual relationship itself is more important than the identities of the parties. In Socrates, Hylas is the *son* of Heracles, and it is Polyphemus who plays the part of his erastēs.

It is remarkable, moreover, that Theocritus, the earliest writer whose text concerning Hylas has survived (but nonetheless a writer of the

Hellenistic period), no longer fully understands the homosexual relationship even as he describes it. Heracles, he says, raised Hylas "as a father [would raise] his cherished son"—and not as an ancient teacher would have done, as an "adoptive father" in the case of foster parentage or as a private hunting instructor in societies that predated the city-state. The relationship of master to disciple in these societies was not that of father to son. By the third century, however, these social realities were no longer perceptible, and the only equivalent that an Alexandrian author can find for a pedagogical relationship of this sort, for the solicitude that Heracles shows for a *pais*, for the cohabitation of master and disciple and the individualized, personalized aspects of the pupil's education, is in the relationship of father to son.

Finally, the fact that this motif is absent from Apollonius's *Argonautica* is not unusual. As Vian rightly observes: "It has often been noted that out of decency the epic does not touch on erotic themes except with the utmost discretion. This is true even of the *Argonautica*, despite the importance in that work of Aphrodite and Eros. [It is the case] in the Lemnian episode; the wedding of Jason and Medea shows the same reserve. . . . Nor is there any explicit suggestion that Heracles feels for Hylas anything other than the virile affection that a hero should feel for a young 'page' (line 131, *opaōn*) for whom he bears moral responsibility (line 1211). Can one even imagine Heracles in love, after his earlier sarcasm toward the ephemeral lover of Hypispyle (lines 865–874)?"[18]

Tailored thus (and I shall say in a moment why I think that what we are seeing here is a tailoring of certain mythological material), the legend follows a typical initiatory pattern. In the course of an adventure that is also a trial (the expedition of the Argonauts), which for him ends early, Hylas is abducted by women. Hence the landing in Chian territory is not an episode of the hero's childhood. A *pais* initially, he is by this point nubile, capable of attracting the opposite sex. He moves from homosexual love, characteristic of the adolescent stage, to heterosexual love, which signifies his promotion to adult status. The sequences are clearly indicated by Apollonius. The Nymphs of Arganthoneion honor Artemis, as do all young girls, or *parthenoi*, prior to marriage, until one of them meets Hylas and falls under the sway of Cypris (Aphrodite), goddess of Cyprus, whereupon she manages easily to lay hold of her man. The metaphor of marriage is clear. For the purposes of myth the story is embarrassing—it is too simple. Artemis ordinarily does not forgive her nymphs their sexual escapades. But this one escapes without difficulty, like any young Greek woman escaping the realm of Artemis through marriage and entering the realm of Aphrodite. As we saw earlier, these same two goddesses frame and punctuate the adventure of Hippolytus.

Thus, Hylas's disappearance is patterned partly on a common theme of initiation, mystical death, "drowning,"[19] and sojourn with a god (e.g., Pelops's sojourn with Poseidon) and partly on the normal outcome of promotion to adult status, namely, marriage.

Hence this legend fully corroborates the argument I am making: Homosexuality was part of the normal initiation procedure and concluded with the end of the youth's education and his promotion to adult status and subsequent marriage.

Undeniably, however, the Hylas legend is a formalization of elements alien to the cycle of Greek initiatory adventures. Without going into a detailed analysis that would take us too far afield, I offer some observations in support of this assertion.

Hylas is not a hero who derives from Greek mythological sources. He has no cult in Greece and appears in no legend other than this one, which unfolds exclusively in Chios in Asia Minor. Furthermore, while Aeschylus and Aristophanes may both have been familiar with the Chian ritual, the annual call to Hylas,[20] their common source was probably Hellanicus, an early fifth-century scholar and collector of myths and traditions.[21] It was the Hellenistic era that made Hylas famous—Apollonius, Theocritus, Euphorion, and Nicander[22]—contemporaneous with the growing importance of Asia Minor after the conquest of Alexander.

Historically, Chios was a colony of Miletus, founded, according to Saint Jerome, in 626/5. But Hylas was as unknown in Miletus as he was elsewhere. Hence the original colonizers must have discovered him in Chios. Our authors are aware of this, as they refer to the Mysians in connection with the ritual of calling out for the hero.

Chios subsequently adopted Hylas as its local hero and took over his cult. Was the associated ritual previously a ritual of initiation? There is no evidence for this. What is more, while the myth has the initiatory form described above, the ritual, as described by our authors, seems to belong to another type of religious behavior.

The people of the country [says Antoninus Liberalis, following Nicander] to this day still offer sacrifices to Hylas beside the well. The priest calls his name three times, and three times the echo answers him.[23]

Strabo speaks of an *oreibasia*, a procession in the mountains, during which the people call out to Hylas.[24] These indications, together with others culled from Latin authors, suggest an annual ritual in which the Chians repaired to the mountains in a *thiasus*, or consecrated group, marched about or ran while calling out the name of Hylas, and accompanied the priest to the well where a sacrifice was made.[25] The meaning of this ritual escapes us. Nilsson, as was his wont, saw this as an agrarian rite of some sort, an interpretation that has fortunately been criticized by Knaack.[26] The theme of rebirth, of the cycle of the seasons or years, may be involved, but nothing is certain. Yet one remarkable coincidence is worth noting: The mountain plays a major role in both the myth and the ritual. The latter is essentially, according to Strabo, an *oreibasia*, mountain race. Apollonius, Nicander, and Euphorion all mention Arganthoneion, the mountain that dominates Chios on the north. Finally, Apollonius explicitly blames Hylas's disappearance on one of the "choirs of nymphs [that] had settled there" on the mountain.

Indeed, the cult of the mountains is typically Anatolian, as Hittite documents have revealed. One mountain mentioned in those documents was known as Hylla. It figures in invocations, paired, as was commonly done, with other mountains that were probably located north of Hatti, that is, northeast of Ankara.[27] The parallel was first noticed by Forrer in 1922,[28] and it may indicate a displacement or derivative of a cult. I would mention, however, that the Hittites often paired sacred mountains that were quite remote from one another. If the mountain Zaliyanu, once paired with Hylla, is in fact, as H. G. Güterbock suggests,[29] in the Ada Dagh, far north of the Hittite capital, Hattysas, it was once paired with Mount Harga, which according to E. Laroche and H. T. Bossert was the Mount Argaeus of the ancients, or present-day Erciyes Dagh, well south of Hattusas.[30] The location of Zaliyanu, which forms a sort of mountainous promontory surrounded by the Halys (present-day Kizil Irmak; Ada Dagh means "mountain-island" in Turkish), is quite similar to that of Arganthoneion, a promontory pointing west into the Sea of Marmara. Hence it is not out of the question that Hylla is the mountain of Hylas. Situated at almost the same distance from Hattusas but to the south, Mount Hazzi (Kasios to the Greeks and Djebel-el-Akra to the Arabs) occupied an important place in Hittite myth and ritual.[31]

In any case Hylas is surely an Anatolian hero, pre-Greek, and cannot belong to the earliest Heraclean cycle.

There is a second point to be made in this connection. Apollonius says that both Heracles and a certain Polyphemus shared an interest in Hylas.

According to Socrates of Argos, Hylas's erastēs was in fact Polyphemus, whereas Heracles was the young man's father.[32] There is every reason to believe that what we see here is an ancient version of the myth, prior to that in which Heracles is the erastēs. Indeed, Heracles played no part in the legendary cycle of Milesian colonization, while Polyphemus was the legendary founder of Chios, a colony of Miletus.[33] Now, even though no Milesian inscription or literary tradition has yet been discovered that attests Polyphemus, we can be sure that he belongs to that city's mythical patrimony. There are three pieces of evidence for this. First, Polyphemus is surely identical to another Greek hero by the name of Euphemus, because the two occur interchangeably in the list of Argonauts;[34] Euphorion and Socrates identify one with the other; according to a scholium of Apollonius, Laonome, sister of Heracles, was given as a wife to either Euphemus or Polyphemus;[35] and finally, their two names, "he who speaks well" and "he who speaks prolifically," are quite similar in form and meaning.

The second piece of evidence is that Euphemus is essentially a Boeotian hero, even though the locale with which he is most closely associated in the classical era is Cape Taenarum in southern Laconia: at some prehistoric time he must have been transferred there by Boeotians. We know that, according to Hesiod, Euphemus was born at Hyria in eastern Boeotia, to Poseidon and Mekionike; according to Pindar he was born on the Cephissus in western Boeotia, to Poseidon and Europa, daughter of Tityus, another Boeotian hero;[36] furthermore, Polyphemus is the son of Elatos, who is the son of Poseidon and, indeed, possibly his hypostasis.[37]

Finally, neither Euphemus nor Polyphemus is attested in the legends of Miletus, but several clues point to their involvement in Miletus. An inscription found at Chios, another Ionian colony in Asia not far from Miletus, mentions "Euphemus, son of Elatos"[38] (which again confirms the assertion that Euphemus and Polyphemus are identical). Boeotian influence is much in evidence at Miletus.[39] The Boeotian Poseidon, father of Euphemus and grandfather of Polyphemus, was known in Miletus.[40] The federal sanctuary of the Ionians, at Cape Mykale just north of Miletus, was dedicated to Poseidon Heliconios, whose title obviously comes from Mount Helicon in western Boeotia.[41]

These observations account for the fact that in a primary Chian version of the myth, Hylas's erastēs is the founder of Chios, Polyphemus. Heracles' role in the story is a later addition, most likely due to the influence of Heraclea of Pontus, a colony of Megara, on its neighbors. This influence is ancient. As early as the fifth century, Hellanicus made

Hylas's father out to be one Theomenes, surely the same person as Theodamas the Dryopian whom Callimachus and Apollonius relate to Hylas.[42] The process was perceived quite early. A poem of Hesiod, the *Marriage of Ceyx*, known from ancient allusions and rare fragments,[43] contained an episode from the Heraclean saga in which the hero, after leaving the ship *Argo* in search of water at the place known as the Aphetes in Magnesia, is abandoned by his companions. This episode has nothing to do with Hylas, Chios, or Mysia. The Aphetes are on the Magnesian peninsula near Iolcus, the port from which the Argonauts departed. But when the similarity was noticed between the story of Heracles abandoned while searching for water and that of Polyphemus the Argonaut searching eternally for his lost Hylas, elements from Hesiod were mingled with the Chian tradition. Hylas became the son or erōmenos of Heracles; his father was Ceyx in Nicander's version[44] or Heracles or Theomenes/Theodamas, the Dryopian who, if Apollodorus's account is to be believed, was Ceyx's enemy and neighbor.[45] Finally, according to Apollonius, there was a relationship between Chios and Trachis, Ceyx's city.[46]

It is possible to establish a rough chronology for these changes. Heraclea was founded in 560; Hellanicus lived from 496 to 411; hence the latest the Heraclean characters could have appeared in the Hylas myth was around 450. The changes must therefore have been made during the first half of the fifth century. Previously, in the sixth or possibly as early as the end of the seventh century (Chios was founded in 626/5), the ancient Anatolian myth of Hylas was incorporated into Greek mythology, in the form of a pedagogical relationship between the Ionian hero Polyphemus/Euphemus and the young mountain god whose name was called out in an annual ritual.

Furthermore, the influence of Heraclea bore unexpected fruit. Euphorion and Socrates, two Hellenistic authors who have left versions of Hylas's adventures, maintain that Heracles was enamored of Euphemus.[47] As Vian has observed, the links between Heracles and Euphemus seem to be tenuous and secondary.[48] The two characters belong to different cycles. Here we have one of many cases of exaggerated and erroneous late interpretations of the relations between Heracles and various other characters; others have already been mentioned. The significance of all this for our purposes is indirect. In the case of Heracles as in that of Apollo, the rich get richer.

FIFTEEN
Traces

According to Sosibius, there was in Sparta a sanctuary whose name, the Elacataeon, derived from that of a hero, Elacatas, in whose honor the Spartans staged the games known as the Elacatia.[1] Sosibius, who is a good historian of Sparta, also tells us that Elacatas was the erōmenos of Heracles.

That is all we know, but this brief mention is all we need. Heracles is exclusively a warrior hero, and in Sparta, as I mentioned earlier, he was regarded as a redeemer; the vanquisher of the usurpers and restorer of the legitimate dynasty. The only rite associated with Elacatas is in fact a contest. Whatever its form may have been, it must have symbolized the paradigmatic battle of Heracles. Elacatas, an obscure hero, eponym of a ritual and a sanctuary, is also related to a group of mythical figures, some famous, some hardly known at all, whose common trait is that all have roots in what we suspect or know to be quite archaic Laconian history. Among the better-known of these mythical figures are Hyacinthus, whose cult at Amyclae dates from the Mycenaean era, and King Tyndareus, whose name represents an ancient, indeed a prehistoric, form of Greek; among the not so well-known are the sons of the usurper Hippocoon, each of whom was honored with a sanctuary in Sparta, and one of whom, Enarsphorus, bestowed his name upon a Messenian locality in the thirteenth century B.C.[2] Elacatas, the erōmenos and no doubt the disciple of Heracles, as Hyacinthus was of Apollo, is also reminiscent of the Theban Iolaus. Among the parallels between the two are the sanctuary, the *agōn*, or contest, and the relationship with Heracles. All of this stems from the very ancient roots of Hellenic religion.

R. Vallois, in an article that has enjoyed astonishing success, attempted to trace the origins of the Olympic Games to an agrarian ritual. His argument was based on tenuous comparisons and a highly selective analysis of the sources. But in the ensuing enthusiasm agrarian roots were ascribed to any number of Greek rites and cults, even though only the most dogmatic of scholars would hold such a hypothesis to be tenable. A case in point concerns a well-known group of cults of Megalopolis in Arcadia, involving five different deities (Heracles, Athena Ergane, Apollo Agyieus, Hermes, and Eileithyia[3]); this was declared to be an agrarian cult, as was the Laconian Elacatia. Why? Because the five gods of Megalopolis were called Ergatai, and Heracles was honored at Sparta by the Ergatia, as he was also by the Elacatia; and because in Greek *ēlakatē* means "distaff."[4] The inanity of this argument is apparent: Athena Ergane is not an agrarian goddess, nor despite her name (derived from the verb meaning "to work") is she a goddess of manual labor; throughout Greece she belongs to the acropolis and is associated with Zeus.[5] Thus even if Athena sometimes carries the distaff as a symbol, this does not concern the Ergane directly, and the association of the Ergatai, the Ergatia, and the Elacatia does not withstand scrutiny. Even if the Egatai of Megalopolis have some connection with the Laconian festival of the Ergatia, which is plausible, this says nothing about the Elacatia, nor is the fact that Heracles is the patron of both festivals enough to establish any particular connection between them, since he is also the patron of a number of other Spartan festivals. Render unto Caesar what is Caesar's: The Lacedaemonian Elacatia belong to a Heraclean and military context. To explain the terms in question, it is better to think of the metaphorical meaning of *ēlakatē*, which is attested quite early, namely, "arrow,"[6] rather than "distaff"; here is yet another parallel between Elacatas and Iolaus.

The facts about the hero Abderus are similar to those about Elacatas. One of the twelve labors that Eurystheus sets as tasks for Heracles is to go to Thrace to kill King Diomedes and seize his ferocious man-eating mares; this, as I have already mentioned, is a transposition of a myth that stemmed initially from Argolis, in which King Diomedes, who plays so large a role in the *Iliad*, is closely associated with horses.[7] In connection with this episode Apollodorus recounts that Heracles, after stealing the mares, gives them temporarily to Abderus, his *erōmenos*. During his absence, they tear the young hero to shreds and devour him.[8]

That is the myth. Here is the ritual. Philostratus explains that at Abderus, a city on the Thracian coast founded, according to legend, by Heracles (and in fact a colony of Teos in Ionia), the eponymous hero was honored with *agōnes* including boxing, pancratium, and wrestling.[9]

So much is clear. A young man took part, along with his master and erastēs, in an expedition that, like all the Labors of Heracles, had initiatory value. Like Pelops he was killed by being torn to pieces and devoured; like Iolaus, Elacatas, and many others he was honored with *agōnes*. There should be no doubt that Abderus, eponymous hero of a Greek city, was also, in conjunction with Heracles, the mythical founder of pederasty there, pederasty that had pedagogical and probative value.

The Latin poet Martial (second half of the first century) echoes a tradition according to which the hero Philoctetes was the erōmenos of Heracles.[10] Greek literature preserves no trace of this legend, yet it may be authentically ancient; in the epic Philoctetes is the heir and keeper of Heracles' bow and arrows.[11] He also lights Heracles' pyre and is thus the only person to take part in the hero's self-sacrifice. It is for rendering this service that Heracles gives him his arms.

Philoctetes is the hero of a famous myth, according to which he is abandoned on the island Lemnus by Greeks on their way to Troy, owing to a wound in his foot that gives off an abominable odor. He remains there for ten years, living on birds that he captures, until one day the Greeks, upon learning that they need Heracles' bow to capture Troy, send Odysseus and Neoptolemus to Lemnus. Martial's assertion comes too late and is too isolated to warrant taking the trouble here to analyze the Philoctetes myth as minutely as we have done or will do for certain other myths. I would simply call attention to its initiatory character. Philoctetes, the heir and therefore surely the disciple of Heracles, hero of the most remarkable of hunts in the wilderness, establishes a connection, in Lemnus, among three initiatory cycles. The first is that of Heracles, whose immolation ends a life entirely devoted to probative exploits and opens the way to divine life. The reason for this "suicide" in immortalizing fire is the unbearable suffering caused by the tunic of the Centaur Nessus. The second initiatory cycle is that of Achilles, whose mother, Thetis, hoping to assure his immortality, initiates him by fire, and who is first the pupil of the Centaur Chiron and later the father of Neoptolemus. We are told that Philoctetes is finally cured thanks to a remedy supplied by Chiron.[12] Furthermore, in Sophocles' *Philoctetes* the young Neoptolemus undergoes an initiation on Lemnus with Philoctetes, an initiation that Pierre Vidal-Naquet, who first made the point, has called an "ephebic" process.[13] Finally, Lemnus is an important stopping place in the voyage of the Argonauts, who stage games there and couple with the women of Lemnus, who only a short while earlier had murdered their husbands. It should be added that the murdered men had fled their wives because Aphrodite had afflicted the women with a disgusting odor.[14]

Philoctetes reigned over the cities of southeastern Thessaly in the Magnesian peninsula at the foot of Pelion.[15] Thus it is possible that in some legend of southern Thessaly he was depicted as the founding hero of homosexuality—initiatory homosexuality to be sure—instead of his Theban counterpart, Iolaus, who was also an archer.

By way of contrast, nothing can be deduced from the traditions reported in the second century by Ptolemy Khennos, who names a whole list of erōmenoi of Heracles: Nestor,[16] Iphitus,[17] Nireus,[18] Adonis,[19] Jason,[20] Corythus,[21] and Stichius.[22] That several of these affairs (with Adonis, Jason, etc.) have a late and artificial air about them casts doubt on the possible value of the others. Finally, a scholium to the *Argonautica* states that Hylas supplanted a certain Phrix or Trinx in the heart of Heracles, but it is impossible to draw any conclusion from such a fragmentary piece of information.[23]

To reiterate: In the case of Heracles as in that of Apollo, the rich get richer.

SIXTEEN

Diocles, Diocles, and Cleomachus

RITUALS

In commenting upon the erotic inscriptions of Thera (alluded to earlier in connection with the discussion of the Carnea), Bethe compared various rituals and sites associated with pederastic myths. The first of these was the myth of Iolaus, the model for a ritual in which Theban erastai and erōmenoi swore to be faithful to one another at the hero's tomb outside Thebes.

Another ritual, known as the Dioclea, was first described in an *Idyll* of Theocritus with the suggestive title "The Beloved," "Aitēs," which in Thessalian means literally, as the poet himself explains, "erōmenos." Theocritus's account is as follows:

> Megarians of Nisaea,
> you champions of the oar,
> live happily, for you above all
> honored the Attic stranger,
> Diocles, lover of his friend.
> And each year in early spring
> boys gather around his tomb
> and contend for the kissing-prize.
> And whoever most sweetly touches
> lip to lip, goes home to his mother crowned
> with garlands. Happy is he
> who judges the kisses for the boys,
> and earnestly he must pray
> to bright Ganymedes that his lips
> will be like the Lydian stone
> where the money-changers try gold
> to see if it is false or true.[1]

Thebes was also the location of the tomb of one Diocles, celebrated for a homosexual love. Little is known about him except for a short mention by Aristotle included in his study of archaic lawgivers.

There was also Philolaus, the Corinthian, who gave laws to the Thebans. This Philolaus was one of the family of the Bacchiadae, and a lover of Diocles, the Olympic victor, who left Corinth in horror of the incestuous passion which his mother Halcyone had conceived for him, and retired to Thebes, where the two together ended their days. The inhabitants still point out their tombs, which are in full view of one another, but one is visible from Corinthian territory, the other not. Tradition says the two of them arranged them thus, Diocles out of horror at his misfortunes, so that the land of Corinth might not be visible from his tomb; Philolaus that it might be visible. This is the reason why they settled at Thebes, and so Philolaus legislated for the Thebans, and, besides some other enactments, gave them laws about the procreation of children, which they call the "Laws of Adoption." These laws were peculiar to him, and were intended to preserve the number of the lots.[2]

Finally, a short distance from Thebes, on the agora of Chalcis in Euboea, stood a no less notable tomb. Plutarch, citing an Aristotle who must be the historian of Chalcis rather than the philosopher,[3] tells the following story but in his son's voice:

"And you know of course how it was that Cleomachus the Pharsalian fell in battle?"

"We certainly don't," said Pemptides and those near him, "but we should very much like to."

"Well," said my father, "the tale's worth hearing. When the war between the Eretrians and Chalcidians was at its height, Cleomachus had come to aid the latter with a Thessalian force; and the Chalcidian infantry seemed strong enough, but they had great difficulty in repelling the enemy's cavalry. So they begged that high-souled hero Cleomachus to charge the Eretrian cavalry first. And he asked his boy-love (erōmenos), who was by, if he would be a spectator of the fight, and he saying he would, and affectionately kissing him and putting his helmet on his head, Cleomachus with a proud joy put himself at the head of the bravest of the Thessalians, and charged the enemy's cavalry with such impetuosity that he threw them into disorder and routed them; and the Eretrian infantry also fleeing in consequence, the Chalcidians won a splendid victory. However, Cleomachus got killed, and they show his tomb in the market-place at

Chalcis, over which a huge pillar stands to this day, and whereas before that the people of Chalcis had censured boy-love, from that time forward they cherished and honored it more than others. Aristotle gives a slightly different account, namely, that this Cleomachus came not from Thessaly but Chalcis in Thrace, to the help of the Chalcidians in Euboea; and that that was the origin of the song in vogue among the Chalcidians,

> Ye boys who come of noble sires and beauteous are in face,
> Grudge not to give to valiant men the boy of your embrace:
> For Love that does the limbs relax combined with bravery
> In the Chalcidian cities has fame that ne'er shall die.

But according to the account of the poet Dionysius, in his "Origins," the name of the lover was Anton, and that of the boy-love was Philistus.[4]

THE UNITY OF THE SEVERAL DIOCLES

Although the initiatory nature of the rituals just described has faded somewhat, it is nonetheless clear. The cluster consisting of the cult at the tomb of Iolaus in Thebes, the Dioclea at Megara, and the "honors" accorded to Cleomachus at Chalcis is absolutely homogeneous. As Bethe, and K. O. Müller before him,[5] saw clearly, all are celebrations of homosexual love between young boys and adult men. The ancients saw the similarity: Aristophanes, in the *Acharnians*, has the Megarians given oaths by Diocles (line 774) and the Thebans by Heracles (line 860) and Iolaus (line 867).

More precisely, Iolaus is a warrior, as are Cleomachus and Diocles. The earliest texts place him at Eleusis (which is why Theocritus calls him a native of Attica), and so does the *Homeric Hymn to Demeter* (perhaps from the late seventh century). He is one of the leaders of the Eleusinians, along with the wise Triptolemus, Diocles the chariot master (*plexippos*), the powerful and (in other respects) irreproachable Eumolpus, and Celeus, the leader of the people.[6] Diocles is thus distinguished by his being a warrior and having to do with horses, as befits an aristocrat of that time. Similarly, Iolaus was a chariot driver and Cleomachus a cavalry leader. Many centuries later Plutarch echoes the *Hymn to Demeter* with a rather obscure assertion. He says that according to some authors Theseus killed Skiron (the Megarian hero) not in his youth, during his glorious march from Troezen to Athens, but later, during the attack on Eleusis, "occupied at that time by the Megarians, after deceiving Diocles, who was in command there."[7] The scholium to Theocritus's text tells the story, based on an Alexandrian poet, of how Diocles fled from Athens to Megara and how he fell in battle while protecting the boy he loved with his shield. This is obviously an aetiological explanation of the feast, revealing its underlying meaning; it was patterned after the story of Cleomachus.

Without going so far as some attempts at rationalization, which explain the presence of Diocles in both Eleusis and Megara by assuming that the hero traveled from one city to the other, we need only remark that the two places were so close together that the presence in both of the same cult and the same mythical figure is hardly surprising.

That said, I think it necessary to look somewhat further afield and to bring the Theban Diocles into the picture as well. As Bethe observed, Aristotle identifies this Diocles with one Olympic victor of 728; this may be a confusion, all the more likely since Eleusinian and Megarian religion and traditions reveal a strong Boeotian influence and suggest the existence of a protohistoric "greater Boeotia," whose outposts in what later became Attica and Megara were symmetric with the Orchomenian possessions in what later became Phocis. Eleusis, as Charles Picard has noted, was in prehistoric times a Theban "way station" en route to the Aegean Sea. Evidence of this is plentiful. According to one tradition, Eleusis was once called Ogygia. Ogygus was a legendary king of Thebes. One of the seven gates of Thebes was called the Ogygian Gate.[8] The river of Eleusis, the Cephissus, bears the same name as the great river of western Boeotia. The Eleusinian family of priests, the Eumolpidae, had many connections with eastern Boeotia.[9] The mysteries celebrated at Eleusis apparently included in their teaching the myth of the union between Poseidon and Demeter that led to the birth of Artemis and the divine horse Areion.[10] But the birth of Areion and the coupling of Poseidon and Demeter are the great myth of the sanctuary of Tilphossa in central Boeotia.[11] At most, it is possible that Eleusis and Megara were Boeotian religious foundations; Demeter Thesmophoros is on the acropolis at Thebes.[12] Car, the first king of Megara, established the cult of Demeter on the acropolis of Caria, and in the Eleusinian myth Demeter, desperate over the loss of her daughter, went to the king of Eleusis, Celeus, whose palace was on the slopes of the acropolis.[13]

The connections between Boeotia and Megara are even more numerous. The name of the city itself may derive from the cult of Demeter introduced by Car, since *megara* in Boeotian refers to the chthonian caves into which young pigs were thrown in the cult of the goddess.[14] A surprising fact is that all, or nearly all, the members of the legendary dynasty of Megara have direct or indirect connections with Boeotia. If Car, the first king, introduced a cult with Boeotian features, that of Demeter of the acropolis, the mythical eponym of the city, Megareus (whose name is in fact an obvious derivative of the place name) is supposed to have come from Onchestus with an army to save Megara from a Minoan attack. Onchestus was a sanctuary in central Boeotia, near Tilphossa. Poseidon, Megareus's father, was worshiped there, and in high antiquity this was probably a border sanctuary between the Orchomenian sphere of influence and territory dominated by Thebes.[15] Besides the Megareus who may have come to Megara from Boeotia, there was a hero named Megara, Heracles' first wife, who was Theban, the daughter of Creon. When Alcathous succeeded Megareus by dint of having slain, on Mount Cithaeron between Attica and Boeotia, a ferocious lion that was responsible for the death of Megareus's son, he became the heir of both Megara and Onchestus. It is as though he absorbed the influence of both extremes of the ancient (Mycenaean) kingdom of Thebes.

The Megarians also possessed the tomb of the hero Manto, daughter of the prophet Polyeidos.[16] She is homonymous, that is to say, identical with, a more celebrated woman of Greek legend, the prophet Manto of Thebes, daughter of Teiresias.

If Diocles died to protect his erōmenos, someone else must have created the festival of the Dioclea in establishing his funerary cult. According to a scholiast on Aristophanes' *Acharnians*, this was the role of Alcathous, king of Megara.[17] This confirms the connection between Diocles and Boeotia: Whether in Eleusis, Megara, or Thebes, the mythical founder of initiatory homosexuality was one and the same person.

This suggests that Philolaus, companion of Diocles until his death, was also legendary. I am assuming that this was the case. The location of the two tombs, one on top of a promontory, the other at the base, is reminiscent of a cult founded by Italiot Greeks and described by Strabo.

In Daunia, on a hill by the name of Drium, are to be seen two hero temples: one, to Calchas, on the very summit, where those who consult the oracle sacrifice to his shade a black ram and sleep on the hide, and the other, to Podaleirus, down near the base of the hill, this temple being about one hundred stadia away from the sea; and from it flows a stream which is a cure-all for diseases of animals.[18]

All of this is reminiscent of Olympia, where the Pelopion, tomb of Pelops, stands at the foot of Cronion, a mountain covered with sanctuaries and tombs.[19] Black rams were also sacrificed to Pelops.[20]

In fact, comparison of the tradition studied here with a Parian myth seems to reveal a rather obscure hero named Philolaus. Apollodorus of Athens, or the author of the *Bibliotheca* attributed to him, recounts that the sons of Minos, namely, Eurymedon, Chryses, Nephalion, and Philolaus, inhabited the island of Paros and attacked Heracles when he visited there. He killed them. Given the fact that their mother was Paria, eponym of the island, it is reasonable to think that this myth founded a ritual, and it is not overbold to assume that this ritual was one of initiation of warriors.[21] This Parian Philolaus may derive from a hypothetical Boeotian, Philolaus: I base this statement in part on philological evidence that large numbers of Ionians from Asia and the islands were natives of Boeotia[22] (a rule that applies to Paros as well) and in part on the fact that all the sons of Minos and Paria have very clear Boeotian affinities, to wit:

Chryses is the name of a legendary king of Orchomenus as well as of a Trojan priest in the *Iliad*, and many characters in the *Iliad* have names taken from the Boeotian and Thessalian onomastic.

Nephalion evokes Nephele, a famous Boeotian hero and wife of Athamas, who is connected with the royal families of Orchomenus and Thebes.

Philolaus occurs only at Thebes in the tradition studied here.

Eurymedon is a name borne by several mythical characters, in general associated with Argolis and eastern Boeotia.

Accordingly, it is reasonable to hypothesize that the pair Philolaus/ Diocles belongs to a very ancient collection of Theban legends associated with an initiation ritual of a military and homosexual character.

The names of all these characters are highly evocative, moreover. If *Iolaus* suggests an army equipped with arrows, thereby indicating his kinship with Heracles, the archer of central Greece, *Philolaus* links the *laus*, or army, with friendship, *philia*, from *philos*, "friend"—and in the historical Thebes of the fourth century there was in fact an army composed of couples of "friends," whose friendship was of a virile, sexual character. *Cleomachus* of Chalcis is "he who fights for glory." Finally, it is reasonable to ask if, in a Boeotia under Theban dominance, which had welcomed the Argive *Heracles*, "the glory of Hera," with such open arms, *Diocles*, "the glory of Zeus," was not created as the alter ego of the former. In this case the attempt was only partially successful: Diocles, fragmented into a Theban of Corinthian origin, an Eleusinian, and a Megarian, never enjoyed the prestige of Heracles. He had to settle for being the founder of local rituals of initiation.

If this view is correct, these three Diocles are in fact only one, and the historical Diocles, the Olympic victor from Corinth, is another, independent personage. Aristotle or his source may have confounded and thus established a connection between him and Philolaus, but this lawgiver seems to have been known only to Aristotle, who knows more about his tomb than about his constitutional works. Is it not remarkable that he is given credit specifically for laws on adoption, given that the founding myths of homosexuality in Thebes mention that it was impossible for the founders to have children and, further, that a primitive institution related to adoption, namely, foster parentage, sometimes included sexual relations between educator and pupil?[23]

ALCATHOUS AND FEMALE INITIATIONS

As I mentioned a moment ago, it was a famous, legendary king of Megara, Alcathous, who was held to be the founder of the Dioclea. He is an interesting character. Everything we know about him links him to the symbolism of initiation. Son of Pelops (the founding hero of an initiatory ritual with homosexual relations between teacher and pupil) and himself the founder of a festival begun by a strictly analogous ritual, he figures in many stories involving deaths, obviously symbolic, of young men. For example, an Aetolian of the same name was, from the time of Hesiod onward, one of the pretenders for the hand of Hippodamia killed by Oenomaus before the victory of Pelops (who is also the hero of a myth of symbolic death).[24]

Alcathous succeeded King Megareus of Megara. Significantly, this prince had an elder son, Timalchus, who was killed by the Dioscuri, and another son, Euhippus, who was torn apart by a lion that plagued Mount Cithaeron.

Megareus promised the hand of his daughter Euaechme to the hero who could kill this lion. This was Alcathous. Note that the two sons of Megareus fulfill a single function, namely, to deprive the king of male offspring; they are two expression of the same need, the heroes of two versions of the same myth.[25] Their death leaves the way clear for Alcathous, much as the death of Alcathous the Aetolian and of twelve other pretenders leaves the way clear for Pelops. It may be that in a primitive version Euaechme was the prize for which rival pretenders vied. This hypothesis gains credence from the fact that the cause of the death of Megareus's "first" son is the Dioscuri, who come to Attica to recover Helen, who has been abducted by Theseus, as well as from a tradition according to which the hero Hippomenes, who outran Atalanta in a race and so succeeded in marrying her, was the son of Megareus.[26] In any case, Alcathous qualifies for a princely marriage and a royal crown through a hunting exploit of a type to which we have devoted considerable attention in the preceding chapters.

There is a recurrence of motifs. Megareus had himself succeeded a previous king, Nisus, by offering him military assistance against the Cretans. The military exploit takes the place of what the hunting exploit represents in the next generation. Of course, Megareus, in this tradition, is the son-in-law of Nisus, having married his daughter Iphinoe. Furthermore, Alcathous, like Megareus, lost his male offspring.[27]

Alcathous is known to have had two sons. One, Ischepolis, participated in the hunt for the boar of Calydon and was one of the few to die in doing so. Just as the death of Euhippus qualified Alcathous, the death of Ischepolis qualified Meleager and Atalanta, the boar's main hunters.[28] The second son of Alcathous, Callipolis, upon learning of the death of his brother, hastened to his father to tell him the frightful news; the king sacrificed to Apollo, on the citadel, and Callipolis in his excitement disrupted the order of the ritual, which sacrilege was immediately punished. Alcathous picked up a burning branch and bludgeoned his son with it.[29]

Here, comparison with the Pelops cycle is inevitable. Pelops in his youth is killed, dismembered, and devoured, and the perpetrator of this "crime" is his father; in the following generation, Chrysippus is killed, either by his own hand out of shame or by one of his half-brothers, Atreus and Thyestes, at the instigation of Hippodamia.

Thus the legendary dynasty of Megara assumes a novel, "matrilinear" form, as is shown by the diagram on page 175. But this pattern meshes with an initiatory symbolism (symbolic death of sons, military and hunting exploits) in such a way that these successions can be explained as the replacement of father-educators by their adoptive sons, pupils, and sons-in-law, in accordance with a relationship between foster parentage

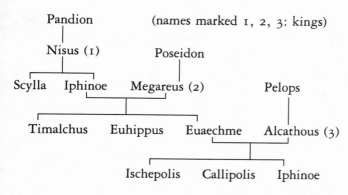

and marriage pointed out by Louis Gernet.[30] Note, too, that the whole process is played out between Poseidon and Apollo, the two great masters of initiation rituals with a sexual component; if Megareus is the son of Poseidon, Alcathous is the son of his pupil; and it is during the course of a sacrifice to Apollo that the second kills his son, much as the young men of Sparta, following the example of Hyacinthus, had to die and be reborn during the Hyacinthia.

Finally, if Alcathous founded the Dioclea, that is, the Megaran initiation ritual for young boys, he was also responsible for an analogous ritual involving young girls. Pausanias said that between the Aesymnion, the sanctuary and communal office, and the *hērōon* of Alcathous, which was also used for municipal activities, stood the tombs of Pyrgo, the first wife of Alcathous, and Iphinoe, her daughter, who, unlike her homonym (older by two generations), died a virgin. Furthermore,

> It is the custom of maidens before marriage to pour libations at Iphinoe's tomb, and sacrifice some of their long hair, as the maidens of Delos used to to Hecaerge and Opis.[31]

I would add that this is just as the sons of the citizens of Agyrion in Sicily offer locks of their hair to Heracles in the temple of Iolaus.

It is probable that in high antiquity the Greeks allowed homosexuality in educational relationships between women as well as men.[32] There is no evidence that this was the case in Megara, but there is no reason why this city should have shunned an institution attested from Sparta to Lesbos. If this is correct, the consecration of a lock of hair on Iphinoe's tomb would be the final fragment, the pale survival, of a once much richer ritual of initiation, just as the extraordinary competition involving kissing the lips of an examiner, which the youths of Megara were forced to undergo, was the survival of an archaic ritual of which Theocritus knew only a watered-down form. Yet he is not unaware of the sexual nature of the examination—he who aspires to serve as an examiner.

EXIGENT ERŌMENOI AND MATTERS OF CHRONOLOGY

No less late and highly developed is the mythical fable according to which the deaths of Diocles (of Megara) and Cleomachus occurred because they wished to demonstrate their contempt for death to their erōmenoi—a sort of romance common enough in late antiquity. Pausanias explains the origins of a cult of Anteros at Athens as follows:

> And they say that the altar in the city called the altar of Anteros is the offering of the resident aliens, for Meles an Athenian, tired of Timagoras, a resident alien who was enamored of him, bade him go to the highest part of the rock and throw himself down. And Timagoras, careless of his life and wishing in all things to gratify the stripling's commands, threw himself down accordingly. But Meles, when he saw Timagoras was dead, was so stricken with remorse that he threw himself down from the same rock, and so perished. And in consequence it was ordained that the resident aliens should worship as a god Anteros, the avenger of Timagoras.[33]

In one of the stories of Conon, the young Cretan Leucocomas sends his lover Promachus into a dangerous trial. Neanthes of Cyzicus recounts an oracle requiring a human sacrifice in Athens. Cratinus, a handsome young man, proposed himself as the victim, whereupon his erastēs, Aristodemos, offered to share his devotion.[34] Similarly, Plutarch, a few paragraphs before his story of Cleomachus, alludes to the example "of Aristogeiton of Athens, Antileon of Metaponte, and Melanippus of Acragas," for

> [these men] rose not against tyrants [respectively, Hipparchus, son of Pisistratus; a tyrant of Metaponte or, according to another source,[35] of Heracleia of Italy; and Phalaris] although they saw how badly they managed affairs, and what drunken tricks they played, yet, when they attempted the chastity of their boy-loves, they retaliated on them, risking their lives, as if they were defending the inviolability of temples and sanctuaries.[36]

Bethe believed that these stories were ancient, dating from the fifth or sixth century.[37] Several stem from a work written by Heraclides Ponticus in the late fourth century,[38] and they clearly attest to the spread of a new outlook in Greece in the fifth and fourth century with the secularization of educational homosexuality, an outlook that we find in the works of Aristophanes, Plato, and Xenophon. The institution waned, the educator and the erastēs became distinct persons, fathers ceased to place their sons with allies who would serve first as masters and then as fathers-in-law, and homosexual relations took on aspects of seduction, of courting of youths by prospective erastai. Adult males would do anything to shine in the eyes of adolescents. More than that, the erōmenos, now a free "sexual object," turned his charms to advantage and refused to give in until his capricious demands had been met.[39] Often these took the form of challenges to run extreme risks, to court death. This is a long way from the primitive spirit of initiation, in which the master had to live in order to instruct his pupil, finish his initiation, help him complete his hunting or military exploit, and marry him off, and in which the death of the erastēs, if such happens to be reported by the myth, is an apotheosis (when the master is not himself a god).

Thus the rituals and myths reported in later literature have often been revised, watered down, tailored to the tastes of an era when individual initiations of aristocratic youths were nothing more than a memory. Yet all the evidence suggests that these later versions are indeed revisions of older myths and not pure inventions: for example, the resemblance between the rites and myths evoked and those that we have studied previously, the antiquity of the personage of Diocles, confirmed by his mention in the *Homeric Hymn to Demeter* and his presence in three nearby cities whose traditions do not coincide, and the explicit reference in most of the myths to legendary eras. In this respect two of the traditions are particularly evocative. Plutarch says, with a perfectly straight face, that the Chalcidians refused to engage in homosexuality until the Lelantine War, that is, until the earliest event reported in their history. For this war, which predates the earliest historic texts, is nothing other than an event in Euboean protohistory. It was in the eighth century, when Chalcis and Eretria fought for control of the plain of Lelantos, that Greece emerged from its prehistory. To say that a practice first appeared "in the period of the Lelantine War" is to situate its origins in the mists of time. Alcathous, moreover, was one of the founders of Megara; he built the city's walls with help from Apollo. Establishing rites, building temples, organizing the city are all related events in mythical time: All take place when the city is founded. In Eleusis, moreover, Diocles is one of the nobles who welcomes Demeter; he is cofounder of the mysteries.

Thus the model that I developed in earlier chapters, through study of the myths of Pelops, Hyacinthus, Cyparissus, Narcissus, Thamyris, and Laius, is further substantiated by the material in this chapter: Cleomachus was the founder of the homosexual initiation ritual in Chalcis, as was Diocles in Megara.

Only the Theban Diocles avoids a similarly glorious fate. This is not surprising, for in Thebes he had rivals: Iolaus for the ritual and Laius for the myth. If, as his name suggests, Diocles was modeled on Heracles, it seems that he was unable to establish himself in his forerunner's fiefdom, yet for reasons unknown to us he caught on in the eastern part of prehistoric Boeotia.

V
Loves and Myths of Dionysus

SEVENTEEN
The Mysteries of Lerna
卐

Bethe drew a parallel between the series of myths involving Iolaus, Diocles, and Cleomachus and the curious tradition reported by certain late authors (all of them Christians) on the subject of Dionysus at Lerna. The most explicit account is found in the *Protrepticus* of Clement of Alexandria.[1]

> Dionysus wanted desperately to go down to Hades, but he did not know the way. Someone named Prosymnus promised to tell him how to go, but in exchange for pay, pay that was not pretty, though it was pretty for Dionysus; the favor asked was erotic, the requested pay was Dionysus himself. The god willingly heard the request, promised to respond if he returned from the underworld, and confirmed his promise with an oath. Informed of the path, he set off. When he came back Prosymnus, who had died, was nowhere to be found. To pay his sacred debt to his lover Dionysus went to his tomb and underwent intercourse. He cut the branch of a fig tree that happened to grow there, carved it to resemble the male member, sat on it and thus fulfilled his promise to the dead man. In the various cities phalli are dedicated to Dionysus as a mystic memorial of this event.

The only other authors who tell the story in so full a fashion are the third-century Arnobius in his work *Against the Gentiles*, and Tzetzes, an eleventh-century Byzantine writer. Does this mean that the whole story is nothing more than a late fable, a Christian calumny against the Pagans? This cannot possibly be the case: When Clement wrote, around 200 A.D., Christianity was still a minority religion in the Roman Empire, and polemicists had to use good arguments or run the risk of refutation. Indeed, historians of religion have frequently recognized the value of the information that Clement provides, and when he speaks of the mysteries "of Aphrodite, of Eleusis or Deo, of Dionysus, or of the Corybantes," he furnishes "details and phrases that constitute an important, if not the major, part of what we know about these subjects . . . together with commentaries, tendentious to be sure, but accompanied by such a wealth of specific facts that some have wondered whether he might not have been initiated himself."[2] The passage by Clement just cited accords well with these remarks, for it tells us some of the content of the mysteries of Dionysus at Lerna. Let the reader judge, with the help of the oldest text on the subject, from Pausanias (the hero is here and elsewhere known as Polymnus).[3]

> I have seen also the well of Amphiaraus and the Alcyonian marsh, where the Argives say Dionysus descended to Hades to fetch up Semele, for Polymnus showed him the descent. There is indeed no end to the depth of the Alcyonian marsh. . . . But the nightly rites which take place near it annually I am not permitted to write for public reading.

Thus Dionysus and Polymnus (who in this expurgated version is of no interest whatsoever) may have been associated with *hieroi logoi*, sacred discourses, which Clement or Arnobius would have had no scruples about revealing to the public.

As it stands, Clement of Alexandria's version bears the mark of Hellenistic romance. The theme of the secret divulged in return for an amorous favor was a commonplace of the time.[4] This does not exclude the possibility that the principal motive is of ancient origin. And for several reasons that I shall explain presently, this was certainly the case.

The lakes and springs of Lerna, formed by the reemergence of rivers swallowed up by the caverns in the mountains of northeastern Arcadia, served as the locale of a number of Argive myths: the battle between Heracles and the Hydra instigated by Hera, the abduction of Kore by Hades, and the descent of Dionysus into the underworld. These motifs are intimately related. For one thing, Demeter and Dionysus are closely associated. The sacred wood, between Mount Pontinus and the sea, near which Kore was abducted and where the mysteries of Demeter Lernaea were celebrated, contains stone statues of Demeter Prosymne and Dionysus Saotes. These two deities are flanked, on the mountaintop, by a temple of Athena founded by Danaos and, on the sea side, by a statue of Aphrodite dedicated by the Danaids.[5] Moreover, Hera, absent from the holy place, figures in the background, because the hero whose name is derived from hers, namely, Heracles, comes here to kill, underneath a plane tree (the sacred wood here is in fact a forest of plane trees, says

Pausanias), an animal that Hera has aroused. Now, at the other end of the plain of Argos, facing the plain, stood the famous temple of Hera, which, as I pointed out earlier, was certainly the birthplace of Heracles. Concerning this sanctuary, Pausanias offers the following noteworthy observations.:

> This temple is on the more level part of Euboea, for Euboea is a mountain, and they say the daughters of the river god Asterion were Euboea and Prosymna and Acraea, and that they were the nurses of Hera. And Acraea gave her name to all the mountain opposite the temple of Hera, and Euboea to the mountain near the temple, and Prosymna to the ground below the temple.[6]

As has long been recognized, these three nurses of Hera are in fact surnames of the goddess. Acraea, "Acropolitan," is the title she received as goddess of Acrocorinthia. Euboea is a variant of the better-known epithet Boopis—Hera has something of the cow about her. It was in Euboea around the Heraeum that the daughters of Proetus, king of Argos, were changed, or thought they were changed, into cows. Finally, Prosymna was, in Pausanias's first text, an epithet of Demeter. Some ancient authors cited by Plutarch speak of Prosymnaea Hera, "Hera of Prosymna."[7]

Hence at the Heraeum, Prosymna is a nurse and the goddess herself; at Lerna, Prosymnus is the erastēs of Dionysus, and Prosymne the goddess Demeter.[8] Io was priest of Hera at Prosymna, but it was at Lerna that she coupled with Zeus.[9] The Heraeum was also a site for the celebration of mysteries, for which the priest drew water from the river Eleutherion,[10] and Eleutherios is a surname of Dionysus. Thus motifs from the two extremities of the Argive plain correspond, and the antiquity of the one set proves the antiquity of the other. Io, the Proitidae, Heracles, and Danaos and her daughters belong to the oldest Argive myths, and Prosymnus-Prosymna and Dionysus, who are so closely related to the others, must be equally ancient.

The antiquity of the pederastic motif is not thereby confirmed, but there is good evidence for it.

Pausanias reports that the mysteries of Demeter Lernaea were founded by Philammon. Now, Philammon was the father of Thamyris, who, as the reader will recall, was, in Apollodorus's version of the myth, the lover of Hyacinthus and the inventor of pederasty. Thamyris is also a singer, eponym of the *thamuriddontes* of Thespiae, and this function evokes the names of Prosymne-Prosymnus and Polymnus (from *hymnos*, "hymn").

We also know that in the feast or feasts of Lerna a certain Glaucus rose from the waters and returned to life.[11] This is not much to go on, but it suggests that the motif of death followed by rebirth, typical of initiations, figured in the ritual of Lerna—but for what festival? Glaucus is more closely associated with Dionysus than with Demeter, and his emergence from a lake is reminiscent of the fact that in the myths of Lerna it is Dionysus who reaches Hades through a bottomless lake, while Kore is kidnapped by the god of the underworld on terra firma (the "Nysean plain" of the *Homeric Hymn to Demeter*) and dragged underground through a slit in the earth. The rebirth of Glaucus must have been a component of the Dionysiac Mysteries of Lake Alcyonian. Other information appears to confirm this hypothesis.

Glaucus

The personage who seems to accompany Dionysus to Lerna is in fact a complex figure in Greek theology and mythology, who is always associated with themes of death and rebirth and, on two occasions known to me, with a story of homosexuality.

Nicander of Colophon recounts in his *Europea*[1] that Glaucus was loved by another, older sea god, Nereus, one of the primordial deities, Hesiod's "Old Man of the Sea."[2]

According to a certain Hedylus, who may have been from either Athens or Samos (even Athenaeus does not know for sure), this same Glaucus hurled himself into the sea out of love for Melicertes.[3] The latter is the hero of a famous myth, according to which his mother (Ino, daughter of Cadmus of Thebes) and he jumped into the sea and became deities of the waters. Ino became the "white goddess," Leucothea; Melicertes was the god Palaemon, protector of shipping. Note that the sea god Palaemon is the cousin of Dionysus (himself the hero in Lerna of a fabulous dive), because Semele was the sister of Ino.

Nicander lived in the second century B.C., and Hedylus too probably lived in the Hellenistic era. It would not be unreasonable to assume that their assertions concerning Glaucus are late speculations of a sort common (as we have seen) in the postclassical period. Here, however, I shall argue the opposite. For these statements correlate with abundant evidence, much of it archaic, all of it having to do with initiation.

Death and resurrection. In the Corinthian legend Glaucus, son of Sisyphus, drinks water from a fountain that makes him immortal. His fellow citizens refuse to believe him, however, and he hurls himself into the sea, where he becomes the sea god of the same name.[4] In the Boeotian version of the same legend, Glaucus was a fisherman from Anthedon on the northern Boeotian coast. By chance he samples a certain herb, which makes him immortal, and he becomes a sea god.[5] This clears up the Lerna myth: These two versions suggest that the god's emergence from the waters of the lake was preceded by a dive—into the underworld, like Dionysus—and that the reemergence signifies the transition to immortality.

Still a fourth version of the myth, better known and richer in detail than the others, helps to clarify the meaning of these promotions to immortality subsequent to a death or sojourn in the underworld.

The story takes place in Crete. Glaucus is here a child, son of Minos, the king of Cnossus. One day he chases a mouse, inadvertently falls into a jar of honey, and drowns. With the aid of soothsayers or of Apollo (two ways of saying the same thing), Minos finds his son and learns from the Couretes that only the man capable of interpreting the meaning of an unusual cow in the royal herd will be able to bring Glaucus back to life. This cow's coat is of three colors, white, red, and black, or else it changes every day from one of these colors to another. Only one soothsayer succeeds at this task: Polyeidos, son of the Argive Coiranos. He explains that the three colors are characteristic of the mulberry, which starts out white, then turns red and finally turns black. Minos then orders Polyeidos to revive his son. To that end he shuts him up in a tomb with the boy's body. Polyeidos is at a loss what to do when a serpent enters the tomb. Polyoidos kills the animal. A second serpent arrives, discovers the death of the first serpent, and goes out again. It soon returns with an herb in its mouth, which, when it touches the other serpent, restores it to life. Polyeidos naturally takes some of the miraculous herb and applies it to Glaucus. An admiring Minos then asks the soothsayer to pass his knowledge on to his son. Polyeidos does so, but, finally liberated and on his way home, he spits into his pupil's mouth, and Glaucus immediately forgets all that he has learned.[6]

This myth, remarkable in many ways, depicts a Glaucus quite similar to the Glaucus of Lerna. In both cases Glaucus dies and is subsequently reborn. Polyeidos, moreover, is a soothsayer closely associated with Dionysus; in Megara it is he who constructs the god's temple. The tombs of his daughters, Manto and Astycratea, stand at the temple entrance. It is interesting to note that, according to the Megarians, Polyeidos came to that city to purify Alcathous after the murder of his son, an event whose significance I discussed in the last chapter. Furthermore, this temple of Dionysus, with the tombs of Polyeidos's daughters, stands right beside the tomb of Iphinoe, where the virgins of Megara were initiated.[7]

Now, the Cretan myth of Glaucus and Polyeidos is, in the most obvious way, the story of an initiation. Everything is there: the mystical death (the honey into which the child falls is a substance that confers immortality[8]), the delegation of power from the father to the teacher, the personal relationship and isolation of master and disciple, education, and resurrection. From what we know of Cretan customs we may assume that a sexual relationship between master and pupil is present but metaphorically transformed. In the Lacedaemonian lexicon the erastēs is called the *eispnēlos*, "he who breathes into," and *eispnei*, "to inspire," "to breathe into," means "to fall in love with."[9] Spitting is an obvious metaphor for sperm.[10]

Studying this myth, Henri Jeanmaire hypothesized that it tells a story of initiation into a sort of Cretan religious confraternity. This was suggested to him by the mention of the Couretes: Epimenides, the great Cretan soothsayer of the sixth century, was described as a "New Courete."[11] This is possible. But Polyeidos, whose father is called Koiranos, literally, the "chief," in a military sense of the word,[12] also presides over the initiations of warriors and hunters. It is he who tells Bellerophon how to subdue the horse Pegasus in order to fight the leonine and ophidian she-goat of Lycia, the Chimaera.[13]

Thus Polyeidos is the master of initiations, in Crete for Glaucus, in Corinth for Bellerophon. This suggests the real nature of Prosymnus/Polymnus of Lerna. This obscure personage has only two functions: He "informs" Dionysus about a path (but quite a path, a *kathodos*, an entry to the Mysteries), much as Polyeidos "indicates" to Bellerophon that he must go to a spring to capture the miraculous horse; and he asks, in return, to have sexual relations with the god, just as Polyeidos spits in the mouth of Glaucus. It is clear, then, that prior to a simplistic rationalization in the Hellenistic period, Polymnus/Prosymnus was nothing less than Dionysus's master and educator. Similarly, at the other end of the Argive plain, Prosymna was a nurse, a *courotrophus*, of the goddess of the Heraeum.

The interpretation is inevitable, and it corroborates the analyses already set forth. Dionysus is the hero of a homosexual adventure, because the myth tells of an initiation. This justifies the originality of this story, which shocked Christian writers. Unlike Apollo, for example, Dionysus is clearly depicted as the erōmenos—to be sure, because the mysteries told the story of the initiation that made him a god. And Prosymnus-Polymnus, the name of the priest or cantor, was his teacher.

To return to Glaucus, does the same hold true as for Dionysus, *mutatis mutandis*, for this sea deity? In other words, if, in Lerna, the divinization of Dionysus was interpreted, surely from very early antiquity, as an initiation with homosexual relations between master and pupil, was this not also true of his companion in these same mysteries? Of course I am assuming that the two traditions reported above by Athenaeus, one concerning the love of Nereus for Glaucus, the other the love of Glaucus for Melicertes, are not late inventions. There is further evidence to support this assumption.

The initiation motifs are intrinsically linked to the character of Glaucus, complex and multiform as that character is. We have just seen this complexity in the different versions of his divinization (from Corinth, Boeotia, and Lerna). It is manifest in this Cretan myth, so archaic in form, in which he becomes the son of a king. Two "other" Glaucuses take part in the probative and initiatory expedition of the Argonauts. "One, an invulnerable warrior, vanishes after diving into the sea, while the other falls from his chariot while racing in the funeral games in honor of Pelias and is torn to pieces by his horses." On this R. Roux correctly comments as follows:

> Two equally ritual deaths precede rebirth and new life. [Glaucus the Cretan] . . . became the lover of Ariadne and finally shared the immortality of the sea gods. There is a whole cycle of royal trials: The dive in the ocean, the honey, the marine plants, the union of the prince with a goddess follow one another in turn. The dismember-ment . . . is merely a variant of these mysteries of apparent death and survival.[14]

There are partial equivalences between one of these two Glaucuses and Diomedes, the warrior king of Argos: It is with Glaucus's shield that Diomedes fascinates the dragon of the Golden Fleece.[15] In a celebrated passage in the *Iliad*, yet "another" Glaucus, this one Lycian but a descendant of Bellerophon (who, like the Cretan Glaucus, was a pupil of Polyeidos), meets the Argive Diomedes on the field of battle; recogniz-ing each other as "hereditary guests," they exchange gifts.[16]

In primitive Greece to refer to the initiation and trial of a warrior is also to refer to homosexuality. I have already shown that in the most explicit account of (the Cretan) Glaucus's initiation, pederasty exists in metaphorical guise.

It would be worth the effort, in this connection, to pay close attention to the relationship between Glaucus and Melicertes. Hedylus, cited by Athenaeus, said that Glaucus was in love with Mericertes and jumped into the ocean because of it. This motivation is a late invention; in high antiquity erastai did not kill themselves for their erōmenoi, except, as in the story of Cleomachus, to set an example of absolute courage. I suspect, however, that what we have here is a Hellenistic interpretation of a truly ancient motif. Nicanor of Cyrene, in a work, whose title, *Metonomasiai*, "Name Changes," alludes to a typical initiation procedure, holds that Melicertes after diving into the water became not Palaemon but Glaucus.[17] Is he simply confusing two closely related maritime figures? No. The connection that he establishes between Melicertes (a Boeotian hero) and Glaucus (who is therefore also Boeotian) also occurs at Corinth, where, as we shall see,[18] a hero by the name of Melissus, father of an Actaeon who was flayed alive by his erastai, threw himself into a "pit" in the temple of Poseidon at Isthmus, a pit that Edouard Will has shown can only have been the sanctuary of Palaemon within Poseidon's enclosure. Given that "another" Actaeon was the hero, in Boeotia, of a famous legend of dismemberment during a hunt, it follows that we find in Corinth and Boeotia a common body of myth, attested by the recurrence of the same characters—Actaeon, Glaucus, Palaemon, and "the honey man," Melissus/Melicertes—and the same motifs: symbolic death by dismemberment or leap into the abyss, the role of honey (the substance of immortality), homosexuality, and immortalization. All of this intrinsically fits together; it is ancient.

Let us now turn our attention to an insular version of the Glaucus story, rich in a different kind of information. Nicander, an erudite poet of the second century B.C., says that Glaucus taught the art of prophecy to Apollo.[19] This is a truly ancient tradition, for Athenaeus cites a lost essay by Aristotle, *The Constitution of Delos*, in which the philosopher states that Glaucus settled at Delos before Apollo with the daughters of Nereus and there engaged in prophecy.[20] Putting together the traditions reported by Nicanor (Glaucus as erōmenos of Nereus), and Aristotle, it is as if, in Delian mythology, Nereus, the primordial sea deity, himself a prophet[21] and a good omen for sailors who caught sight of him, had been the erastēs and hence the master of Glaucus. Later, Glaucus, with the Nereides for his companions (the erōmenos becomes the son-in-law of the erastēs) established himself as a prophet at Delos. His pupil and successor was Apollo. In other words, in some lost Delian myth, might he not have been the erastēs of the young god, as Admetus seems to have been in the oldest Delphic mythology?

NINETEEN
Dionysus, the Twice-Born
卍

No one can possibly doubt that Dionysus is an initiate, a model for novices in various social institutions of ancient Greece. I refer the interested reader to the essays collected by Henri Jeanmaire in his book *Dionysos*[1] and will not here explore this important aspect of his character. There is simply too much material for the size and purpose of the present study. I shall call attention to just two points.

In the precise context of Argive ritual and myth, all that we know relates to the theme of mystical death, death followed by rebirth. This is the case, first of all, with Dionysus himself, whose journey to Hades can obviously be interpreted as a journey into death. It is also the case with Semele, his mother, who died even before the god was born and whom he restores to life once he has the age and capacity to do so. And it is the case, too, with Glaucus, whose connection with the god is unknown to us, but who is cast in the Corinthian, Boeotian, and Cretan accounts already cited as a hero of initiation who dies and is born again. Finally, it is true also of Polymnus/Prosymnus in a metaphorical sense, in that his death does not prevent him from being the erastēs par excellence and for all eternity of the god, via the phallic symbol in the wood of the fig tree. Moreover, Dionysus is par excellence the "twice-born" figure of Greek mythology. According to a widespread but not exclusive tradition, Semele, a mortal thunderstruck by the splendor and fire of Zeus, dies in pregnancy, and the god saves the fetus by placing it in his thigh.[2] Thus Dionysus is twice "born," once to his mother and a second time to his father. The tradition is ancient. Taking liberties with etymology, Euripides interprets the word *dithyrambus*, used to describe Dionysus, as a derivative of *dithyrus*, "having two doors," to signify the divine child's double birth.[3] Elsewhere he is characterized as *digonos*, "of double birth."[4] This notion and this latter term are strongly reminiscent of an important sociological concept of ancient India, at the other end of the Indo-European world. The members of the first three *varna*, or leading "castes," the Brahmans, the Ksatriya, and the Vaisya, undergo an initiation that confers upon them the title *dvija*, "twice born," which distinguishes them from the fourth caste, the Sudra, and by extension from the out-castes.[5] The reader may be surprised to find a direct comparison between a specific aspect of a character as rich and complex as Dionysus and a foreign institution before we have examined the relation of this theme to the Dionysiac character as a whole. Examining that relation would certainly be more sound methodologically. But the classical Dionysus is invested with the symbolism of Orphism and civic religion,[6] and we are fortunate to be able to turn instead to a god of the second rank but with ancient roots in Greek theology. He was known to the Mycenaeans,[7] and we can best understand the nature of this primitive Dionysus by investigating certain localities such as Megara and Argos. In Argos, at any rate, it was indeed themes of death and rebirth that were stressed, apparently, in the mysteries of Lake Alcyonia. Through Polyeidos and Glaucus Dionysus is associated with initiatory themes in Crete and Megara; in Megara he is connected with the initiations of both females (the tomb of Iphinoe stands near his temple) and males (Polyeidos purges Alcathous of the murder of his son). Here the "twice-born" image is one of the deepest, most archaic aspects of the ritual and accords with an institution fully homologous to the Indian one. Finally, we know that Greek mythology often contains scattered, isolated, distorted traces of institutions that other peoples, both Indo-European and non-Indo-European, knew in reality; hence it is not out of the question that the early stages of Dionysus's "life" (relationship to his mother, death of his mother, relationship to his father, "double birth") represent the only trace of an Indo-European pattern of initiation.

At all events, Bethe's theory seems to be borne out. The myth of Dionysus, erōmenos of Polymnus/Prosymnus, which so scandalized Christian writers, is an element of a ritual in which youths celebrated their initiation (which, like the god's initiation, involved mystical death and rebirth) at the master's tomb (as at the tomb of Diocles in Megara). If this is correct, then this initiation, or its final phase, is none other than the mysteries of Dionysus, which Pausanias had wished to conceal. Is it reasonable to assume that the festivals celebrated nearby at the sanctuary of Demeter Lernaea, like the Attic Thesmophoria, concerned only women and that the mysteries of Dionysus were their masculine counterpart? In that case, Dionysus, dead and reborn, would be the Argive counterpart of Hyacinthus. The local founder of the homosexual initiation ritual, he was the patron of the testing of young Argive males. But, in an inversion of the Laconian pattern, Dionysus is the erōmenos because the tomb is that of the educator, while at Sparta the tomb of the Amyclaeon is that of the erōmenos Hyacinthus. Leaving this inversion aside, the structure, the relations between the characters, and the behavioral model are the same.

VI
Cretan Stories

As one might expect, several texts describe homosexual relations between characters in the Cretan cycle of myths. Here as elsewhere, however, these stories are not always part of authentic local tradition. In more than one case late, Hellenistic, purely literary inventions link heroes who originally had nothing to do with each other or whose relations were of an entirely different nature.

TWENTY
Loves of Minos
🪟

The mythographer Apollodorus recounts that Asterios, king of Crete, adopted the sons of Europa by Zeus, namely, Minos, Sarpedon, and Rhadamanthus. In adulthood the three men quarreled over a boy named Miletus, son of Apollo and Areia, daughter of Cleochus. Because the youth preferred Sarpedon, Minos went to war, triumphed, and conquered the entire island. Sarpedon fled to Lycia and Miletus founded the city of Miletus in northern Lycia. Apollodorus points out that, according to other authors, the young man whom the three sons of Europa loved was named Atymnios and was the son of Zeus and Cassiopeia.[1]

Nicander tells the story this way in book II of his *Metamorphoses*, of which Antoninus Liberalis has given a summary.

> Apollo and Akakallis, daughter of Minos, had a child in Crete named Miletus. Fearing the anger of Minos, Akakallis exposed her child in the forest, where, on orders from Apollo, she-wolves came often to protect and suckle the infant in turns. Later, some ox-drivers found the child, took him in, and raised him as their own. The boy grew up into a strong and handsome young man. Minos, seized with desire for him, wanted to take him by violence. So on advice of Sarpedon Miletus sailed by night for Caria where he founded the city of Miletus and married Eidothea, daughter of Eurytus, king of the Carians.[2]

If the group consisting of Minos, Sarpedon, and Rhadamanthus is ancient, being attested in the Hesiodic *Catalogues*,[3] the remainder of both stories is late invention. Miletus, whose name is obviously derived from the place name, is not attested prior to the second century B.C. in the words of Apollodorus and Nicander.[4] The idea of a rivalry between two princes for the love of a young man is in keeping with the transformation of male homosexuality into a sexual game, not with the Cretan initiatory institution. The conflict between Minos and Sarpedon is primarily political in origin, as in Herodotus in the fifth century,[5] and this is probably based on a very old tradition.[6] The Cretan origin of the hero Miletus is similarly based on elements of the highest antiquity, since Pausanias states that it is the Milesians' own tradition that has the native sovereigns Anax and Asterios followed by a Cretan conqueror, Miletus, and Greek Ionian colonizers,[7] and this has been amply confirmed by archeological research, which has shown that Miletus was colonized first by Minoans and later by Mycenaeans.[8] Yet it is clear that the account given by the Hellenistic and Roman authors in various versions is an amalgam and synthesis of disparate elements. The Milesians first of all wrote their eponymous hero, Miletus, into the story and established a relationship between him and traditions of a pre-Hellenic Cretan influence in their city.[9] Once this Cretan origin was established, authors linked the hypothetical "departure" of Miletus from Crete to the now analogous adventure of Sarpedon, who emigrated from Crete to Lycia. All that remained was to fabricate a story for this Miletus, to trace his imaginary life history, which was done by drawing on the Cretan theme of the child abandoned and raised by an animal[10] and on the then fashionable notion of conflict between erastēs and erōmenos or between rival erastai. Nothing in all this teaches us anything real about the mythical origins of Cretan pederasty.

There is also a sexual interpretation of the relations between Minos and Theseus. Anthenaeus attributes this interpretation to one Zenis or Zeneus, a historian of Chios, his native island; according to this author, Minos reacted violently to the death of his son Androgeos in Attica because he was in love with Theseus, and he later gave him his daughter Phaedra as a wife.[11]

In spite of appearances this story is not entirely absurd. Besides the "vulgate," or classical Attic version of the story of Theseus (in which Minos does not know Theseus, who has anonymously joined the young men and women whom the Athenians are to deliver to the king of Cnossus and who later leaves the Labyrinth surreptitiously with the help of Minos's daughter Ariadne), there is another version, which establishes a more direct relationship between the Cretan king and the sons of the king of Athens. It is known primarily through a hymn of Bacchylides. On board the ship carrying them to Crete Minos and Theseus clash in a round of typical heroic boastfulness. To Minos, who claims to be the son of Zeus, Theseus responds that he is no less noble, being the son of Poseidon. To prove his point and provoke his antagonist, Minos obtains a thunderbolt from Zeus. Then he throws his ring into the sea and challenges Theseus to go and find it to prove his kinship with Poseidon. The son of Aegeus immediately dives in, and dolphins lead him to an undersea palace, where he is received by Poseidon and Amphitrite. He returns to the ship carrying the gold ring and a crown given him by Amphitrite (without rancor, the mother of Theseus being the human Aethra).[12]

Since Theseus is a young man and Minos an accomplished king as well as Theseus's father-in-law according to a universally attested tradition, it would be pleasant to assume that in an authentic ancient version of the story the relations between Minos and Aegeus's son were those of teacher to foreign pupil, just as the vulgate in which the Phlegyan Phorbas is the enemy of Apollo suggests a parallel version in which one is the pupil of the other. Furthermore, the absence of founding myths of homosexuality in Attica suggests that the compilers of Athenian mythology, whose essential works date for the most part from the sixth century, deliberately eliminated all references to pederasty, in keeping with social and ideological notions of which we can see other effects.[13] In other words, it is possible, in the absence of contradictory evidence, that the most ancient Athenian tradition presented the relations between the two characters in non-antagonistic terms, in accordance with a model of which we find a trace, for example, in the relations between this same Minos and another Attic hero, Daedalus. Moreover, Minos, who before supplying Theseus with a spouse sets him two initiatory trials, that of the ring[14] and later the military and hunting trial of the fight with the Minotaur, does indeed appear to be the young man's teacher and examiner.

But merely because something is possible does not prove that it was so, and there is nothing prior to the late Hellenistic work of the obscure Zenis or Zeneus to corroborate the interpretation suggested above. It cannot, therefore, be used in the present research. Note simply that if what I am arguing here is correct, namely, that each Greek province in protohistorical times possessed its own myth of the foundation of pederastic rituals of initiation, then Attica must have had such a myth prior to eliminating it from its traditions, and this myth may have belonged to the Theseus cycle, since Theseus was in fact the founder of most of the Attic military and initiatory rituals. In that case this tradition may have been preserved outside Attica, for example at Chios, of which Zenis/Zeneus wrote the history. In any case it does not appear to be Cretan.[15]

TWENTY-ONE

The Judge and the Warrior

A third story depicts Rhadamanthus as the erastēs of Talos, a typical Cretan hero. This story has in its favor the authority, and the antiquity, of the poet Ibycus of Rhegium, an author who flourished in the middle of the sixth century.[1] The assertion is therefore ancient, but what value are we to ascribe to it? No other text confirms this tradition, and the relationship between Talos and Rhadamanthus was, as far as we can see, especially complex.

Ever since the Homeric poems Rhadamanthus was a legendary Cretan, son of Zeus, brother of Minos, and in some ways connected with central Greece (the *Odyssey* says that he traveled to Euboea on Phaeacian ships; later he was said to have married Alcmene in Boeotia; a Cretan city, Gortyn, and a Boeotian city, Erythrae, have his sons for eponyms).[2] From Hesiod onward he was famous as a "just man" and teacher of justice.[3] Talos, in the "vulgate" (Apollodorus, Apollonius of Rhodes, Plato, etc.), is a man of bronze, whose primary function is to watch over the isle of Crete and prevent strangers from landing there.[4] He has long been recognized as a Cretan and Dorian solar hero.[5] Thus these two characters would seem to have nothing in common.

However, closer inspection, taking account (as one must always do) of "variants" that differ from the vulgate, reveals curious relations between them. To begin with, Pausanias, following Cinaethon, proposes the following genealogy: Kres, eponym of Crete, was the father of Talos, who was the father of Hephaestus, who was the father of Rhadamanthus.[6] It is generally believed that the mention of Hephaestus is an ancient error for Phaestus, for the god of fire had no cult or mythological role in Crete,[7] whereas Phaestus is the eponym of the famous city of the same name near Gortyn in southern Crete.[8] Thus one of the oldest Greek traditions links Talos and Rhadamanthus in a diachronic order that is reminiscent of the text considered here: Talos is from a generation prior to Rhadamanthus, whereas according to the "vulgate" both are contemporaries of Minos.

Another connection between them is mentioned in a dialogue attributed to Plato, the *Minos*, where it is stated that "Rhadamanthus was not trained [by Minos] in all the royal art, but in an auxiliary part, namely, how to preside over tribunals. It was to him that Minos entrusted the keeping of the laws in the city; for the rest of Crete it was Talos."[9] King Minos hereby establishes a division of labor between two prosecutors for the purpose of "keeping order" in Crete. Note that Rhadamanthus and Talos again become contemporaries, but their legends, distinct in the common tradition, are here totally intertwined, since both represent complementary aspects of the same function.

A third connection between the two characters involves a curious coincidence. According to one tradition Rhadamanthus had several companions, named Anios, Oenopion, Euanthes, Staphylus, Thoas, etc.; according to another tradition, Oenopion, king of Chios, who is the son of Ariadne (daughter of Minos) and Dionysus (or Theseus), has as his sons Euanthes, Athamas, Melas, Salagos, and Talos.[10] In these genealogies Anios is specifically a hero of the island of Delos, Athamas reigned over Coroneia in Boeotia, Euanthes in Thrace, Thoas is a legendary king of Lemnos, Oenopion is a legendary king of Chios, etc.: Talos/Rhadamanthus is "the" Cretan.

Thus Rhadamanthus and Talos are closely related in a variety of ways, apparently as conjoined aspects of the sovereignty embodied in Minos. The least that can be said is that the variation in the expression of their relationship is such that yet another tradition, that of Ibycus, may represent as well as the others an authentic and ancient Cretan form. How, in that case, is it to be interpreted?

I shall not press this line of inquiry further here. It should be obvious that, in order to understand the precise implications of the complementarity between Talos and Rhadamanthus, one would have to study in detail not only the various symbolic aspects of both figures (juridical, royal, infernal, and agrarian in the case of Rhadamanthus,[11] solar, military, and technological in that of Talos) but also the structure of Minos's sovereignty, since their functions depend on and are subsumed by those of Minos. This is a great deal of work for a result that will inevitably be tenuous and uncertain.

I shall make only one point, which tends to support the argument of the present work. Like Rhadamanthus, Talos has strange affinities with central Greece. For one thing, Oenopion, his father in the text cited above and his son in other texts, is certainly a native Boeotian hero, as is shown by his relations with Dionysus and Orion.[12] More than that, there is "another" Talos in Greek tradition, this one Athenian. There is a well-known story about the Athenian artist and technician Daedalus, who goes to work for Minos and builds the Labyrinth at Cnossus. Apollodorus writes:

> He had fled from Athens, because he had thrown down from the Acropolis Talos, the son of his sister Perdix; for Talos was his pupil, and Daedalus feared that with his talents he might surpass himself, seeing that he had sawed a thin stick with a jawbone of a snake which he had found.[13]

Pausanias, who calls the hero Calos, and Diodorus, who attributes to him the invention of the metal saw, the potter's wheel, the mason's compass, and still other items, tells the same story.[14]

The connections between this Talos and the previous one are obvious. The Cretan man of bronze was in fact according to some authors the work of Daedalus and according to others of Hephaestus, who, especially in Attica, was the divine equivalent of Daedalus.[15] As Marie Delcourt points out, "the mysterious, disturbing character of metal works can be fully appreciated in the legend in which the Cretan Talos, instead of killing strangers by stoning, crushes them against his body and leaps with them into an incandescent grave in which they perish."[16] Thus one of the two Taloses is the material work of Daedalus, and the other, his disciple, is his metaphorical "work." And both, subjects as well as objects of the forge, embody metallurgical mysteries.

These connections are duplicated at a symbolic level that confirms the homogeneity of this group of legends. According to Apollodorus, Talos the Athenian is the son of a sister of Daedalus named Perdix. But, in a different tradition from the one represented by this author and the others I cited along with him, the name Perdix is given to the artisan-pupil himself—sometimes with the explanation that he was given this name because when Daedalus hurled him from the Acropolis, Athena out of pity changed him into a partridge (*perdix*).[17] Here we touch symbolism deriving from the most ancient Greek sources, as Marie Delcourt has shown in her study of Hephaestus. In high antiquity the blacksmith was a magician, and transformation into a bird and possession of avian powers were universal attributes of primitive magicians. In fact, in the

Daedalus cycle, apart from the hero himself, who fashioned wings to escape from Crete, the theme of being hurled from a height only to be transformed into a bird occurs three times: once in the story of Talos/Perdix, again in the celebrated adventure of Icarus, Daedalus's son, and finally in connection with a character mentioned only by Ovid[18] and named Daedalion, literally, "son of Daedalus," though he is cast by Ovid as a son of Apollo. This Daedalion, in despair over the death of his daughter Chione, leaps from the top of Parnassus, but Apollo transforms him into a sparrow-hawk.

In the same study Marie Delcourt shows that when a magician dives into water or leaps into the air, it is a symbol of initiation.[19] This explains the significance of the transformation into a bird; it symbolizes that the apprentice magician has mastered his technical and magical powers and joined the "brotherhood" of initiates who, by nature, are superior to other men.

Talos, inventor and pupil of Daedalus, leaps from a height and is transformed into a bird, and is therefore a novice undergoing and completing his initiation. All these traits can be carried over to the Cretan Talos. A wine bowl from Ruvo depicts the death of Talos, who bears

> no apparent wound, under the gaze of Medea, who holds a cup, suggesting both a poisoning and an evil spell. The Man of Bronze is a handsome young man whose white body has been touched up with brown varnish to suggest metal . . . and coins of Phaestus, several of which have the name Talos inscribed on them, show a winged man running with a stone in each hand, sometimes accompanied by a dog.[20]

Recall that Rhadamanthus is also connected with Phaestus and that in Pausanias's text, in which Talos, son of Kres, is the father of Hephaestus, the name Hephaestus may have been erroneously substituted, owing to an error in the tradition, for Phaestus.

What can we conclude from all this? Ibycus's curious assertion is not confirmed by other texts. But upon analysis the connections between Talos and Rhadamanthus turn out to be numerous and systematic. Moreover, Talos turns out to be a young man, fresh from his initiatory trials and—by way of his "Attic homonym"—a pupil of Daedalus, a relationship which, in Crete at any rate, would surely have included a sexual aspect (Attic tradition leaves the question in doubt).

I should point out, moreover, that the symbolism of homosexual initiation turns up in other ways throughout this group of legends. The Parnassian Daedalion commits suicide because his daughter Chione ("snow") dies. She had dared to compare herself to Artemis, and the goddess would not forgive her. Previously, however, she had given birth to two heroes: Autolycus, whose father is Hermes, and Philammon, whose father is Apollo.[21] This Philammon has already been mentioned twice in this book: first as father of Thamyris, the musician inventor of homosexuality in a certain Greek tradition, and second as creator of the mysteries of Demeter at Lerna. "Another" Chione is the mother of Priapus, the phallic god.[22] Still "another," the daughter of Boreas, the North Wind, was the mother, with Poseidon, of the hero Eumolpus. This story is worth noting. For fear of her father (this Chione, like her homonyms, is an unwed mother) she hurls her newborn into the sea, and Poseidon saves it (think of the stories of Theseus and Hephaestus) and turns it over to one of his daughters. Later this Eumolpus becomes king of Eleusis and fights the Athenians with the help of Phorbas, or, less explicitly in our texts, of Diocles. Both are heroes of stories in which homosexual initiation figures as an important theme.

TWENTY-TWO
The Handsome Ganymedes

The last Cretan tradition that I will examine is the most famous. It concerns the loves of Zeus and Ganymede, a hero whom I shall call by a name closer to the Greek form, Ganymedes.

At the beginning of the *Laws* Plato expresses himself very clearly on this point.

> The pleasure of males with males, or females with females, is contrary to nature and a boldness of the first rank in the surrender to pleasure. And we all charge the Cretans that they made up the tale (*mythos*) of Ganymede; they were convinced, we say, that their legislation came from Zeus, so they went on to tell this story against him that they might, if you please, be following his example when they indulged in this pleasure too.[1]

The Athenian who utters these words is here speaking to a Lacaedemonian and a Cretan, and he is not contradicted. This raises two problems: First, how ancient is the interpretation of the relationship between Zeus and Ganymedes as sexual, and second, is the myth in fact of Cretan origin?

The *Iliad* mentions Ganymedes twice. In book V, Diomedes is speaking of the horses of Aeneas.

> These are of that strain which Zeus of the wide brows granted
> once to Tros, recompense for his son Ganymedes, and therefore
> are the finest of all horses beneath the sun and the daybreak;
> and the lord of men Anchises [father of Aeneas] stole horses from this
>   breed,
> without the knowledge of Laomedon putting mares under them.[2]

In book XX Aeneas sets forth his genealogy for Achilles.

Dardanos in turn had a son, the king, Erichthonios,
who became the richest of mortal men, and in his possession
were three thousand horses who pastured along the low grasslands,
mares in their pride with their young colts; and with these the North
    Wind
fell in love as they pastured there, and took on upon him
the likeness of a dark-maned stallion, and coupled with them,
and the mares conceiving of him bore to him twelve young horses.
. . . Erichthonios had a son, Tros, who was lord of the Trojans,
and to Tros in turn there were born three sons unfaulted,
Ilos and Assaracus and godlike Ganymedes
who was the loveliest born of the race of mortals, and therefore
the gods caught him away to themselves, to be Zeus's wine-pourer,
for the sake of his beauty, so he might be among the immortals.
Ilos in turn was given a son, the blameless Laomedon,
and Laomedon had sons in turn, Tithonos and Priam,
Lampos, Klytios and Hiketaon, scion of Ares;
but Assaracus had Kapys, and Kapys' son was Anchises,
and I am Anchises' son, and Priam's is Hector the brilliant.[3]

I cite this genealogy in full because it mentions, in addition to
Ganymedes, two other men who were loved by gods. This fact is not
without interest.

The author of the *Iliad* mentions no sexual relationship between Zeus
and the son of Tros. In this respect, two subsequent texts, from the
seventh century, the *Little Iliad* and the *Homeric Hymn to Aphrodite*,
remain in the strict Homeric tradition. That is why it is generally held
that it was not until the sixth century that two poets, Ibycus of Rhegium
and Theognis of Megara, gave a sexual turn to Ganymedes' service with
Zeus. For Theognis, in fact, the love of young men first became pleasur-
able with Zeus's abduction of Ganymedes, and he refers to this to justify
his own loves.[4] Indeed, from this point on, ancient tradition is almost
unanimous in interpreting the relationship between Zeus and
Ganymedes as homosexual.[5]

That is why Bethe, for example, argues that pederasty was unknown
to Homer and that it was in Crete, under Dorian influence, that the
cupbearer of the gods was transformed into the erōmenos of Zeus. He is
followed on this point by authors as different as Jeanmaire, who believes
that the first attestation of this form of the myth is in Theognis, and
Dover, who attributes it to Ibycus.[6]

Consideration of the *Homeric Hymn to Aphrodite* will show how mis-

taken this conception is. I am obliged to say, despite the respect that I
have for its exponents, that it is based on a profound misunderstanding
of the nature of Homer's work. It is completely illusory, in fact, to
believe that what is not mentioned in the work of "Homer" did not exist
in Homer's time and, conversely, that what is mentioned did exist. The
authors of the Homeric poems are not "objective" observers of their
times, and on many occasions they were altogether partial.[7] It is undeniable that in various literary genres there exists a kind of implicit moral
code that prohibits discussion of certain subjects. We saw earlier, for
example, how the *Iliad* glosses over internal conflict among the Atridae.
In the same way, Greek, and later Roman, epic poets always refused to
discuss homosexuality. For example, I have noted that as late as the early
Hellenistic period Apollonius of Rhodes, in telling the story of Hylas,
Polyphemus, and Heracles, describes in detail the relationship between
master and disciple without the slightest mention of its homosexual
aspect, in contrast to all other sources (including the poem of Theocritus, a contemporary of Apollonius), simply because Apollonius was
writing an epic work; he had to accommodate himself to the tacit
morality of the genre.[8] Similarly, consider the contrast in fifth-century
Athens between tragedy, in which allusions to homosexuality are very
rare indeed, and comedy, vase paintings, and philosophy, in which they
are common currency. In other words, had there been a Plato, a Theocritus, or an Aristophanes contemporary with "Homer," the position of
Bethe, Jeanmaire, Marrou, Dover, and others would be untenable.

What do we actually find in the *Hymn to Aphrodite*, a work that has
been dated without hesitation as belonging to the final third of the
seventh century?

Ganymedes is mentioned in the following context: The Trojan prince
Anchises is enraged when he learns that the marvelous woman who had
come to join him on Ida is none other than Aphrodite, since the love of
gods is fatal to mortals. The goddess reassures him:

> "What is more, of all mortal men those of your race come closest to
> the gods in fine and imposing appearance. It was for his beauty that
> Zeus carried off the blonde Ganymedes, who lived among the immor-
> tals and served as cupbearer to the gods in Zeus's abode. He was a
> marvel to behold, and all the immortals honored him, who poured the
> dark nectar into a golden bowl. As for Tros, a cruel sorrow filled his
> heart, and he knew not where the divine tempest had taken his son.
> He cried endless tears. It came to pass that Zeus felt pity for him and

gave him as compensation for the abduction of his son brisk-stepping horses, the very same that carried the immortals. Zeus made him a gift of these, and on Zeus's orders Argeiphontes the messenger told him in full detail that he was immortal and exempt from old age, just like the gods. After receiving the messages of Zeus, Tros never cried again. His heart was filled with joy, and joyously he drove his horses as fast as the wind. Another of your race equal to the immortals was Tithonus, who was carried off by Aurora of the golden throne.''[9]

It is immediately apparent that the *Hymn* in no way differs from the *Iliad*, not in its themes or in its discretion or in its terms. The stories of Anchises, Ganymedes, and Tithonus are all mentioned in the *Iliad*.[10] As for Ganymedes' beauty, it is specifically and repeatedly mentioned in the passage of book XX already cited—to such a degree that to deny the homosexuality or at least homophilia of the author of these verses is something of a paradox.[11] But if there is no explicit mention of pederasty in either the *Hymn* or the *Iliad*, it is nevertheless implicitly necessary and obvious. The context is in fact decisive—and it can only be regretted that nothing similar could be included in the context of the epic. Aphrodite responds to Anchises after having had sexual relations with him, and she responds on this precise point, which is the cause of the hero's anguish.

> "Ah! I grab your knees and beg in the name of Zeus who carries the Aegis, do not allow me to live impotent in the midst of other men. Take pity on me, for the man who sleeps with immortal goddesses will never see his life bear fruit!"[12]

The danger is indicated with stark clarity; it comes not from frequenting or sharing meals with the gods but from having sexual contact with them. Now, Aphrodite responds first by revealing to Anchises that she is going to have a child by him and then by reminding him that two members of his family had been granted immortality after similar contacts (for had these contacts not been similar, they would not have been convincing). The poem therefore compares three couples, whom it treats as equivalent: Anchises-Aphrodite, Ganymedes-Zeus, and Tithonus-Aurora. This makes sense only if Ganymedes and Zeus had relations comparable to those between Anchises and Aphrodite or Tithonus and Aurora.

What is true of the *Homeric Hymn to Aphrodite* is true also of the *Iliad*:

The former is merely an extension of the latter. And, as Dover has rightly observed, [13] the emphasis on Ganymedes' beauty in the *Iliad*'s book XX, which is praised in terms similar to those used in the *Hymn* and in Theognis, clearly suggests an erotic preoccupation on the poet's part.

I therefore have no hesitation in concluding that the myth of Ganymedes was already known, in the form under discussion here, during the Homeric era. The silence of "Homer" on this point is not a relevant fact, and what little he does say tends to support this interpretation.

If this is correct, R. F. Willetts's interpretation of the myth of Ganymedes is of the utmost importance for the present study. Willetts, following Jeanmaire, compares the myth of Ganymedes with the Cretan custom discussed at the beginning of this book.

> The aristocratic *élite* who practiced the custom may have derived their ultimate origin from the chosen band of youths whom Evans supposed to exist at the court of Minos. The myth of Ganymedes, according to Plato, was said to have originated in Crete; and there was a tradition that Minos, not Zeus, was the ravisher. [14] But all this later sophistication must be set beside the original form of the myth, where Ganymedes is not the bedfellow but the cupbearer of Zeus. He was chosen by the gods; he was blessed with immortality; his father was compensated for his loss. He was the young initiate chosen for special office. [15]

I shall omit discussion of Evans's hypothesis concerning bands of youths in the Minoan palace, whose existence is far from certain, and I do not agree with his assertion concerning the original form of the myth. The connection with the Cretan initiates, on the other hand, is quite interesting, and Willetts's interpretation is supported by a number of parallels. The death of Heracles, for example, is his abduction to heaven and his promotion to the status of a deity. It is worth noting that this promotion goes along with his marriage to Hebe, Zeus's daughter, who preceded Ganymedes as a servant to the gods—here as in the *Hymn to Aphrodite*, the gift of immortality coincides with a sexual contact, and Ganymedes merely confirms the habit. The death of Hyacinthus preceded his resurrection, which was also an ascent to heaven. The novice's serving the master is a general feature of the initiatory process. Jeanmaire points out that Ganymedes' serving of drinks is suggested by the Cretan ritual in which the erastēs gives his pupil three ritual objects upon completion of testing: an ox to sacrifice, military gear, and a drinking cup.[16] Of these three items the myth of Ganymedes preserves—can preserve—only the third. The second is eliminated, since the divinized hero is henceforth confined to his function as servant and erōmenos, while the first is simply inverted: Instead of the new warrior sacrificing an ox to Zeus, Zeus gives horses to the old king, father of the young novice.

But to judge the depth of the association between the myth and the custom, we need to know whether or not the myth is of Cretan origin. The assertions of Plato, to which his Cretan interlocutor has no answer, and of the historian Echemenes, a specialist on Crete cited by Athenaeus, imply that the myth of Ganymedes was regarded by Cretans as the founding myth of their homosexuality from the early fourth century on. Plato says even more: If "all" Greeks agreed that the Cretans, and not Homer, Ibycus (of Rhegium), or Theognis (of Megara), were the inventors of the myth of Ganymedes, then that myth must have been of incalculable antiquity in Crete.

It is quite possible that "Homer" borrowed from Cretan mythology. Nineteenth-century German philologists showed that many characters in the Homeric poems have doublets in the mythology of Boeotia and Thessaly, which suggests that the authors of these epics drew widely and freely on local traditions. The myth of the judgment of Paris, which underlies the *Iliad*, in which it is merely mentioned[17] (proof among many others that the *Iliad* is not a compendium of the mythology of its time), is certainly of Lacedaemonian origin.[18] The genealogy of the princes of Troy is a composite of disparate motifs. Along with purely local eponyms, such as Ilos, Dardanos, and Tros, certain names, such as Assaracus and possibly Capus,[19] may be of local origin, but the majority come directly from Greece. Hector is an old Theban hero;[20] Anchises, Aeneas, and Alexandros (another name for Paris) are Peloponnesian.[21] There may well also be elements of Cretan origin. The *Odyssey* contains a catalogue of loves between mortals and gods. To Hermes, who reproaches Calypso for keeping Ulysses with her, Calypso responds that this is jealousy on the part of the gods, as evidenced by two stories from times past, one concerning the love of Orion and Aurora, which Artemis ended by murdering the hero, the other concerning Demeter and Iasion, "in the field of the third plowing," which roused Zeus to such fury that he unleashed a thunderbolt against Iasion.[22] Hesiod's *Theogony* specifies the locale of this second affair.

Demeter, shining goddess, joined in love
With Iasion the hero, on the rich
Island of Crete, they lay on fallow land
Which had been plowed three times.[23]

Here, Iasion is not struck by a thunderbolt and the outcome of the coupling of man and goddess is a happy one; Plutos, their son, is agricultural wealth personified. We can make out the primitive form and value of the myth: The plowman makes the earth fertile, the sexual act is an obvious metaphor for plowing (a reversible metaphor), and on the plane of myth the paradigmatic plowman who encounters the goddess herself is thereby sanctified. The coupling with the goddess confers immortality, and the thunderbolt is another way of expressing this immortalization.[24]

The theme of coupling between mortal and deity is therefore attested in Crete in remote antiquity. The Lacedaemonians joined Hyacinthus and Apollo, the Chians Cyparissus and Apollo. The Cretans may have joined Ganymedes and Zeus.

The theme of service is reminiscent of an aspect of the Cretan ritual, as I mentioned a moment ago. Furthermore, Jeanmaire points out that the importance of horses in Ganymedes' story may reflect a Cretan preoccupation with horses since, according to Ephorus, "the horsemen (Hippeis) of Crete possess horses, while those of Sparta have none [meaning, they no longer have any]."[25]

Athenaeus, however, suggests a possibility other than Crete for the origin of the myth. Echemenes, he says, attributed the abduction of Ganymedes to Minos.

But the Chalcidians assert that Ganymedes was carried off by Zeus in their own country, and they point out the place, calling it Harpagion; in its grow excellent myrtle trees.[26]

The myrtle is a sexually marked tree that frequently appears in rituals of initiation and marriage. Near the temple of Aphrodite Kataskopia, where Phaedra went to watch Hippolytus exercising in the stadium of Troezen, there still stood in Pausanias's time a myrtle whose leaves Phaedra had shredded with one of her hair pins. The context is that of ephebic trials, of love and conformity with the social models that new generations were obliged to reproduce.[27] In Crete, in the festival in honor of Britomartis, "the myrtle is not touched," according to Callimachus; "the nymph's cloak caught on a branch of the tree while she was fleeing, which explains her great anger toward it."[28] The Chalcidian pretension is thus rooted in an ancient ritual practice.

According to Plutarch, the Chalcidians attributed the foundation of their homosexual rituals to Cleomachus. I pointed out earlier how this legend seems to be based on an adaptation of the Boeotian theme of the feast in the presence of initiatory hero and founder, Iolaus or Diocles, even though an onomastic change undercuts this implication. In fact, human names ending in -cles, -laus, and -medes, attested since the Mycenaean period,[29] seem to be older than those ending in -machus. And Cleo- as the first syllable of a composite is not Mycenaean either. Cleomachus is surely recent and secondary; his purpose is to tell the Thebans that the founder of initiatory homosexuality was not named Diocles, Iolaus, or Heracles. But then, if the Chalcidians felt a historical need to reject a Theban contribution, and if (as it is my purpose here to show) institutional pederasty dates from prehistoric times in Chalcis as elsewhere, then there may have existed a local ritual and myth prior to Cleomachus and prior to the Theban contribution. Ganymedes, an ancient hero whose name has an archaic structure, may have been the hero of this myth, the model for this ritual.

The Cretan and Chalcidian pretensions are not irreconcilable. The Couretes, mythical projection of the kouroi, or young men undergoing probation, as Jeanmaire has shown in detail in his book Couroi et Courètes, are associated with three specific sites in Greece: Aetolia, Chalcis, and Crete.[30] Ganymedes served Zeus as the Couretes served the mother of the gods and perhaps also Zeus.[31] He may be one of them.

At this point it is easy to arrange these various facts to form a coherent pattern. I have assumed that initiatory pederasty is of Indo-European origin. Mythical rites and models were brought to Greece by the first Hellenes around 2000 B.C. Some centuries later, several waves of Greeks streamed into Crete, bringing their language, institutions, and religions to the island. Among these Greeks one important group may have—must have—come directly from Euboea. This is a simple, unproblematic, and fruitful hypothesis. With them these Euboeans brought not only ritual homosexuality, which they shared with other Greeks, but also the Couretes and Ganymedes. Over the centuries Ganymedes was relegated to the second rank in Euboea, whereas along with the Couretes he enjoyed considerable success in Crete, where the author of the Iliad borrowed his name and associated him with Troy.

The parallel between Ganymedes and the Couretes could be explored in greater detail. Here I must limit myself to a few speculative observations. They suggest that the cupbearer of Zeus was a founding hero of initiatory homosexuality in Crete and, even earlier, in Greece.

VII
Heroes

Meleager the Solitary

In a famous passage of the *Erōticos* Plutarch assures us that "not only are the most warlike nations most amorous, as the Boeotians, the Lacedaemonians, and the Cretans, but also, of the old heroes, who were more amorous than Meleager, Achilles, Aristomenes, Cimon, and Epaminondas?"[1]

The first two of these names are legendary characters, the other three historical. But this is not the most pertinent distinction among them. In tradition Aristomenes has taken on so many elements of myth that so far as we are concerned he belongs more to legend than to history.

Meleager and Aristomenes share one negative trait that distinguishes them from Achilles. The traditional image of Achilles is of a man inseparable from his friend Patroclus. Whether or not this friendship involved a sexual relationship is a question that I shall take up in a subsequent chapter. For now let us accept the common hypothesis that the relationship between Achilles and Patroclus as depicted in the *Iliad* was not pederastic and was not described as such until some centuries later. Such a reinterpretation was possible, of course, only because the Homeric poems showed such a close relationship between the two friends. This is not the case with the traditional images of Aristomenes and Meleager. Neither is associated with a comrade-in-arms whose existence would allow a secondary interpretation of the sort assumed between Achilles and Patroclus. While it is possible that Plutarch, writing at the end of a millennial literary tradition, reports a late or evolved state of the Achilles legend, it is hard to see what sort of rereading or reinterpretation could have served as the basis for his assertions concerning the other two heroes.

By contrast, it may well be that Plutarch is here reporting elements of genuinely ancient traditions, lost to us. In fact, to take the most explicit case, Aristomenes is treated at length only in the work of the Cretan poet

Rhianus, who lived in the third century B.C. and based his story
on Messenian traditions. Rhianus's poem is completely lost, however.
The content of his work is available to us only through Pausanias, an author roughly contemporaneous with Plutarch. So Pausanias abridged
Rhianus, who had collected Messenian traditions concerning the hero,
about whom other brief stories were current in the Greek world, such as
at Rhodes and in Boeotia. It should be clear how much has been lost. For
us, works from around 100 A.D. at the earliest (Plutarch and Pausanias)
are chronologically the earliest sources we have concerning Aristomenes.
They may reflect many reinterpretations and modifications of tradition
or, equally possibly, they may report a primitive version. Elsewhere I
have pointed out how, contrary to a position that has been defended on
several occasions by other writers,[2] certain of Rhianus's pseudohistorical
traditions are authentically derived from a very ancient past. All or
nearly all of the names of ancient Messenian kings that he gives are found
in the Pylian onomastic from the Mycenaean era but not (and the point is
crucial, for it brings out the full significance of the coincidence) in other
Mycenaean onomastics, from Cnossus or elsewhere.[3]

The case of Meleager is different, for he is a hero whose name has been
known since the *Iliad*. Yet nothing written about him then or since
would justify a secondary interpretation of his character along the lines of
the reinterpretation of the Achilles character mentioned above. In the
case of Meleager and many other mythological heroes, including the best
known (e.g., Heracles[4]), very late sources have disclosed very archaic
aspects of character. Hence it is perfectly possible that Plutarch, in the
passage cited, is reporting an ancient tradition.

It is interesting to observe that both Achilles and Meleager are typical
military heroes. We cannot analyze the nature of their pederasty as we
did for Hyacinthus, Iolaus, and others, since Plutarch, our only source,
gives no details, but we may assume that homosexual traditions associated with them were useful if we can determine the significance of the
related myths in regional symbolism.

Meleager is the hero of Calydon, the principal city of Aetolia. The
symbolism that defines him in the texts makes him one of the richest,
most archaic characters in all Greek mythology. For the most part his
image is subsumed in a concept: He is primarily a hunter and warrior.

A passage from book IX of the *Iliad* alludes to both aspects of his
character.

The Couretes and the steadfast Aetolians were fighting
and slaughtering one another about the city of Calydon,
the Aetolians in lovely Calydon's defence, the Couretes
furious to storm and sack it in war. For Artemis,
she of the golden chair, had driven this evil upon them,
angered that Oeneus had not given the pride of the orchards
to her, first fruits; the rest of the gods were given due sacrifice,
but alone to this daughter of great Zeus he had given nothing.
He had forgotten, or had not thought, in his hard delusion,
and in wrath at his whole mighty line the Lady of Arrows
sent upon them the fierce wild boar with the shining teeth, who
after the way of his kind did much evil to the orchards of Oeneus.
For he ripped up whole tall trees from the ground and scattered them
     headlong
roots and all, even to the very flowers of the orchard.
The son of Oeneus killed this boar, Meleager, assembling
together many hunting men out of numerous cities
with their hounds; since the boar might not have been killed by a few
     men,
so huge was he, and had put many men on the sad fire for burning.
But the goddess again made a great stir of anger and crying
battle, over the head of the boar and the bristling boar's hide,
between Couretes and the high-hearted Aetolians. So long
as Meleager lover of battle stayed in the fighting
it went the worse for the Couretes, and they could not even
hold their ground outside the wall, though they were so many.
But when the anger came upon Meleagros, such anger
as wells in the hearts of others also, though their minds are careful,
he, in the wrath of his heart against his own mother, Althaea,
lay apart with his wedded bride, Cleopatra the lovely,
daughter of sweet-stepping Marpessa, child of Euenos,
and Idas, who was the strongest of all men upon earth
in his time; for he even took up the bow to face the King's onset,
Phoebus Apollo, for the sake of the sweet-stepping maiden;
a girl her father and honoured mother had named in their palace
Alcyone, sea-bird, as a by-name, since for her sake
her mother with the sorrow-laden cry of a sea-bird
wept because far-reaching Phoebus Apollo had taken her;
with this Cleopatra he lay mulling his heart-sore anger,
raging by reason of his mother's curses, which she called down
from the gods upon him, in deep grief for the death of her brother,
and many times beating with her hands on the earth abundant

she called on Hades and on honored Persephone, lying
at length along the ground, and the tears were wet on her bosom,
to give death to her son; and Erinys, the mist-walking,
she of the heart without pity, heard her out of the dark places.
Presently there was thunder about the gates, and the sound rose
of towers under assault, and the Aetolian elders
supplicated him, sending their noblest priests of the immortals,
to come forth and defend them; they offered him a great gift:
wherever might lie the richest ground in Calydon,
there they told him to choose out a piece of land, an entirely
good one, of fifty acres, the half of it to be vineyard
and the half of it unworked ploughland of the plain to be furrowed.
And the aged horseman Oeneus again and again entreated him,
and took his place at the threshold of the high-vaulted chamber
and shook against the bolted doors, pleading with his own son.
And again and again his honored mother and his sisters
entreated him, but he only refused the more; then his own friends
who were the most honored and dearest of all entreated him;
but even so they could not persuade the heart within him
until, as the chamber was under close assault, the Couretes
were mounting along the towers and set fire to the great city.
And then at last his wife, the fair-girdled bride, supplicated
Meleager, in tears, and rehearsed in their numbers before him
all the sorrows that come to men when their city is taken:
they kill the men, and the fire leaves the city in ashes,
and strangers lead the children away and the deep-girdled women.
And the heart, as he listened to all this evil, was stirred within him,
and he rose, and went, and closed his body in shining armor.
So he gave way in his own heart, and drove back the day of evil
from the Aetolians; yet these no longer would make good
their many and gracious gifts; yet he drove back the evil from them.[5]

The image of the invincible warrior and practiced hunter is solidly
constructed. To the author of this text Meleager is the guarantor of his
city's security, a professional warrior. But he is also a solitary, savage
warrior and here represents what ought not to be done. Phoenix,
Achilles' teacher, recounts this story to his pupil in order to persuade
him to rejoin the battle that he had forsaken. The era of the Homeric
poems was in fact the period during which the city slowly came into its
own—first as the aristocratic city and later, in the centuries that followed, as the democratic city-state, in which civic solidarity outweighed
individual passions. An individualistic warrior like Meleager had no

place in the Greece that was then being formed. But let us get back to the structure of the myth.

Quite obviously, "Homer" has posed in "national" terms a problem that in his day and milieu was no longer "social." The Couretes he mentions are the brothers of the mother, in other words, the adult members of another *genos*. In primitive Greece marriages were made between noble *genē* of different localities; family exogamy was complemented by geographical exogamy, exhibiting an openness to the outside world that the Greece of the city-states would reject. Hence Meleager's uncles do not belong to the same *genos* and do not come from the same locality as Meleager himself. In this way, a conflict that is essentially intergenerational becomes a conflict between Calydon and "another" Aetolian "tribe." In fact, as R. Roux points out, "the hunt for the boar of Calydon is a couretic exploit; before quarreling the *kouroi* of the noblest Greek blood had reinforced the valiance of the virtuous Couretes in a joint expedition that, its purpose being to capture a skin, is analogous in more than one way to the adventure of the Argonauts."[6] Subsequent literary tradition in fact included Meleager among the Argonauts.

The Couretes, whose name is derived from *kouroi*, are essentially young men undergoing initiation. Here the term is applied to adult men belonging to the same generation as the hero's mother. They participate in the hunt that demonstrates the hero's valor. Now it is clear what they must be. Matrilinear uncles of Meleager who take part in the hunt but allow their nephew and his companions (his *agele*, as one would say in terms of Cretan sociology) to kill the animal, they can only be the masters of the *kouroi*. Included in the initiatory process, they are still, institutionally speaking, Couretes. If the myth never mentioned homosexuality in the Meleager cycle, one would in fact situate it at this level: between the hero and an older member of his mother's family.

Apollonius of Rhodes clearly understood the nature of Meleager. "He [Jason] it was whom Oeneus sent, now that he was grown up, to guard his child; so while yet a youth (*kourizōn*) he entered that brave band of heroes."[7]

The scholium defines *kourizōn* as *akmazōn eti*, "one who is in the full flower of youth."[8]

We must assume, though this is no longer obvious to the author of the *Iliad*, that victory in the hunt, success in the trial set by Artemis, makes Meleager eligible to marry, to move from the childhood phase to the adult phase of which Aphrodite is in large part the patron. Promoted to the rank of warrior, Meleager becomes the equal of his uncles the Couretes; this is certainly one of the cruxes of the conflict. And the battle that follows, between the Couretes full of their privileges and the youths of Meleager's cohort demanding equality with their uncles, is none other than a mythically dramatized version of the combats between distinct but proximate age cohorts which we find embodied in the conservative institutions of certain Greek cities in the classical era.[9]

Meleager has only to wish for victory in order for victory to be his—he is the Aetolian Heracles. The mythology of warfare as well as hunting completely envelops him. If, in the *Iliad*, he is the son of the chariot driver Oeneus, in later texts he is cast as the son of Ares.[10] Now, as F. Vian points out in his study of the warrior function in Greek mythology, "all the male children of Ares are warriors, generally savage and terrifying warriors." For example, Diomedes of Thrace and Cycnus, who blocked the road between northern Thessaly and Delphi, were both killed by Heracles, their counterpart and enemy. Phlegyas, leader of the Phlegyans, also fought with Heracles. Oenomaus and Euenus killed their daughters' suitors, and the daughter of the latter was Marpessa, mother-in-law of Meleager. Finally, in Aetolia, there was Meleager himself.[11] In the family of Meleager we find a certain Toxeus, whose name is derived from the word for bow, a woman named Gorgo, a warrior hero and hypostasis of Athena,[12] and Tydeus, father of Diomedes of Argos, "homonym" of Diomedes of Thrace. All three—the father, the son, and the homonym—are paradigmatic warriors. Tydeus, who like Meleager murders his own relatives, also acquires a wife after a successful hunt for a boar.

Logically enough, Meleager is associated with military cults and rituals. In the great sanctuary of Athena Alea at Tegaea in Arcadia the teeth of the Calydonian boar were preserved, and on the pediment Meleager and other heroes of the hunt were represented.[13] By his name the son of Oeneus is linked to the type of the "black hunter," Melanion in Arcadian tradition and Melanthus in Attic tradition. The essential role of this black hunter was that of hero in the founding myth of Attic ephebia, which we now know, thanks to the work of Jeanmaire, P. Roussel, C. Pélékidis, and P. Vidal-Naquet, "was rooted in ancient practices of apprenticeship, in which young men learned their future role as citizens and fathers—in short, as members of the community."[14]

There can be no doubt that in Aetolia Meleager was a military hero. He was probably the founder of some archaic form of warfare, and his image was no doubt reinforced by stories such as those told about

VII
Heroes

TWENTY-THREE
Meleager the Solitary

Heracles or, as we shall see in a moment, Aristomenes. A distinction should be made between these hypothetical but probable tales and other stories that, though real, are artificially associated with this particular hero. For example, there are stories from outside Aetolia that in literary tradition link him to the Argonauts (heroes native to Thessaly) and Atalanta (an Arcadian and surely also a Boeotian hero but alien to the Aetolian cycle). These further stories extended the Homeric text and strengthened the image of Meleager as an initiatory hero. It is not difficult to imagine that his mythology was somewhat richer in his native country and that he was the hero of etiological myths of military institutions. Once again we can guess at the place of a local founding myth of institutional homosexuality.[15] The character of Meleager and the patterns of primitive pederasty in the myths are such that it seems reasonable to assume that Plutarch drew upon a very ancient Aetolian tradition. This is only a hypothesis; still, the attribution of homosexual practices to Meleager can only strengthen my thesis.

TWENTY-FOUR

Aristomenes the Creator

When Aristomenes was born, Messenia was already in the hands of the Spartans. His entire life is epitomized in the story of his military adventures against the invader. His martial nature is hardly surprising, for in conquered and exploited Messenia, a man could stand out only by doing battle with the conqueror. This constraint is such that the existence of military motifs in Aristomenes' life is not significant by itself. What is significant, however, is the symbolic importance that Aristomenes assumes in the eyes of the Messenians. He is a hero honored by a cult and war songs, and he was so much a type that his story is not so much a biography as a panoply of heroic imagery.

For Messenians Aristomenes was the son of Nicomedes. But a tradition, probably attested by Rhianus—who made inquiries in Messenia three centuries before Pausanias—makes him the son of Pyrrhus, son of Achilles, an invincible warrior and cult hero in Laconia, where he was held to be the inventor of the "pyrrhic," a martial dance.[1] He belonged to a group of youths from the Andania region who raised the flag of rebellion against the Messenian nobility. The sociological detail is worth noting. His first exploit was to cross, alone, the Taygetus mountains between Messenia and Laconia and to enter by night the sanctuary of Athena Chalcioecus at Sparta, on the Acropolis, where he hung a shield bearing the inscription "Aristomenes to the goddess, spoils of the Lacedaemonians."

Before this, according to Pausanias, there was a battle with the Derai in Messenia, in which mythology took precedence over history.

And the battle was an undecided one, but they say Aristomenes exhibited in it preterhuman bravery, so that they elected him king after the battle, for he was of the family of the Aeptyidae [the ancient Messenian royal dynasty], and though he was for refusing they also appointed him commander in chief.[2]

For Aristomenes was indeed a superman, an uncommon warrior. Here the tradition takes up an old Indo-European warrior theme. In another battle described by Pausanias—a veritable historical remake—the chronology is confused and heroes from different eras are pitted against each other. Aristomenes defeats three Lacedaemonian armies, one by one, and then "he dashed in amongst them with more formidable fury than one could have expected from one man."[3]

Aristomenes is a warrior belonging to the same family as the Irish Cuchulain, the Scandinavian *berserkir*, and the earliest Roman Horatius: a violent type subject to murderous rages that, according to certain very interesting texts, transform men into wild animals or deformed creatures.[4] The rationalist Pausanias does not credit these exploits; he omits details and indicates his doubts as to their reality. They are all the more significant as a result.

A savage and murderous warrior, a solitary figure who, like Sparta's young elite soldiers belonging to the Krupteia, the harshest and fiercest branch of the military, crosses a mountain by himself and strikes by night, Aristomenes is also the original organizer of the modern Messenian army. As we have just seen, he refuses kingship (thereby attesting his qualitative association with the warrior function) and accepts the apparently new post of general-in-chief with discretionary powers, analogous to the Latin *dictator*. In describing the battle action Pausanias tells us what Aristomenes did as a military leader.

> Eighty picked men of the Messenians about the same age as himself were in close attendance upon him, and each of them thought himself highly flattered to be posted near Aristomenes: and they were very keen at detecting in a glance one another's ideas and especially their leader's plans in the very germ.[5]

This organized military unit, in which the exploits of individuals are subordinate to the discipline of the group, is none other than the phalanx. Patterning the organization of his regiment after Spartan military institutions, Aristomenes created the Messenian phalanx. In fact, in his earlier description of the first Messenian War Pausanias describes a battle between the Messenians and the Spartans in which only the Spartans are organized as hoplites. Marcel Detienne has clearly brought out the contrasting types of behavior.

On the Messenian side each man rushed the enemy on his own, and disorder reigned supreme. To accomplish great personal deeds, to charge the enemy ranks like men possessed—such was the warrior ethos of the enemies of Sparta. By contrast, the Spartans, despite their love of combat, took great care to preserve the order of the ranks. They advanced shield to shield, pressed together in a compact group. No one responded to the provocations of the Messenians, and no one left his post to finish off a fleeing enemy. The conflict between Messenians and Spartans was a battle between archaic warriors (like those immortalized in the *Iliad*) and hoplites.[6]

Under Aristomenes the Messenians modernized. They adopted the techniques that had worked so well for their adversaries. Aristomenes was thus the patron of both types of warfare. He was a solitary hero who penetrated the heart of the enemy's city in an act of provocation, a wild warrior who pursued his vanquished adversaries like a madman, and also the organizer of Messenia's first hoplitic army. This is a contradiction only in appearance. In Attica the mythical model for the ephebe's behavior as hoplite was a solitary warrior of the type of the wild hunter of the *eskhatiai*, Melanthus. In Sparta the young men who took part in the Krupteia, a wild nocturnal, daring, and quasi-individualistic form of hunting and warfare, also served in the hoplitic elite corps, the Hippeis.[7] Aristomenes combines both types of martial behavior, in reality complementary, in his person.

A conquering hero in a war that lasted ten years, Aristomenes became the Messenians' model warrior, assuming traits that had once belonged to other heroes. In fact, it is certain that the Messenians and Laconians, closely related peoples, initially shared some of their military heroes. It makes sense that the Messenians eventually cast off those divine "protectors" who repeatedly favored their adversaries.

Following his exploits (not all of which need be recounted here[8]), Aristomenes became the hero of the Messenian resistance. Pausanias cites the refrain of a war song which he says was sung in Messenia in his own time: "To the mid plain and high mountain at Stenyclaros did Aristomenes pursue the Lacedaemonians."[9]

He was also honored, finally, by a heroic cult, which one suspects was military. After the victory of Epaminondas over the Spartans with the help of the Messenians, the Theban leader helped his allies found a new city, Messena.

And when all was in readiness the Arcadians furnished victims, and

Epaminondas and the Thebans sacrificed to Dionysus and Apollo Ismenius in the accustomed manner, and the Argives to Argive Hera and Nemean Zeus, and the Messenians to Zeus of Ithome and Castor and Pollux, and the priests of the Mysteries to the Great Goddesses and Caucon. And with one consent they invoked the heroes to come and dwell with them, especially Messene the daughter of Triopas, and Eurytus and Aphareus and his sons, and of the Heraclidae Cresphontes and Aepytus. But most unanimous of all was the cry for Aristomenes. And that day they devoted to sacrifices and prayers, and on the following days they raised the circuit of the walls, and began to build their houses and temples inside the walls.[10]

Aristomenes is alone; he has no appointed companion-in-arms or celebrated master. We do not know how pederasty figured in his story. His role as creator of the phalanx is worth noting. Composed of youths of his own age group, in one sense it transformed an *agele* into a military organization. In Crete and in nearby Laconia the promotion of an *agele* to a corps of warrior-citizens was accompanied in myth or ritual by homosexual practice.[11] It is quite possible that Aristomenes, paradigmatic hero of the Messenian military, was like Meleageros in Aetolia the patron of pederastic military rituals. One can even say that, knowing the symbolism of promotion in Sparta and the internal structure of the Theban phalanx,[12] Messenia *required* a mythical creator of military homosexuality. Aristomenes was tailor-made for the purpose.

TWENTY-FIVE

Actaeon of Corinth

The story of Actaeon (whom I shall call Actaeon of Corinth to distinguish him from the more famous Boeotian figure with the same name) is told by two anonymous authors, one of whom is the writer of the *Erōtikai Diēgesis*, "Love Stories," attributed by tradition to Plutarch but whose numerous errors and simplistic concerns betray an impostor, and the other, the scholiast of the *Argonautica* of Apollonius of Rhodes.

A man named Pheidon, who was striving to make himself ruler of the Peloponnesians and wished his own native city of Argos to be the leader of all the other states, plotted first against the Corinthians. He sent and asked of them the thousand young men who were the best in vigor and valor; and they sent the thousand, putting Dexander in command of them. Now Pheidon intended to make an onslaught upon these young men, that Corinth might be weakened and he might have the city in his power, for he considered that it would be the most advantageous bulwark of the whole Peloponnesus, and he confided this matter to some of his friends, among whom was Habron. Now he was a friend of Dexander and told him of the plot, so before the onslaught was made the thousand young men escaped safely to Corinth; but Pheidon tried to discover the betrayer of his plot and searched for him with great care. So Habron was frightened and fled to Corinth with his wife and his servants, settling in Melissus, a village in Corinthian territory. There he begot a son whom he called Melissus from the name of the place. This Melissus had a son named Actaeon, the handsomest and most modest youth of his age, who had many lovers, chief of whom was Archias, of the family of the Heracleidae, in wealth and general influence the most outstanding man in Corinth. Now when he could not gain the boy by persuasion, he determined to carry him off by force. So he got together a crowd of friends and servants, went as in a drunken frolic to the house of Melissus, and tried to take the boy away. But his father and his friends resisted, the neighbors also ran out and pulled against the assailants, and so Actaeon was pulled to pieces and killed; the assailants thereupon went away. But Melissus took his son's body and exhibited it in the market-place of the Corinthians, demanding the punishment of the men who had done the deed; but the Corinthians merely pitied him and did nothing further. So, being unsuccessful, he went away and waited for the Isthmian festival, when he went up upon the temple of Poseidon, shouted accusations against the Bacchiadae, and reminded the people of his father Habron's benefactions, whereupon, calling upon the gods to avenge him, he threw himself down from the rocks. Not long afterwards the city was afflicted by drought and pestilence, and when the Corinthians consulted the oracle concerning relief, the god replied that the wrath of Poseidon would not relax until they inflicted punishment for the death of Actaeon. Archias knew of this, for he was himself one of those sent to consult the oracle, and voluntarily refrained from returning to Corinth. Instead he sailed to Sicily and founded Syracuse. There he became the father of two daughters, Ortygia and Syracusa, and was treacherously murdered by Telephus, who had been his beloved and had sailed with him to Sicily in command of a ship.[1]

The scholium to the *Argonautica* gives the affair a slightly different historical setting, but the central theme remains the same.

"Bacchis was the son of Dionysus and lived in Corinth. His descendants, who were expelled from Corinth because of Actaeon's death, were of noble blood. Here is the reason for their expulsion. Melissus, benefactor of the Corinthians (he had saved them from defeat at the hands of Pheidon, king of Argos), had been rewarded by them. Now, one night, the Bacchiadae came to Actaeon's house intending to seize the boy. His parents protested and Actaeon was torn to pieces. Just before the Isthmian Games, Melissus leapt upon the altar and pronounced numerous curses against the Corinthians if they did not avenge the boy's death. After uttering these words he jumped into the pit that opened up at his feet. The Corinthians saw to it that the murder of Actaeon did not go unavenged, and on orders of the god expelled the Bacchiadae." So it was that Archias went off to found Syracuse and Chersicrates Corcyra.[2]

The Bacchiadae and the Heraclidae are of course identical. The first term denotes a group of aristocratic families with allegedly common Heraclean ancestors, which dominated Corinth in the archaic period.

Pheidon was a famous king of Argos, the man who brought that city to
its peak of political power. The affair took place, therefore, within the
very highest Peloponnesian aristocracy. This is all that can be concluded
from the historical information. The founding of Syracuse and Corcyra
took place in the second half of the eighth century, whereas the expulsion
of the Bacchiadae, according to the scholium a byproduct of the drama,
occurred a hundred years later. Pheidon's dates are similarly inaccurate.
According to ancient tradition he was both the victor over the Spartans at
Husiai, supposedly in 669–68, and the father of a man who is supposed
to have been in his thirties in 580.[3] Thus there are two chronologies of
Pheidon's life, one "early" and one "late," between which it is difficult to
choose.[4] Actually it scarcely matters which is correct. Although some
authors have viewed the story in question as a "historical novel" based on
actual events,[5] I tend to agree with Edouard Will when he argues that
"the story of Actaeon must be seen not as a tale resulting from the
accretion of details *subsequent* to some historical event but rather as the
projection onto a vaguely defined event of a myth or combination of
myths that existed *beforehand*."[6]

The most ancient version seems to link the affair to the expulsion of
the Bacchiadae. An elegy of Alexander of Aetolia, in a brief allusion that
suggests the popularity of the story, says that the son of Melissus was a
"cause of joy for Corinth and of mourning for the Bacchiadae." This
alludes to a version that can only be that of the scholiast of the
Argonautica.[7] But the events of the seventh century, like those of the
eighth, predate the first written historical chronicles of the Greeks. Like
the Lelantian and Messenian wars, they inaugurate history, and as such it
was easy, in keeping with their founding role, for purely mythological
material to be added to memories of them. The story of Actaeon is a pure
myth, and Edouard Will was right to have treated it as such. I shall here
follow the analysis that he gives in his remarkable book *Korinthiaka*, a
landmark in contemporary history of early antiquity.

Authors of the Roman era remarked (and modern authors have rightly
followed suit[8]) that the story of the Corinthian Actaeon is largely reminiscent of the story of the more overtly mythological hero of the same
name, who was torn to pieces by his dogs. According to the most
widespread version, Actaeon, son of Aristaeus and Autonoe, daughter of
Cadmus (founder and first king of Thebes), was so given to hunting and
so good at it, that one day he came upon the goddess Artemis bathing
naked in a well. To set eyes upon what the Greeks called the "shameful
parts" of the virgin goddess was evidently to impugn her chastity, and in

her wrath she transformed Actaeon from hunter into hunted, into a stag, following which her fifty dogs devoured the son of Aristaeus.[9]

This Actaeon is a Boeotian hero: he was honored by a cult at Orchomenus, and the well where he encountered Artemis was said to lie on the road between Plataea and Megara.[10] The Plataeans honored him as a founding hero[11] and grandson of Cadmus.

The central element common to the myths of both Actaeons is the hero's dismemberment—what was called, in Greek Ritual, (dia)sparagmos.[12] Hence the death of the Boeotian Actaeon can help to shed light on that of the Corinthian one.

Will points out another resemblance that parallels the previous one. The father of Actaeaon (the Corinthian Actaeon) was called Melissus, "the man of honey." The father of the other Actaeon, Aristaeus, a cultural hero, was the inventor of techniques of husbandry and hunting and above all of beekeeping.[13] With respect to both birth and death, the homology between the two Actaeons is therefore complete.

A further, sociological rather than mythological parallel can be seen between the adventure of Actaeon the son of Melissus and the Cretan pederastic ritual.[14] Henri Jeanmaire, for example, points out that pseudo-Plutarch's version depicts Archias surrounded by a kōmos, a group of joyful companions: "The abduction set two groups against each other in a battle that was generally a sham, one group consisting of the hero's friends, the other of the abductors' friends." The same social groups participated in the Cretan ritual, and their behavior was not very different. The erastēs—himself a member of the local aristocracy— announced to the young man's "friends" his intention to abduct him three or more days in advance. Immediately after the kidnapping, these "friends," in fact the members of the youth's agele, of his own age cohort and social class, pursue the erastēs and recapture the young man, but gently, "merely in conformity with the custom," writes Strabo. Then they return the youth to the erastēs, provided he offers the necessary moral and aristocratic guarantees. Their "show of resistance does not end till the youth is received into the Andreium to which the ravisher belongs."[15] It is only then that the "friends" of the erastēs are allowed to intervene. They do not take part in the abduction, the only major difference between the Cretan and the Corinthian adventure. The social context is the same, and the Cretan ritual includes the survival of a "custom" which can only have been a more serious type of struggle—a struggle of which Actaeon's story in fact gives us a glimpse. Bethe noted that the Cretan ritual allowed for the possibility of a refusal on the part of the erōmenos's "friends." Formalized and undramatic, the Cretan ritual nevertheless still evokes a practice whose form in primitive Corinth the myth in question enables us to make out.

Finally, the religious elements in Actaeon's story are rather interesting. In examining the text of the scholium to Apollonius, according to which Melissus "leapt upon the altar" and "jumped into the pit that opened up at his feet," Will makes an interesting comparison. Melissus's suicide apparently took place on the Isthmus of Corinth, since pseudo-Plutarch places it at the temple of Poseidon were the Isthmian Games were held. In this region there is known to have been a sanctuary in which an altar stood close to a pit, at least in early antiquity. This was called the Palaemonion, temple of Palaemon, a sea god linked to Poseidon. This pit was a *khasma gēs*, an "abyss in the earth," the site of Palaemon's tomb, where mysteries and *orgia* where celebrated. There are some specific similarities between Melissus and Palaemon: Both committed suicide by means of a leap, or *katapontismos*; furthermore, prior to his death and divinization, Palaemon had another name, Melicertes, the "honey eater" or "honey gatherer."[16] Finally, if Actaeon the Boeotian is the grandson of Cadmus, so is Melicertes. His father is Athamas, king of Orchomenus, and his mother is Ino, daughter of Cadmus.

It was for Melicertes, after his tragic death, that the Isthmian Games were instituted.[17] This takes us back to the context of initiatory myths and rituals. The myth of Ino and Melicertes seems to underlie an initiatory ritual,[18] and the fact that the ritual of the Palaemonion was nocturnal[19] is no objection to this interpretation, despite what Will says:[20] the death-divinization of Melicertes/Palaemon is reminiscent of the quite similar death-divinization of Glaucus and of Dionysus's dive into Hades, which were celebrated nearby, at Lerna, by nocturnal mysteries that were probably initiations.[21]

Furthermore, Poseidon, the avenger of Melissus and Actaeon, beneficiary of the Isthmian Games, was one of the gods who created initiatory homosexuality, in particular in the myth of Pelops. Related to this, in one version of the myth it was at the temple of Poseidon Isthmius that Oenomaus placed the finish line of his race with Pelops.[22] "On the other hand," writes Will, "when it comes to relating Melissus's leap to Actaeon's death, I confess that I am unable to propose an explanation."[23]

There is no insuperable problem, however. Recall the meaning of the death of Actaeon the hunter, son of Aristaeus. Pupil, like his father, of the Centaur Chiron, Actaeon did not participate in all areas of production. Aristaeus was the inventor of the pit (for trapping game) and the fish net as well as of beekeeping, husbandry, milk processing, and the techniques of vine growing. All that Actaeon remembered from his instruction was how to hunt. Cadmus, in Euripides' *Bacchae*, exhorts Pentheus to recognize the divinity of the god that he refuses to worship, Dionysus.

> "Do you know the sad fate of Actaeon, who while hunting one day in the plain was torn to pieces by ravenous hunting dogs he himself had trained, because he boasted of being a greater hunter than Artemis! Fear his fate!" [24]

Compare to this the song of the elders in the chorus of Aristophanes' *Lysistrata*, on the subject of one of Actaeon's simulacra.

> There is one story I want to tell you that I heard myself as a child. There was a young man named Melanion who fled to a desert in order to avoid marriage. He lived in the mountains and hunted hare with nets that he made himself. So great was his horror of women that he never returned home. [25]

Vidal-Naquet comments that such a hunter "appears to be an ephebe, but an ephebe who has failed, in a sense a Hippolytus. . . . [We have here] an aspect of the very common myth of the somber, solitary hunter, a misogynist or someone who attempts to take advantage of Artemis, which in either case is a violation of the rules of social behavior. This is a well-known type, that of the hunter Orion, none other than the inventor, according to Oppian, of nocturnal hunting." [26]

If Aristaeus is the model, moreover, then Orion is the counter-model, unable to behave correctly in society or to strike a proper relation to the world. [27]

By contrast, Aristaeus is the man of honey, and honey, produced by bees, was for the Greeks the ideally pure substance, reflecting the purity of the bee, the complete agriculturalist. Melissus, in another context, is also the man of honey. By refusing to kill Dexander, his father carried respect for the social conventions to an extreme of total honesty.

This positive model was, willingly or unwillingly, turned upside down by the sons. One Actaeon was torn to pieces by his dogs when he failed to confine hunting to what it should have been in the Greece of the city-states, namely, a form of recreation and a supplemental, probative means of procuring food. [28] The other died because of a human error, an overstatement, a violation of social rules on one side or the other. As the story of Melissus has come down to us, in the form of a pseudohistorical romance, the blame is laid squarely with the kidnappers, the abominable Bacchiadae, whose expulsion is heralded by the tragedy of Actaeon. In proof of immanent justice, Archias will in turn be killed by his erōmenos—who is also his pupil, to whom the command of a ship had been entrusted. What we suspect and know about homosexual rituals, primarily through comparison with the evidence for Crete, inclines us to a different judgment about the primitive form of the myth. The Bacchiadae were unacceptable to Melissus as erastai for his son precisely because their power and prestige were on the wane. In their days of glory, however, a society that presumably accepted the same criteria of selection that were used in Crete would surely have had no complaints as to the aristocratic and moral excellence of a young Bacchiad. In terms of the social underpinnings of the myth, therefore, Actaeon is culpable. He shuns the relationship with his erastēs, much as Hippolytus and Melanion shun women in the song from *Lysistrata*. He is torn apart by his friends—those of his own age cohort together with the somewhat older companions of the erastēs—much as Actaeon of Boeotia is devoured by his own dogs and Hippolytus is dragged over the rocks by his horses. His boundless pride turns against him and destroys him. Similarly, Narcissus, in the Thespian myth, dies because he has refused the love of Ameinias.[29]

The *katapontismos* possesses an entirely positive virtue: It confers immortality and signifies initiation. Melissus and Melicertes, leaping into a pit or into the sea, connote the proper functioning of social rules. The *(dia)sparagmos*, tearing apart, of Hippolytus and Actaeon denounces the violation of those rules.

Thus the myth of Actaeon is, in a negative sense, a *reductio ad absurdum*, the founding myth of a form of initiatory homosexuality. This is demonstrated by the whole mythic and religious context, which remains closely related to the still-living institution of fourth-century Crete. Corinth and Crete, both Dorian colonies, attest once more to the prehistoric and clearly Indo-European (rather than Minoan) origins of this institution.

TWENTY-SIX

Eurybatus and the Monster of Delphi

🔳

Probably in the second century A.D., an author of whom we know nothing but the name, Antoninus Liberalis (which is mentioned twice in his only surviving manuscript), composed in Greek prose a small corpus of *Metamorphoses*, taken from various authors of the Hellenistic and, in a few cases, earlier periods. In general, these stories belong in substance to the earliest Greek myths, but they have been rewritten in keeping with the literary tastes of the Hellenistic and Roman periods and, reworked and reinterpreted, have lost their primitive character. Still, it is easy to guess what the primitive versions of these myths must have been. I shall here study two of these stories. Others have already been examined. The first is a fragment of Delphic mythology.

VIII: Lamia or Sybaris. Nicander tells this story in book IV of his *Metamorphoses*.

Not far south of the foothills of Parnassus stands a mountain called Kirphis, hard by Krisa. On this mountain there is even today an immense cave in which an enormous monster used to live; it was called Lamia or Sybaris. This monster daily raided the fields and carried off men and beasts. The Delphians wondered if they would have to leave their land and asked the oracle to tell them where they ought to go. The god told them that they would be delivered from the scourge if instead of fleeing they agreed to expose, near the cave, a young man chosen from the families of the city. The Delphians did as the god asked. Lots were drawn and Alcyoneus, son of Diomus and Meganeira, was chosen. His father had no other child, and the child was handsome in character as well as physique. The priests crowned him and led him in a procession to the cave of Sybaris. Eurybatus, son of Euphemus, of the race of the river Axius, a valiant young man, had left the land of the Couretes on the instigation of the god and happened upon the troop that was taking the child away. Gripped by love for Alyconeus, he asked the Delphians the reason for this procession and rebelled at the idea of not being able to defend the young man with all his might and allowing him to die a lamentable death. He therefore snatched the wreaths from the head of Alcyoneus and, placing them on his own head, invited the priests to take him instead of the boy. When the priests took him to the cave, he ran in, snatched Sybaris from her lair, dragged her out into the open, and hurled her off the cliff. Sybaris fell near the foothills of Krisa and struck her head. She died of this wound and vanished. From the rock upon which she fell there sprang a well that the people of the country call Sybaris.[1]

Kirphis, a mountain situated not far from Parnassus, to the south, near Krisa but surely also near Delphi, can only be the range that separated Delphi from the gulf of Corinth, at the eastern end of which Krisa was in fact situated. This range faced Delphi across the Pleistus valley and was therefore a sort of opposite of Parnassus.[2] Eurybatus was a hero who stemmed from Ozolian Locris or western Locris, for an inscription reveals that Eurybatus's father was one "Euphamus," a demiurgic hero who stemmed from Ozolian Locris or western Locris, for an inscription reveals that Eurybatus's father was one "Euphemus," a demiurgic hero honored there by a cult,[3] and through this region flowed the Axius looking for a geographical interpretation of the expression "the land of the Couretes," even if the author, somewhat ignorant of Locrian cults and geography, was probably thinking of the Couretes of Aetolia. In fact, Eurybatus, a young warrior, is a Courete, an armed *kouros* in the prime of life.

The story, as I said, is a fragment of Delphic mythology. One can even say that it is a humanized, modifed version of other myths.

According to the Delphic "vulgate," known to us through the *Homeric Hymn to Apollo*, the prologue to the *Eumenides*, and a passage from *Iphigenia among the Taurians*, the "first prophet" at Delphi was the earth, Gaea. A monstrous beast symbolized her presence. According to Euripides "a great snake, spangled of back, bright of eye, coiled in the dark shadow of laurel leafage, a monster out of primeval earth, controlled the chthonic oracle."[4] The *Hymn* evokes "the well with the beautiful waves (Kastalia) where the lord, son of Zeus, killed with his powerful bow the female dragon—the enormous giant beast, the wild monster that did so much harm on earth to men and their fine-hoofed sheep; it was a bloody scourge."[5]

The Delphic founding myth was enacted every eight years in the festival of the Septerion or Stepterion.[6] For our purposes it is enough to

note that the hero of the ritual, a human representing Apollo, was a
kouros amphithalēs, that is, a young man whose father and mother were
still alive, that the serpent inhabited a hut representing the cave in
which, according to certain texts, the chthonian monster lived,[7] and that
the *kouros*, upon returning from an exile symbolizing Apollo's exile to
Thessaly, was crowned with laurel. Thus all the details in Antoninus
Liberalis's account have mythical and ritual counterparts, and that
account must therefore be seen as a plagiarism of the Delphic myth.
Indeed, Pausanias, in the first century, recorded at Delphi a tradition
according to which Lamia, daughter of Poseidon, was the mother of the
first Delphic Sibyl.[8] Given that Poseidon was the consort of Gaea in the
"pre-Apollonian" phase of the oracle,[9] it follows that Lamia, as the
female dragon, is a hypostasis of the earth, here in her function as
primordial priest. Similarly, the sacred spring, Kastalia, is another
manifestation of Gaea. In the geography of the Delphic sanctuary, the
chthonian deities are grouped together around the spring.[10]

The myth of Alcyoneus and Eurybatus is therefore a transposition of
the great Delphic myth. Eurybatus, the human equivalent of Apollo,
wearing a crown, kills a female dragon that has been terrorizing the
region of Delphi, and the vanished dragon gives birth to a spring. But,
geographically speaking, the theme has been shifted southward (to
Mount Kirphis, alter ego of Parnassus) and westward (to Krisa, Locris).
Why this transformation?

Apollo, the paradigmatic *kouros*, acts at Delphi as the model initiate.
His victory over the dragon is the probative act that, according to the
archaic sociological code, marked his transition from erōmenos to
erastēs. This is not made explicit in the myth, however. A powerful and
influential god,[11] Apollo has, in the vulgate, no erastēs. On the contrary,
he is the erastēs of numerous heroes. This trait cannot be transposed to a
mortal; in the mortal world every erastēs is a former erōmenos. This is
the truth that the story of Eurybatus restored through an obvious
plagiarism of the myth of reference.

The ancient conceptions that we see underlying the story were no
longer understood by Greeks of later periods, however. In Hellenic
culture the image of the erastēs as master and educator had given way to
another image, that of the erastēs as lover of a handsome adolescent.
Eurybatus's original motivation, which was surely to show Alcyoneus
what to do and encourage him to emulate his teacher, has disappeared,
replaced by motives of a purely psychological, erotic sort; Eurybatus acts
for love. Earlier, in discussing the Taifali, I mentioned the remarkable

story of Bödhvar Bjarki and Höttr. Here, too, a monster has been
wreaking havoc in the region inhabited by the heroes. He comes every
year during the annual festival, until Bödhvar kills him. Then he brings
the animal back to life and tells his protégé, Höttr, hitherto horribly
timid, to take a sword and "kill" the monster one more time. The young
man does so and acquires the courage to engage in combat with his
teacher and subsequently to take his place among the king's warriors.
This Scandinavian tale is quite close, in my view, to the Delphic
adventure. The man- and animal-eating monster in the latter turns out,
when Eurybatus goes to his cave, to be as passive as the Scandinavian
monster. Eurybatus runs toward him, grabs him, drags him out, hurls
him into the abyss. He is all façade. The trial is symbolic. It seems likely
that Alcyoneus will be as successful as Höttr. But the story ends
abruptly, with an explanation of place names.

   In the vulgate, Admetus is in no sense the erastēs of the god, and, at
Delphi, Apollo is both his own master and his own pupil. His exploit
brings together forms of behavior that the authentic initiation ritual
keeps separate. In this respect, one might say that Antoninus Liberalis's
story is an analysis whose purpose is to make the myth explicit so as to
enable mortals to pass the job of initiatory instruction from one to
another. Alcyoneus, the equivalent of the *kouros amphithalēs* of the
Stepterion, and Eurybatus, the slayer of the chthonian monster, are two
complementary hypostases of Apollo.

TWENTY-SEVEN
Cycnus of Aetolia
𖥔

Elsewhere Antoninus Liberalis tells the following story:

Apollo and Thyria, daughter of Amphinomos, had a child, Cycnus. He was handsome, but his character was crude and unpleasant. He exhibited an extraordinary passion for hunting and lived in the country midway between Pleuron and Calydon. Many loved him for his beauty. But Cycnus out of vanity granted none of them their wishes and quickly became an object of hatred for his other lovers, who abandoned him. Phylius was the only one to remain faithful to him. Yet Cycnus treated him, too, with extreme violence. At this time there appeared in Aetolia an enormous lion that preyed on men and flocks. Cycnus ordered Phylius to kill this beast without a weapon. Phylius promised to do it, and here is the stratagem he used to gain his end. Knowing when the lion would return, he filled his stomach with food and wine and, when the beast approached, vomited it all up. The hungry lion ate this food and was dazed by the wine. Then Phylius wrapped his garment around the lion's throat. He killed it, slung it over his shoulder, and took it to Cycnus, and this success brought him much renown. But Cycnus set him another trial even stranger than the first. Huge vultures had appeared in this land, that massacred many people. Cycnus ordered him to capture these birds alive by some ruse and to bring them back to him. Phylius was wondering how to carry out this order, when an eagle that had snatched a hare let it fall to earth half dead at the instigation of the gods before carrying it off to its aerie. Phylius tore it to pieces, smeared himself with its blood, and lay stretched out on the ground. Then the birds dived at him, thinking that he was dead, and Phylius grabbed two by the feet, captured them, and took them to Cycnus. And Cycnus then set him a third trial even more difficult than the other two: to capture a bull with his bare hands out of its herd and take it to Zeus's altar. At a loss, Phylius asked Heracles to help him. He was in the midst of praying to Heracles when two bulls appeared.

In rut over a cow, they knocked horns and finally both fell to earth. Phylius, seeing them prostrate, tied the legs of one and took it to the altar, but at Heracles' injunction . . . he refused to obey the young man's orders. A frightful thought took hold of Cycnus when he found himself spurned against his expectation. Demoralized, he jumped into a lake named Konope and disappeared. Seeing him die, his mother Thyria jumped into the lake after her son. And by the will of Apollo both became birds living in the lake. After their disappearance the lake changed its name and became the Lake of the Swans; many of these birds come there at plowing time. Near the lake is the tomb of Phylius.[1]

Ovid had earlier alluded briefly to this legend, with some modifications. Cycnus's mother is called Hyrie, which is surely the correct form of the name, since Stephen of Byzantium mentions an Aetolian city called Hyria.[2] Cycnus does not jump into the lake, which in this version does not yet exist, but rather leaps from a cliff and is changed into a swan during his fall. Finally, the lake is formed from the tears of Hyrie, who ultimately becomes identified with it.[3] On these three points Ovid is certainly closer to the original version, but out of confusion with other heroes named Cycnus he sets the scene in Thessaly, whereas Antoninus places it in Aetolia, which is confirmed, independently of his text, by the names Hyrie and Lake Konope (an ancient Aetolian city was named Konopos, literally, "place where mosquitoes are found"). Antoninus's geographical detail enables us to identify the lake as present-day Angelokastron, north of Pleuron. It is therefore likely that the reference to a tomb of Phylius is an authentic detail—and a relevant one, for it proves that the legend is original, not a copy of Heracles' legend, say, but a story rooted in the "sacred geography" of Aetolia.

Phylius differs from Heracles in one essential respect. Heracles is a hero of strength, while Phylius is a hero of ruse. Heracles faces the lion of Nemea in single combat and strangles it to death; Phylius kills a lion by cunning (ancient authors held that animals could not tolerate wine, and we are told of wild animals being captured after becoming drunk[4]). Phylius captures the vultures by feigning death, whereas Heracles downs the birds of Lake Stymphalus with arrows. Phylius is therefore not a doublet of Heracles. That he invokes Heracles is not surprising, since the Argive hero was the patron of athletes and a model for champions performing initiatory exploits. For it is nothing other than an initiation that is in question here; the threefold trial, each stage more difficult than the last, is a recurrent feature of Indo-European initiatory combat,[5] and the use of cunning in hunting is a constant feature of Greek education, even during the classical period, when the teaching of hoplitic combat to ephebes avoided feint and ruse, which were seen as secretive, individualistic, and unfair tactics.[6] Outside the Greek world, there was an exact equivalent for the bare-handed capture of animals such as lions, vultures, and bulls in the Taifale initiation, which required the novice to down a bear or capture a boar single-handed.

There is a further difference between Phylius and Heracles. Heracles, a common Indo-European type (in Greece, as I have pointed out, of Argive origin), performs his deeds alone, whereas Phylius acts out of love for a beautiful boy. In the text of Antoninus, Phylius obviously sets himself up as the child's educator, so that the trials that he faces do not relate to his own initiation and promotion to adult status (for otherwise, in the primitive conception that underlies the whole text without its author's knowledge, he could not have fallen in love with Cycnus). Rather, these trials are models, indicating what a docile erōmenos must do in ord·r to prove himself ready to assume the prestigious role of adult warrior. True, we are told that "as erastēs of Eurystheus, who orders him to perform his feats, Heracles seems to be the prototype for the character of Phylius."[7] Here we have a good example of the pitfalls inherent in a philological approach overly concerned with matters of chronology. To be sure, the Phylius legend, which is not attested until Ovid, in the Augustan period, comes after the Hellenistic interpretation of the Heraclean cycle, according to which the motivation for Heracles' labors was his love for Eurystheus. But as I pointed out a moment ago, the Phylius legend is original, in terms of both geography and narrative form; it has nothing to do with the Heraclean typology.

It is, moreover, entirely possible that the Phylius legend, of ancient Aetolian origin, was like so many other legends subjected to reinterpretation in the Hellenistic era, at which time a reference to pederasty may have been added. I doubt that this was the case, however. Though there certainly was reinterpretation of the legend, it had to do with the transformation of an institutional, pedagogical relationship into an affective, erotic relationship. In fact, the love between Heracles and Eurystheus is absurd, since both are the same age and one is a warrior, the other a king, while the (unrequited) love between Phylius and Cycnus makes good sense; Phylius is one of numerous erastai who court Cycnus, and he is a powerful hunter, a man in the prime of life. Cycnus is a *pais*—already grown, it seems, since he has a passion for hunting—

an adolescent, say. In plain words, Phylius is of an age to be an erastēs, and Cycnus is the normal age of an erōmenos. The pair differ in this respect from Heracles and Eurystheus and resemble, rather, Heracles and Iolaus, undeniably a couple of ancient date.

For further proof of the authenticity of the legend and of its independence of both Hellenistic literature and Heraclean models, consider the various mythological characters who bear the name Cycnus or Cygnus. He is an ancient pan-Hellenic hero like many others, including Heracles and Phorbas; like Phorbas, Cycnus gave rise to different personages in different regions of Greece. All are accursed warriors, *hubristes*—wild, impious men. One was invulnerable and fought Achilles (in the rationalized versions that have come down to us, because he came to the aid of the trojans; but he is an authentic Greek, not so much through his father Poseidon as through his mother, Calyce, daughter of the Thessalian Aeolus and ancestor of the first kings of Elis). The hero must have suffocated under this one until Poseidon transformed him into a swan (a trace, perhaps, of a homosexual myth).[8] "Another," more famous Cycnus, son of Ares, was a bloodthirsty brigand who preyed, depending on the version, on Macedonia around the river Echedorus, Thessaly around the city of Pagasae (near Iolcus), or farther south, near the sanctuary of Athena at Itonos. Like Phorbas, he attacked travelers on the road to Delphi. Apollo, insulted, induced Heracles to travel along the road that was obstructed by this savage warrior, and the two heroes clashed in a memorable battle. The author of *Heracles' Shield*, attributed to Hesiod, took this occasion to describe Heracles in arms and the marvelous motifs on his shield.[9] There is no doubt that Heracles' intervention is a later addition; none of the hero's exploits is situated in northern Greece.

Thus the Cycnus of Ovid and Antoninus Liberalis is related to a local Aetolian elaboration of a northern Greek myth. The conceptual homology is complete: If the Thessalian Cycnus is a *hubristēs*, a violator of the rules of society, the Aetolian Cycnus is an obsessive hunter, like Hippolytus and others. Just as Hippolytus shuns the heterosexual love that should normally accompany his accession to adulthood, Cycnus refuses to be an erōmenos, even though this is a necessary stage in socialization. Cycnus the Thessalian violates society's rules by killing pilgrims, a sacrilege against religion and humanity; Cycnus the Aetolian errs by devoting too much of his life to hunting and by failing in his relations with other people.

There is still another similarity between the fierce warrior of Pagasae and the child who sends his erastēs into daunting battle. No ancient

author alludes explicitly to a pederastic relationship between Cycnus and
another person, for such a relationship does not conform to the literary
image of a lonely and powerful warrior. However, in what must be
interpreted as a clue to another, lost literature, Theocritus, at the very
beginning of the Hellenistic period, raised the following question:
"Who would know of the Lycian princes, or Priam's long-haired children, or Cycnus, white-skinned as a woman, if poets hadn't sung the old
battles of heroes." [10]

Which Cycnus is Theocritus referring to? Is it Achilles' enemy,
celebrated in the *Cyprian Songs*? This is the opinion put forward by the
scholiast, and he may be right. Or is it the enemy of Heracles, immortalized in *Heracles' Shield*? No matter—this Cycnus, this formidable hero
able to hold his own with the greatest of Greek champions, was "white-
skinned as a woman." One could hardly allude more clearly to his youth
and potential status as an erōmenos.

The metamorphosis into a bird during the course of a fall is interpreted in several myths as a symbolic death representing an initiatory
transition. In Ovid's story does it stand for Cycnus's final acquisition of
civic status? For this to be so one has to assume the existence of an ancient
version of the legend in which the young man is less hostile to Phylius's
desire and, as in the case of Eurybatus and Alcyoneus, the heroic acts of
Phylius are followed by similar acts of Cycnus, meeting the challenge.
Such a version would conflict not only with the letter of the texts and
their underlying conceptions but also with the image of Cycnus
throughout Greece as a transgressor of the rules of society. The metamorphosis into a swan seems out of place in this context. In fact, once
initiatory symbolism ceased to be a living reality, the Greeks were quick
to see metamorphosis, as well as leaps from the heights into the sea, as a
form of punishment. In fact, there are several instances of hunters like
Hippolytus, hostile to love (and hence unduly devoted to hunting),
whose lives end in this manner. [11]

This makes the meaning of the story clear. The legend of Phylius and
Cycnus told young Aetolians both what they must not do (namely,
immerse themselves in an activity that was merely the symbol of a status
and disobey their teachers) and what they must do (hunt with cunning).
Because Cycnus disobeys, he disgusts his people's warriors—his potential erastai—and is condemned to vanish into nature. I suppose that the
uncontrollable tears of Hyrie/Thyria, the mother, which also condemned her to lose her identity in nature, to become confounded with
the waters of a lake, punished her unwarranted intimacy with an adoles-

cent who, having refused integration into the world of men, remained attached to society's feminine, maternal, and infantile values. Furthermore, the tomb of Phylius, the material proof of the tale, suggests its symbolic usefulness. We already know the uses to which similar tombs, of Iolaus and Diocles, were put. On the outskirts of Iolcus in Thessaly once stood the tomb of Cycnus, but Apollo caused it to be destroyed by the waters of the Anayros. Both may have been the scene of initiation rituals with a pederastic component.

TWENTY-EIGHT
Antheus
咼咼

The Greeks of Asia were familiar with a legendary character named Antheus, whose mythic function was simply to have been an erōmenos. Two texts, a millennium apart, mention him.

The first Antheus was a hero of the city of Assesos, in the Miletus region of Ionia. Alexander of Aetolia says that he was the son of a king and had been loved by Hermes. But Parthenius, who reports this fact in chapter 14 of his *Erōtika*, is more familiar with an entirely different story about this same Antheus. In this version he is a native of Halicarnassus in Doris who lived as a hostage at the court of the Milesian tyrant Phobius, whose wife, Cleoboea or Philaichme, fell in love with him. Since the rules of hospitality obliged him to respect Phobius, Antheus resisted Cleoboea's advances, and the tyrant's wife decided to avenge herself. She tossed a golden cup into a well and asked Antheus to go fetch it. While he was down in the well, she threw a heavy rock after him. Shortly thereafter she hanged herself out of remorse.

Twelve centuries after Parthenius, Tzetzes, in a scholium to Lycophron's *Alexandra*, speaks of another Antheus, a Trojan belonging to the family of the hero Antenor, who was loved by Paris and Deiphobus and whom Paris accidentally killed in the course of a game.[1]

In Greece Hermes was the protector of gymnasia; in Athens the festival of young boys, or *paides*, was known as the Hermaia. It is not surprising that homosexual loves were attributed to Hermes as they were to Apollo. The first Antheus, Antheus of Assesos, is fully characterized by his dual role as son and erōmenos, especially since his erastēs is the god Hermes. He is an adolescent whose myth is a paradigm for the youth of Assesos.

The second Antheus, removed from the Greek geographical context and incorporated into literature, conforms entirely to the model. Paris and Deiphobus are above all mature men, adults, the first being the abductor of a woman and the second being one of the most powerful

Trojan warriors. It is probably no accident that they are linked here, since they are none other than the two successive Trojan husbands of Helen.[2] Antheus has his place in their love lives when, still young, they lack access to reproductive, heterosexual love—before, that is, Paris's abduction of the wife of the king of Sparta (in keeping with Spartan marriage ritual) granted them such access. According to a tradition that is not uniquely Greek, the perfect erastēs is a young man, a recent initiate, who takes advantage of his newly acquired social status by treating younger boys as women. Marriage, a serious business, comes only later. In this context, the accidental death of Antheus has exactly the same place, and probably also the same significance, as that of Hyacinthus; in the course of a game, he is killed by his erastēs, and one suspects that in another version of the story it is after this murder that Paris leaves for Sparta. In other words, the death of Antheus signifies Antheus's promotion to the status previously occupied by Paris and the end of Paris's function as erastēs. The motif, though attested at a late date, is nonetheless ancient. Parthenius's Antheus also dies young, and though we do not know the fate of Alexander of Aetolia's Antheus, the beloved of Hermes, we do know that in several spots Hermes presided over *agōnes*, ephebic competitions similar to those involved in the Hyacinthia.[3]

Antheus has another trait in common with Hyacinthus: His name is linked to spring vegetation. There was a Dionysus Antheus at Patras, and Pausanias maintained that his name derived from an ancient city called Anthea.[4] But the existence of a Dionysus Antheus, "of the flowers," in Attica[5] suggest another etymology.[6] There is a connection between Dionysus Antheus and the hero of the same name, yet "another" Antheus, who appears in the *Dionysiaca* of Nonnus of Panopolis as companion of Dionysus. This Antheus is a native of Lyctus in Crete, and is killed by the Indian king Deriades.[7] Antheus bears the name of a flower, and this name is the title of a god of vegetation. Hence he belongs to the same family as Hyacinthus, Cyparissus, Narcissus, Carpus, etc., all heroes for whom the reference to the plant kingdom signifies initiatory death and resurrection. Antheus was certainly the mythical founder of initiatory homosexuality in Assesos. Then literature took hold of him, though without losing the authentic meaning of the story, as Tzetzes' note attests.

TWENTY-NINE
From Kainis to Kaineus
㘞

The analyses given here of Greek pederastic myths can help us to understand a famous legend that, strictly speaking, is not homosexual in its subject matter. I say this because it is all too homosexual in spirit. It is one of the most popular legends of all antiquity.[1] Here is the context: Peirithoos, king of the Lapithae, a people (mentioned several times already) who lived along the banks of the Peneus in northern Thessaly, is celebrating his marriage to Hippodamia, daughter of Adrastus, in the company of several heroes as well as some Centaurs, to whom he was related through his father. But when the wine takes effect, the Centaurs can no longer control what, at bottom, constitutes their true nature: They attempt to kidnap Hippodamia and other Lapith women. A fierce battle ensues, from which the Lapithae, aided (in derivative Attic versions) by Theseus, emerge victorious. One of the combatants, himself a Lapith, is called Kaineus. Apollodorus gives the gist of what we know about him. "Caeneus was formerly a woman, but after Poseidon had intercourse with her, she asked to become an invulnerable man; wherefore in the battle with the centaurs he was unconcerned about being wounded and killed many of the centaurs; but the rest of them surrounded him and by striking him with fir-trees buried him in the earth."

Both Georges Dumézil, in his *Problème des Centaures*, and Marie Delcourt, in her study of hermaphrodism, detected in this myth an evocation of a ritual in which men disguished themselves as women.[2] Dumézil, in comparing the Greek Centaurs with the Indian Grandharva, describes the hero Ila, who was condemned by a deity to change sex every month and thus was indirectly the cause of the transformation of his companions into female Centaurs, or Kimpurusi. Delcourt compares the story of Kaineus mainly with the Cretan myth of Phaestus's daughter, whose sex her mother, Galatea, had hidden from her father. At puberty she persuaded the goddess Leto to change her daughter into a man, Leucippus.[3] Both comparisons make sense in a broad context, but the reasons for transvestism differ considerably from case to case. The Cretan myth is the basis of the local marriage ritual, but there is no question of Kaineus's marrying. Ila changes sex periodically, thereby connoting the changing of time, the rhythm of the years and months. The metamorphosis of Kaineus is irreversible and intransitive (those authors who say that Kaineus regains his original sex when he dies are all Roman, of very late date—they have taken a common belief and incorporated it into the myth).[4]

What Kaineus signifies, connotes, and expresses in Greek mythology is neither marriage nor the change of seasons but war, pure and simple. Kaineus is the type of the warrior, the Lapith hero (the only authentic hero named in the tradition of the battle with the Centaurs), as invulnerable as Talos and Achilles. A parallel but different version of his story narrates his death as follows: A proud prince, he places his spear in the middle of the agora and demands of his subjects that they worship it as though it were a god. He himself honored only his spear, to the detriment of all other gods. Outraged, Zeus unleashes a horde of Centaurs against the *hubristés*.[5] In the *Iliad* the contingent of Lapithae was commanded, as was fitting, by "Polypoites, stubborn in battle, son of Peirithoos whose father was Zeus immortal." But "not by himself, for Leonteus was with him, scion of Ares, Leonteus, son of high-hearted Koronos the son of Kaineus."[6] The king is on the side of Zeus, the specialist warrior on the side of Ares—a pertinent opposition in remote Greek antiquity.

Thus Kaineus reminds us first of all of Achilles, another Thessalian. Also invulnerable, a model warrior, not known to have married during his life on earth, a hero with a celebrated spear,[7] Kaineus lived disguised as a girl in the women's quarters of King Lycomedes of Scyros. This confirms the initiatory interpretation of the myth of Kaineus's sex change.

Above all, the story reminds us of Pelops. In both myths, the erastēs is a god, Poseidon, and the erōmenos demands in return for his favors a gift that will enable him to reveal and realize his true nature. Pelops asks for a chariot that will gain him Oenomaus's daughter and kingdom. Kaineus wants the invulnerability of the invincible warrior. The parallel may extend still further, for there are obscure connections between the Thessalian marriage of Pierithoos and the Pisatan, Olympic marriage of Pelops. Both, in fact, marry a Hippodamia, "mistress of horses," whose name expresses what the husbands accomplish, for one is victor over the Man-Horses and the other over the king whose horses cannot be defeated by mortal or honest means. None of this is important for present purposes, however. In Thessaly we need only observe that if Kaineus was first Kainis, the reason is that his initiation as a warrior, in the arms of Poseidon, required it.

We have yet to examine a celebrated myth, probably the only myth that from very early times contained a reference to homosexuality not involving initiation. What, then, was going on? I shall discuss this question in the final chapter.

THIRTY

Achilles, Patroclus, and Homeric Love
🫧

That there was a sexual aspect to the friendship between Achilles and
Patroclus has been a commonplace since the fifth century B.C. The orator
Aschines, in his indictment of Timarchus, accused of debauchery,
looked for examples of honorable homosexuality in tradition and cited
the precedent of Achilles. Though Homer does not say so, it is obvious
that the hero loved Patroclus, for their relationship was based on affection (*eunoia*) to such a degree that it could only have been sentimental.
Moreover, Achilles, manifesting the naturally protective feelings of an
erastēs for his erōmenos, had promised Menoetius to bring his son home
alive.[1] In the *Symposium* Plato has Phaedrus argue that Achilles was the
erōmenos of Patroclus and that it was out of love that he came to his
rescue and avenged his death.[2] Xenophon, who plainly represents the
antipederastic current in Greek thought, argues in his *Symposium* against
these assertions.

> Moreover, Niceratus, Homer portrays Achilles so gloriously taking
> revenge for Patroclus' death not as his boyfriend but as his comrade.
> Orestes and Pylades, Theseus and Peirithoos, and many other excel-
> lent demigods are praised in song not because they slept together but
> because they had the greatest admirartion for each other and together
> performed fine deeds.[3]

Culminating this long tradition, Plutarch also numbered Achilles
among the heroes who practiced homosexuality.

On this score the ancients were divided, and so are modern scholars.[4]

That "Homer" says nothing about a sexual relationship between the
two heroes is obviously not proof that no such relationship existed,
Bethe's opinion to the contrary notwithstanding. It is true that epic
poetry, following the moral dictates of its tradition, eschews all mention
of homosexuality. As we saw earlier, the *Homeric Hymn to Aphrodite*,

composed shortly after the "Homeric" period, speaks of Ganymedes in such a way that, while nothing is said about sexuality per se, the text would make no sense if there were no physical relations between Zeus and the hero. It seems likely that the founders of the epic tradition shared, though not necessarily to the same degree, the doubts about homosexuality expressed much later, in the classical period, by Xenophon, and evident in the state of mind that led the Athenians to pass laws against pederasty.[5] While not ignorant of homosexual practices they chose to say nothing about them, judging them unworthy of appearing in poems whose purpose was to celebrate men's intellectual and physical prowess. To reiterate, it is likely that the myth of Ganymedes had a sexual component from the beginning. The poet left it up to his audience to understand his allusion.

One problem is revealed by the difference of opinion between Aschines, who believed that Achilles was the erastēs, and Plato, who thought that this role fell to Patroclus. To this Xenophon had a pertinent response: Greek homosexuality is fundamentally a *paiderastia*, a love of young boys. Hence such pairs from epic and myth as Achilles and Patroclus, Theseus and Peirithoos, Orestes and Pylades signify only virile friendships and not relationships between erastēs and erōmenos. If there is any possible doubt as to the identity of the erastēs, that is proof that the couple in question does not conform to the common image of homosexuality. A passage from the *Iliad* states that Patroclus is older than his friend.[6] Plato no doubt based his curious view of the matter on this passage. But it would have violated social norms for Patroclus to have been the erastēs. Achilles is clearly the dominant member of the couple, and nearly all authors other than Plato therefore make him the erastēs.

These observations accord well with the major thesis of this book. If, as abundant evidence seems to suggest, Greek pederasty derives from a pedagogical institution, then the relationship between Achilles and Patroclus, which is nothing but comradeship between warriors of the same generation, cannot also be sexual.

The Achilles-Patroclus relationship was apparently first interpreted as homosexual in the fifth century. Plato blames the playwright Aeschylus for making Achilles the lover of Patroclus. The bulk of Aeschylus's work is of course lost. It included a trilogy, *Myrmidones, Nereides,* and *Phryges,* together with a satyric drama, *The Redemption of Hector;* the first tragedy is presumably the source for the sexual interpretation so often alluded to by later authors. Two surviving fragments leave no room for doubt, and their crudity is shocking in Attic tragedy. The first, cited by Plutarch in his invaluable *Eróticos*, says: "You had no reverence for the holiness of thighs, ungrateful after all our frequent kisses."[7] The second speaks of *homilia*, "association" but also "coitus," "of your thighs."[8] These words are probably uttered by Achilles standing over the cadaver of Patroclus, whom he blames for not having remained alive at his side. Bodily contact is here evoked with a clarity not matched, it seems to me, before Solon, who celebrated the erastēs with these words: "So long as he loves boys in the lovely bloom of youth, / [Desiring] the sweetness of thighs and mouth."[9]

An author of the Homeric era might, I think, have seen a homosexual aspect of Achilles' life in another context, chiefly in connection with his education. In the *Iliad* one man has a (weak) authority over him: old Phoenix, whom Peleus has asked to accompany his son. But Phoenix is advanced in years, and Achilles himself is too old to be an erómenos. The Greek champion is no longer fifteen; he is a man still young but already an adult, at a peak of strength and swiftness. Achilles' real teachers are known only from post-Homeric texts, and they are noteworthy. One is the Centaur Chiron, in whose charge the young boy is placed to learn what every man must know. The other is the king of the Island of Scyros, Lycomedes, with whom the adolsecent is "hidden" in order that he may undergo the initiatory trials that will make him eligible for marriage and combat (interpreting the texts, of course, according to criteria no longer intrinsic to them). One would expect in both cases attestation of a homosexual aspect. This is not the case, and the only issue here is surely the way in which classical antiquity received the traditions.

Here, for example, is the account given by Apollodorus of Athens:

> When Thetis had got a babe by Peleus, she wished to make it immortal, and unknown to Peleus she used to hide it in the fire by night in order to destroy the mortal element which the child inherited from its father, but by day she anointed him with ambrosia. But Peleus watched her, and, seeing the child writhing on the fire, he cried out; and Thetis, thus prevented from accomplishing her purpose, forsook her infant son and departed to Nereids. Peleus brought the child to Chiron, who received him and fed him on the innards of lions and wild swine and the marrows of bears, and named him Achilles, because he had not put his lips to the breast;[10] but before that time his name was Ligyron.
>
> After that Peleus, with Jason and the Dioscuri, laid waste Iolcus;

and he slaughtered Astydamia, wife of Acastus, and, having divided her limb from limb, he led the army through her into the city.

When Achilles was nine years old, Calchas declared that Troy could not be taken without him; so Thetis, foreseeing that it was fated he should perish if he went to the war, disguised him in female garb and entrusted him as a maiden to Lycomedes. Bred at his court, Achilles had an intrigue with Deidamia, daughter of Lycomedes, and a son of Pyrrhus was born to him, who was afterwards called Neoptolemus. But the secret of Achilles was betrayed, and Odysseus, seeking him at the court of Lycomedes, discovered him by the blast of the trumpet. And in that way Achilles went to Troy.[11]

These childhoods of Achilles come in many variations, but the sense of all is the same. They yield an image of a typical *kouros* of archaic times, whose life consists of education and rites of passage. Among the latter, the disguise of the hero as a girl, which immediately precedes heterosexual union, paternity, and departure for war, is undeniably reminiscent of the homosexual initiation rituals of the Greeks. We saw this earlier in connection with Hymenaeus. Crete, the site of the pederastic ritual that formed the point of departure for this study, is the source of several tales of men being disguised as women and of clothing being exchanged between the sexes in connection with matrimonial rites and myths.[12] Here, surely, what prevents Lycomedes (whose name, based on the word for wolf, is typical of masters or heroes of Greek initiations[13]) from being, explicitly, the erastēs of Achilles is simply the form of the legend. Since the "feminine" phase of Achilles' life is interpreted as an attempt at camouflage, the internal economy of the legend required that the man in whose home this stratagem is adopted be ignorant of what is going on. Could a Greek of the classical era maintain that a prince of his country deliberately hid a young man in the women's quarters? Thus Lycomedes cannot have sexual relations with the adolescent, or, more generally, play the role of teacher and patron, because Achilles is still so feminine in appearance, and is taken to be a young girl.

One would also expect a sexual strain in the Centaur story. Note that the situation in which young Achilles finds himself, isolated in the mountains with Chiron, eating the entrails and marrow of wild animals, is reminiscent of the probative isolation of the young Cretan erōmenos with his erastēs. As Frazer remarks in his commentary on the passage from Apollodorus cited above, "the flesh and marrows of lions, wild boars, and bears were no doubt supposed to impart to the youthful hero who partook of them the strength and courage of these animals."[14]

According to Philostratus, Chiron fed Achilles honeycombs and fawn's marrow;[15] the *Etymologicum Magnum* speaks of buck's marrow.[16] The reference to bucks or fawns is a weak form (more realistic in historical Greece) compared with the stronger reference to lions, boars, and bears, which would have been plausible, however, in primitive Greece.[17] In other words, in the Achilles legend alone we have both types of hunting trials—bear and wild goats—that occur in the stories told by Strabo and Ammianus and cited at the beginning of this book.

Yet no text explores the institutional aspects of the situation, which involves the classical interpretation of the Centaurs. The Centaurs were forest and mountain creatures, qualitatively different from men (meaning Greek men of the city-state, "political animals," as Aristotle put it). Models of savagery, they were distinct from humans and gods, as well as from the animals, whose function it was to mediate between humans and gods, primarily through sacrifice. Because of their place in the order of things, the Centaurs were excluded from participation in a relationship as socialized, as human, as pederasty.[18] This conception of them occasionally led to their being accused of homosexuality. In Aristophanes' *The Clouds* the "son of Xenophantus," that is, the Athenian Hieronymus, is called a "madman," a "long hair," a "wild man," and compared to a Centaur. The scholiast explains that his madness was to fall passionately for young men and to spend his days pursuing them.[19] Similarly, Hesychius defines the word "Kentauros" as meaning "brute," "savage," "pederast," "ass."[20] We are a long way from Chiron and Achilles. These Centaurs define debauchery, and, as lovers of pleasure of all kinds, like the Satyrs, they prey on people of either sex, provided they are good-looking. Indeed, Chiron, along with Pholus, is the good Centaur, the friend of Heracles, the only Centaur whose reputation is free of the blemish of debauchery.

Apollodorus and other authors say that Achilles went to join Chiron in his tenth year. His stay with Lycomedes would last another ten years. Here, myth and literature make free with chronology. In the authentic ritual, time was measured in months, or at most in annual cycles. In any case, Achilles leaves his master prior to adolescence, that is, prior to the age at which young Greeks normally experienced passive homosexuality.

It is not impossible that a primitive version of the myth conformed more closely to the ancient initiatory practice. The Tehran cave graffiti that I mentioned earlier in discussing the Carnea combine well-known erotic inscriptions with the names of certain deities, who served in one way or another as patrons of probative, pedagogical, and initiatory rituals. Among them, the only "hero," apart from the Dioscuri, is Chiron.[21] There is no question that in Thera he presided over an educational program that included homosexual practices. Hence it is conceivable that in some lost myth Chiron had several relations—positive and honorable relations, to be sure—with his pupils.

The foregoing observations do not exhaust the subject of Homeric love. There may be something else to be learned from the relationship of Achilles and Patroclus in the *Iliad*.

In an article, W. M. Clarke took a fresh look at the whole question, basing his answers, not like Xenophon and myself on sociological probabilities, but on the Homeric text itself. He called attention to certain of the poet's descriptions of Achilles and his friend, and these are indeed interesting to consider.

In book XVI Achilles asks the gods to rid the world of all humanity except for Patroclus and himself. Aristarchus, the Alexandrian editor of the Homeric poems, rejected these lines, according to Scholium A because he regarded them as the interpolation of some rhapsodist who wanted to prove that the two heroes were lovers. The latest editors (Leaf, Mazon) do not reject the passage, because, as Wilamowitz pointed out long ago, it accords well with the context.[22] Clarke observes that the *Iliad* often suggests that the relationship between the sons of Peleus and Menoetius was so close that they appeared to be not two men but one, and Aristarchus evidently thought it unwise to eliminate all such allusions.[23]

In book XXIV Achilles mourns his friend. The Alexandrian editors, Aristarchus and Aristophanes of Byzantium, both rejected the passage. But the violence of Achilles' feelings is expressed in the final books of the poem in other ways, all of which suggest that the affection between the two heroes was extreme.[24] At the beginning of book XIX, Thetis finds her son "lying in the arms of Patroclus / crying shrill."[25] This, says Clarke, was absolutely unparalleled behavior toward a corpse.[26] He further notes that, apart from the couple Achilles/Patroclus, Homer uses sentimental words only in speaking of women.[27]

The ancients held that these texts alluded to pederasty. Clarke accepts this interpretation and adds a passage which, in his opinion, is more than an allusion, in which Thetis says to Achilles:

"My child, how long will you go on eating your heart out in sorrow and lamentation, and remember neither your food nor going

to bed? It is a good thing even to lie with a woman
in love. . . ."[28]

If the other passages signify a homosexual relationship, then this one
does in fact suggest Thetis's opposition not only to her son's exaggerated
despair but to his love. Clarke concludes that homoeroticism, if not
homosexuality, is patent in the *Iliad*, which lacks only the word and not
the thing itself. One may compare this to the discussions in the Platonic
dialogues, where physical love is not mentioned directly but everyone
knows that that is what is being talked about.[29]

I think that Clarke's moderate conclusion can be accepted as correct.
If, in fact, one rejects the interpretation of the last passage cited, which is
justified only to the extent one believes that the rest of the text conveys
an image of authentic homosexuality, it still reflects much more of an
emotional relationship between two men than many cultures, including
our own, will accept. Indeed, this man who cries for his friend, who
stretches out beside him and holds him in his arms, and who, at the
height of his rage, envisages a humanity reduced to just two persons—
this man is close, undeniably close, to his successors of the classical era,
to the best known Greeks of the fifth and fourth centuries, for whom
friendship between men occasions greater, more authentic, more intense
emotions than affection between a man and a woman. In addition to
Plato, in whose work the theme recurs frequently, listen to Protogenes,
one of the speakers in Plutarch's *Erōticos*, a thousand years after Homer.

If, however, we ought to give the name of love at all to this passion,
then it is an effeminate and bastard love, that exercises itself in the
women's quarters as bastards do in the gymnasium of Cynosarges,[30] or
rather, just as they say there is a genuine mountain eagle, which
Homer called "black, and a bird of prey," while there are other kinds
of spurious eagles, which catch fish and lazy birds in marshes, and
often in want of food emit a hungry wail: so too there is a single
genuine love—the love of boys.[31]

Along the way, authors of the early fourth century extolled the merits
of an army made up of couples of erastai and erōmenoi.[32] Thus there is
continuity from Homer up to the late Hellenistic period, and one can
only wonder how Bethe and others, ignoring the conventions of a literary
genre, could have posited a radical break between the earliest Greek

poets, still free of "Dorian" influence with its pederastic components, and their successors. The emphasis on virile friendship leads, similarly, to initiatory homosexuality and, between men of the same age cohort, to intimacy of the sort exemplified by Achilles and Patroclus. That is why the oldest Greek literary text provides an example of both the former (if that is the correct interpretation of the Ganymedes myth) and the latter.

The textual evidence does not permit us to say more; to do so in the absence of adequate proof would be to extrapolate from the sources.

Yet it is worth noting that such an extrapolation would solve many problems. Assuming that a society in which both pedagogical pederasty and homoerotic friendship were practiced must have seen the one influence the other in such a way that friendship would have become sexualized (independent of the fact that the friendship between Achilles and Patroclus was in fact sexualized in the mind of the poet), and given, further, that such an influence was probable since the Homeric milieu had to be one of the most advanced in Greece, the reasons for the ideological rejection of homosexuality in the oldest poems become clear. For it is true that, no matter how much we suspect pederasty in the subtext of these poems, their authors refused to speak of it directly, a taboo that is easier to understand if we assume that some men, still few in number, disapproved of a practice they regarded as debauched even though it was part of a widespread and prominent institution. This hypothesis is supported by the fact that we find, in the early seventh century on one of the Ionian islands, Archilochus of Paros heaping sarcasms on a "shameless invert."[33] In fact, what the literary sources reveal is not an emergent new phenomenon but the end of a period of discreet silence (the ninth and eighth centuries B.C.—Homer and Hesiod), in circumstances that imply that homosexuality was an ancient practice. Echoing the sentiments of the Ionian Archilochus is his contemporary Tyrtaeus, a Spartan, who praises the beauty of a young man "lovely (*eratēs*) in the eyes of men, desirable (*eratos*) to women."[34] In the second half of the century, the *Hymn to Aphrodite* alludes implicitly but unmistakably to homosexuality. At the beginning of the sixth century homosexuality, plainly pedagogical in function, became a common subject of literature in the poems of Sappho and Alcaeus at Lesbos, Alcman at Sparta, Solon at Athens, and later Theognis at Megara and Anacreon at Teos.[35] It is as if initiatory homosexuality exceeded its institutional boundaries even before Homer, ultimately yielding practices similar to those we know existed in classical Athens. Not until the seventh or six centuries were authors able to overcome their initial inhibitions and to speak both of traditional homosexuality, pedagogical in its purpose, and of the other kind of homosexuality, which was in fact becoming increasingly common. All of these matters are worthy of further attention, and I plan to devote another book to them.

Conclusions

The foregoing review of myths is nearly exhaustive. I have, however, omitted various myths whose treatment of homosexuality is obviously recent and artificial. For the sake of completeness and to avoid misunderstanding, here is a brief review.

Athenaeus reports the affirmation by Licymnios of Chios, who flourished around 420 B.C., that Hypnos, "sleep," was in love with Endymion.[1] This is an obvious metaphor, a purely literary invention, reflecting the well-known myth according to which Endymion fell into an eternal sleep atop Mount Latmus.[2] Nothing here is useful for the purpose of mythological research.

Athenaeus also mentions the love of Bacchus for Adonis.[3] Regardless of when this tradition originated, Adonis, a Phoenician god, does not belong to the fund of Greek religious sources. The fact that he has been linked, for whatever reason, to Bacchus/Dionysus has nothing to do with the mythical origins of Greek homosexuality.

Phanocles, a writer of elegies of the third century B.C., says that Orpheus loved the Boread Kalais.[4] So far as I know, there is no ancient link between these two characters. The isolation of Kalais, who is arbitrarily separated from his brother Zetes, can only be a literary invention. It is only because both are Argonauts and native heroes of northern Thrace that the connection seemed justified.

In the third century A.D. Philostratus alluded to the love of Achilles for another hero of the *Iliad*, Antilochus, son of Nestor.[5] No tradition, Homeric or otherwise, corroborates this notion. In fact, in the *Iliad* Antilochus is an accomplished warrior of the same generation as Achilles. He is too old to be an erōmenos. But an author of the third century cannot be expected to have known this.

In Alexandrian bucolic poetry it was often assumed that the god Pan was in love with the shepherd Daphnis. No wonder! Daphnis is a literary creation of the time, the model shepherd of a mythical countryside; Pan, god of the mountains where Daphnis grazes his flocks, is his sworn protector.[6]

In the fifth century, at the end of antiquity, in the last Greek epic, Nonnus recounts the loves of Calamus, "reed," and Carpos, "fruit," and, in the same vein, the love of Dionysus for Ampelos, "vine"![7]

Instances of legendary homosexuality are especially abundant in Ptolemy Chennos, who was cited earlier. We find an interminable series of erōmenoi of Heracles, a love of Zeus for Priam, king of Troy (to whom the god gave, according to Ptolemy, a golden vine;[8] obviously, this "tradition" is the product of a twofold confusion, for prior tradition has this gift going to Tros, Priam's ancestor,[9] not to pay Tros for sexual services but to compensate him for the abduction of his son, Ganymedes). Ptolemy Khennos also reports another love of Zeus for a hero named Euphorion known only to Ptolemy,[10] the love of the (Thessalian) Centaur Chiron for the young (Boeotian) god Dionysus,[11] and finally the love of Hermes for Polydeuces, brother of Castor.[12] None of this is ancient. Yet these pseudomythological love affairs take place in an initiatory setting. Pausanias, in his description of Laconia, explains that the Dioscuri, born at Pephnos on the west coast of the province, were carried by Hermes to Pellana, where they received their education.[13] Given the role of pederasty in Spartan civic training, it is possible that the idea of sexual relations between Hermes and the Dioscuri is ancient—but in that case, why separate Polydeuces from his brother? So sentimental an interpretation of the myth must be of late date. Of Chiron Ptolemy says that he taught Dionysus the sacred dance and Bacchic rites and initiated him into the mysteries. Whatever its age, this conception of the love between the two conforms to ancient patterns. Finally, the story of Euphorion also combines archaic features with late sentimental treatments. The son of Achilles and Helen (married, after their death, in the Isles of the Blessed) and equipped with wings, Euphorion tries to escape from Zeus, who has fallen in love with him. But the god strikes him down on the island of Melos with a thunderbolt. The nymphs of the island bury him, and Zeus, outraged, turns them into frogs. Recall that in Crete, on the coins of Phaestus, Talos is represented as a young man with wings, running with his dogs. Melos is not far from Crete, also a Dorian island. Helen, moreover, was honored by a cult on another Dorian island, Rhodes,[14] as well as in Sparta,[15] of which Melos was a colony, and where Achilles was also worshiped.[16] In short, the death of Euphorion may be the Melian equivalent of the death of Hyacinthus or Talos. Would only that there were evidence for this in an author more reliable than Ptolemy Khennos.

Table I summarizes the detailed discussions of the foregoing chapters. The results are clear: Whenever a myth is ancient or there are good reasons for assuming that it is, it always connotes an initiation. The power of the model even determines the structure of more recent myths; this supports rather than weakens my argument. It is not until the end of the classical period, and even more in Hellenistic times, when the number of stories mentioning pederasty was on the rise, that we find myths using pederasty apart from any initiatory context.

To be sure, whenever the inhabitants of a region of Greece named a founder of homosexuality, they placed him in the remote past, in the "Heroic Age" of mythical, or semilegendary, Greek prehistory. In itself this proves nothing. But it is worth noting that if by chance the people of the region considered the local founder of pederasty to be a fully human historical figure, closer to them in time than the heroes who predated the Trojan War, he is always a warrior from the very earliest historical times, from that obscure period when oral tradition is still the only witness to events. The Lelantine War is surely a historical fact, but did Cleomachus really exist? Did the Chalcidians really need someone to show them a practice that they previously ignored or abhorred, when the spot where Ganymedes was abducted by Zeus was located within their borders, and when this abduction (given the parallel between Ganymedes and the Couretes) took place in circumstances suggesting that this location may have been chosen in remotest antiquity? Recall that the Athenian verbs for "to practice pederasty" included *lakōnizein, khalkidizein, khiazein,* and *siphniazein,* all derived from place names, and that the expression "in the Cretan way" was common in Athens, as if the vice were peculiar to the people of Lacedaemonia, Chalcis, Chios, Siphnos, or Crete and had been introduced into Athens by some unfortunate contagion. In fact, of course, Athens was one of the centers of Greek pederasty from its earliest days, since the subject is prominent in the poetry and laws of Solon.[17] In creating and using such expressions the Athenians were behaving no differently from the French and English, who use the expressions "French leather" and *"capote anglaise"* to describe the same object (a condom), which was invented, incidentally, by a Venetian physician during the Renaissance. Similarly, by projection, Cleomachus became a Thessalian.

TABLE I

ERASTĒS	ERŌMENOS	PAGES	VERY OLD MYTH	INITIATORY	FOUNDING MYTH FOR	REMARKS
Poseidon	Pelops	59–70	+	+	Pisatis	
Laius	Chrysippus	67–70	+	+	Thebes	
Apollo	Hyacinthus	81–93	+	+	Sparta	
Zephyrus	"	81	?	?		
Thamyris	"	82	?	+?	Thessaly?	
Apollo	Cyparissus	82, 96, 100	+	+	Chios & Orchomenus	
Ameinias	Narcissus	82–83	+	+	Thespiai	inv.
Calamus	Carpus	85, 260	–	–		at Chios inv.
Apollo	Admetus	102–108	+	+	Delphi	
Apollo	Hymenaeus	108–112	?	+	Thessaly?	
Thamyris	"	109	?	+	" ?	
Hesperus	"	109	?	?		
Argynnus	"	109	?	+	Boeotia? (or Dionysus)	
Agamemnon	Argynnus/Argennos	109	?	+	Boeotia?	
Apollo	Carnos/Carneus	114–120	+	+	Sicyon	
Apollo	Branchus	113–114	+	+	Didyma (whence Miletus)	
Apollo	Helenus	114	–	+		

Apollo	Leucatas	121–122	–?	–?	Leucade?	str.
Apollo	Phorbas	125–129	+?	+?	Orchomenos	str., inv.?
Apollo	Hippolytus	131–135	+?	+	Troezen	
Heracles	Iolaus	143–152	+	+	Thebes, Thespiae, Agyrion	
Heracles	Admetus	153	–	–		
Eurystheus	Heracles	154	–	–		
Heracles	Hylas	155–162	–	+	Chios	str.
Polyphemus	Hylas	157, 160–162	–	+	Chios	str.
Heracles	Euphemus	162	–	–		
Heracles	Elacatas	163–165	+	+	Sparta	
Heracles	Abderus	164–165	–?	+	Abderus	
Heracles	Philoctetes	165	?	+	Thessaly?	str.?
Heracles	Nestor	166	–	–		str.
Heracles	Iphitus	"	–	+?		
Heracles	Nireus	"	–	+?	Syme?	str.?
Heracles	Adonis	"	–	–		str.?
Heracles	Jason	"	–	–		
Heracles	Corythus	"	?	+?	?	str.?
Heracles	Stichius	"	?	–	Aetolia	str.?
Heracles	Phrix/Trinx	"	?	?,?	?	str.?
Diocles	Philolaus	168	+	?	Thebes?	str. s.d.
Cleomachus	x	168–169	+	?	Chalcis	
Anton	Philistus	169	?	+		
Timagoras	Meles	176	+?	?	Athens	

(continued)

TABLE I (continued)

ERASTĒS	ERŌMENOS	PAGES	VERY OLD MYTH	INITIATORY	FOUNDING MYTH FOR	REMARKS
Leucocomas	Promachus	29, 176	+ ?	+	Leben/Cnossus	
Cratinus	Aristodemos	176	+ ?	?		(Athens)
Polymnus/ Prosymnus	Dionysus	181, 187	+	+	Lerna, Argos	
Nereus	Glaucus	185, 188, 189	?	+ ?	Delos?	
Glaucus	Melicertes	185	?	+	Corinth?	
Minos	Miletus/ Atymnios	197–198	−	+ ?	Miletus	str.
Sarpedon Rhadamanthus						
Minos	Theseus	198–199	+ ?	+	Athens?	
Rhadamanthus	Talos	200–203	+ ?	+ ?	Crete	
Zeus	Ganymedes	205–213	+	+	Crete, Chalcis	
Minos/ Tantalus		209	?	?		
Meleager	x	217–223	+ ?	+ ?	Aetolia	
Aristomenes	x	224–227	−	+	Messenia	str.

Archias	Actaeon	228–234	+	+	Corinth	inv.
Eurybatus	Alcyoneus	235–238	+	+	Delphi	
Phylius	Cycnus	239–244	+	+	Aetolia	inv.
Hermes/Paris/ Deiphobus	Antheus	245–246	+	+	Assessos	
Achilles	Patroclus	250–258	?	+		
Orpheus	Calais	259	–	–		
Hypnos	Endymion	259	–	–		
Dionysus	Adonis	259	–	–		
Achilles	Antilochus	259	–	–		
Zeus	Euphorion	260	+?	+	Melos?	
Zeus	Priam	260	–	–		
Chiron	Dionysus	260	–	+		
Pan	Daphnis	259–260	–	+		
Dionysus	Ampelos	260	–	–		
(Poseidon)	(Kainis/ Kaineus)	247–249	+	+	northern Thessaly	

Notes to table:

+ = yes; – = no; x = anonymous or unknown; str. = secondary structuration on initiatory model; inv. = characters or facts inverted relative to a discernible primary version.

In many cases mythological analysis, occasionally with the help of archeology, can supply an approximate date for the elaboration of a myth, and generally that date lies in the farthest reaches of the accessible Greek past. Hyacinthus was the hero of Amyclae. His cult there dates from Mycenaean IIIc, the twelfth century B.C.[18] But it has often been noted that the tomb of Vapheio, which despite ancient pillaging is one of the most beautiful and richest of the Mycenaean world, was associated with Amyclae, and the objects that it contained suggest a local plant cult,[19] in other words, a Minoan type of cult, the Minoans having made abundant use of plant symbols to encode their religious and mythological concepts. It dates from the fifteenth century.[20] Moreover, the onomastic series Hyacinthus–Narcissus–Cyparissus points to a pre-Greek linguistic stratum, as we saw earlier. In this case the chronology and origins are particularly obscure, but we are surely talking about early Greek prehistory, for the adoption of these heroes by the Hellenes in Laconia, eastern Boeotia, and (before Chios) western Boeotia must have occurred as Greek culture itself was being formed.

The Pelopion, at Olympia, dates from the eleventh century B.C. But the cults of Olympia are certainly older. And even earlier, the mythology that relates the Tantalids and the kings of Thebes, the masters of Olympia and the eastern Boeotians, belongs to a tradition whose origin is connected with the formation of the Mycenaean Pisatid on the lower Alpheus. This, as I have tried to show, involved the settlement, probably on a large scale, of Boeotians in the northwestern Peloponnesus. First evident from mythological and hydronymic comparisons, this is supported by two items of historical evidence, one, from the late twelfth century, preserved in the archives of Pylos in Messenia, the other, from the early fourteenth century, preserved in an impressive Egyptian document. Thus we must go back to the fifteenth century or even to the first Mycenaean communities of the sixteenth century.

In Boeotia and roundabout, the dispersion of the several Diocles, together with the fact that one of them is Megarian, even though the mythology of Megara links its heroes (including Alcathous, founder of the Diocleia) to Thebes and Onchestus, suggests a protohistorical period in which the geography of central Greece was quite different from what it was in historical times. The power of Thebes then extended as far as Megara, Eleusis, and perhaps Athens on the east, Euboea (partially included) on the north, and Onchestus on the west. This could have occurred only at a time when Athens was still a city of secondary importance and before Megara became the outpost of the Peloponnesian Dorians to the north, that is, prior to the twelfth century B.C. One can say even more: the tablets of Thebes (probably from the second half of the fourteenth century[21]) mention the temple of the Potnia at Amarynthus, meaning Artemis Amarynthus in southern Eubeoa.[22] This dates the political apogee of Mycenaean Thebes.

At an unknown date the Euboeans brought to Crete the Couretes and with them, probably as one of them, Ganymedes. The date of the transfer is unknown, but it can only have been prior to the Dorian occupation of Crete; the Couretes were too important there, and too widespread, to have been introduced in historical times. It is not unreasonable to assume that Euboeans participated in the Mycenaean Hellenization of Crete.[23] But that is not all. The character Cleomachus seems to be a fairly recent onomastic innovation, subsequent, in any case, to the Mycenaean period. Why invent him when the place known as the Harpagion, where Zeus was supposed to have seized Ganymedes, was still being pointed out in Chalcis in historical times? The resemblance between the suspected ritual surrounding the tomb of Cleomachus and the attested rituals surrounding the tombs of Iolaus at Thebes and Diocles at Megara served as the grounds for the following simple and consistent hypothesis: that it was Boeotians who established this ritual in Chalcis during the time when they ruled the city, that is, during the Mycenaean period. Later, deliberately throwing off the Theban influence, the Chalcidians abandoned the legendary founder imposed on them by their conquerors and were therefore obliged, since the ritual remained and the place continued to be sacred, to invent a new founder. This hypothesis has two consequences for the chronology: For Thebes it follows that the rituals of the Diocles–Iolaus–Cleomachus group already existed by the fourteenth century, the latest date at which the Thebans could have taken the myth and ritual, to Chalcis; on the Chalcidian side, it was not in the fourteenth century that Ganymedes was transported to Crete, for the local founder at that time was a Boeotian hero (Iolaus?[24]), nor was it afterward, for this Boeotian was succeeded by Cleomachus. Ganymedes and the Couretes were therefore brought to Crete by the first Mycenaean settlers on the island (perhaps the second half of the fifteenth century).

I further pointed out the importance of homosexual myths associated with Orchomenus in western Boeotia, with the lands of the Lapithae in northern Thessaly, and with Iolcus in southern Thessaly. There is no inscription that would confirm a Mycenaean chronology, but archeology reveals a similar situation. These three regions were heavily populated, very important in the Mycenaean period, and unimportant thereafter (except for the area around Iolcus in the Hellenistic period).[25]

I shall omit a similar summary of results concerning the pedagogical aspects of homosexual behavior. On every page of this book it has been clear that erōmenoi are pupils, disciples, apprentices. The erastai are their masters, teachers, and models. Whenever the myths are explicit, we find that the master's social rank is as eminent as that of his pupil. Frequently the master concluded a sojourn in the bush with a gift: a chariot, invulnerability (better than the armor given to the Cretan page), or prophetic knowledge. The symbolism of initiation is omnipresent. The disciple, the beloved, dies, only to be reborn, explicitly or otherwise, or he performs an exploit that proves his prowess. He then accedes to the status of adult man. He becomes a trained warrior or a king, he marries, and he excels in those areas where his erastēs was master. Philoctetes is an archer, Pelops wins the chariot race that ends at the altar of Poseidon Hippius, Hyacinthus ascends to heaven.

These traditions are manifestly ancient, as are their heroes, in many cases heroes solely of these initiatory myths. It is interesting to note how many portraits of asocial youths, hubristic hunters scornful of women, were composed from the material of pederastic myths: Narcissus, Actaeon, and Hippolytus were all erōmenoi or former erōmenoi. It is probable that this type of character dates back to the first centuries of the first millennium B.C., the period when the city-state (*polis*), with its own system of values hostile to aristocratic individualism, was first established. Thus there may also have been a time when Actaeon and Narcissus were good students, respectful of their teachers; but that was the second millennium B.C.

I have, I hope, drawn from mythology all that it has to give on this subject. Cretan and Taifali values were used throughout to interpret the true meaning of the genuinely archaic myths. Other information, from Greece itself, has been used to confirm these interpretations. Other Indo-European peoples contributed their stones to the reconstruction of a vanished social practice, with the Cretan and Taifale evidence serving as pillars upholding the entire edifice. I hope to devote another book to this rich fund of materials.

In the mean time, the results obtained thus far confirm the hypothesis I proposed in Part 1: that Greek pederasty, far from being a sociological or psychological "accident" of limited scope in space and time, in fact stemmed from the earliest imaginable Greek past. It was not a monstrous innovation but a mere generalization of a practice institutionalized among the Greeks and other Indo-European peoples. A sexual morality different from our own, it was based on a powerful tradition representing one of humanity's fundamental sexual options.

NOTES

Where no title or an abbreviated title is given, refer to the bibliography or either of the two lists of abbreviated authors and titles (one for classical works and the other for journals and reference works).

INTRODUCTION

1. See, for example, for Greece, the works by Jane Harrison, H. Jeanmaire, A. Brelich, C. Pélékidis, and P. Vidal-Naquet cited in the bibliography; for the Germans, the works by Lily Weiser, O. Höfler, and L. Cahen.
2. See, for example, Georges Dumézil, *H.M.G.*, and Mircea Eliade, *Initiation*.
3. Sigmund Freud, *Trois essais*, sections 1.7, 2.5, 3.5, etc., concerning the "polymorphous perversity" of infantile sexuality.
4. Such a restrictive definition of "normality" is a typical feature of racism. In this respect there is a battle to be fought, following the lead of Kate Millett, for example, against the division of the population into a "heterosexual majority" and a "homosexual minority." This can be done by criticizing the notions that underlie such a distinction.
5. Cf. the works of G. Dumézil, E. Benveniste, and M. Gimbutas cited in the bibliography.

CHAPTER ONE

1. The manuscript is missing a line at this point, which "may have indicated the occasion for the abduction or the lover's *andreia* membership, for one does not guess immediately that the trial to which he is about to subject himself is intended solely to win approval of his erōmenos by his peers" (Lasserre, p. 103, n. 1).
2. Aristotle, *Pol.*, II.9.7 (1269b 26–31).
3. Diodorus V.32.7; Strabo IV.4.6 (199); Athenaeus XIII.603a.
4. Bouché-Leclercq, p. 340 n.
5. Cf. Dumézil, *H.M.G.*, pp. 130–32.
6. Dover, p. 16.
7. Cf. Buffière, pp. 318–19, 611–13.

8. Plutarch, *Life of Lycurgus*, XV.4.
9. Cf. Jeanmaire, *C.C.*; Pélékidis; Brelich, *P.P.*
10. Cf. Tacitus, *Germania*, XXVIII and XXX.
11. Cf. Dumézil, *Dieux des Germains*, pp. 111–12; *H.M.G.*, pp. 100–101.
12. In Chapter 2.
13. For the meaning of this sacrifice, see the section "Three Gifts" in Chapter 2. On the symbolism of hunting in ancient Greece, see Vidal-Naquet, "Chasse et sacrifice"; Schnapp; Brelich, *P.P.*, p. 77.
14. Cf. e.g. K. Meuli, "Ein altpersischer Kriegsbrauch," in *Gesammelte Schriften* (Basel, 1975), vol. 2, pp. 699–729. In the Germanic world, the victory over the bear among the Taifali corresponded to the murder of an enemy among the Chatti (Tacitus, *Germania*, XXXI).
15. Cf. Vernant, *P.G.G.A.*, pp. 10–29.
16. See n. 7.
17. See Tacitus, *Germania*, V; Musset, I, p. 56.
18. See Beck.

CHAPTER TWO

1. See Höfler; Weiser; De Vries, *Altgerm.*, vol. 1, pp. 499–502; Eliade, *Initiation*, pp. 180–86, with bibliography, p. 185, n. 8 (L. Weiser, C. Clemen, G. Dumézil, A. Endter), etc.
2. Respectively vol. 2, p. 91, and vol. 3, p. 177, in the Belles Lettres (Budé) edition.
3. 1 Cor. 11:25, etc. See also Aristophanes, *Knights*, 120; Ctesias, quoted by Athenaeus, XI.464A.
4. Athenaeus, XI.502b. He also knows Ephorus's account (see XI, 782c).
5. XI.470e–472e.
6. Gernet, "Droit et prédroit," p. 178.
7. Ibid., pp. 189–90.
8. See M. Durry, "Les femmes et le vin," *R.E.L.*, 33 (1955): 108–13; F. Graf, "Milch, Honig und Wein. Zum Verständnis der Libation im griechischen Ritual," in *Perennitas. Studi in memoria di Angelo Brelich* (Rome, 1980); Bremmer, p. 286.
9. Aelian, *V.H.*, II.38. See also Athenaeus, X. 429b.
10. Athenaeus, X.425a; *Sch. Il.*, I.470.
11. *Od.*. XV.141; cf. also *Il.*, I.470.
12. Theophrastus, frag. 119; Sappho, frag. 169 Reinach.
13. Amerias, in Athenaeus, X.424f.
14. Diodorus of Sicily, XII.14.5.
15. Plutarch, *Life of Pyrrhus*.
16. See Chapter 22; Bremmer, p. 286.
17. Cahen, p. 38.
18. Apd., II.5.7; Diodorus IV.13.4; Pausanias, I.27.9–10 and V.10.9; Tzetzes, *Chil.*, II.293–4; Hyg., E., 30; schol. to Statius, *Theb.*, V.431; Virg., *Aen.*, VIII.294ff.

19. Evans, *P.M.*, vol. 4, p. 3979; Willetts, *Cults*, pp. 112, 116.
20. See Chapter 28.
21. Bremmer, p. 185; cf. Graf, pp. 14–15; references at n. 114 in this chapter; and Willetts, p. 115.
22. Dumézil, *Mariages*, pp. 245–58, with references.
23. Willetts, p. 115.
24. Deubner, p. 160.
25. Yoshida, 1965.
26. This is one of the main points of Dumézil's work. For the most recent account, see his *Scythie*, which gives references to earlier works.
27. Yoshida, 1965, p. 33.
28. Hdt., IV.5.
29. Hdt., IV.7.
30. *Le premier homme et le premier roi dans l'histoire légendaire des Iraniens*, Leyden-Uppsala, 1917, vol. 1, pp. 137–38.
31. "La préhistoire indo-iranienne des castes," *Journal Asiatique* 216 (1930): 114–24.
32. "Traditions indo-iraniennes sur les classes sociales," *Journal Asiatique* 230: 532–34.
33. Dumézil, *Scythie*, p. 172.
34. Quintus Curtius, VII.8.17–18, in Dumézil, ibid., pp. 172–73; earlier in *J.M.Q.* I, p. 54.
35. Yoshida, 1965, pp. 34–35.
36. Cf., e.g., L. H. Gray, *Spiegel Memorial Volume* 1908: 160–68; C. Kérényi, *La religion antique*, French translation (Paris, 1957), pp. 133–36.
37. See. L. Gerschel, "Structures augurales et tripartition fonctionnelle dans la pensée de l'ancienne Rome," *Journal de psychologie* 45 (1952): 47–78. "Often" is saying too much, however; the ox more commonly denotes the first function. For Greece and Rome in other contexts, see the end of the preceding section, "Three Gifts." For Iran, see Dumézil, *Dieux des Indo-Européens*, pp. 17, 19.
38. Yoshida, "Survivances," pp. 36–38.
39. Dumézil often pointed this out. For a recent statement, see my article "Les trois fonctions," pp. 1155–56.
40. Ibid., pp. 1156–76.
41. Ibid., pp. 1164–70.
42. See Strabo, VI.3.5 (281).
43. Lyc., *Alex.*, 852–55.
44. Yoshida, 1965, p. 36. Cf. my article "Les trois fonctions," p. 1168.
45. Strabo, VI.3.5 (281).
46. A slight Minoan influence can be detected in the Western Mediterranean. See, for example, J. Bérard, *La colonisation de l'Italie méridionale et de la Sicile dans l'Antiquité* (vol. 2, 1957), pp. 490–92; M. Cavalier, "Les cultures préhistoriques des îles Eoliennes et leur rapport avec le monde égéen," *B.C.H.* 84 (1960): 319–46; R. W. Hutchinson, *Prehistoric Crete* (London, 1962), pp. 113–15.
47. Cf. Wuilleumier, pp. 486–87.
48. Strabo, VI.3.2–3(278–80), based on Antiochus of Syracuse (frag. 13) and Ephorus (frag. 216 *F.G.H.*; Artt., *Pol.*, V.7.2(1306 b31); Polybius, XII. 6b.5, XII.6b.9; Dionysus of Halicarnassus, XIX.1.1–2; etc.
49. Sergent, "Les trois fonctions," p. 1169, based on Hatzopoulos, p. 56.

50. Pliny, *N.H.*, XXXIII.4.

51. Lyc., *Alex.*, lines 886–96.

52. D. A. Tuganov, Kto takie Narty?" ("Who are the Nartes?"), *Izvestija Osetinskogo Instituta Kraevedenija* 1 (1925): 373; cited by Duméil, *M.E.* I, p. 458.

53. Dumézil, *M.E.* I, pp. 455–75; Dumézil, *Scythie*, pp. 169–224.

54. Dumézil, *Scythie*, pp. 205–6, and cf. pp. 227–31.

55. Dumézil, *J.M.Q.* I, pp. 257-58; Dumézil, "Triades," pp. 183–85; Dumézil, *M.E.* I, pp. 493–96; Sergent, "Les trois fonctions," pp. 1173–76.

56. *Rep.*, 399e.

57. Sergent, "Les trois fonctions," pp. 1174–75, where I am following Ollier, p. 240.

58. The parallel between the Cretan concepts and those put forward by Plato in the *Republic* is pointed out by F. Lasserre, p. 103, n. 2.

59. Strabo X.4.16 (480).

60. Dumézil, *M.V.*, pp. 79–97; Dumézil, *Dieux des Indo-Européens*, pp. 41–54; Dumézil, *Dieux souverains*, pp. 55–85.

61. X.4.17 (481), and cf. his description of Crete, X.4.9–14 (477–79).

62. *Laws of Gortyn*, II.1–17; Willetts, *Code*, p. 10; Dover, p. 189.

63. For example, Lasserre, p. 96, n. 3; Effenterre, *Crète*, pp. 75–104 (though on the specific point of homosexuality, this author admits (p. 79) the accuracy of Ephorus's account and recognizes the value of Jeanmaire's interpretation).

64. See the beginning of this chapter.

65. Sergent, "Les trois fonctions," p. 1171; "envy" is characteristic of the third function in one Iranian tradition; see Dumézil, *Scythie*, p. 189.

66. Sergeant, "Les trois fonctions," p. 1176.

67. Plato, *Laws*, 636b–d.

68. Ibid., 836b.

69. Tim., frag. 144 Jacoby; Heracl. Pont., 508.

70. *Pol.*, II.10. (1272a 23–6).

71. *Anacreontea*, XXXII.

72. Strabo, X.4.12 (478).

73. Conon, *Narr.*, 16.

74. Bethe, pp. 453, 456, 455. Cf. Cic., *Repub.*, IV.3 for Crete; Plut., *Lyc.*, XVIII, for Sparta; Plut., *Erot.*, 761c, for Thessaly; Pausanias of Athens in Plato, *Symposium*, 178e.

75. Hesych., X.4080.

76. Cf. Dover, pp. 38, 187–88.

77. Dover, p. 187.

78. Plut., *Lyc.*, XV.4.

79. The principal texts are Herodotus, I.65; Ephorus, in Strabo X.4.17–19 (480–82); Artt., *Pol.*, II, 10.22 (1271b); Polybius, VI.46–47; Luc., *Anach.*, 39. Cf. Ollier, pp. 39–41.

80. The basic study of this phenomenon is that of Guy Dickins; a good summary is in Michell, pp. 25–27.

81. Gerschel, cited by Dumézil., *J.M.Q.* IV, pp. 170–76, based on Plut., *Lyc.*, V.10; VIII.1; XII.1.4. and 8.

82. We have, thanks to Plutarch and Athenaeus, fragments of many classical and

Hellenistic authors who wrote about Sparta or discussed the work of Lycurgus: Sosibius, Oenomaus, Hippias, Philostephanus, Demetrius of Phalerum, Hermippus, Timaeus, Appolodorus, Molpis, Polycrates, and others.

83. Hdt., I.65 and VI.56–60; Plato, *Laws;* Artt., *Pol.*, II (1269b–1271b) and V, 11 (1313a25–33); Xen., R.L.

84. Cf. Hdt., I.65, and especially the fragment of the *Eunomia* of Tyrtaeus known to Plut., *Lyc.*, VI.10 (frag. 4 Edmonds).

85. Diodorus VII.12.2

86. This is clearly stated in the *Republic,* III. 399e, IV. 442a, and in the *Timaeus*, 69e–73d. Cf. my "Les trois fonctions," pp. 1173–76. For Indian parallels, see Dumézil, *J.M.Q.* III, pp. 41ff., and *Dieux des Indo-Européens*, p. 22. For other countries, see Dumézil, *Tarpeia*, pp. 287–88.

87. Sergent, "Les trois fonctions," pp. 1164–65.

88. Note this point of similarity between the rituals of Therapnae involving Menelaus and Helen and the initiation ritual. This may shed light on the meaning of the former.

89. Tyrtaeus, who alludes to this, flourished around 650. Cf. Dickins, p. 9; Huxley, pp. 41ff.; Forrest, *Sparta*, pp. 35ff. Opposing this view, see Toynbee, *Problems,* pp. 235, 284–85; Finley, "Sparta," pp. 143–60; Oliva, pp. 66–70; T. Leuschan, "Die Entstehung des spartanischen Staates," *Klio* 30 (1937): 269–89, who sees this as a consequence of the Second Messenian War and/or of social crises of the seventh century. The complete absence of any reference to the ephor (magistrates) in the Rhetrai casts doubt on this interpretation.

90. Dickins, pp. 12–16; Den Boer develops this argument in the second part of his work on Sparta.

91. Boardman, 1973, fig. 47.

92. Dover, p. 204.

93. Besides Greek tradition (e.g., Strabo, X.4.18 (482), concerning Althaemenes, the Dorian colonizer of Crete), there is now confirmatory archeological evidence; cf. M. S. F. Hood and J. N. Coldstream, "A Late Minoan Tomb at Ayios Ioannis near Knossos," *B.S.A.* 63 (1968): 205–18, esp. pp. 205, 210.

94. See among others A. Meillet, "Quelques hypothèses sur des interdictions de vocabulaire dans les langues indo-européennes," in *Linguistique historique et linguistique générale* (Paris, 1958), pp. 281–91; Gauthiot, on the names of the bee and the hive, *Mem. Soc. Ling.* 16: 264ff.; J. Vendryes, on the Latin word *mundus*, ibid. 18: 305ff.

95. *Galmuda*: S. Reinach, in *R.A.* 1886: 59–60; discussion by L. Weisgerber, *Bericht der Römisch-Germanischen Kommission,* p. 201; Weisgerber, "Galatische Sprachreste," in *Natalicium, Festschrift Geffcken* (Hamburg, 1931), p. 201; C.–J. Guyonvarc'h in *Ogam* 6 (1954): 144. *Malini*: cf. Chantraine, *D.E.,* p. 681.

96. Respectively, Athenaeus, 663a, Apollodorus, III.3.5, Praxilla, frag. 5 Page; and Ibycus, frag. 8 Page, and Theognis, 1347. Bremmer, p. 285.

97. Cf. n. 79.

98. See the end of Chapter 22.

99. X.4.20 (482).

100. H. Rose, *Primitive Culture in Greece*, p. 122; Michell, p. 220; Willetts, *Society*, p. 19; among others.

101. Aristotle, *Pol.*, II.10.5 (1272a1–4).
102. Dem. Skepsis, in Athenaeus, IV.173f; Pausanias, VII.1.8.
103. Cf. Graf, p. 11, with references, and more recently A. J. Beattie in *Kadmos* 14 (1975): 43–47.
104. On this point cf. Hubert, II, pp. 219, 250.
105. Sosicrates, in *F. Grill.* III B. 461.F7 (Athenaeus, XIII. 561e).
106. Plutarch, *Pelops*, XIX.
107. Bremmer, p. 285; and J. Le Goff, *Pour un autre Moyen Age* (Paris, 1977), p. 147, n. 1 (translated by Arthur Goldhammer as *Time, Work and Culture in the Middle Ages* (Chicago, 1978).
108. Bethe, p. 459.
109. Roheim, pp. 42–44.
110. Baumann and Westermann, p. 212.
111. M. Griaule and G. Dieterlen, *Le renard pâle*, vol. 1 (Paris, 1965), p. 34.
112. Theocritus, VII (*Thalusia*), 78–86, and scholia.
113. *C.C.*, p. 453. Concerning the Cretan ritual of social integration, see pp. 459–60.
114. Lasserre, p. 104, n. 1; cf. Willetts, *Society*, pp. 155–56.
115. Cf., e.g., Plato, *Lysis* 204b–e, 206d; and Plato, *Euthyd.*, 300c–d.
116. Ael., *Hist. Anim.*, IV.1; Plut., *Erot.*, 761c and *Pelopidas*, XVIII. Cf. Bethe, pp. 446–47, and Bremmer, p. 287.
117. Rhianus, frag. 1 (*Anth. Pal.*, XII. 38); Dover, p. 99; Bremmer, p. 287.

CHAPTER THREE

1. P. Näcke, "Die Homosexualität im Orient," *Archiv für Kriminalanthropologie und Kriminalstat. von Gross* 12: 353ff.; R. Schmidt, *Liebe und Ehe in Indien* (1904), pp. 530ff.; E. Carpenter, "Beziehungen zwischen Homosexualität und Prophetentum," *Jahrbuch für sexuelle Zwischenstufen unter Berücksichtung der Homosexualität,* suppl. 1911; Brelich, *P.P.*, pp. 35, 84–85, 120–21; Westermarck, vol. 2, pp. 460–65.
2. See Chapter 4.
3. Subincision, or subcision, is a ritual operation performed by Australasian tribes; it involves cutting the penis along the urethra at the base or near the glans in order to make it bleed, enlarge it, and make it more "beautiful." See the description by R. Dadoun in the foreward to his translation of Roheim, pp. 18–19.
4. Moscovici, p. 258, based on Roheim, pp. 107, 165, 209.
5. Deacon, pp. 260–61.
6. Ibid., p. 171.
7. Ibid., p. 261.
8. Ibid., p. 261–62.
9. Ibid., p. 171.
10. Jensen, p. 82.
11. A. C. Haddon, in Williams, p. xxvi.

12. Ibid., p. xxviii, based on G. Landtman, *The Folk-tales of the Kiwai Papuans* (Helsingfors, 1917), pp. 78–80.
13. Williams, pp. 188, 200, and 200 n. 1.
14. Williams, pp. 200–203.
15. Chelmes, p. 109.
16. See Chapter 4.
17. Jensen, pp. 78–79, based on Wirz, vol. 2, pt. 3, p. 35 n.
18. Cf. Brelich, *P.P.*, p. 94, n. 130, with numerous ethnographic references; Eliade, *Initiation*, pp. 147, 158, 73–74, 79–80; Van Gennep, *Rites*, pp. 144, 149, 157. There exist several other traces of this in Greece. For the Germans, see, e.g., Dumézil, *Dieux des Germains*, p. 112.
19. Jensen, p. 101, based on Parkinson, pp. 657–59.
20. Van Gennep, *Rites*, p. 119.
21. Ibid., p. 244, based on Parkinson, p. 611.
22. Cf. S. Iwaya-Tokio, "Die Päderastie in Japan," *Jahrbuch für homosexuelle Zwischenstufen* 4 (1902): 265–71, and Nanshok'-Okagami, *Histoires péderastiques de Saikak'* (vol. 1., pp. 67ff.), cited by Bethe, pp. 472–73.
23. The only known exception in which the active member is the initiate was reported by Roheim in Australia; cf. Brelich, *P.P.*, p. 35. On one Melanesian island adult men lie on their stomachs during initiation and present their buttocks to the novices, but it is not certain that this is a symbolic act of pederasty (H. P. Duerr, *Traumzeit* (Frankfurt, 1978), p. 98. Concerning the general nature of initiatory coitus (anal intercourse with the master taking the male part), cf. Brelich, *P.P.*, p. 85, and Bremmer, p. 280.
24. See the latter part of Chapter 2.
25. Cf. chap. 2, n. 100; and Van Gennep, *Rites*, pp. 244–45; Bremmer, p. 292, who discusses the polemic between H. Wagenvoort and G. Dumézil in the early 1950s concerning the value of comparisons between Roman customs and Melanesian customs (bibliography at n. 122 of Bremmer's article, p. 298). This is a question of level; the religions and ideologies of Mediterranean antiquity cannot be reduced to the forms of Pacific neolithic societies. Institutions are more amenable to such reduction, because the social constraints to which they correspond are recurrent, even in societies of very different types.
26. Cf. Vian, *Thèbes*, pp. 186, 226–28, 234, on the subject of Pelops, whose myth can be summed up as one of initiation (see Chapter 5). Epimenides, the great Cretan sage of the seventh century, was tattooed. Cf. Vernant, *M.P.*, p. 300, n. 44.
27. For the Namba, see Deacon, p. 261, and for Greece, see Buffière, esp. pp. 100, 101–3, 113–16, and 225–35 for Macedonia; and compare, for the Celts, Diodorus and Athenaeus, cited in Chapter 1 n. 3.
28. Deacon, p. 261; for Greece, see Meier, Dover, and Buffière.
29. Devereux, "Pseudo."
30. Which Devereux, a psychoanalyst, has always affirmed, since in his view an unhappy homosexual who comes to his office should leave a happy heterosexual.
31. Deacon, p. 171.

CHAPTER FOUR

1. Cf. Westermarck, vol. 2, pp. 465ff.
2. *Education,* vol. 5, pp. 62–63.
3. M. Foley, "Sur les habitations et les moeurs des Néo-Calédoniens," *Bull. Soc. Anthr. Paris,* 3d series, vol. 2, p. 606; cited by Westermarck, vol. 2, p. 460.
4. Even in Sparta, where young married couples did not live together, custom tolerated, or, rather, induced secret, nocturnal, ostensibly clandestine relations between men (Plut., *Lyc.,* XV. 7–11); ethnology provides numerous examples of similar situations. These young men are not sexually frustrated. Furthermore, according to Plutarch, it was common for a child to be born before the couple began living together. Note that a fourth-century comic poet, Eubolous, envisioned a military origin of homosexuality. Because Greeks laid siege to Troy for ten years, he says, without women, they took to homosexual practices (frag. 120, cited by Dover, pp. 135, 193). But the event is mythical. By contrast, it was in the fourth century, after the Peloponnesian War, that professional armies and lengthy occupations of conquered territory first developed. Then and only then did the barracks' phenomena occur from which Euboulos derived his notions.
5. Lévi-Strauss, *A.S.,* p. 140.
6. This is the object of Brelich, *Guerre.*
7. G. Bateson, *La cérémonie du naven* (Paris, 1971), p. 142.
8. Moscovici, pp. 302–4.
9. Moscovici uses this term to refer to any group, human or not, in which the males of a species live together.
10. Moscovici distinguishes "the other issue, male homosexuality, [which] allows men to live in the female world without violating the rules in force or compromising their application" and which "forms prior to the demarcation represented by initiation." One finds such practices among the "female males" of certain North American tribes. This "homosexual masculinity," which is due to an affirmed desire to remain among males and not to a shortage of women, was also noticed by Bethe, p. 440, and Dover, pp. 193–94. J. Winthuis, *Einführung in die Vorstellungswelt primitiven Völker* (Leipzig, 1921), p. 38, understood that the initiate is female because he is not yet a man (cited by Brelich, *P.P.,* p. 35).
11. Cf. Moscovici, pp. 113–20, 227–48.
12. Cf. Langaney, pp. 119–126.

INTRODUCTION: PART II

1. Excellent examples may be found in the works of Louis Gernet (e.g., "Fosterage," and "Ancient Feasts," pp. 13–47, in *Anthropology*; "The Mythical Idea of Value in Greece," pp. 73–111 of the same; "Law and Prelaw in Ancient Greece," pp. 143–215 of the same); and Glotz, *Ordalie.*
2. See n. 1 of the general introduction to this book.
3. The data have been collected most recently by Buffière, pp. 89–91, 95–99.
4. Bethe, p. 441.
5. Devereux, "Pseudo"; Dover, pp. 57, 188, 195–96.

6. See Chapters 22 and 30.
7. Cf. F. Hampl, "Die Iliad ist kein Geschichtsbuch," *Serta philologica Aenipontana* 1962: 37–63.

CHAPTER FIVE

1. *Il.*, II.100-108 (English translation by Richmond Lattimore; transcription of proper names has been modified).
2. Frag. 190, 191, 193.11 M.-W.
3. Pindar, *Ol.*, I.23–56 and 65–96.
4. Pausanias, V.1.6–7, 3.1, 4.7, 6.4, 10.2, 13.4, 16.5–6; VI.4.2, 21.1–2, 21.4, 21.6. Strabo, VIII.3.3 (337), 3.7 (339), etc.
5. For the fall, see n. 6; for murder, see Euripides, *Orestes*, 988ff.; Apd., *Epit.*, II.7; for the thunderbolt, cf. Paus., V.20.6-8; according to Diodorus, IV.73.6, Oenomaus committed suicide.
6. Apd., *Epit.*, II.7; schol. Ap. Rh., *Argon.*, I.752; Tzetzes, schol. to Lyc., *Alex.*, 156; schol. to Eur., *Orestes*, 998; Servius, *Commentary* to Virg., *Georg.*, III.7; *Mythologie Vaticane*, I.21; *Myth. Vat.*, II. 146; Hyg., *F.*, 84. The scholium to the *Argonautica* refers to Pherecydes of Athens, who is thus the first attestation of the myth (frag. 37a *F.G.H.*).
7. Detienne and Vernant, *Mètis*, esp. pp. 167–241.
8. If one agrees with Hatzopoulos, p. 72, that the Hippeis are the same youths as the Kruptoi but at a slightly different age. Concerning the Krupteia, a form of service that elite youths in Sparta were obliged to perform, see Plut., *Lyc.*, XXVIII.2–4; schol. Plato, *Laws*, 633b–c; Heracl. Pont. in *F.H.G.*, vol. 2, p. 210.
9. See Part 3.
10. Schol. Pindar, *Ol.*, I. 37 and 40c; Paus., V.13.4–6; Lyc., *Alex.*, 152f.; Lucian, *Salt.*, 54; Tzetzes, at Lyc., *Alex.*, 152; Nonnos, *Narr.*, in Westermann, *Myth. Graeci, Appendix Narrationum*, vol. 57, p. 380; Servius, at Virg., *Aen.*, VI.603, and at Virg., *Georg.*, III.7; Hyg., *F.*, 83; Pliny, *N.H.*, XXVIII.34.
11. Apd., *Epit.*, II.3.
12. See Buffière, pp. 261–66.
13. Delcourt, "Tydée," p. 143; for an earlier treatment see Dumézil, *Festin*, p. 91.
14. *Origines*, pp. 13–14.
15. Claude Lévi-Strauss deserves the credit for his masterly demonstration that this is the case. See his "La structure des mythes," in *A.S.*, pp. 227–56, and his several volumes collected under the title *Mythologiques* (1964, 1967, 1968, 1971).
16. *Electra*, 509–11.
17. *Orestes*, 988–92.
18. Schol. to Sophocles, *Electra*, 504. Cf. Lacroix, p. 335.
19. Herrmann, pp. 18–22.
20. Herrmann, pp. 23–25; Yalouris, p. 178; Lévêque, "Continuité," pp. 27–32; cf. the remarks of G. Roux, "Samothrace, le sanctuaire des Grandes dieux et ses mystères," *Bull. Ass. G. Budé*, March 1981: 2–23.
21. Herrmann, pp. 18–19; Yalouris, p. 181; Lévêque, "Continuité," pp. 28, 32.
22. See my article "Mythologie et histoire," pp. 62–63.

23. Roux, *Delphes*, pp. 33–34; Defradas, pp. 147–48, based on Lerat, *R.A.*, 1938, pt. 2: 198ff., 200, fig. 8.
24. Snodgrass, pp. 422–23.
25. Ibid., pp. 416–36.
26. For a good account of the principal motifs and of similar legends see F. M. Cornford, "Origins of the Olympic Games," included in Harrison, *Themis*, pp. 212–53.
27. Athenaeus, XIII.602f–603a. Athenaeus then goes on to discuss Celtic homosexuality; see Chapter 1, n. 3.
28. Apd., *Bibl.*, III.5.5.
29. Gernet, "Fostérage," p. 24, n. 2, rightly calls attention to traces of the institution in Elis, in the legend of origin of the Iamidae, the family of Olympian soothsayers.
30. See, e.g., Gernet, "Marriages of Tyrants," *Anthropology*, pp. 289–302; Vernant, "Introduction," pp. 11–12.
31. Gernet, *"Fostérage,"* pp. 20, 22–28.
32. Apd., II.5.5–6; III.5.6.
33. Hes., frag. 190, M–W.
34. Schol. to Eur., *Phen.*, 1760, based on pseudo-Peisandros.
35. *Schol. Il.*, II.105; Hyg., *F.*, 85.
36. Hyg. *F.*, 9

CHAPTER SIX

1. Robert, *Oidipus*, vol. 1, pp. 149–67.
2. Frag. 157 Jacoby.
3. A. D. Trendall and T. B. L. Webster, *Illustration of Greek Drama* (London, 1971), pp. 3, 16–18; Dover, p. 198.
4. Hdt., IV. 147–49. Cf. Vian, *Thèbes*, pp. 216–25, who along with A. Puech and F. Chamoux is here following C. Robert.
5. Hdt., IV. 149; concerning the chronology of events, see the end of this chapter.
6. Aeschylus, *Seven*, 742–48; EUR., *Phen.*, 12–22.
7. Vian, *Thèbes*, pp. 216–25.
8. Cf. Aristotle, *Pol.*, II.10.9 (1272a).
9. Cf. "Argument" of Euripides' *Phoenician Woman* (C.U.F. edition). This was no doubt the subject of Euripides' lost play *Chrysippus*; cf. also contemporary vase paintings.
10. Cf. Vian, *Thèbes*, p. 226; Bethe, p. 448.
11. L. Legras, *Les légendes thébaines dans l'épopée et la tragédie grecques* (Paris, 1905), pp. 34–35, 39–40, 50–52; Bethe, *Theban. Helden.*, pp. 12ff.; T. Zielinski, "De Euripidis Thebaide Posteriore," *Mnemosyne* 52 (1924): 189–205, 194–95; Vian, *Thèbes*, p. 226.
12. *Od.*, XI.271–80; cf. *Il.*, XXIII.679–80.
13. Herodotus, IV.147–49.
14. Cf. Desborough, *P.P.*, p. 214; the oldest document of the Hellenic phase is a protogeometric vase.

15. Ephorus, *Hist.*, book I, in *F. Gr. Hist.* IIA 70 F 16, based on schol. to Pindar, *Pyth.*, v. 101b. (French translation in F. Vian, *Thèbes*, p. 217). The fifth *Pythian* and seventh *Isthmian* odes of Pindar contain earlier allusions to the event.

CHAPTER SEVEN

1. Cf. *Il.*, XXIV.602–17, and the note of Paul Mazon, vol. 4 of the C.U.F. edition, p. 161.
2. *Il.*, XXIV.615; Strabo, XIV.5.28 (680); Ael. Aristides, XVII.3–5, etc. (complete list of references in Sakellariou, *Migration*, p. 266).
3. Mayer, *Gig. u. Tit.*, p. 87; Wilamowitz, *Eur. Her.*, vol. 2, pt. 2, p. 96; Wilamowitz, *Glaube*, vol. 1, p. 65; Delcourt, "Tydée," p. 143.
4. Tzetzes, at Lyc., *Alex.*, 433; Schol. to Ap. Rh., *Argon.*, III.1242.
5. Cf. Grimal, genealogical table, p. 268, and references to corresponding words.
6. Diodorus, IV.73.1. This name is sometimes considered to be a simple epithet of Ares. In any case, on names of this type, all warriors, see Vian, *Géants*, p. 169.
7. Vian, *Thèbes*, pp. 107–9.
8. I studied them in detail in my thesis, *Royauté*, pp. 166–68; see summary in my "Mythologie et histoire," pp. 84–85.
9. Sergent, *Royauté*, pp. 168–9.
10. Ibid., pp. 85–93, and my "Liste de Kom el-Hetan," pp. 149–51.
11. *Royauté*, pp. 165–67, 169, and "Liste de Kom el-Hetan," p. 146.
12. K. A. Kitchen, "Theban Topographical Lists, Old and New," *Orientalia, n.s.* 34 (1965): 3–5; E. Edel, "Die Ortsnamenlisten aus dem Totentempel Amenophis III," *Bonner Biblische Beiträge* 1966: 33–60; Kitchen, "Aegean Place-Names in a List of Amenophis III," *Bull. Am. School of Oriental Research* 481 (1966): 23–24 (with references to the letters of W. F. Albright dated 18 and 19 June 1965) (Other references in my "Liste de Kom el-Hetan," p. 126, n. 1).
13. Sergent, "Liste de Kom el-Hetan," pp. 144–48.
14. Ibid., pp. 162–65.
15. I should add that the name Tantalus seems to have been used by Cretans and Messenians in the second millennium (Cnossus, tablet As 707.2; Pylos, Eo 224.7, Ep 306.1).

CHAPTER EIGHT

1. Boardman, *Eros*, p. 103; an amphora of Douris, discovered at Tarquinia, c. 480, shows intercrural coitus between Zephyrus and Hyacinthus, the former lying on top of the latter. On p. 102, another cup by the same painter, with red figures, c. 480, shows the same figures standing erect and engaged in intercrural coitus.
2. *Il.*, II.595.
3. Apd., I.3.3.
4. Cf. Bissinger, *Welche Blume hat man sich unter dem hyakinthus zu denken?* (Leipzig,

1880); C. Garlick, "What was the Greek hyacinth?" *Class. Review* 35 (1921): 146ff.; Chriassi, pp. 157–59.

5. *Myth. Vat.*, II.181; Ovid, *Met.*, X.215.

6. Ovid, *Met.*, X.106–42; Servius, at Virgil, *Aeneid*, III.64, III. 680; Servius, at *Georgics*, I.20; Servius, at *Ecl.*, X.26; Probus, at *Georgics*, II.84; Nonnus, *Dion.*, XI.364.

7. Ovid, *Met.*, III.339–46.

8. Conon, *Narr.*, 24.

9. Probus, at Virg., *Ecl.*, II.48.

10. P. Kretschmer, *Einleitung in die Geschichte der griechischen Sprache* (Göttingen, 1896); A. Fick, *Vorgriechische Ortsnamen als Quelle für die Vorgeschichte* (1905), pp. 58, 153ff. Since these pioneering works the bibliography on the subject has grown to impressive proportions. See, in particular, on the subject of the Anatolian origins of these formations, the studies by E. Laroche: "Notes de Toponymie Anatolienne," *Gedenkschrift Paul Kretschmer* (Vienna, 1957), vol. 2, pp. 1–7, esp. p. 1; "Etudes de toponymie anatolienne," *Rev. Hitt. et As.* 69 (1961): 57–98, esp. pp. 76–77; "Linguistique anatolienne," *Minos* 11 (1970); 112–29.

11. Picard, *Luttes*, p. 21.

12. See the end of Chapter 12; and especially Vidal-Naquet, *Chasseur noir*, pp. 177–72.

13. Ovid, *Met.*, III.349–510.

14. Herodotus, I.56.

15. A. von Blumenthal, *Hesychstudien* (Stuttgart, 1930), p. 8; H. Krahe, *Die Sprache der Illyrier* (Wiesbaden, 1955), vol. 1, p. 46; cf. Chantraine, *D.E.*, p. 788.

16. Paus., III.15.10.

17. See bibliography under Mellink.

18. It is based entirely on an "agrarian" interpretation of the festival and the myth, concerning which see the following.

19. Besides Mellink, Piccirelli and Chirassi have also treated this subject.

20. Frazer, *Atys*, pp. 36–39; Nilsson, *G.F.*, pp. 130–31.

21. *Jardins*, pp. 96–100, 110–14.

22. Luc., *Dial. Deor.*, 16 (14).

23. See the opening of this chapter. For Erato, see schol. Eur., *Phoen.*, 347.

24. Isidore, XVII.9.15.

25. Servius, at Virgil, *Ecl.*, V.48; Nonnos, *Dionys.*, XI.370–481.

26. Marrou, *Education*, pp. 50, 57; Buffière, pp. 65–88; Bethe.

27. Ovid, *Met.*, X.171–73.

28. On this topic see Chapter 5, n. 8; and Michell, pp. 128–30; Brelich, *P.P.*, pp. 155–57; Jeanmaire, *C.C.*, pp. 540–45.

29. Philostr., *Imag.*, I.4.

30. Chirassi, p. 169, n. 1.

31. Dover, p. 75, with references: Hyacinthus seized by Zephyrus.

32. Mellink, p. 14, based on *Eph. Arch.*, 1892, p. 14 and plate IV.2.

33. Ibid., based on *Eph. Arch.*, 1892, pl. III.5.

34. Ant. Lib., 9; Ovid, *Met.*, V.663–78; Paus., IX.29.4.

35. *Il.*, II.595–600.

36. An Athenian artist of the second half of the fourth century; cf. Overbeck, *Gr. Plastik*, vol. 1, pp. 71ff.
37. Paus., III.19.3–5.
38. Cf. n. 20.
39. XIX.104.
40. See the excellent description by Ollier, pp. 31–32, based on numerous allusions in Aristophanes, Plato, Demosthenes, Plato (the comic playwright), Theophrastys, Plutarch, etc.
41. E.g., the Chatti, in Tacitus, *Germania*, XXXI; for the hero Starcatherus, cf. Dumézil, M.E. II, p. 50; and the origin of the name of the Lombards, Langobardi, "people with long beards."
42. *P.P.*, p. 148.
43. See the close of Chapter 1.
44. E.g., Luc., *Dial. Deor.*, 16 (14); Isid., XVII.9.15.
45. Ovid, *Met.*, X.209–13.
46. Conon, *Narr.*, 24.
47. Pliny *N. H.*, XXI.170; Dioscor., IV.62; cf. also Galen, xii, 146 Kühn.
48. Frazer, *Atys*, p. 38; Piccirelli, p. 113, n. 59.
49. Gruppe, p. 124; Mellink, pp. 48, 52–53; Nilsson, *G.F.*, p. 140, n. 4; Dietrich, p. 135.
50. She is known from inscriptions: Collitz-Bechtel, 3501, 3502, 3512.
51. For this notion see the classic work of Eliade, *Aspects du mythe*.
52. *Lyc.*, XIV.1–7.
53. See the section "The Hyacinthia" of this chapter.
54. For Lesbos, see Marrou, *Education*, 59–62; for Sparta, Calame, vol. 2, pp. 86–97.
55. Ollier, pp. 63–74, after Plato, *Laws*, I.637c; VI.781a–b; VII.806c. Cf. *Rep.*, VIII.548b; Aristophanes, *Lys.*, on Lampeto the Laconian woman, 79–82, 142–44, 183, 198, 206; Aristotle, *Pol.*, II.9 (1269b12–1270a10).
56. Cf. Brelich, *P.P.*, pp. 240–94.
57. Ritual theft of cheese by a group of youths, which another group attempts to prevent by whipping them. This eventually developed into a public flagellation, the *diamastigosis*. See Xen., *R.L.*, II.9; Plutarch, *Arist.*, XVII; Plato, *Laws*, I.633b; Paus., III.16.10; Hyginus, *F.*, 261; Luc., *Anach.*, 38; Plutarch, *Lyc.*, XVIII, and *Inst. Lac.*, 239d; *Nic. Dam., F. Gr. Hist.* IIA 90 F 103 (z); Philostr., *Life of Apollonius*, VI.20.
58. Paus., III.10.7; IV.16.9.
59. Schol. Call., *H. Zeus*, 77; cf. Paus., III.18.9 and 19.4.
60. Diodorus, V.73; Paus., IV.34.6; Hesychius and Suidas, s.v. *Kourotrophos*; Orpheus, Hymns, 36, 8. *Schol. Od.*, XIX.71.
61. See the close of this section.
62. Plut., *Lyc.*, XV.4.
63. *G.F.*, pp. 139–40.
64. Schol. Pindar, *Ol.*, I.149.
65. Müller, *Dorier*, vol. 1, Pt. 2, p. 358; Rohde, I, p. 144; Wide, pp. 290–94; H. Treidler, s.v. *Polyboia*, in *R.E.*, vol. 21, pt. 2, cols. 1581–83; Fougères, col.

305; Nilsson, *G.F.*, pp. 130-31; Piccirelli, p. 113 and n. 95 (who for circumstantial reasons transforms Hesychius's definition of Polyboea so that Kore becomes Persephone and Artemis becomes Artemis/Hecate).

66. Paus., IV.3.10; IV.33.5. He is an expert with the bow (Paus., IV.2.3).

67. Paus., II.19.8.

68. Clem. Al., *Protr.*, III.45.3.

69. Ibid., III.45.4, based on Ptolemy.

70. Herodotus, IV.34–35.

71. Brelich, *P.P.*, p. 303.

72. See note 68.

73. Paus. X.24.6.

74. *Protr.*, III.45.1–4. Also Oedipus at Colonus in the sacred wood of the Eumenides, Phylacus and Autonoos with Athena Pronaea at Delphi, Calamites at Athens near the Lenaeon, Deucalion near the Olympeion, Aristomachus alongside the temple of Dionysus at Marathon, etc.

75. Enmann, p. 33; cf. Delcourt, *Cultes*, pp. 60–61.

76. *H.H.Ap.*, 448–50; cf. Hes., *Theog.*, 347; Ap. Rh., *Arg.*, I.

77. Kiechle, *L.u.S.*, P. 177, and Dietrich, p. 134, have rightly pointed this out.

78. Polybius, VIII.30.

79. Unger, p. 33; Fougères, p. 306; Greve, in Roscher, vol. 1, pt. 2, cols. 2761–62; Stengel, in *R.E.*, vol. 9, pt. 1; Ziehen, in *R.E.*, vol. 3A, col. 1518; Mellink, p. 25; Piccirelli, p. 110; with hesitation, Farnell, vol. 4, p. 267. In favor of three days, see Rohde, I, pp. 142–44; Wide, p. 288; Nilsson, pp. 130–31, 135–37; Frazer, *Atys*, pp. 37–38; Pareti, p. 27; How-Wells, pp. 288–89; Roveri, p. 230; Jeanmaire, *CC.*, p. 527.

80. Ath., IV.139d–f, which cites Polycrates via the grammarian Didymus of Alexandria (first century A.D.).

81. Paul., III.19.3.

82. *C.C.*, pp. 527–29.

83. Paus., III.18.6; Ath., IV.138e–139b.

84. Xen., *Ages.*, II.17.

85. *Helen*, 1465–75.

86. Brelich, p. 135; Chirassi, p. 172.

87. *P.P.*, pp. 142–44.

88. Paus., III.16.1–2, and cf. Euripides, *Helen*, 1465.

89. Plut., *Lyc.*, XVI.13.

90. To borrow J.-P. Vernant's phrase.

91. For instance, the members of Laconian religious associations included a *stephanopō-lis*, or "crown seller," and a *psilipoios*, "maker of garlands or palm crowns" (Tod-Wace, p. 19, no. 203); on crowns in Spartan rituals, see Theocr., XVIII.43ff.; Pamphilos in Ath., XV.678a; Sosibius, ibid., 678c. On similar cases of sacrifices without crowns, see Jeanmaire, *C.C.*, p. 528 (on the Pyanopsia of Athens and the Thesmophoria); Mellink, p. 38, on the sacrifice to the Kharites at Paros, based on Apd., III.15.7.

92. Cf. Eur., *Helen*, as well as Hesychius, s.v. *Hekatombeus*, which according to Hesychius is the name of the month in which the Hyacinthia were held, and

Strabo, VIII.4.11 (302); and *I.G.*, vol. 1, 161, which attests a festival of the Hecatombaea in honor of Apollo, in Laconia.

93. The large number of reliefs with which the Magnesian Bathycles graced the Amyclaeon can be grouped under four heads: apotheosis, education, marriages, and contests (*agones*), generally involving initiation. On this point see Jeanmaire, *C.C.*, pp. 530–31. This is further evidence that the essential nature of the myth and ritual was initiatory and not agrarian (Paus., III.18.10–16). Chimaera in Greek means simply "goat": cf. *Il.*, VI.181; Hes., *Theog.*, 322–23; Xen. *Anab.*, III.2.12; Xen., *Hell.*, IV.2.20; Xen., *R.L.*, XIII.8 (in which Xenophon states that when the Spartan army encountered an enemy army, a goat was sacrificed to the music of flutes, while the soldiers crowned one another and polished their weapons. The sacrifice was intended for Artemis Agrotera; cf. the citation from *Anabasis*. In other words, for a *military* action the Spartans sacrificed a *goat* to Artemis the *hunter*. The Cretan evidence and the myth of Bellerophon suggest that these three things are related through the symbolism of initiation).

94. See the section "Cretan Pederasty" in Chapter 2.

95. Atalanta (Apd., III.9.2) and Paris (Apd., III.12.5).

96. For example, Polyphontes (Ant. Lib., *Met.*, 21), Cephalus (cf. Grimal, p. 84), and Crimisus (Grimal, p. 103).

97. For example, Crimisus (see n. 96) and Callisto (Paus., VIII.3.6; Apd., III. 8.2).

98. Eur., frag. 767; Aristophanes, *Lys.*, 645, and schol.; Bekker, *An.*, 444.

99. This cannot be rigorously demonstrated by linguistic means (cf. Chantraine, *D.E.*, p. 110), but Arcas is the son of Callisto (Apd., III.8.2; Paus., VIII.4.1).

100. Herodotus, I.66, and earlier Alcaeus, frag. 245 Reinach.

101. Ovid, *Met.*, III.402ff.

102. Cf. Roux, *Delphes*, pp. 43, 132.

103. Strabo, XIV.1.20(639).

104. Hesychius and *Et. M.*, s.v. Ἀοία.

105. Cf. Paus., VIII.6.5; Wide, p. 268.

106. Diodorus, V.66.

107. Paus., II.15.2.

108. Paus., II.11.6; Ps. Hippocr., *Ep.*, 11; Wide, p. 268.

109. On the cypress see in general Murr, pp. 122ff.

110. *H.H.Dem.*, 8–16.

113. *O.C.*, 683.

112. Reinach, III, pp. 54–55.

113. See n. 110.

114. Since Narcissus is a pre-Hellenic word, representing what may be a Cretan or "Anatolian" linguistic stratum, whereas Laius is a Greek word meaning "left," on which see Lévi-Strauss, *A.S.*, p. 236. At Thespiae the role is filled by Iolaus.

115. For example, a village there is called Kopros, as is a village on the Gulf of Eleusis (once under Theban domination), and a son of Haliartos, eponymous hero of Haliarte, a Boeotian city near Orchomenus. Poiessa, one of the cities of Chios, has the Kharites for poliad deities; so does Orchomenus. A hero of the island is called Damon or Demonax; his female equivalent, Demonassa, is a daughter of Amphiaraos (a hero buried and worshiped in Boeotia), wife of Thersandros and

mother of Autesion, the last two Theban kings of the Cadmus family; finally, Chios, eponym of the island, was said to be the son of Apollo and Melia, which is the name of a well in Thebes, worshiped as a divinity in the temple of Apollo Ismenios at the gates of the city.

116. Inscription in *S.G.D.I.*, vol. 1, 463. The town is mentioned in *Il.*, II.519; Paus., X.26.5 (which identifies it with Antikura); Steph. Byz., s.v.; J. F. Lazenby and R. Hope Simpson, *Catalogue of the Ships in Homer's Iliad* (Oxford, 1970), p. 40.

117. See Chapter 12.

118. Ovid, *Her.*, XX and XXI; Ovid, *Tristes*, III.10.73ff.; Ant. Lib., *Met.*, I; Call., frag. 102 Schn. -69 Pfeiffer.

119. On the *kottabos* game, see Buffière, pp. 585–88.

CHAPTER NINE

1. *Pyth.*, IV.126.
2. Apd., I.8.2.
3. Ibid., I.9.16.
4. Ibid., III.10.4.
5. V.47–52. Also see Plut., *Numa*, IV.8.
6. Cf. Vian, introduction to *Argonautica* of Apollonius of Rhodes, vol. 1, pp. xxvi–xxviii.
7. Apd., III.6.1.
8. G. D. Beazley, "Two Swords," *Bull. Vereeniging. Ant. Beschaving*, the Hague, 1939.
9. Apd., III.13.6.
10. Vian, *Thèbes*, p. 120, and pl. I (Louvre, inv. CA 1961 no. 2).
11. Hitching of wild beasts also serves, no doubt more generally, to indicate divine power (ibid., pp. 120–21).
12. Ibid., pp. 142–43.
13. *Il.*, II.711–15.
14. Plut., *Q. Gr. 12 (Mor.* 293c); Pluto, *Def. or.* 21 (*Mor.* 421c).
15. *Il.*, VII.452–53; *Il.,* XXI.441–57; Apd., II.5.9.
16. Rohde, I, p. 436, n. 3; J. G. Frazer, *Pausanias*, V. p. 40; Frazer, *Apollodorus*, vol. I, pp. 218–19; Eliade, *Traité*, pp. 332–49; Vian, *Thèbes*, pp. 114–15.
17. Apd., III.4.1; Schol. AD to *Il.*, II.494; Lycus, in *F. Gr. Hist. IIIB 380 F5*.
18. *Hes., Theog.*, 793–804.
19. Apd., III.6.7; Phlegon, *Mirabilia*, 4; Tzetzes, at Lyc., 683; Eustathius, at *Od.*, X.492; *Sch. Od.*, X.494; Ant. Lib., *Met.*, XVIII; Ovid. *Met.*, III.316ff.; Hyg., *F.*, 75.
20. Cf. Jeanmaire, *C. C.*, p. 559.
21. Eur., *Hipp.*, 34–37; Eur., *Or.*, 1643–45; cf. Vian, *Thèbes*, p. 115, n. 3, which says that one may "compare ostracism, which lasts for ten years."
22. Jeanmaire, *C.C.*, pp. 389–91, 403.
23. *H.M.G.*, pp. 63–96; *M.E.* II, pp. 117–25.
24. *Thèbes*, p. 116.
25. *Il.*, XXI.441–57.

26. *Thèbes*, p. 117.
27. Porphyrus, *V. Pyth.*, 16.
28. Fontenrose, pp. 86, 91, 313 (n. 72), 592 (theme 8A); Delcourt, "Tydée," pp. 144–45.
29. See the discussion of the *Iliad* and *Homeric Hymns* near the beginning of Chapter 22.
30. *Isyllos*, pp. 57–58, and *Gr. Tr.*, vol. 3, pp. 71ff.
31. *S.v. Admetou Kore.*
32. Schol. to Eur., *Alc.*, 16.
33. Hyginus, *F.*, 14.
34. See esp. Paus., II.35.4–5, the basis for Wiliamowitz, *Glaube*, vol. 1, pp. 337ff.; Malten, pp. 188–89.
35. Malten; Jeanmaire, *Dionysos*, pp. 281–85.
36. Grimal, s.v. *Admète*, p. 11.
37. II.763–67; XXIII.288.
38. *Il.*, IX.158; cf. Jeanmaire, *C.C.*, p. 403.
39. Ant. Lib., *Met.*, 23; Hesiod, frag. 256 M.-W.
40. Suidas, s.v. *Thamuris.*
41. XIII.603d.
42. Ibid.
43. Clem. Al., *Protr.*, II.38.2; Steph. Byz., s.v. *Kōpai* and *Argunnos.*
44. Hes., frag. 70.33 M.-W. And cf. Sakellariou, *Migration*, pp. 117–18.
45. See Dover or Buffière, pp. 89–91, 7–9, 30, 208, 556–57.
46. *Antiope*, fr. 184, 185, 187 Nauck.
47. *Symposium*, 179d.
48. Dover, pp. 74–75.
49. Delcourt, *Hermaphrodite*, pp. 7–8.
50. Apd., III.10.3, which may in this case be following an Orphic tradition.
51. Frags. 7 and 171 M.-W.

CHAPTER TEN

1. Conon, *Narr.* 33; Lucian, *De domo*, 24, *Dial. Deor.*, 6; for Smicrus see Lact. Plac., schol. at Statius, *Theb.*, VIII.198.
2. Ptol., 151b 34–37; Apollo gave the soothsayer an ivory bow so that he could wound Achilles in the thigh.
3. See the close of Chapter 15 and the opening of Conclusions.
4. Frag. 7 Bergk, in Schol. to Theocr., *Idylls*, V.83a; Paus., III.13.5–4.
5. Cf. in particular Ant. Lib., *Met.*, XVII ("Leucippus," on which, cf. the beginning of Chapter 29); and on the city of Lato in the eastern part of the island, see Willetts, *Cults*, p. 176.
6. Cf. Wide, p. 86; Willetts, *Cults*, p. 265; Brelich, *P.P.*, pp. 148–53, 179–87; Hatzopoulos, pp. 140–57.
7. Apd., II.8.3; Paus., III.13.3; Diodorus, V.9; Conon, *Narr.*, 26; Schol. to Pindar, *Ol.*, XIII.17.
8. Conon 26 in Photius, *Bibl.*, Cod. 186(135a).

9. Apd., II.8.2; Schol. Theocr., V.85.
10. Paus., II.10.2, 11.2, III.13.4–6, 21.8, 24.8, 25.10, 26.5 and 7; IV.31.1, 33.4; *Eph. Arch.*, 1892, pp. 620, 265; etc.
11. Schol. Theocr., V.83. Also Cos (Brelich, *P.P.*, p. 182), whose population was of Argive origin.
12. Cf. Dieuchidas, in Schol. Aristoph., *Wasps*, 875; Bekker, *An.*, 305, 21; Athenaeus, IV.141e,f; cf. Hatzopoulos, pp. 143–46.
13. That is, in the Hellenistic era. See the close of Chapter 16.
14. Cf., e.g., Vian, *Thèbes*, pp. 194–98.
15. See, e.g., Vian, Ibid., pp. 138–39; Kiechle, *L.u.S.*, 26.
16. Paus., II.6.7, 11.2, 13.1, 28.3, 38.1; Strabo, VIII.8.5 (389); Nic. Dam., frag. 38; Diodorus, frag. IV.
17. Call., *H. Ap.*, 17–94; cf. Nilsson, *G.F.*, pp. 126–29.
18. Thuc., V.54.2–3; *I.G.*, IV.620 (Kaibel, *Epigr.*, 465); Nilsson, *G.F.*, p. 124.
19. Gernet, "Fostérage."
20. No tradition states this explicitly, but in this book see Chapter 13 on Iolaus and pp. 188–189 on Theseus, and Gernet, "Fostérager," pp. 19–21, 24–25.
21. Hiller, *Thera*, vol. 1, p. 275.
22. Paus., III.14.6.
23. Inscription 12/3 513a–b, from the second or first century B.C. Cited by Brelich, *P.P.*, p. 186.
24. Paus., II.11.2.
25. Bethe, pp. 452–53; Jeanmaire, *C.C.*, pp. 455–58; Bremmer, p. 283.
26. Cf. Brelich, *P.P.*, p. 184.
27. Inscription no. 336, from the second half of the third century.
28. Jeanmaire, *C.C.*, pp. 524–26; Brelich, *P.P.*, pp. 148–53, 179–87.
29. Based on Demetrius of Skepsis in Athenaeus, IV 141e–f.
30. Paus., III.13.3–5.
31. Cf. Athenaeus, IV.141e–f, and Nilsson, *G.F.*, p. 188; Brelich, *P.P.*, p. 148, based on Bischoff, in *R.E.*, s.v. *Kalender*, col. 1578e, and s.v. *Karneia*, cols. 1992–93.
32. Hatzopoulos, pp. 140–54.
33. Plut., *Lyc.*, XV.1–3.
34. Brelich, *P.P.*, p. 153.
35. Ibid., which is based on the text of Demetrius. On the *sphaireis*, see esp. Paus., III.14.6.
36. Nilsson, *G.F.*, p. 120; at Cos the cycle was triennial.
37. Hatzopoulos, pp. 21, 147, 288–89.
38. Hesychius, s.v. *Staphulodromoi*; Bekker, *An.*, vol. 8, p. 305.
39. *C.I.G.*, vol. 5, 1387 and 1338.
40. Conon 26 (in Photios, *Bibl.*, (Cod. 186); cf. Nilsson, *G.F.*, pp. 121–22; Brelich, *P.P.*, p. 151; Hatzopoulos, pp. 143–46; Jeanmaire, *C.C.*, p. 525.
41. Bekker, An., vol. 1, 305, 15; Hatzopoulos, p. 148.
42. Brelich, *P.P.*, pp. 152, 182–83.
43. *Alcestis*, 446–54.
44. Paus., III.18.16 (Alcestis and Acastus are children of Pelias). Brelich, *P.P.*, p. 152.

45. *I.G.*, 12/3, 333, and suppl., 294; see discussion by Nilsson, *G.F.*, p. 125, with interpretations by Hiller von Gärtringen and Studniczka.
46. *H. Ap.*, 85–86.
47. Nilsson, *G.F.*, based on Call., *H. Ap.*, 89ff.; and cf. *S.G.D.I.*, vol. 3, 4833.
48. Call., *H. Ap.*, 79.
49. Call., *H. Ap.*, 20–22.
50. Herodotus, IV.147–58.
51. See Vürtheim, p. 239; and references in my article "Mythologie et histoire," p. 94, n. 107.
52. See my "Mythologie et histoire," p. 69.

CHAPTER ELEVEN

1. Serv. at Virg., *Aen.*, III.271; similarly Photios, s.v. *Leukates*.
2. Strabo, X.2.9 (452); cf. Thuc., III.94.2; Ael., *N.A.*, XI.8; Ovid, *Tristia*, III.1.42, V.2.76; Prop., III, 11, 69; Ptol. Chennos, see below, Chapter 15, n. 18.
3. Strabo, X.2.9.
4. Concerning the universality of this rite, see Frazer, *Le bouc emissaire*, trans. P. Sayn (Paris, 1925).
5. Helladius of Byzantium in Photios, *Bibl.*, Cod. 279 (p. 534a 2-12); 539; Diogenes Laertius, II.44; Hesychius, s.v. *kradiēs nomos;* Tzetzes, *Chil.*, V.729; etc; see Vernant, *Mythe et tragédie*, pp. 117–21.
6. References in Vernant, ibid., p. 119.
7. Ibid., pp. 120–21.
8. On the *Koruthalia* and Artemis Korythalia, see Jeanmaire, *Dionysus*, p. 14, and *C.C.*, p. 258, 522–23; Nilsson, *G.F.*, pp. 182–89.
9. Plutarch, *Theseus*, XVIII.1–2.
10. Menander, *The Leucadian*, frag. 258 Körte-Thierfelder, in Strabo, X.2.9, following passage cited at the opening of this chapter.
11. *Ordalie.*
12. Apd., II.4.7.
13. Glotz, *Ordalie*, p. 46.
14. Diodorus, V.62.1-4, and *Cyprian Songs*, p. 29, frag. 17 Kaibel.
15. Apd., II.2.2, and III.10.3; Paus., III.13.8; earlier, Pherecydes, in *F. Gr. Hist.* 13.
16. Paus., X.14.1; Tzetzes at Lyc., 232; Schol. to Pindar, *Ol.*, II.147; *Sch. Il.*, I.38.
17. See Grimal's article, s.v., p. 84.

CHAPTER TWELVE

1. *Numa*, IV. 708.
2. Cf. Plut., *De E Delph.*, 285b–387c, and *Def. or.*, 413c–415e, 418b, 406f.

3. Plut., *Erōt.*
4. Paus., II.6.3.
5. Vian, "Triade," pp. 219–22.
6. E.g., Jeanmaire, *C.C.*, p. 477; Sakellariou, *Peuples*, p. 108.
7. Plato, *Laws*, 666e; Aristotle, *Hist. Anim.*, VIII.24.1.
8. Polemon, in Macrobius, V.19.
9. Xen., *Equitation*, V.1; and in a related sense, Aristotle, *Pol.*, VII.2 (1324 b16); Strabo 15.1.52 (709); Lucian, *As.*, 51.
10. Paus., V.1.11; Diodorus, IV.69.2.
11. *Suppl.*, 680ff.
12. See my article "Frontières de l'Elide," pp. 23–24.
13. On which see Dumézil, *I.R.*, p. 102.
14. Cf. Vian, "Fonction guerrière," pp. 63–68.
15. Diodorus, V.58.5, Zeno of Rhodes, in *F. Gr. Hist.*, IIIB 523 F 1; cf. Athenaeus, VI.262e–f.
16. *Sch. Il.*, XXIII.660; Ovid, *Met.*, XI.413; Paus., IX.36.2, and X.7.1.
17. Jeanmaire, *C.C.*, p. 427.
18. Hesychius, s.v. *Phorbanteion*; Eur., *Eurystheus*, frag. 854; and Paus., I.38.2.
19. Diodorus, IV.69.1.
20. Vian, "Triade," pp. 223–24.
21. Paus., IX.34.5; Steph. Byz., s.v. *Argunnos*.
22. *Pyth.*, III.60; on Lakereia, see Grégoire, Goossens, and Mathieu, pp. 17–18, 21, 33.
23. Apd., III.5.5.
24. Steph. Byz., s.v. *Gurton*.
25. Cf. Vian, "Triade," pp. 215, 221–22.
26. Hesiod, frag. 59 M.–W. (Strabo 9.5.22; 14.1.40); Call., *H. Dem.*, 30–32; Ovid, *Met.*, VIII. 751, 872; Diodorus, V.61.
27. Paus., VII.26.5.
28. Paus., II.36.4.
29. Herodotus, I.174; Schol. to Theocr., XVII.69. On this group of cultural and geographical correlations, see the early work of Müller, *Dorier*, vol. 1, pp. 262, 400; Wide, p. 45 (with Laconian parallels); Vollgraff, p. 194.
30. Diodorus, IV. 58.7.
31. Vollgraff, p. 194.
32. On Cadmus, for example, see Vian, *Thèbes*, pp. 114–51.
33. Paus., X.11.1
34. Athenaeus, X.416b, based on Hellanicus, *Deukalioneia*; Call., *H. Dem.*, 24ff.; Lyc., *Alex.*, 1396, and Tzetzes at line 1396; Ovid, *Met.*, VIII.738–878.
35. Hellanicus, see n. 34 (*F. Gr. Hist.* I 4 F 7).
36. Vollgraff, p. 194.
37. Do not be surprised. All the major temples in Greece reveal traces of trifunctional theology—whether at Athens, Thebes, Orchomenus, Sparta, Samothrace, Troezene, Delphi, Erythrae (Asia Minor on the Ionian coast), or Aegion (the federal temple of the Achaean league). See my article "Les trois fonctions," pp. 1164–67; in a subsequent article I shall examine the case of Eleusis; for Therapnae see ibid., pp. 1164–65. What I have just said makes it reasonable to include

Amyros in the Dotion plain, Argos, and surely Didymoi in Argolis as well as Cnidus. Trifunctionality was often expressed through a trivalent goddess—e.g., Athena at Athens, Aphrodite at Thebes (and probably also in Arcadia), Hera at Sparta, the Kharites at Orchomenus. Triopas, Phorbas, and Erysichthon express the same idea in different ways.

38. Cf. Soph., *Trach.*, 512; Aristoph., *Fr.*, 47, 495.
39. For example, L. Méridier, in vol. 2 of the C.U.F. edition of Euripides' works, pp. 10–12.
40. The tomb mentioned by Pausanias, I.22, is obviously a fairly recent limitation of the Troezenian tomb.
41. Paus., II.32.3.
42. Ibid.
43. Paus., II.31.6.
44. Paus., II.32.1.
45. At Argos, the temple of Athena Oxyderkes (Paus., II.24.2); at Methone that of Athena Anemotis (Paus., IV.35.8); in addition, a temple of Apollo Epibaterios at Troezene (Paus., II.32.2). On the connection between Diomedes and Athena, cf. Call., *Pallas's Bath*, 35; *Il.*, V.595–854; Paus., II.24.2; Strabo 6.3.9 (284) (on Athena Achaea in Daunia).
46. Paus., I.22.2; Gernet, "Fostérage," p. 19.
47. Paus., I.22.2 and II.32.3
48. Paus., II.32.3.
49. Vol. 2 of the C.U.F. edition of Euripides' works, pp. 11–12, based on Paus., II.32.1.
50. Eur., *Hipp.*, 1425–26; Paus., II.32.1
51. Apd., *Epitome*, I.19; Diodorus, IV.62.3–4; Paus., II.32.1
52. Claud., XXVIII.165–73; Nonnus, *Dion.*, XXXVIII.424.
53. Paus., III.12.9.
54. Cf. Propertius, I.1; Paus., VIII.6.4; on Parthenopaeus, Aeschylus, *Seven*, 532–46; see Vidal-Naquet, *Chasseur noir*, pp. 171–73. Note, too, that it is in Attic tradition that Melanion becomes a wild hunter and misogynist (Aristophanes, *Lysist.*, 781–96). In Peloponnesus, on the other hand, Melanion rehabilitates Atalanta, a young hunter who is hostile to men and marriage. Parthenopaeus is their son, proof of his success. The fact that the monuments to Aulon and Hippolytus stood close together in Sparta then becomes significant. It evokes the possibility that the ephebe may go astray by reference to Atalanta and probably also to Hippolytus and Melanion, while the presence of a descendant of Atalanta alludes to the necessary correction. For young Spartan boys and girls tempted by deviance and marginality, it signifies, "Even they!"
55. *Hipp.*, 58–87, 614–68, 996–69, 1092–94, 1240–41, 1389–1441. Méridier, C.U.F. edition of Euripides' works, vol. 2, pp. 20–21.
56. On this passage cf. Calame, vol. 2, esp. pp. 11–12.
57. *Hipp.*, 1–57, 1283–1439. The opposition is rightly emphasized by Méridier, op. cit., pp. 22–24, but he fails to see the connection with marriage rituals that Hippolytus in fact establishes. Yet this is explicit; cf. lines 58–87 and 99–106, 113–20, 1268–81ff.; cf. Vidal–Naquet, *Chasseur noir*, p. 171.
58. Paus., II.32.3; Eur., *Hipp.*, 228–31, 110–12, 1131–33, 1219–20.

59. He is known through inscriptions: cf. Will, *Korinthiaka*, p. 136; Wicherley, "Neleion," *B.S.A.* 1960: 60, based on *I.G.*, vol. 2, pt. 2, 4605. One also finds him in Trieste (Malten, p. 187, fig. 7), Byzantium, etc.
60. Cf. n. 54; Méridier, op. cit. at n. 55, p. 20.
61. Paus., II.32.2.
62. Paus., II.27.4.

INTRODUCTION: PART IV

1. Hes., Theog., 921–22, 950–52; Diodorus, IV.39.3.
2. References and bibliography in Gérard-Rousseau, pp. 34–35 (Hephaestus), 38–39 (Ares), 44–45 (Artemis), 72–74 (Zeus), 74–76 (Dionysus), 85-88 (Hermes), 94–96 (Hera), 164 (Paean, cf. Apollo), 181–85 (Poseidon); the author's curious restrictions are rightly corrected by Lévêque, "Syncrétisme," pp. 42–53.
3. PY Tn 316 v. 9; cf. Gérard–Rousseau, p. 95.
4. Cf. Apd., I.3.71. In Mycenaean, she was called Diwija/Diuja (Gérard-Rousseau, pp. 67–70).
5. Cf. Chantraine, *D.E.*, s.v. *Héra*, p. 416. Several authors favor an etymology via the root *yer*, "year"; e.g., Schröder, *Gymnasium*, pp. 60ff.; van Windekens, *Glotta* 36 (1958): 309ff.; and most recently W. Pötscher, "Hera und Heros," *Rh. Mus.* 104 (1961): 302–55, and "Der Name des Herakles," *Emerita* 39 (1971): 169-84.
6. Strabo, VIII.6.10 (372).
7. See my article "Mythologie et histoire," pp. 69–70.
8. Hera is apparently absent from Cnossus; at Pylos she was worshiped in the Diwieion (literally, "sanctuary of Zeus").
9. Paus., VIII.26.1–3.
10. References and onomastic coincidences in Sakellariou, *Colonisation*, pp. 98–101.
11. See my *Royauté*, pp. 121–22, 124; cf. my "Liste de Kom el-Hetan," pp. 136–38.
12. Diodorus, IV.9.4; Apd., II.4.5.
13. See my "Mythologie et histoire" p. 69 and nn. 112, 113, 114, with references to E. Meyer, M. P. Nilsson, P. Mazon.
14. Nilsson, *Mycenaean Origin*, pp. 206–20.
15. Dumézil, *I.R.*, pp. 30–31, 37; Dumézil, *H.M.G.*, pp. 89–94; *M.E.* II, pp. 117–24.
16. Diodorus, IV.10.6–38.2.
17. "Les trois fonctions," p. 1167.
18. The other Diomedes, king of Thrace and son of Ares, like his homonym was a protégé and worshiper of Athena. Note that Eurystheus sent Heracles to Thrace to do battle with his man-eating mares. Diomedes king of Argos and his father Tydeus are closely associated with horses and with cannibalistic themes. See esp. Delcourt, "Tydée," pp. 150–56.
19. At the Ladon in Elis, Heracles catches and kills the doe with feet of brass (Apd., II.5.3); the dragon of the Hesperides is called Ladon (Ap. Rh., IV.1394).
20. Geryoneus has three bodies, Cerberus three heads, the Hydra nine heads; on which see Vian, "Typhée," pp. 34–35; Dumézil, *H.M.G.*, pp. 21–22, n. 2.
21. Cf. Dumézil, *H.M.G.*, pp. 58–63, 77–78.

22. Ibid., pp. 105–6, 108–12.
23. Through the Aegean Master of the Animals; cf. Demargne, *Crète dédalique*, pp. 289–90; Mylonas, *Mycenae*, pp. 123–25.
24. Apd., II.4.6; Ps. Hes., *Shield*, 77–89.
25. Diodorus, IV.10.2–6.
26. Diodorus, IV. 10.4–5 (the same episode as that mentioned in the preceding note).
27. Apd., II.6.1–2; Diodorus, IV.30.1–3; and *Od.*, VIII.224–27.
28. The myths concerning Phorbas and the Phlegyans are among the grounds for these hypotheses.
29. See Picard, *Luttes*, pp. 12–19.
30. This is suggested by: the hydronymic series of rivers named Cephissus, one in Phocis and eastern Boeotia, another flowing into the Gulf of Saronica at Eleusis, a third flowing north to south across the plain of Athens; the legend according to which the tomb of Oedipus, king of Thebes, is located at Colonus on this third Cephissus (a local tradition, as is rightly observed by F. Chapouthier, "Notice" to the C.U.F. edition of Euripides' *Phoenicians*, vol. 5, p. 137); and the introduction into the Attic cycle of Theban heroes (Aegeus, here the father of Theseus, at Thebes the eponym and ancestor of the powerful Aegidae) or more exotic heroes (Phorbas), taken out of context. And, negatively, the apparent absence of a palace complex in Mycenaean Athens.
31. Suggested by the close connections between Megaran mythological heroes and Theban mythology, and by the recurrence of certain anthroponyms: Megareus is a Theban hero; Alcathous, king of Megara, comes from Onchestus, a Boeotian sanctuary once on the border between Theban and Orchomenian territory; Megara, wife of Heracles, is a Theban; Diocles is a Theban hero and a Megarian hero; etc.
32. Many traditions suggest that this is the case. E.g., Lycus and Nycteus, sons of Hyrieus and hence of Boeotian origin, are given as Euboeans by Euripides, *Heracles*, 32, and Apollodorus, III.5.5, according to which they kill Phlegyas, the traditional enemy of Thebes (being the eponym of the Phlegyans, the Orchomenian warrior caste), while still in Euboea, before going to Thebes. Antiope, daughter of Nycteus, Theban in the myth, is the lover of Epaphos, a Euboean hero (cf. Strabo, X.1.3 (445). Dionysus, grandson of Cadmus, the founder of Thebes, was raised in Euboea by Aristaeus (also a Boeotian hero) and Macris. The giant Tityus, grandson of Orchomenus (Pher., frag. 15) or of Minyas, king of Orchomenus, is honored by a cult in a Euboean grotto (Strabo, IX.3.14 [(423)]; Rhadamanthus, a Cretan hero, has affinities with Euboea (where he visited Tityus) and with Boeotia (where he married Alcmene, widow of Amphitryon). Recently the discovery and decipherment of fifty-odd Mycenaean tables in Thebes confirmed that Thebes belonged to Euboea. One tablet mentions the sending of *amarutode* wool "to Amarynthus" (TH Of 25.2); Amarynthus, in the southern part of the island, was the location of an important temple of Artemis (Paus., I.31.5) and at the beginning of the first millennium was the center of the Euboean federation. Excavation has confirmed that the city was Mycenaean (J. Chadwick, "The Linear B Tablets," in *The Thebes Tablets II* [*Minos* 1975, pt. 4: 88–107], p. 94.

CHAPTER THIRTEEN

1. *Erot.*, 761d.
2. *Life of Pelopidas*, XVIII.5.
3. *Ol.*, IX.98–99.
4. Paus., VIII.31.23, 1.
5. Pindar, *Nem.*, III. 36–37; Apd., II.5.2; Ovid, *Met.*, VIII.310; Hyg., *F.*, 14; Ps. Hes., *Shield*, 74–478.
6. *Heracleidae*, 88, 216.
7. Plut., *Life of Pelopidas*, 18–19; *Erot.*, 761c; Polyaenus, II.5.1.
8. Iolaus used his uncle's horses for this; Paus., V.8.3–4.
9. Hyg., *F.*, 273.
10. *Isthm.*, I.16–31; translation R. Lattimore.
11. *Isthm.*, VII.1–2 and 9. Here Pindar characterizes Iolaus as *hippometis*, literally, "intelligent in the driving of horses." On *métis* in chariot-driving, cf. Detienne and Vernant, *Mètis*, pp. 176–200.
12. *Isthm.*, V.32–34. Same grouping in *Pyth.*, XI. 59–62.
13. *Ol.*, IX.98–9.
14. Paus., VII.2.2, IX.23.1 and 27.6; Diodorus, IV.29; Hyperochus, *Historia Cumana*, in Festus, p. 266M = *F. Gr. Hist.* IIIB 576 F 3. Further, Apd., II.4.9–10 and 7.6–7; Athenaeus, XIII.556f; Tzetzes, *Chil.*, II.221ff.; Strabo, V.2.7 (225).
15. Diodorus, IV.29.5 and 30.2; Strabo, ibid.; Paus., X.17.4.
16. *Od.*, VIII.36. Other references and studies of this series in Roux, *Argonautes*, pp. 129, 135; Vian, *Thèbes*, p. 186; Astour, p. 78.
17. Diodorus, IV.29.4; similarly Apd., II.7.6, says that seven Thespiades remained at Thespiae and three at Thebes.
18. Antiochus of Syracuse, frag. 13 Jacoby, in Strabo, VI.3.2 (278).
19. Simplicius, *Comm. to Aristotle, Gr.*, ed. Diels, 9, p. 707, 31ff.
20. Eust. at Dion. Per., 458; Solinus, V.1–2; Schol. to Dion. Per., ibid.
21. Paus., I.29.4, IX.23.1, VII.2.2
22. Paus., IX.26.4, for example.
23. L. Méridier in the C.U.F. edition of Euripides, vol. 1, p. 180.
24. Pindar, *Pyth.*, IX.79; Eur., *Heracl.*, 793ff.
25. Schol., to Pindar, ibid.
26. Eur., *Heracl.*, 796, 851ff.; Ovid, *Met.*, IX.394–401, 430–31.
27. Roux, *Argonautes*, pp. 134–35.
28. Pindar, *Isthm.*, I.30; on the Spartoi and this passage from Pindar see Vian, *Thèbes*, p. 167.
29. Cf. Jeanmaire, *C.C.*, pp. 490–97; Vian, *Gèants*, p. 186; Lejeune, "Guerre," p. 31, and *R.P.G.* 1965: 1–15; Heubeck, *Studi Linguistici Pisani*, vol. 2, pp. 535–36; Sergent, "Représentation," pp. 3–5ff.; Benveniste, *Instit.* vol. 2, pp. 90–95.
30. Chantraine, *D.E.*, s.v. *ios*, p. 466; and s.v. *iocheaira*, p. 467.
31. Paus., IX.40.3, based on Hes., frag. 252 M.-W.
32. Diodorus, IV.24.4–6.
33. Cf. Gernet, "Law and Prelaw," pp. 153–54; Nilsson, *G.F.*, pp. 449–50.

34. On these rites there is an abundant bibliography, including, Labarbe, "Koureion"; Gernet, "Ancient Feasts," pp. 22–23; Vidal-Naquet, *Chasseur noir*, p. 155.
35. Bethe, p. 452.
36. Ibid., p. 450.
37. Hiller, *Thera*, vol. 1, p. 152, vol. 3, pp. 67–69; *Atlas*, 3–4; Bethe, pp. 449–50.
38. Cf. Bethe, p. 455; opposing, Dover, p. 198, but without examination of the question, based solely on the fact that homosexual interpretations of Greek myths became widespread at a late date.
39. Which surely dates back to at least the beginning of the Mycenaean period; see my article, "Mythologie et histoire," p. 84, after Vian, *Thèbes*, pp. 88, 137–38, 232–33.

CHAPTER FOURTEEN

1. *Erot.*, 761e.
2. In the *Iliad*, Eumelos, Admetus's son, has the best horses, for they were fed by Apollo (II.763; and cf. XXIII.258–59).
3. Apd., I.9.15; cf. Méridier, op. cit. (at chapter 13, n. 23 above), pp. 46–47.
4. According to Servius, on Virg., *Aen.*, IV.694; Hesychius, s.v.; Suidas, s.v. *Phrunikhos*; Méridier, op. cit., pp. 47–48. Opposing, L. Bloch, "Alkestisstudien," *Neue Jahrb. f. das klass. Altert.* 1901:114.
5. Ath., XIII.603d.
6. See n. 12 to the introduction to Part 4.
7. Amphitryon, the human father of Heracles, though of royal blood (son of Alcaeus, king of Tiryns), never reigned. He was involved in three military campaigns against the Taphians or Teleboeans—all warrior exploits, obviously. It is also said that he taught his putative son how to drive a chariot, and that he died by his son's side in the Thebans' battle against Orchomenian attackers. Although he comes close to becoming king of Mycenae when he kills Electryon, who had made him regent, this does not make him "royal" (for his involuntary murder he is exiled to Thebes). Rather, he resembles the typical Theban regent, whose connections with the military caste have been demonstrated by F. Vian, *Thèbes*, pp. 177–201. For a good study of Amphitryon, with references, see Grimal, s.v., pp. 33–34.
8. *Thèbes*, pp. 76–236.
9. See the end of the introduction to this part, with nn. 25–26.
10. Hatzopoulos, pp. 52–56, notes that all Spartan allusions to the Heraclean myth relate to this legend.
11. Wilamowitz, *Eur. Her.*, vol. 1, pt. 1, pp. 310, 78.
12. Dover, p. 198.
13. Bethe, p. 455.
14. Idyll 13, 1–20.
15. For the priority of Theocritus: H. Tränkle, *Hermes* 91 (1963): 503–505; A. Köhnken, *Apollonios Rhodios und Theokrit* (1965), which contains a general study of the question; P.E. Legrand, *Bucoliques grecs*, vol. 1, Theocritus (Paris: C.U.F., 1972), p. 86; F. Vian, "Introduction" to Apollonius, *Argonautiques*

(Paris: C.U.F., 1974), pp. 40–48. For the priority of Apollonius, see Serrao, *Studi su Teocrito* (1971), pp. 109–50.

16. *Argon.*, I.1177–1357; quoted here are lines 1177–78, 1208–15, 1223–33, and 1345–57.

17. Euphorion, frag. 75, 76 (J.U. Powell, *Collecteana Alexandrina*); Socrates of Argus, *F. Gr. Hist.* IIIB 310 F 15, based on Schol. to Ap. Rh., *Argon.*, I.1207; Phanocles, *Erōtes*, (Powell, *Coll. Alex.*) (for Hylass and Argynnus together, cf. Plut., *Brut. rat. uti.*, 990e and Martial, VII.15.1–2; Simylus, based on *Et. M.*, 135, 30; Cephalion, in *F. Gr. Hist.* IIA 93 F 1 (p. 440).

18. Vian, op. cit., (at n. 15), p. 41.

19. Which is probably a rationalization: cf. Roux, *Argonautes*, pp. 142–44; and *R.E.*, s.v. *Hylas*, vol. 11, col. 110.

20. Line 1055 of Persians contains an allusion to this rite, according to Cinaethon, in Schol., to Ap. Rh., *Argon.*, I.1357, and similarly, line 1127 of Aristophanes' *Ploutos*, according to the scholia.

21. Hell., in *F. G. Hist.* IA 4 F 131(b), based on Schol. to Ap. Rh., *Argon* I.1207.

22. See preceding notes; for Nicander, frag. 48 Schn., in Ant. Lib., *Met.*, XXVI.

23. Ant. Lib., *Met.*, XXVI.

24. Strabo, XII.4.3 (564). [With an implied etymology of Hylas from *hylas*, "woods."-Tr.]

25. Cf. Val. Flacc., III.336ff.; Solinus, 42, 2; Servius, to Virg., *Ecl.*, VI.43. And *R.E.*, s.v. *Hylas*, vol. 11, col. 111.

26. Nilsson, *G.F.*, p. 430; Knaack, p. 868.

27. Gonnet, no. 112, p. 133, and no. 148, p. 144.

28. Forrer, in *Z.D.M.G.* 76 (1922): 219; cf. Gonnet, no. 77, p. 124.

29. Gonnet, no. 148, p. 144, citing Güterbock, *J.N.E.S.* 20 (1961).

30. Gonnet, no. 74, p. 123, citing Bossert, *Orientalia* 23 (1954): 131, and Laroche, "Toponymie," p. 78.

31. Gonnet, no. 154, pp. 146–47.

32. Cf. n. 17.

33. Ap. Rh., *Argon.*, I.1321 and 1345–47, IV.1472. Nymphodoros and Kharax in Schol. to Ap. Rh., *Argon.*, IV.1470 and I.1321.

34. For the scholiast of Ap. Rh., *Argon.*, I.1241 and I.40, the hero in question is clearly Euphemus; cf. *R.E.*, s.v. *Hylas*, vol. 11, col. 114.

35. Schol. to Ap. Rh., *Argon.*, I.1241.

36. Hes., frag. 253 M.-W.; Pindar, *Pyth.*, IV.45–46. On the question of the origin of Euphemus see Vian, op. cit. (at n. 15), pp. 45–46; Wide, pp. 42–44; Kiechle, *L.u.S.*, pp. 26–27.

37. Schol. to Ap. Rh., *Argon.*, I.40. Cf. Wide, p. 44.

38. *R.E.G.*, vol. 3, pp. 207ff., cited by *R.E., loc. cit.* at n. 28.

39. Sakellariou, *Migration*, pp. 67–72, 266–67.

40. Ibid., p. 72. There was a month called Taureios at Miletus and in its colonies Kyzikos, Olbia, and Sinope. This indicates a cult of Poseidon Tauros. This cult is attested in Thebes (Ps. Hes., *Shield*, 103–4), and the scholiast indicates that sacrifice was made to Poseidon Tauros in Boeotian cities, especially Onchestus.

41. Herodotus, I.148.

42. Call., Schol., to Ap. Rh., *Argon.*, I.1212; Ap. Rh., *Argon.* I.1212–13.

43. Frag. 263–69 M.-W.; *R.E., loc. cit.*, col. 114; Vian, op. cit. (at n. 15), pp. 43, 47–48.
44. Frag. 48 Schn., in Ant. Lib., *Met.*, XXVI.
45. Apollodorus, II.7.7.
46. Ap. Rh., *Argon.*, I.1212–13.
47. Euphorion and Socrates, refs. in n. 17.
48. Op. cit. (at n. 15), p. 45.

CHAPTER FIFTEEN

1. Hesychius, s.v. *Elakatia*.
2. Sergent, "Mythologie et histoire," p. 62.
3. Paus., VIII.32.4.
4. Vallois, "Jeux Olympiques," p. 312.
5. Cf. Paus., I.34.3 (Athens), III.17.4 (Sparta), VI.26.3 (Elis), V.14.5 (associated with Zeus, Olympia); Amandry, p. 207 (with Athena Pronaea at Delphi).
6. Chantraine, *D.E.*, s.v., *elakate*, p. 409, with references.
7. See n. 18 to the introduction to Part 4.
8. Apollodorus, II.5.8. Abderus is also mentioned as the erōmenos of Heracles by Ptol., 147b.
9. Philostr., *Imag.*, II.25.
10. *Epigrams*, II. 84.
11. Diodorus, IV.38.4, which is inspired by the *Little Iliad*.
12. Tzetzes, *Posthomerica*, 571–95, based on Leskhes, *Little Iliad*.
13. *Annales E.S.C.* 1971: 623–38, reprinted in Vernant, *Mythe et tragédie*, pp. 159–84. On Philoctetes and the Centaur myths see Dumézil, *Le problème des Centaures* (Paris, 1929), pp. 188–89.
14. See Dumézil, *Lemniennes*, for references and interpretation of ritual. On connections between the myths of Philoctetes and the Lemnians see Dumézil, *Centaures* (cited in no. 13), p. 189.
15. *Il.*, II.716–18.
16. Ptol., 147e. Philostratos, *Her.*, 696, also mentions Nestor as erōmenos of Heracles. This is a late invention to explain that Nestor was the only son of Neleus spared by the hero. In the earlier tradition this was justified in a totally different way: The young man lived with the sons of Asclepius in Gerenia in southeastern Messenia (a good example of foster parentage), hence outside the kingdom of Pylos, when Pylos was taken. See Apollodorus, I.9.9, II. 7.3.
17. The tradition could be authentic, given that Iphitus, one of the sons of King Eurytus of Oechalia, was the only one to agree to give his sister Iole to Heracles, who had won her in an archery contest. Despite this relationship and this bargain, the tradition assures us that Heracles later killed Iphitus, for which several explanations are given, all indicating that the murder was indeed the fundamental element. The circumstances are strongly reminiscent of an initiation ritual. But since it was also said that Heracles, after receiving an insult, took Oechalia by force, killed Eurytus and his sons, and spared only Iphitus, it may be that some

later author made Iphitus Heracles' erōmenos for the same reasons that Nestor was cast in the same role.

18. Ptol., 147b. This probably comes from the fact that, according to the *Illiad* (II.673–74), Nireus was "the most beautiful man who came beneath Ilion / beyond the rest of the Danaans next after perfect Achilles." That said, since Ptolemy adds that certain authors make Nireus the son of Heracles, it is possible that an authentic tradition previously related the two characters. Nireus was king of the island of Syme in the *Iliad,* and in historical times the inhabitants of this island were Dorians, worshiper of Heracles. It is worth noting that "another" Nireus was the hero of a myth that would not spoil the series just examined: In despair of love (homo- or heterosexual?) he threw himself from the promontory of Leucadia and was "miraculously" saved by fishermen. This myth is at once hortatory, apotropaic, and initiatory (Ptol. Heph., VIII, in Westermann, *Myth. gr.,* p. 159, 13ff.).

19. 147b.

20. Ibid. The association of Heracles with the Argonauts is secondary.

21. Ibid. This is probably an Iberian, inventor (as his name suggests) of the helmet.

22. 152b. This may be an authentic tradition. Stichius, supposedly an Aetolian, is unknown elsewhere, and his myth is summed up for us in his connection with Heracles. A hard-hearted hero, he was the erōmenos of Heracles, who one day in a rage killed him and then massacred his own children. This death looks much like an initiation. It was also said of Iphitus that he was killed by Heracles in a rage.

23. Schol. to Ap. Rh., *Argon.,* I.1207b. Roux, *Argonautes,* p. 311, n. 22, assumes that he is a sort of spring genius, like Hylas. But are their origins the same?

CHAPTER SIXTEEN

1. Theocr., XII.27–38.

2. Aristotle, *Pol.,* II.21 (1274a32–65); English translation by Benjamin Jowett.

3. This is the opinion of Jacoby, *F.G. Hist.* IIIB 3 19 F 423, and Schwartz, *R.E.,* s.v. *Aristoteles,* no. 14. A similar view is found in Dover, p. 182. Disagreeing is V. Rose, frag. 98 of Aristotle.

4. *Erot.,* 17 (*Mor.,* 760e–761b).

5. Müller, *Dorier,* vol. 2, pt. 2, p. 289; Bethe, p. 451.

6. V.153 and 474–75.

7. Plutarch, *Theseus,* X.4.

8. Steph. Byz., s.v. *Ogugia*; cf. Paus., IX.38.7; Eur., *Phen.,* 1113; Aeschylus, *Persians,* 37; Soph., *Oedipus,* 1770; Ap. Rh., *Argon.,* III.1178; on Ogygus other references and study in Vian, *Thèbes,* p. 230. Picard, *Luttes,* p. 12.

9. Picard, *Luttes,* pp. 18–21.

10. Ibid., p. 22.

11. Cf. Vian, *Thèbes,* pp. 107–8.

12. Paus. IX.16.3. On this goddess see Vian, ibid., pp. 135–39.

13. Picard, *Luttes,* p. 14.

14. Paus., I.39.5; Picard, ibid.

15. Paus., I.39.5–6; on the religious importance of Onchestus in primitive Boeotia,

cf. *Homeric Hymn to Apollo*, 230–38; Vian, *Thèbes*, p. 139, with references cited at note 8.

16. Paus., I.43.5.
17. Schol. on Aristoph., *Acharnians*, 774.
18. VI.3.9 (284).
19. Paus., VI.20.6.
20. Paus., V.13.1
21. Apd., II.5.9, III.1.2. Cf., in Athens, Androgeos, the other son of Minos, whose murder established the Theseia (Jeanmaire, *C.C.*, pp. 528–29).
22. Cf. Sakellariou, *Migration*, esp. table pp. 266–67.
23. I should add that if Cleomachus copies Iolaus and Diocles at Chalcis, the erōmenos of his doublet Anton probably copies Philolaus.
24. Hes., frags. 11.4, 259(a), 259(b).4 M.–W.
25. Paus., I.41.3–4, 42.4, 43.2, 4-5.
26. Schol. to Theocr., III.40.
27. Paus., I.43.4.
28. Paus., I.42.7, 43.2.
29. Paus., I.42.7, 43.5.
30. Gernet, pp. 19–21; 24–25.
31. Paus., I.43.4; cf. Plut., *Q. Gr.*, 16 (*Mor.*, 295a–b); according to Pausanias, the first Iphinoe is the daughter of Nisus and a woman named Abrota; Plutarch mentions a woman named Habrote, daughter of Onchestus, who presides over the dressing of Megaran women, who change their clothing style only when told to do so by an oracle. Abrota/Habrote and Iphinoe therefore do in fact preside over female rites of passage.
32. See Chapter 8, n. 54.
33. I.30.1. Cf. also Suidas, s.v. *Meletos* (Aellan frag. 69 Hercher, 147).
34. *F. G. Hist.* IIA 84 F16, based on Athenaeus, XIII.602c–d.
35. Phaenias of Eresos, frag. 16 Wehrli (= Parthenius VII).
36. *Erot.*, 760b–c. On Aristogeiton, see Buffière, pp. 108–13. The hero of Metaponte is named Antileon. Phaenias points out that the tyrant (for him, of Heracleia, a city close to Metaponte) was Antileon's rival for the handsome Hipparinus. Plutarch calls Melanippus the rival of Phalaris, tyrant of Agrigentum. According to Athenaeus, XIII.602b, citing Heraclides Ponticus, *Erotika*, frag. 65 Wehrli, Melanippus was the erōmenos, and the erastēs was named Khariton; cf. also Ael., *V.H.*, II.4. On this type of story, cf. also Plato, *Symposium*, 179e–180a, on Achilles and Patroclus; Dover, p. 191; and Buffière, pp. 113–21.
37. Bethe, p. 455.
38. See n. 37 and Dover, ibid.
39. Cf. e.g. Buffière, pp. 178–82, 310–18, and Dover.

CHAPTER SEVENTEEN

1. *Protr.*, II.34.3–5. Other sources: Paus., II.37.5; Westermann, pp. 348, 368; Tzetzes, on Lyc., *Alex.*, 212 Arnob., *Adv. Nat.*, V.28.

2. C. Mondésert, "Introduction" to *Protrepticus* in the Sources Chrétiennes collection (Paris, 1949), p. 33.
3. Cf. n. 1.
4. Mondésert, op. cit. (in n. 2), p. 91, n. 8.
5. Paus., II.36.8 through 37.2.
6. II.17.1–2.
7. Agathon and Timotheus in Plut., *Fl.*, XVIII.3.
8. Cf. *R.H.R.* 1927: 386; and Picard, *Congrès d'Histoire des Religions* 1928: 233–34, 254–55.
9. Grimal, s.v. *Io*, p. 233.
10. Paus., II.17.1.
11. Glotz, *Ordalie*, p. 54.

Chapter Eighteen

1. Cited by Athenaeus, VII.296f.
2. Hes., *Theog.*, 233–234.
3. Athenaeus, VII.297a.
4. Schol. to Plato, *Rep.*, 611d.
5. Athenaeus, VII.296b–e, based on Theolytus of Methymna, Mnaseas, Alexander of Aetolia, and Aischrion of Samos.
6. Apollodorus, III.1.3, 3.1.
7. Paus., I.43.5.
8. Cf. Jeanmaire, *C.C.*, pp. 444–48.
9. Whence "to copulate" in Sparta; cf. Ael., *V.H.*, III.12, and Bethe, p. 454.
10. This is a universal—throughout the world spit impregnates. See, e.g., Dumézil, *Scythie*, p. 216. Compare the Papuan custom, attested among the Marind-anim (Roheim, p. 201) and the Baruya (M. Godelier, *La production des Grands Hommes* (Paris, 1982), pp. 99–94), according to which novices, during initiation, consume the sperm of their teachers. According to a tradition reported by Servius, Apollo had given the gift of prophecy to Cassandra, but since she refused to give herself to him, he spit in her mouth to take back or at least to alter the prophetic meaning of the gift (Serv. on Virg., *Aen.*, II.247). An Amerindian example of equivalence between sperm and saliva may be found in Lévi-Strauss, *Origine des manières de table* (Paris, 1968), p. 173. The equivalence is heightened by the fact that the Greeks and many other peoples believed that sperm originated in the neck (on this question see R. B. Onians, *The Origins of European Thought About the Body, the Mind, the Soul, the World, Time, and Fate* Cambridge, 1953, pp. 109–119).
11. Plut., *Solon*, XII.7. Jeanmaire, *C.C.*, p. 444–47.
12. A meaning obscured in classical Greek, since *koiranos* is an old Indo-European word disconnected from its ancient sociological contexts. Consider, however, the etymology: The word comes from *koryo-*, "army," from which come the Gothic *harjis* and Old Icelandic *herr*, Old High German *hari*, German *Herr*, Lithuanian *karias*, and Old Prussian *karjis*, all words with the same meaning; a derivative is *koryo-no-s*, "chief of the army," for which there are two and only two attestations: one is this word *koiranos*, the other the Icelandic *Herjan*, another name for Odhinn.

Thus the etymology does indicate a warrior meaning, and it would have been appropriate to give a hero a father with this name only before the word had acquired the vague meaning that it has in historical Greek. Cf. Benveniste, *Institut.*, vol. 1, pp. 112–15 (which oddly enough takes no account of the profound social changes that occurred between the Mycenaean and Homeric periods and, earlier, between Indo-European and Mycenaean times); and Chantraine, *D.E.*, s.v. *Koiranos*, p. 553.

13. Pind., *Ol.*, XIII.75ff.: Polyeidos sent Bellerophon to capture the marvelous horse at the Peirene fountain.
14. Roux, *Argonautes*, p. 219.
15. Ibid., p. 330.
16. *Il.*, VI.119–236.
17. Athenaeus, VII.296e.
18. See Chapter 25.
19. Nicandros, *Aitolika*, cited by Athenaeus, 296f.
20. Athenaeus, VII.296c.
21. Hes., *Theog.*, 233; on which see M. Detienne, *Les maîtres de vérité dans la Grèce archaïque*, 2d ed. (Paris, 1973), pp. 29–49, with other texts.

CHAPTER NINETEEN

1. See Jeanmaire, *Dionysos*, pp. 136, 173–75, 209, 388, 406.
2. Eur., *Bacch.*, 524–25; Apollodorus, III.4.3; *Schol. Il.*, XIV.325. Lucian, *Dial. deor.*, 12 (9), and Diodorus, IV.2.3, present things differently.
3. Eur., *Bacch.*, 524–529; cf. Harrison, *Themis*, p. 33.
4. Anth., IX.524.
5. J. Jolly, s.v. *Initiation (Hindu)*, in *E.R.E.*, vol. 7, p. 323.
6. See Detienne, *Dionysos Slain* (Baltimore, 1979).
7. At Pylos, in the genitive, *Diwonusojo*, Xb 1419.1 and Xa 102.

CHAPTER TWENTY

1. Apollodorus, III.1.2; (Ps.) Clement, *Homilies*, V.18 and 15; *Reconn.*, X.22; Schol. to Ap. Rh., *Argon.*, II.178, based on Hellanicus, in *F. Gr. Hist.* IA 4 F 95,
2. Ant. Lib., *Met.*, XXX.1–2.
3. Frags. 140 and 141.13–15 M.-W.
4. Apd., III.1.2; Nic., frag. 46 Schn., in Ant. Lib., *Met.*, XXX.1–2.
5. I.173.
6. Vian, *Thèbes*, pp. 241–42, shows that a fragment from Hesiod featuring Minos, Sarpedon, and Rhadamanthus classifies them trifunctionally.
7. VII.2.3.
8. Sakellariou, *Migration*, pp. 333–35; Hope Simpson, *Gazetteer*, p. 193, with bibliography of works through 1965. Since then, G. Kleinger, *Alt. Milet* (Wies-

baden, 1966); Kleinger, *Die Ruinen von Milet* (1968); and chronicle of excavations in *A.J.A.* 1969: 211; 1971: 169; 1972: 175–76, 1974: 114; 1975: 207, 270.

9. There is continuity from Cretan habitation to Mycenaean habitation and the geometric city of the archaic and classical eras. Traditions concerning the city could therefore be maintained, e.g., in the Milesian *genos*, the Euxantides, whose eponym, Euxantos, was taken to be the son of Minos and the father of Miletus (Apd., III.1.2, who spells the name Euxanthius; Schol. Ap. Rh., *Argon.*, I.185). A similar thing happened with the hero Atymnius, who in Apollodorus's version replaced Miletus as erōmenos of the Cretan sovereigns. This hero was associated with two geographical areas, Crete (Apollodorus and Solinus, XI.9; Nonnos, *Dion.*, XI.258, XII.217, XIX.182, XXIX.28), and southwestern Anatolia (a Lycian, in *Il.*, XVI.317; a son of Emathion and Pedasia, whose name is linked to Pedasus, an Anatolian city, according to Quintus of Smyrna, II.300); and there was a city named Tymnos or Atymnus and another called Tymnessos (Steph. Byz., s.v.).

10. On this theme see M. Delcourt, *Oreste et Alcméon*, pp. 55–56, and Héphaistos, p. 42. The theme may have existed for a long time in Cretan mythology. A seal from Middle Minoan II from Cnossus shows a small boy with a goat or ewe. The relationship between them is not clear enough, however, to justify the assertion that this seal depicts a legend in which an animal nurses a human being (Mellink, p. 76, with references). It was in Crete that the divine goat Amalthea nursed the child Zeus with her milk.

11. Ath., XIII.601f.

12. Bacchylids, XVII.

13. Cf. Chapter 30.

14. There are many traces in Greek mythology of initiation by fire and water. See, e.g., Delcourt, "Tydée," p. 144, and *Héphaistos*, pp. 41–42, 143; Vernant, *M.S.*, p. 123; on the myth in question here, see Gernet, *Anthropology*, p. 91.

15. Dover, p. 200, holds that the tradition reported by Athenaeus is one of many Hellenistic inventions.

CHAPTER TWENTY-ONE

1. Ibycus, frag. 28 Page (32 Bergh-Athenaeus XIII, 603d); cited by Dover, p. 200.

2. *Od.*, VII.323–24; Apd., II.4.41; Diodorus, V.79.1 (on Erythras); Paus., VIII.53.5 (on Gortus).

3. Hes., frag. 14.13 M.-W.

4. Apd., I.9.26; Ap. Rh., *Argon.*, IV.1639–40 (and schol. on that passage), Zen., V.85; Ps. Plato, *Minos*, 320b.

5. Wide, pp. 248, 250; Cook, vol. 1, pp. 718–20; Frazer, *Dieu qui meurt*, p. 63; Willetts, *Cults*, pp. 52, 100–1, 248–49; opinions are based in particular on the notation in Hesychius's lexicon: "Talos: the sun."

6. Paus., VIII.53.5.

7. Cf. Willetts, *Cults*. By contrast, Hephaestus is mentioned often in non-Cretan sources as being associated with Crete. He gives Talos to Minos (Apd., I.9.26), or he makes Talos, whom Zeus gives to Europe (*Sch. Od.*, XX.302; Eust., on *Od.*,

1839.9; Ap. Rh., *Argon.*, IV.1641); in the *Iliad*, XVIII.590–92, Hephaestus decorates the shield of Achilles with the motif of a dancing place for choirs of young girls, similar to that which Daedalus had built at Cnossus for Ariadne. In my opinion this has to do with Mycenaean traditions, for a fourteenth-century Cnossian tablet proves that the god was known to the Mycenaeans: The anthroponym *apaitijo* of KN L588.1 is a derivative in *-ijo* of *Apaito*, i.e., the form of the god's name as attested in Dorian and Aeolian: Hephaestus/Aphaistos (cf. Gérard-Rousseau, pp. 34–35, with references). In other words, the Mycenaean conquerors of Crete brought the god of fire with them, just as they brought Daedalus (KN Fp 1.3 and Fs 723) and Zeus. This dates the formation of this group of legends. Hephaestus, not much honored in Dorian territory (Pausanias mentions no cult or sacred image of this god in Laconia, Messenia, Argolis, Corinthia, or Megaris), was subsequently neglected and forgotten by the Dorian inhabitants of Crete.

8. Correction of Malten accepted by Delcourt, *Héphaistos*, pp. 40, no. 2, and 160.

9. *Minos*, 320b. Note that Talos was then a warrior (cf. Vernant, *M.P.*, pp. 32, 35) and that he here replaces Sarpedon in the trifunctional group of masters of Crete; see Chapter 20, n. 6.

10. Paus., VII.4.6; Diodorus, V.79.2.

11. This latter aspect may originally have been the principal one; on this point cf. Vian, *Thèbes*, pp. 241–42.

12. Dionysus was born in Thebes; his mother Semele was the daughter of Cadmus.

13. Apd., III.15.8.

14. Paus., I.6.5; Diodorus, IV.76.4–7. Note that Talos is here the matrilateral nephew of Daedalus and that he therefore belongs to another *genos*.

15. Apd., I.9.26; Simonides, frag. 63 Page (in Schol. to Plato, *Rep.*, 337a); Zen., V.85; *Sch. Od.*, XX.302; Eust., on *Od.*, 1839.9; Ap. Rh., *Argon.*, 1641 (cf. Grimal, s.v. *Talos*, p. 435).

16. Delcourt, *Héphaistos*, p. 161 (after Frazer, *Dieu qui meurt*, p. 264, n. 181).

17. Athenaeus, IX.388f; Ovid, *Met.*, VIII.236–259; Hyg., *F.*, 39, 274; Serv., on Virg., *Georg.*, I.143; Serv., on Virg., *Aen.*, VI.14; Apd., III.15.9; Diodorus, IV.76; Soph., lost tragedy the *Kamikoi*.

18. *Met.*, XI.339–45.

19. *Héphaistos*, pp. 115–20; after H. Usener, *Sintflutsagen* (1899); J. Hubaux, *Le plongeon rituel* (1923); Jeanmaire, *C.C.*, pp. 326–328. see also Glotz, *Ordalie*, esp. pp. 45–46.

20. Delcourt, *Héphaistos*, p. 161, with references. The wine bowl, of unknown origin, dates from the sixth century.

21. Ovid, *Met.*, XI.303–17.

22. Schol. to Theocr., I.21. On Priapus and pederasty see Buffière, pp. 128–29.

CHAPTER TWENTY-TWO

1. *Laws*, I.636c–d.

2. V.265–69 (Lattimore translation).

3. XX.219–25, 230–40.

4. Ibycus, frag. 8 Page; Theognis, 1345.

5. Pind., *Ol.*, I.40–45; *Ol.*, X.105; Eur., *Orestes*, 1392, and *Cycl.*, 582–87; Artph., *Peace*, 724; Plato, *Phaedrus*, 255c; and *Laws* (cf. n. 1); Theocr., XII (*Aites*), 80; Apd., III.12.2; Ap. Rh., *Argon.*, III.115; etc. Figurative representations: Sichtermann, Bonghi Jovino, Schwarz, Kaemph-Dimitriadou.

6. Bethe, p. 449; Jeanmaire, *C.C.*, p. 455; Dover, p. 196. Buffière, p. 373.

7. For example, the "Catalogue of Ships" (*Iliad*, book II) mentions Elis but not Pisatis and Olympia, the object of a major political conflict in the eighth century (cf. my article "Frontières de l'Elide," p. 28), or Cythera, no doubt for the same reason, Sparta having seized it in ancient times, when Sparta first developed a navy. No Attic cities are mentioned except for Athens (at a time when the integration of those cities into the state formed by Athens was certainly a problem). Furthermore, the ancient power of Orchomenus is minimized, and Orchomenus is said to have ruled over Aspledon alone (II.511). In any case, the author flatters the powers of his own time (Elians over Pisatans, Thebes against Orchomenus, Athens).

8. See Vian's "Introduction" to the *Argonautica* (cited at Chapter 14, n. 15). Vernant, *M.S.*, p. 129, writes on a similar problem: "In general Homer exhibits a very positive attitude toward defilement. In this respect and others he showed a positive determination to ignore certain aspects of religious thought." This tradition persisted until the time of the Latin epic; homosexuality is never mentioned in the *Aeneid*, with one exception, and there Dumézil has shown the Homeric influence (*Mariages*, pp. 232–33 and cf. p. 219).

9. *H.H.Aphr.*, 200–219.

10. On Tithonus see *Il.*, XI.1–2.

11. Cf. Dover's observations, p. 196.

12. *H.H.Aphr.*, 187–90.

13. Dover, p. 196. On the correlations between immortalization and sexual union between a human and a god, see Rohde, I, p. 79, and Delcourt, "Tydée," pp. 148–50. Cf. also Buffière, p. 352.

14. Echemenes, *F. Gr. Hist.* IIIB 459 F 1, based on Athenaeus, XIII.601e–f; similarly Dosiadas, in Schol. Town. *Il.*, XX.234.

15. Willetts, *Cults*, pp. 116–17. Cf. Evans, *P.M.*, vol. 4, pp. 397–99.

16. *C.C.*, p. 455.

17. *Il.*, XIV.26–30.

18. Cf. my article "Les trois fonctions," p. 1169.

19. Kretschmer, *Einleitung*, p. 185, n. 1.

20. Aristodemos of Thebes, in *F.Gr. Hist.* IIIB 383 F 7 (and commentary by Jacoby); Paus., IX.18.4; Preller-Robert, vol. 1, p. 82, and vol. 3, pp. 2, 985; Vian, *Thébes*, p. 90, n. 2; Sakellariou, *Migration*, pp. 192–94, with other references (Dümmler, Bethe, Gruppe, Staehlin, Pfister, J. Valeton, P. Lauer), and opposing (Crusius, Cauer, Wilamowitz, H. M. Chadwick, Kroll, Drerup, J. A. Scott, Farnell, Halliday, Nilsson).

21. For Anchises see Paus., VIII.12.8–9 (Anchises buried in Arcadia and eponym of a mountain), and cf. *Il.*, XXIII.296–99 (an "other" Anchises is from Sicyon). In Arcadia Anchises was earlier linked to Aphrodite. Aeneas was raised by a brother-in-law named Alcathous—like the son of Pelops—married to his sister Hippodamia—the name of Pelops's wife. And the name of the hero in Greek (cf. Perpillou, pp. 185–86). As for Alexandros/Paris, he is a hero of Therapnae, in which he

figures in Helen's trifunctional marriage; see my "Les trois fonctions," pp.
1164–65. He is to be compared with the hero Alexandra (identified with Cassandra), known from ancient texts (Pindar, *Pyth.*, XI.31; Paus., III.19.6.; cf. Wide,
p. 12, and R. Stiglitz, "Alexandra von Amyklai," *J.Oe.A.I.* 40 (1953): 72–83),
whose temple has recently been found (cf. Tod-Wace, pp. 176–77, and *B.C.H.*
1957: 548, 1961: 685, 1962: 723). Similarly the Trojan soothsayer Helenos, twin
brother of Cassandra (*Il.*, VI.76, etc.), is paired with Helen.

22. *Od.*, V.125–28.
23. *Theog.*, 969–71 (this passage is generally held to be an interpolation).
24. Delcourt, "Tydée," pp. 148–50.
25. Strabo, X.4.18 (482); cf. Jeanmaire, *C.C.*, p. 455. The question actually seems
more complex: if the Lacedaemonian Hippeis no longer fought on horseback in
historical times, they nevertheless seem to have been responsible for providing the
army with a horse (cf. Chrimes, p. 496), besides which the Cretan horsemen
mentioned by Ephorus were unknown both to Aristotle (in his critical study of
Cretan institutions) and in the island's epigraphy. Furthermore, Plato says explicitly that horsebreeding in Crete was rare (*Laws*, VIII.834b–c); Willetts, *Society*,
pp. 155–56, concluded that by the fourth century there was no longer an
equestrian class in Crete, except perhaps as a local survival.
26. Ath., XIII.601f. The abductor was Tantalus, according to Mnaseas, *Sch. Il.*,
XX.234; cf. Eust., 1280, 11.
27. Paus., II.32.3.
28. Call., *H. Art.*, 201–2.
29. See Chadwick-Baumbach, pp. 210 (names in -*klewes*), 216–17 (names in -*llawos*),
221 (names in -*medes*). On p. 219 we find names whose root is *makh-*.
30. Strabo, X.3 (462–474), an entire section devoted to this question.
31. In service of the mother of the gods, see Strabo, X.3.7 (466), 12 (468); in service of
Zeus, Strabo, X.3.11 (468); *Hymn of Palaecastro*, in Jeanmaire, *C.C.*,
pp. 432–33.

CHAPTER TWENTY-THREE

1. *Erot.*, 761d.
2. E.g., L. Pearson, "The Pseudo-History of Messenia and Its Authors," *Historia* 11
(1962): 397–426; Sakellariou, *Migration*, p. 264; Michel Austin and Pierre
Vidal-Naquet, *Economics and Social History of Ancient Greece*, translated and revised
by M. M. Austin (Berkeley, 1977), p. 252.
3. See Sergent, *Royauté*, pp. 160–61; summarized in my "Mythologie et histoire," p.
82 and 223.
4. See Dumézil, *H.M.G.*, p. 89, concerning the ancient origins of the life of Heracles
as told by Diodorus of Sicily.
5. Il., IX.529–99 (Lattimore translation; proper names were restyled).
6. Roux, *Problème*, p. 148.
7. Ap. Rh., *Argon.*, I.194–96.
8. Schol. to line 195; cf. Roux, *Problème*, p. 138.

9. E.g., probably in Crete: See Strabo, X.4.20 (482); in Elis, Paus., V.16.2–3; in Sparta at the Gymnopaedea, Pluto., *Ages.*, XXIX.3.
10. Vian, "Fonction guerrière," p. 56.
11. Ibid., p. 54.
12. Delcourt, "Tydée," pp. 160–61. after O. Müller.
13. Paus., VIII.45.6.
14. Vidal-Naquet, *Chasseur noir*, pp. 156–61, and bibliography.
15. Ap. Rh., *Argon.*, 190–93, mentions a Laocoon, uncle and educator of Meleager: Is this a trace of the supposed myth?

CHAPTER TWENTY-FOUR

1. Paus., III.24.10, 25.1; Schol. to Pindar, *Pyth.*, II.127.
2. Paus., IV.15.4.
3. IV.16.4.
4. Cf. Dumézil, *H.M.G.*, pp. 121–35. On Cuchulain's warrior deformities see *Les exploits d'enfance de Cûchulainn*, trans. C. Guyonvarc'h, *Ogam* 11 (1959): 335.
5. IV.16.3.
6. Detienne, "Phalange," p. 139, based on Paus., IV.8.1–11. The passage is interesting for the date of the phalange organization; cf. "Phalange," p. 140.
7. See Vidal-Naquet, *Chasseur noir*, esp., on the identity of the Hippeis and Kruptoi, p. 78, n. 8.
8. Cf. the preceding and following references to book IV of Pausanias. On one of these exploits, clearly legendary, namely, the Spartans' plunge into the pit of the Kaidas, see my article "Partage du Péloponèse," 2d part (1978), pp. 8–9.
9. Paus., IV.16.6.
10. Paus., IV.27.6–7.
11. See Brelich, *P.P.*, pp. 199–204.
12. See the opening of Chapter 13.

CHAPTER TWENTY-FIVE

1. Ps. Plut., *Erotl.Dieg.*, 2 (*Mor.*, 772c–773b).
2. Schol. to Ap. Rh., *Argon.*, IV.1212, translated by E. Will, Korinthiaka, p. 181.
3. Cf., most recently, C. Mossé, *La tyrannie dans la Grèce antique* (Paris, 1969), pp. 23–25, with references to G. Glotz, E. Will, Andrewes; and Huxley "Argos," p. 593.
4. Mossé does not choose between the two; Will, *Korinthiaka*, pp. 251 ff., and Huxley, "Argos," prefer the "late" chronology.
5. Vitalis, Andrewes, Wilamowitz, Hanell, Maass: see references in Will, *Korinthiaka*, p. 182.
6. Will, *Korinthiaka*, p. 182.
7. M. Cuvigny, in Ps. Plut., *Erot. Dieg.*, p. 115, C.U.F. edition, based on Parthenius, *Erot.*, XIV, citing Alexander of Aetolia.

8. Plut., *Sert.*, I.4; Diodorus, VIII.10; Maxim of Tyre, *Diss.*, 18.1 Hobein (24.1 Duebner); Wilamowitz, Hanell, Maass, cf. n. 5.

9. Apd., III.4.4; Hyg., *F.*, 181; Nonnos, *Dion.*, V.287ff.; Ovid, *Met.*, III.131–252; Paus., I.44.8, IX.2.3; Eur., *Bacch.*, 337; Diodorus, IV.81.

10. Paus., IX.2.3, 38.4.

11. Plut., *Artist.*, XI.3.

12. Cf. Harrison, *Themis*, p. 15; Jeanmaire, *C.C.*, pp. 560–62, and *Dionysos*, pp. 82–83, 201, 206, 252–57, 341, 385, 494; Vian, *Thèbes*, p. 135; Will, *Korinthiaka*, p. 182.

13. Pindar, *Pyth.*, IX.59–67; Ap. Rh., *Argon.*, II.500–520; Virg., *Georg.*, IV.317ff.; cf. Will, *Korinthiaka*, p. 183, after Maass, and, on Aristaeus, Detienne, "Orphée," pp. 8-13, 18–19.

14. Bethe, p. 448; Jeanmaire, *C.C.*, pp. 451, 561–62; Will, *Korinthiaka*, p. 183.

15. See the opening of Chapter 1.

16. I have already mentioned this hero and his homophilic relation with Glaucus. *-kertes* comes from *keiro*, which can mean "to eat rapidly" (this is the meaning preferred by Carpenter, p. 124), but more commonly means "to cut," the basis for Maass's interpretation, cited by Will, *Korinthiaka*, p. 169.

17. Scholia to Pindar, *Isthm.*, pp. 350–52 Abel.

18. Will, *Korinthiaka*, pp. 179–90.

19. Plut., *Thes.*, XXV.5.

20. Will, *Korinthiaka*, p. 186.

21. Recall that sacrifice was also made at night or in the evening to Pelops and Hyacinthus.

22. Compare also the tradition according to which Laius abducted Chrysippus and took him to the Nemean Games, dedicated to Zeus, which were held at the other end of Corinthia (Isthmia lies to the northeast, Nemea to the south).

23. Will, *Korinthiaka*, p. 187.

24. *Bacch.*, 337–40. The warning is here addressed to Pentheus, king of Thebes, who refused to allow Dionysus into the city, which is why he is ultimately torn to pieces by the Bacchae accompanied by the dogs of Lyssa, "rage," on Cithaeron, the same mountain where the tragedy of Actaeon unfolds. This explains why Actaeon is mentioned several times in Euripides' play: He has prophetic value (see lines 230, 1227, 1291). Cf. Grégoire's note on p. 256 of the C.U.F. edition. On Actaeon, see also Ovid, *Met.*, III.131–54 (which fails to understand the meaning of the myth); Aeschylus, frag. 241; Apd., II.4.4; Nonnos, *Dion.*, V.289–300.

25. Lines 781–96.

26. Vidal-Naquet, *Chasseur noir*, pp. 171–72.

27. Detienne, "Orphée."

28. Pentheus is torn apart by the Bacchae *and* the dogs of "rage": Jeanmaire points out (*C.C.*, p. 560; after Reinach, III, p. 25) that the dogs of Actaeon may represent ritual actors disguised as animals; it is said that they were later changed into men. According to Eustathius cited by Lobeck, *Aglaoph.*, p. 1189, they became the Telkhines, magicians, who, as it happens, become in another myth enemies of Apollo, who takes on the form of a wolf to fight them (Servius, on Virg., *Aen.*, IV.377). This is another connection between the two Actaeons, especially since Jeanmaire believes that when pseudo-Plutarch's text speaks of Archias and his

companions as coming to abduct Actaeon in a *kōmos* we should interpret that as meaning that they come "wearing masks" (attested in Dionysiac rituals). See Jeanmaire, *C.C.*, p. 561. In fact, masks figure in several Greek initiation rituals (e.g. in the Spartan Carnea; in a female ritual at Letrino, Paus., VI.22.8–9; etc.), and the idea is attractive here. Opposing, Buffière, p. 94, and Dover, "Eros," p. 37, but without extensive discussion.

29. On the Bacchiadae and their influence in ancient aristocratic Greece, recall that the Philolaus who took refuge in Thebes was a Bacchiad.

CHAPTER TWENTY-SIX

1. Antoninus Liberalis, *Metamorphoses*, from the French translation by Manolis Papathomopoulos (Paris: C.U.F., 1968), pp. 14–15.
2. On this placement see ibid., p. 86, nn. 2 and 3 references cited.
3. *I.G.*, vol. 9, pt. I(1), p. 335, inscription of Galaxidi; cf. Papathomopoulos, op. cit. (at n. 1), p. 87, n. 9, with which I disagree as far as the location of the Kouretis is concerned.
4. *Iphig. Taur.*, 1245–47.
5. *H.H.Ap.*, 303–4.
6. Plut., *Q. Gr.*, 12 (*Mor.*, 293c); *Def. or.*, 418a; Strabo, IX.422; Steph. Byz., s.v. *Deipnias*; Ael., *V.H.*, III.1; Ps. Plut. *De Mus.*, 1136a; Schol. to Pindar, *Arg. Pyth.*, 3. The correct form seems to be Septerion (from *sebomai*, "to venerate"), which is given in all the manuscripts of Plutarch and corroborated by Hesychius, s.v., who defines the word as "purification." But since the Renaissance many editors have put Stepterion, which gives a simple meaning: "festival of crowns." On this question see Defradas, p. 98.
7. Plut., *Def. or.*, 418a.
8. Paus., X.12.1.
9. Cf. Roux, *Delphes*, pp. 19–22, 26–30, 39–40.
10. Amandry, pp. 207–8; and cf. my article "Les trois fonctions," pp. 1166–67.
11. Cf. *H.H.Ap.*, 127–36.

CHAPTER TWENTY-SEVEN

1. Ant. Lib., *Met*; in Papathomopoulos, op. cit. (at Chapter 26, n. 1), pp. 21–22.
2. References and summary of discussions in Papathomopoulos, op. cit., p. 98, n. 2.
3. Ant. Lib., *Met.*, VIII, 371–81.
4. J. Aymard, *Essai sur les Chasses romaines* (Paris, 1951), pp. 463–64.
5. Cf. introduction to Part 4, n. 20; noted by Papathomopoulos, op. cit., p. 99, n. 11.
6. On this point see the fundamental observations of Vidal-Naquet, *Chasseur noir*, pp. 171–74.
7. Papathomopoulos, op. cit., p. 100, n. 15, who, following S. Eitrem, *Die göttlichen Zwillinge bei den Griechen* (Kristiania, 1902), p. 70, regards Phylius as being copied from Heracles, which in my view is incorrect.

8. Pind., *Ol.*, II.147; Schol. to Aristoph., *Fr.*, 963; Schol. to Pindar, *loc. cit.*; Schol. to Theocr., XVI.49; Athenaeus, IX.393e; Hyg., *F.*, 157 and 273; Ovid, *Met.*, XII.72–145; Sen., *Troj.*, 183, and *Agam.*, 215; Eust., 116.26, 167.23, 1968.45; Palaiphat., *De Incred.*, 12; Tzetzes, *Anteh.*, 257. On Calyce and her Elian offspring see Apd., I.7.3 and 5. Since the Elians came originally from Aetolia, the Cycnus of Aetolia establishes a connection between Calyce, mother of the "Trojan" Cycnus, and the Calyce of the legendary Elian dynasty, which confirms that this hero was in fact part of the ancient Aetolian cycle.

9. Ps. Hes., *Shield*, esp. lines 57–67. Another Thessalian Cycnus was associated with the isle of Tenedos opposite Troad, which is again reminiscent of the Trojan Cycnus.

10. Theocr., XVI (the *Kharites*), 48–50.

11. This is the subject of C. Gallini, "Katapontismos," *Studi e materiali di Storia delle Religione* 34 (1963): 78.

CHAPTER TWENTY-EIGHT

1. Tzetzes, on Lyc., *Alex.*, 1342.
2. Cf. Chapter 2, n. 49.
3. Cf. Pindar, *Ol.*, VI.79, and *Pyth.*, II.10; for the Hyacinthia, see Chapter 8, n. 93.
4. VIII.21.2.
5. Paus., I. 31.2.
6. Cf. Roscher, vol. 1, s.v. *Antheus.*
7. Nonnos, *Dion.*, XXXV.383, XXXII.187.

CHAPTER TWENTY-NINE

1. Apd., *Epit.*, I.22; Ap. Rh., *Arg.*, I.57–64, and Schol. to 57; *Sch. Il.*, I.264; Plut., *Stoic. absurd.*, 1 (*Mor.*, 1057c–d), and *Prof. virt.*, 1 (*Mor.*, 75a–b); Lucian, *Gallus*, 19, and *Salt.*, 57; Apostolius, *Cent.*, IV.19; Palaiphat., *De Incred.*, 11; Ant. Lib., *Met.*, XVII; Virg., *Aen.*, VI.448ff.; Ovid, *Met.*, XII.459–532; Hyginus, *F.*, 14; Servius, on *Aen.*, ibid.; Lact. Plac., on Statius, *Achill.*, 264; *Première Myth. Vat.*, 154; *Seconde Myth. Vat.*, 108; *Troisième Myth. Vat.*, 6.25.
2. Dumézil, *Problème des Centaures*, pp. 180–81; Delcourt, *Hermaphrodite*, pp. 53–55.
3. Ant. Lib., *Met.*, XVII.
4. Servius and *Première Myth. Vat.*, see n. 1.
5. *Sch. Il.*, I.264; Schol. to Ap. Rh., *Arg.*, I.57.
6. *Il.*, II.740–41 and 745–46. Note the animal aspect of this warrior kinship: Kaineus, who is closely related in both versions of his myth to the Man-Horses, has Coronos, the Crow, for a son, whose own son's name is based on the word for lion. On this point, and on Coronos as Argonaut, see Roux, *Argonautes*, p. 206–7.
7. *Il.*, XVI.140–44; his father Peleus had received him from Chiron. Statius, *Achill.*, I.260–63, draws a parallel between the two heroes, as do Jeanmaire, *C.C.*, pp. 359, and Brelich, *Eroi*, p. 286. See also Vian, "Fonction guerrière," p. 67, and

Vernant, *N.P.*, p. 35 and n. 73. On heroes who worship their lances, see Roux, *Argonautes*, pp. 206–8, 212–13.

CHAPTER THIRTY

1. Eschine, *Contra Tim.*, 132–33, 142–50.
2. Plato, *Symposium*, 179e–180b.
3. Xenophon, *Symposium*, VIII.31. See also Athenaeus, XIII.601a; Plut., *Erot.*, 751c, 761d; Theocr., *Idylls*, XXIX.31–34; Martial, II.43.9; Luc., *Erot.* 54. Fragments and references collected by R. Beyer, *Fabulae Graecae quave aetate puerorum amore commutatae sint* (Weida, 1910), pp. 52f., 73.
4. Those who believe in a homosexual relationship between the two heroes include Symonds, p. 80; Clarke; Robinson and Fluck, p. 19; Licht, p. 452. For these authors, the homosexuality of Achilles is proven because Agamemnon offers him two young men as part of his compensation (*Il.*, XIX.193–94 and 247). Opposed to this view are Bethe, esp. p. 455; W. Kroll, in *R.E.*, s.v. *Knabenliebe*, vol. 21, cols. 199–230; Levin; Dover, pp. 197–98; Buffière, pp. 373–74. I was unable to consult D. J. Sinos, *Achilles, Patroklos and the Meaning of Philos* (Innsbruck, 1979).
5. See Buffière, pp. 167, 179–217, 401–405; Flacelière, pp. 66–67.
6. XI.786.
7. *Erot.*, 751c, frag. 228b Mette (135 Nauck). The fragment is also given by Athenaeus, XIII.602e.
8. Frag. 229 Mette (136 Nauck/; Luc. *Erot.*, 54). On the meaning of the *homilia*, Aristotle, *Pol.*, II.10 (1272a25), cited above, p. 25. Mention is also made of a vase painting attributed to Euphronius around 500, in which Achilles, treated in the then habitual manner as *erōmenos*, grooms his friend Patroclus; Buffière, p. 370, and reproduction, p. 237.
9. Frag. 25 West and Edmonds, (Plut., *Erot.*, 751c).
10. A hopeless attempt to explain the name of the hero by *a-* ("without") plus *kheilē* ("lips"); similarly, *Et. Ma.*, p. 181, s.v. *Akhilleus*, and Eust., on *Il.*, I.1, p. 14.
11. Apd., III.13.6–8.
12. See Delcourt, *Hermaphrodite*, pp. 7–18; Jeanmaire, *C.C.*, pp. 153, 321.
13. *C.C.*, pp. 573–74, 585; Vian, *Thèbes*, pp. 185–86.
14. Apollodorus, Loeb Classical Library Edition, vol. 2, p. 71, n. 2.
15. *Heroicus*, XX.2.
16. *Et. M.*, p. 181, s. v. *Akhilleus*.
17. The presence of lions on Olympus, Pinde, and other Balkan mountains is affirmed explicitly, often with precise geographical detail, by Herodotus, VII.124–26; Xen., *Cyrop.*, II.1; Aristotle, *Hist. Anim.*, VI.31 (597b 7), and VIII.28 (606b 15); and Paus., IX.40.4 and VI.5.4–5; see the recent study by Helly, pp. 273–82.
18. For these observations I thank my colleague Noël Arnaud, who is currently working on the place of the Centaurs in Greek symbolism; cf. B. Schiffler, *Die Typologie des Kentauren in der antiken Kunst* (Frankfurt, 1976); and A. Schnapp, *Dictionnaire des Mythologies* (Paris, 1981), s.v. *Centaures*.
19. Lines 348–49.
20. Hesych., s.v. *Kentauros*. X.2223–27. Dover, p. 38.

21. *I.G.*, vol. 12, p. 360.
22. Wilamowitz, *Ilias und Homer* (Berlin, 1916), pp. 121–22; Clarke, p. 384.
23. Clarke, p. 385.
24. XXIV.6–9 (rejected by Aristarchus, according to Aristonikos in Scholium A, and Didymus in Scholium AT): Achilles mourns Patroclus, which recurs in XIX.315–21, XXII.387–90, XXIV.3–5 and 10–11.
25. *Il.*, XIX.4–5.
26. Clarke, p. 393.
27. Clarke, p. 388.
28. *Il.*, XXIV.128–30.
29. Clarke, p. 396; Cf. Flacelière, p. 167; Buffière, pp. 391ff. G. Dumézil has called my attention to the passage in the *Odyssey* in which Telemachus, welcomed to Pylos by Nestor, sleeps in the palace entry hall in "a fine bed near the bed of Peisistratos, captain of Spearmen," Nestor's unmarried son, while Nestor himself sleeps "in his own inner chamber where his dear faithful wife had smoothed his bed" (III.399–403, Fitzgerald translation). Then Peisistratos accompanies Telemachus as far as Sparta, where they again sleep together, and again a parallel is drawn between them and a married couple (IV.302–305). Athena finds them thus (XV.45). Peisistratos cannot be a typical erōmenos: Though quite young, he is "a leader of warriors" and old enough to participate in sacrifice (III.456). But why is he depicted as Telemachus's nighttime companion? It is tempting to see this as "routine homosexuality." Like Achilles and Patroclus, Telemachus and Peisistratos are almost the same age and in a country where homosexuality between both males and females seems to have been widely practiced in early times (in Lesbos and Sparta at any rate), to put a young man together with a very young adult like Telemachus is not much different from putting him with a young woman. In this sense see Clarke, p. 383; Oka, who sees Telemachus as the erōmenos here. Opposing, Bethe, p. 441; Millar and Carmichael; Buffière, pp. 373–74.
30. Name of the only gymnasium in Athens open to Athenians of illegitimate birth or with foreign mothers (Plut., *Them.*, I.3–4).
31. *Erot.*, 750f–751a.
32. Plato, *Symposium*, 178e–179a; Xen., *Symposium*, VIII.32–35.
33. *Epode* II (frags. 177–87 Lasserre and Bonnard). The few surviving words of this poem are commented on by André Bonnard (C.U.F. edition of the *Fragments* of Archilochus (Paris, 1968), pp. 55–56) as follows: Archilochus "denounces his adversary [Kheidos, frag. 185] as an invert by linking him to the troupe of Sabaziens [frag. 182] devoted to the goddess Cotytto, who is the patron of homosexuals and whose cult at this time may have been celebrated in an underground sanctuary at Paros. He paints him as a 'horn player,' which he may or may not have been, because these musicians were also believed to indulge in homosexual behavior. The very rare word used in fragment 181 [*muklos*] denotes the lasciviousness of women: Applied to a man it is clear that it makes him a homosexual. Similarly, the people in fragment 183, who wear a typically feminine hairstyle (although the adjective is in the masculine), are also suspect." If these interpretations are correct, if the Thracian goddess Cotytto was indeed honored at Paros and associated with the cult of Sabazios as early as the beginning of the seventh century (Archilochus must have been about twenty years old at the time of

the colonization of Thasos, hypothetically dated at 684; cf. Bonnard, op. cit., "Introduction," p. viii), and if, finally, one can deduce from Archilochus's language, his allusion to the Sabaziens, and his insults that male homosexuality already numbered among the debauched practices of which the gods in question were patrons, this would confirm that pederasty and inversion were a social reality of the primitive Ionian world. This again indicates that the silence of the epic poets on this point does not signify a late appearance of homosexuality. Curiously, Dover, p. 195, overlooks this text of Archilochus and draws sweeping conclusions from this oversight.

34. Frag. 10, 27–30, from Edmonds, p. 71. Dover, ibid., says that this is a Homeric theme taken from *Il.*, XXII.71–73. But the context is totally different, and the vocabulary, merely esthetic in the *Iliad*, becomes plainly erotic in Tyrtaeus's poem. Dover's parallel is not well founded and neither is his conclusion.

35. Cf. for Sappho, Marrou, *Education*, pp. 80–83; for Alcaeus, Buffière, pp. 246–49; for Alcman, Calame, vol. 2; for Solon, Buffière, pp. 242–45; for Anacreon, Buffière, pp. 251–56; for Theognis, Buffière, pp. 267–77.

CONCLUSIONS

1. Athenaeus, XIII.564c.
2. Sappho, frag. 165 Reinach, based on Schol. to Ap. Rh., *Arg.*, IV.57; Nicander, *Europa*, II; Theocr., III.49–50, etc.
3. X.456a.
4. Phanocles, frag. 1, 1–6 (T. U. Powell, *Collectanea Alexandrina*, pp. 106–7; Buffière, p. 385).
5. *Imag.*, II.7.
6. *Anth.*, IX.338 (attributed to Theocritus), IX.341 (from "the garland" of the poet Meleager), VII.535 (the same), IX.556 (Zonas of Sardis); *Bucoliques grecs* (Paris: C.U.F., 1967), p. 126 (Ps. Theocr., *Epigrams*, II and III); from which *Et. M.*, 13, 48; Bekker, *An.*, pp. 200, 21; 339, 23. See Buffière, pp. 364–65.
7. *Dion.*, XI–XII.
8. Ptol., 152b9.
9. Buffière, p. 266, n. 59.
10. 149a20–3.
11. 150a2.
12. 152b40.
13. Paus., III.26.2.
14. Paus., III.19.10.
15. Paus., III.15.3; Eur., *Hel.*, 1661ff.; Theocr., XVIII ("Epithalamium of Helen"); etc. Tod-Wace, pp. 117–18.
16. Paus., III.20.8, 24.15.
17. Cf. Chapter 30, n. 35; for the laws, Plut., *Solon*, I.6, *Erot.*, 751b; Hermias of Alexandria, *On Plato's Phaedrus*, 231e; and cf. Eschine, *Contra Timarkhos*, 138. For the verbs cited here, see Photios, Suidas, Eustatius, s.v.
18. R. Hope Simpson, *Gazetteer*, p. 97, with references.
19. T. W. Allen, *The Homeric Catalogue of Ships* (1921), p. 24; J. F. Lazenby and

R. Hope Simpson, *The Catalogue of the Ships in Homer's Iliad* (Oxford, 1970),
p. 78; Mellink, p. 138.

20. E. Vermeule, *Greece in the Bronze Age* (Chicago, 1964), pp. 127–130.

21. See J. Chadwick, "The Linear B Tablets," in *The Thebes Tablets II* (*Minos* 1975, pt.
4:88–107); and the discussion of J. Raison, "La Cadmée, Knossos et le Linéaire B.
A propos de plusieurs ouvrages ou articles récents et d'un livre de S. Syméono-
glou," *R.A.* 1977: 79–86.

22. See the introduction to Part 4, n. 32.

23. See the conclusion of Chapter 22.

24. If the Boeotian hero who in my view is interpolated into the history of Chalcidian
homosexuality between Ganymedes and Cleomachus, explaining why the former
was replaced by the latter, was in fact Iolaus, this would explain the cult of Iolaus,
along with Heracles, at Agyrion in Sicily. This village was on the banks of the
Symaethus south of Etna. It was the Chalcidians who colonized the rich plain of the
Symaethus after driving out the Sikeles. Six years after settling in Naxus, east of
Etna, they founded Catana and Leontini, cities that enabled them to control the
plain (Thuc., VI.3.3–4; cf. Diodorus, XIII.53.1; Polyaen, 5.5). This was roughly
contemporary with the start of the Lelantine War (second half of the eighth
century).

25. Cf. R. Hope Simpson, *Gazetteer*, pp. 115–21, 150–64, 143–47.

ABBREVIATIONS:
Ancient Authors and Works

Ael.: Aelianus,
  N.A. or *Hist. Anim.*: *On nature* or *History of Animals*
  V.H.: *Varied Histories*
Ael. Aristides: Aelius Aristides
Aesch., *Seven*: Aeschylus, *Seven Against Thebes*
Anth. Pal.: *Palatine Anthology*
Ant. Lib., *Met.*: Antoninus Liberalis, *Metamorphoses*
Apd.: Apollodorus, *Bibliotheca*
  Epit.: Epitome
Ap. Rh., *Arg.* or *Argon.*: Apollonius of Rhodes, *Argonautica*
Arnob., *Adv. Nat.*: Arnobius, *Adversus Nationes*
Artph., Aristoph.: Aristophanes,
  Lys., Lysist.: *Lysistrata*
  Fr.: *Frogs*
Artt., *Pol.*: Aristotle, *Politics*
  Hist. Anim.: *Historia animalium*
Ath.: Athenaeus, *The Deipnosophists*
Call.: Callimachus,
  H. Art.: *Hymn to Artemis*
  H. Dem.: *Hymn to Demeter*
  H. Zeus: *Hymn to Zeus*
  Frag. Schn.: *Fragments*, ed. O. Schneider
Cic., *Repub.*: Cicero, *Republic*
Claud.: Claudian
Clem. Al., *Protr.*: Clement of Alexandria, *Protrepticus*
Conon, *Narr.*: Conon, *Narrations* (summarized by Photinus in his *Bibliotheca*,
  cod. 186, printed in F. Jacoby, *F. G. Hist.* IA26.
Dem. Skepsis: Demetrios of Skepsis
Dion. Per.: Dionysius the Perigete
Dioscor.: Dioscorides
Et. M.: *Etymologicum Magnum*
Eur.: Euripides,

Alc.: *Alkestis*
Ant.: *Antigone* (lost tragedy)
Bacch.: *The Bacchae*
Cycl.: *The Cyclops*
Hel.: *Helen*
Heracl.: *The Heraclidae*
Hipp.: *Hippolytus*
Or.: *Orestes*
Phen.: *The Phoenician Women*
Suppl.: *The Suppliants*
Eust.: Eustathius, *Commentary on Homer*
Frag. M.-W.: see Hes.
H.H.Ap.: *Homeric Hymn to Apollo*
H.H.Aphr.: *Homeric Hymn to Aphrodite*
H.H.Dem.: *Homeric Hymn to Demeter*
Hdt.: Herodotus, *Histories*
Hell.: Hellanicus
Heracl. Pont.: Heraclides Ponticus (fragments in F. Wehrli, *Die Schule der Aristoteles*)
Hes.: Hesiod,
    Theog.: *Theogony*
    Frag. M.-W. or M.-W. alone: *Fragmenta Hesiodea*, ed. R. Merkelbach and M. L. West
Hesych.: Hesychius of Alexandria, *Lexicon*
Hyg., *F.*: Hyginus, *Fables*
Il.: Homer, *Iliad*
Isid.: Isidore of Seville, *Etymologies*
Lact. Plac.: Lactantius Placidus, *Commentaries on Ovid and Statius*
Luc.: Lucian,
    Anach.: *Anacharsis*
    As.: *The Ass* or *Lucius*
    Dial. Deor.: *The Dialogue of the Gods*
    Salt.: *On Dance*
Lyc., *Alex.*: Lycophron, *Alexandra*
Nic. Dam.: Nicolas of Damascus
Nonnus, *Dion.*: Nonnus of Panopolis, *Dionysiaca*
Od.: Homer, *Oydssey*
Ov., *Met.*: Ovid, *Metamorphoses*
    Her.: *The Heroidae*
Palaiphat., *De Incred.*: Palaiphatus, *De Incredibilia*
Parthenius, *Erot.*: *Erōtica Pathēmata*
Paus.: Pausanias, *Description of Greece*

Pher.: Pherecydes of Leros
Philostr., *Imag.*: Philostratus of Lemnos, *Imagines*
  Life Apoll.: *Life of Apollonius of Tyana*
Photius, *Bibl.*: Photius, *Bibliotheca*
Pind., *Isthm.*: Pindar, *Isthmian Odes*
  Nem.: *Nemean Odes*
  Ol.: *Olympian Odes*
  Pyth.: *Phythian Odes*
Plato, *Euthyd.*: Plato, *Euthydemus*
  Rep.: *Republic*
Pliny, *N.H.*: Pliny, *Natural Histories*
Plut.: Plutarch,
  Arist.: *Life of Aristides*
  Brut. rat. uti: *Bruta animalia ratione uti*, or *Gryllus* (*Moralia*, 985d–993a)
  De E Delph.: *De E apud Delphos* (*Mor.*, 384c–394d)
  Def. or.: *De defectu oraculorum* (*Mor.*, 409e–439a)
  Erot.: *Eroticos* (*Amatorius*) (*Mor.*, 748e–771e)
  Inst. Lac.: *Instituta Laconica* (*Mor.*, 236f–240c)
  Lyc.: *Life of Lycurgus*
  Mor.: *Moralia*
  Prof. virt.: *Quomodo quis suos in virtute sentiat profectus* (*Mor.*, 75a–86b)
  Q. Gr.: *Quaestiones Graecae* (*Mor.*, 291d–305a)
  Sert.: *Life of Sertorius*
  Stoic. absurd.: *Compendium argumenti Stoicos absurdiora poetis dicere* (*Mor.*, 1057c–1058e)
  Them.: *Life of Themistocles*
  Thes.: *Life of Theseus*
Polyean.: Polyeanus, *Strategemata*
Porphyry, *V. Pyth.*: *Life of Pythagoras*
Prop.: Propertius, *Elegies*
Ps. Arist.: Pseudo-Aristotle
Ps. Hes., *Shield*: Pseudo-Hesiod, *Heracles' Shield*
Ps. Hippocr., *Ep.*: Pseudo-Hippocrates, *On Epidemics*
Ps. Plut., *Erot. Dieg.*: Psuedo-Plutarch, *Erotikai Diegesis* (*Mor.*, 771e–776a, *Amatoriae narrationes*)
Ptol.: Ptolemy Khennos, (summarized by Photius in his *Bibliotheca*, cod. 190)
Sch. Il.: *Scholia to the Iliad*, ed. G. Dindorf
Sch. Od.: *Scholia to the Odyssey*, ed. G. Dindorf
Sen., *Troj.*: Seneca, *The Trojan Women*
  Agam.: *Agamemnon*
Soph., *O.C.*: Sophocles, *Oedipus at Colonus*
  Trach.: *The Trachiniaes*

Statius, *Achill.*: *Achilleid*
 Theb.: *Thebaid*
Steph. Byz.: Stephen of Byzantium, *Ethnika*
Strabo: Strabo, *Geography*
Tac., Germ.: Tacitus, *Germania*
Theocr.: Theocritus, *Idylls*
Thuc.: Thucydides, *Histories*
Tim.: Timaeus
Tzetzes, *Anteh.: Antehomerica*
 Chil.: *Chiliades*
Virg., *Aen.*: Virgil *Aeneid*
 Ecl.: *Eclogues*
 Georg.: *Georgics*
Xen., *Ages*: Xenophon, *Agesilas*
 Anab.: *Anabasis*
 Cyrop.: *Cyropedia*
 Hell.: *Hellenica*
 R.L.: *The Republic of the Lacedaemonians*
Zen.: Zenobius

SOURCES FOR
ENGLISH QUOTATIONS

Where possible I have used standard English translations of classical texts. In a few cases it was necessary to retranslate from French translations of the original Greek or Latin.—Trans.

Ammianus Marcellinus, *Rerum Gestarum*, tr. J. C. Rolfe (Cambridge, Mass., 1972).

Apollodorus, *Bibliotheca*, tr. J. G. Frazer (New York, 1921).

Apollonius Rhodius, *The Argonautica* (London, 1889).

Aristotle, *The Basic Works*, ed. R. McKeon (New York, 1941).

Athenaeus, *The Deipnosophists*, tr. C. B. Gulick (Loeb Classical Library, New York, 1928).

Callimachus, *Hymns*, tr. W. Dodd (London, 1755).

Diodorus of Sicily, *Works*, tr. C. H. Oldfeather (Cambridge, Mass., 1935).

Euripides, *Iphigenia in Tauris*, tr. R. Lattimore (Oxford, 1973).

Euripides, *Plays*, tr. R. Lattimore et al. (Chicago, 1955).

Herodotus, *The Histories*, tr. A. De Sélincourt (London, 1954).

Hesiod, *Theogony*, tr. D. Wender (London, 1973).

Homer, *The Iliad*, tr. R. Lattimore (Chicago, 1951).

Homer, *The Odyssey*, tr. R. Fitzgerald (New York, 1963).

Ovid, *Metamorphoses*, tr. F. J. Miller (New York, 1916).

Pausanias, *Description of Greece*, tr. A. R. Shilleto (London, 1900).

Pindar, *The Odes*, tr. R. Lattimore (Chicago, 1947).

Plato, *Collected Dialogues*, tr. B. Jowett et al. (New York, 1961).

Plutarch, *Morals*, tr. R. A. Shilleto (London, 1888).

Sophocles, *Plays*, tr. F. Ferguson (New York, 1965).

Strabo, *Geographies*, tr. H. C. Hamilton (London, 1856).

Theocritus, *The Idylls*, tr. B. Mills (West Lafayette, Ind., 1963).

Xenophon, *The Whole Works of Xenophon*, tr. A. Cooper et al. (London, 1832).

ABBREVIATIONS:
Journals, Collections, and Reference Works

A.A.A.: *Archaiologika Analekta ex Athinôn.*
A.J.A.: *American Journal of Archaeology.*
A.K.: *Antike Kunst.*
A.M.: *Mitteilungen des deutschen archäologischen Instituts zu Athen.*
B.C.H.: *Bulletin de Correspondance Hellénique.*
B.S.A.: *Annual of the British School at Athens.*
C.A.F.: see Kock (bibliography).
C.I.A.: *Corpus Inscriptionum Atticarum.*
C.U.F.: Collection des Universités de France, de L'Association G. Bude.
D.H.A.: *Dialogues d'Histoire Ancienne.*
E.R.E.: Hastings, J., ed. *Encyclopaedia of Religion and Ethics.* 13 vols.
F.Gr.Hist.: Jacoby, F., ed. *Fragmente der griechischen Historiker.* 1923.
F.H.G.: Müller, C. and T. *Fragmenta Historicorum Graecorum.* 1841–70.
I.G.: *Inscriptiones Graecae.*
J.D.A.I.: *Jahrbuch des deutschen archäologischen Instituts.*
J.H.S.: *Journal of Hellenic Studies.*
J.N.E.S.: *Journal of Near Eastern Studies.*
J.Oe.A.I.: *Jahreshefte des österreichischen archäologischen Instituts.*
J.R.S.: *Journal of Roman Studies.*
P.d.P.: *La Parola del Passato.*
P.G.G.A: see Vernant (bibliography).
R.A.: *Revue Archéologique.*
R.E. Wissowa, G., W. Kroll, et al. Paulys *Real-Encyclopädie der klassischen Altertumswissenchaft.* New ed.
R.E.A.: *Revue des Etudes Anciennes.*
R.E.G.: *Revue des Etudes Grecques.*
R.E.L.: *Revue des Etudes Latines.*
R.H.R.: *Revue d'Histoire des Religions.*
S.E.G.: *Supplementum epigraphicum graecum.*
S.G.D.I.: see Collitz-Bechtel (bibliography).

S.M.S.R.: *Studi e materiali di storia delle religioni.*

S.V.F.: von Arnim, H. *Stoicorum Veterum Fragmenta.* 1903.

T.A.P.A.: *Transactions and Proceedings of the American Philological Association.*

Z.D.M.G.: *Zeitschrift der deutschen Morgenlandischen Gesellschaft.*

BIBLIOGRAPHY
With Key to Abbreviated Citations Used in Notes

AMANDRY: Amandry, P. *La mantique apollonienne à Delphes. Essai sur le fonctionnement de l'oracle.* Salem, N.H., 1976.

ASTOUR: Astour, M. C. *Hellenosemitica. An Ethnic and Cultural Study in West Semitic Impact on Mycenaean Greece.* Leyde, 1965.

BAUMANN and WESTERMANN: Baumann, H., and D. Westermann. *Les peuples et les civilisations de l'Afrique.* Followed by *Les langues et l'éducation.* Translated from German by L. Homburger. Paris, 1967.

BECHTEL, *Gr. dial.*: Bechtel, F. *Die griechischen Dialekte.* Berlin, 1921.

BECK: Beck. H. *Das Ebersignum im Germanischen, ein Beitrag zur germanischen Tier-Symbolik.* Berlin, 1965.

BEKKER, *An.*: Bekker, E. *Anecdota Graeca.* Berlin, 1814–21.

BENVENISTE, *Instit.*: Benveniste, E. *Indo-European Language and Society.* Baltimore, 1973.

BETHE: Bethe, E. "Die dorische Knabenliebe, ihre Ethic, ihre Idee." *Rhein. Mus.* 62 (1907): 438–475.

—, *Theban, Helden.*: Bethe, E. *Die thebanischen Heldenlieder, Untersuchungen über die Epen des thebanisch-argivivischen Sagenkreises.* Leipzig, 1891.

BOARDMAN, *Eros*: Boardman, J. *Eros in Greece.* London, 1978. Eva R. Szilagyi. Budapest, 1976.

—, 1973: Boardman, J. *Greek Art.* Vol. 2. London, 1973.

BONGHI JOVINO: Bonghi Jovino, M. "Una tabella capuana con ratto di Ganimede." *Hommages à M. Renard.* Vol. 3, pp. 66–78. Brussels, 1969.

BOUCHÉ-LECLERQ: Bouché-Leclerq, A. *L'astrologie grecque.* Paris, 1899.

BRELICH, *Guerre*: Brelich, A. *Guerre, Agoni e Culti nella Grecia arcaica.* Bonn, 1961.

—, *P.P.*: Brelich, A *Paides e Parthenoi.* Rome, 1969.

BREMMER: Bremmer, J. "An Enigmatic Indo-European Rite: Paederasty." *Arethusa* 13, pt. 2 (1980): 279–98.

BUFFIÈRE: Buffière, F. *Eros adolescent. La pederastie dans la Grèce antique.* Paris, 1980.

BUSOLT: Busolt, G. *Griechische Geschichte.* Vol. 2, pt. 3. Gotha, 1892.

CAHEN: Cahen, M. *La libation. Etude sur le vocabulaire religieux du vieux scandi-nave*. Paris, 1921.

CALAME: Calame, C. *Les choeurs de jeunes filles in Grèce archaïque*. Vol. 1, *Morphologie, fonction religieuse et sociale*. Vol. 2, *Alcman*. Rome, 1977.

CARPENTER: Carpenter, R. *Folk Tale, Fiction and Saga in the Homeric Epics*. Berkeley, Los Angeles, 1958.

CHADWICK-BAUMBACH: Chadwick, J., and L. Baumbach, "The Mycenaean Greek Vocabulary." *Glotta* 41 (1963): 157–271.

CHANTRAINE, *D.E.*: Chantraine, P. *Dictionnaire étymologique de la langue grecque. Histoire des mots*. Paris, 1968, 1974, 1977, 1980.

CHELMES: Chelmes, J. "Notes on the Bugilai, British New Guinea." *Journal of the Royal Anthr. Inst. of Gr. Britain and Ireland* 34 (1904).

CHIRASSI: Chirassi, I. *Elementi di cultura precereali nei miti e riti greci*. Rome, 1968.

CHRIMES: Chrimes, K. M. T. *Ancient Sparta*. Manchester, 1949.

CLARKE: Clarke, W. M. "Achilles and Patroclus in Love." *Hermes* 106 (1978): 381–396.

COLLITZ-BECHTEL: Collitz, H., et al. *Sammlung der griechischen Dialekt-Inschriften*. Göttingen, 1884–1915.

COOK: Cook, A. B. *Zeus, A Study in Greek Religion*. Cambridge, 1914–40.

DEACON: Deacon, A. B. *Malekula, A Vanishing People in the New Hebrides*. London, 1934.

DEFRADAS: Defradas, J. *Les thèmes de la propagande delphique*. Paris, 1964.

DELCOURT, *Cultes*: Delcourt, M. *Légendes et cultes de héros dans la Grèce ancienne*. Paris, 1942.

———, *Héphaistos*: Delcourt, M. *Héphaistos ou la légende du magicien*. Paris, 1957.

———, *Hermaphrodite*: Delcourt, M. *Hermaphrodite. Mythes et rites de la bissex-ualité dans l'Antiquité classique*. Paris, 1958.

———, *Oreste et Alcméon*: Delcourt, M. *Oreste et Alcméon. Etude sur la projection légendaire du matricide*. Paris, 1959.

———, "Tydée": Delcourt, M. "Tydée et Mélanippe." *S.M.S.R.* 37 (1966): 169–80.

DEMARGNE, *Crète dédalique*: Demargne, P. *La Crète dédalique*. Paris, 1947

DEN BOER: Den Boer, W. *Laconian Studies*. Amsterdam, 1954.

DESBOROUGH, *P.P.*: Desborough, W. R. d'A. *Protogeometric Pottery*. Oxford, 1952.

DETIENNE, *Dionysos*: Detienne, M. *Dionysus Slain*. Baltimore, 1979.

———, *Jardins*: Detienne, M. *Les jardins d'Adonis*. Paris, 1972.

———, "Orphée": Detienne, M. "Orphée au miel." *Quaderni Urbinati di Cultura Classica* 12 (1971): 7–23.

———, "Phalange": Detienne, M. "La Phalange. Problèmes et controverses." In *P.G.G.A.*, pp. 119–142.

DETIENNE and VERNANT, *Mètis*: Detienne, M., and J.-P. Vernant. *Les ruses de l'intelligence, la Mètis des Grecs*. Paris, 1974.

DEUBNER: Deubner, L. *Attische Feste*. Berlin, 1932. Reprint. 1956.

DEVEREUX, "Pseudo": Devereux, G. "Greek Pseudo-Homosexuality and the 'Greek Miracle.'" *Symbolae Osloenses* 42 (1967): 69–92.

DE VRIES, *Altgerm.*: De Vries, J. *Altgermanische Religiongeschichte*. 2 vols. Berlin, 1956–57.

DICKINS: Dickins, G. "The Growth of the Spartan Policy." *J.H.S.* 32 (1912): 1–42.

DIELS: Diels, Hermann. "Alkmans Partheneion." *Hermes* 31 (1896): 339–374.

DIETRICH: Dietrich, B. C. "The Dorian Hyacinthia: A Survival from the Bronze Age." *Kadmos* 14 (1975): 133–142.

DOVER: Dover, K. J. *Greek Homosexuality*. London, 1978.

———, "Eros": Dover, K. J. "Eros and Nomos." *Bulletin of the Institute for Classical Studies London* 11 (1964).

DUMÉZIL, *Dieux des Germains*: Dumézil, G. *Gods of the Ancient Northmen*. Berkeley, 1973.

———, *Dieux des Indo-Européens*: G. Dumézil, *Les dieux des Indo-Européens*. Paris, 1952.

———, *Dieux souverains*: Dumézil, G. *Les dieux souverains des Indo-Européens*, Paris, 1977.

———, *Festin*: Dumézil, G. *Le festin d'immortalité*. Paris, 1924.

———, *H.M.G.*: Dumézil, G. *Heur et malheur du guerrier*. Paris, 1969.

———, *I.R.*: Dumézil, G. *Idées romaines*. Paris, 1968.

———, *J.M.Q.* I: Dumézil, G. *Jupiter-Mars-Quirinus*. Vol. 1, *Essai sur la conception indo-européenne de la societé et sur les origines de Rome*. Paris, 1941.

———, *J.M.Q.* III: Dumézil, G. *Jupiter-Mars-Quirinus*. Vol. 3, *Naissance d'Archanges*. Paris, 1945.

———, *J.M.Q.* IV: Dumézil, G. *Jupiter-Mars-Quirinus*. Vol. 4, *Explication de textes indiens et latins*. Paris, 1948.

———, *Lemniennes*: Dumézil, G. *Le crime des Lemniennes*. Paris, 1921.

———. *Mariages*: Dumézil, G. *Mariages indo-européens*. Followed by *Quinze questions romaines*. Paris, 1979.

———, *M.E.* I: Dumézil, G. *Mythe et épopée*. Vol. 1. Paris, 1968.

———, *M.E.* II: Dumézil, G. *Mythe et épopée*. Vol. 2. Paris, 1971.

———, *M.V.*: Dumézil, G. *Mitra-Varuna. Essai sur deux représentations indo-européennes de la souveraineté*. Paris, 1940.

———. *Scythie*: Dumézil, G. *Romans de Scythie et d'alentour*. Paris, 1978.

———, *Tarpeia*: Dumézil, G. *Tarpeia. Essais de philologie comparative indo-européenne*. 6th ed. Paris, 1947.

———, "Triades": Dumézil, G. "Triades de calamités et triades de délits à valeur fonctionnelle chez divers peuples indo-européens." *Latomus* 14 (1955): 173–185.

EDMONDS: Edmonds, J. M. *Greek Elegy and Iambus*. Vol. 1. London and Cambridge, Mass., 1968.

EFFENTERRE, *Crète*: Effenterre, H. van. *La Crète el le monde grec de Platon à Polybe*. Paris, 1948.

ELIADE, *Aspects du mythe*: Eliade, M. *Aspects du mythe*. Paris, 1963.

————, *Initiation*: Eliade, M. *Rites and Symbols of Initiation; The Mysteries of Birth and Rebirth*. New York, 1965.

————, *Traité*: Eliade, M. *Traité d'histoire des religions*. Paris, 1968.

ENMANN: Enmann, A. "Kypros und der Ursprung des Aphroditekultus." *Mem. Acad. Imp. Sciences St. Pétersbourg*. 7th series, vol. 34, pp. 886ff.

EVANS, *P.M.*: Evans, A. J. *The Palace of Minos at Knossos*. 4 vols. London, 1921–35.

FARNELL: Farnell, L. R. *The Cults of the Greek States*, 5 vols. Oxford, 1896–1909.

FINLEY, "Sparta": Finley, M. I. "Sparta." In *P.G.G.A.*, pp. 143–160.

FLACELIÈRE: Flacelière, R. *Love in Ancient Greece*. Translated by James Cleugh. Westport, Conn., 1973.

FONTENROSE: Fontenrose, J. *Python, A Study of Delphic Myth and its Origins*. 1959.

FORREST, *Sparta*: Forrest, W. G. *A History of Sparta, 950–142 B.C.* London, 1968.

FOUGÈRES: Fougères, G. "Hyacinthia." In C. Daremberg and E. Saglio, *Dictionnaire des antiquités grecques et romaines*. Vol. 3, columns 304–306. 1900.

FRAZER, "Two Dedications": Frazer, D. M. "Two Dedications from Cyrenaica." *B.S.A.* 57 (1962): 24–27.

FRAZER, *Apollodorus*: Frazer, J. G., ed. and trans. *Bibliotheca*, by Apollodorus. 2 vols. London, 1921. Rev. ed. London and Cambridge, Mass., 1967.

————, *Atys*: Frazer, J. G. *Adonis, Attis, Osiris*. 2 vols. New York, 1980.

————, *Dieu qui meurt*: Frazer, J. G. *The Dying God*. New York, 1980.

————, *Rameau d'or*: Frazer, J. G. *The Golden Bough*. 13 vols. New York, 1980.

FREUD, *Trois essais*: Freud, S. *Three Essays on the Theory of Sexuality*. New York, 1982.

GÉRARD-ROUSSEAU: Gérard-Rousseau, M. *Les mentions religieuses dans les tablettes mycéniennes*. Rome, 1968.

GERNET, *Anthropologie*: Gernet, L. *Anthropology of Ancient Greece*. Baltimore, 1981.

————, "Droit et prédroit": Gernet, L. "Droit et prédroit dans la Grèce ancienne." *Année sociologique* 1948–49. Reprinted in Gernet, *Anthropologie*, pp. 175–260.

————, "Fostérage": Gernet, L. "Fostérage et légende." in *Droit et société dans la Grèce ancienne*, pp. 19–28. Paris, 1955; 2d ed. 1964.

————, "Frairies": Gernet, L. "Frairies antiques." *R.E.G.* 41 (1928). Reprinted in Gernet, *Anthropologie*, pp. 21–61.

GIMBUTAS: Gimbutas, M. *The Gods and Goddesses of Old Europe.* 1974.

GLOTZ, *Ordalie*: Glotz, G. *L'ordalie dans la Grèce primitive, étude de droit et de mythologie.* Salem, N.H., 1979.

GONNET: Gonnet, H. "Les montagnes d'Asie Mineure d'après les textes hittites." *Revue Hittite et Asianique* 26 (1968): 93–170.

GRAF: Graf, F. "Apollon Delphinios." *Museum Helveticum* 36 (1979): 2–22.

GRÉGOIRE, GOOSSENS, and MATHIEU: Grégoire, H., R. Goossens, and M. Mathieu. *Asklepios, Apollon Smintheus et Rudra, Etudes sur le dieu à la taupe et le dieu au rat dans la Grèce et dans l'Inde.* Brussels, 1949.

GRIMAL: Grimal, P. *Dictionnaire de la mythologie grecque et romaine.* New York, 1969.

GRUPPE: Gruppe, O. *Griechische Mythologie und Religiongeschichte.* Salem, N.H., 1969.

HARRISON, *Themis*: Harrison, J. *Themis. A Study of the Social Origin of Greek Religion.* Cambridge, 1912. Reprint. New York, 1962.

HATZOPOULOS: Hatzopoulos, M. *Le culte des Dioscures et la double royauté à Sparte.* Unpublished thesis. Paris, 1970.

HELLY: Helly, B. "Des lions dans l'Olympe!" *R.E.A.* 70 (1968): 271–285.

HERRMANN: Herrmann, V. "Zur ältesten Geschichte von Olympia." *A.M.* 77 (1962): 3–34.

HILLER, *Thera*: Hiller von Gärtingen, F. *Thera. Untersuchungen, Termessungen und Ausgrabungen in den Jähren 1895–1898.* 3 vols. Berlin, 1899.

HÖFLER: Höfler, O. *Kultische Geheimbünde der Germanen.* Frankfurt-am-Main, 1934.

HOPE SIMPSON, *Gazetteer*: Hope Simpson, R. *A Gazetteer and Atlas of Mycenaean Sites. Supplement* to *Bulletin of the Institute of Classical Studies* London 16 (1965).

HOW-WELLS: How, W. W., and J. Wells. *A Commentary on Herodotus.* Vol. 2. Rev. ed. Oxford, 1957.

HUBERT, I and II: Hubert, H. Vol. 1, *Les Celtes et l'expansion celtique jusqu'à l'époque de La Tène.* Vol. 2, *Les Celtes depuis l'époque de La Tène et la civilisation celtique.* Paris, 1932. Reprint. 1974.

HUXLEY: Huxley, A. L. *Early Sparta.* London, 1962.

————, "Argos": Huxley, A. L. "Argos et les derniers Téménides." *B.C.H.* 82 (1958): 588–601.

JEANMAIRE, *C.C.*: Jeanmaire, H. *Couroi et Courètes.* Lille, 1939.

————, *Dionysos*: Jeanmaire, H. *Dionysos, histoire du culte de Bacchus.* Paris, 1951, Rev. ed. 1970.

JENSEN: Jensen, A. E. *Beschneidung und Reifezeremonien bei Naturvölkern.* Stuttgart, 1933.

KAEMPF-DIMITRIADOU: Kaempf-Dimitriadou, S. "Zeus und Ganymed auf einer Pelike des Hermonax." *A.K.* 22 (1979): 49–54.

KAIBEL, *Epigr.*: Kaibel, G. *Epigrammata graeca ex labidibus conlecta.* Berlin, 1878.

KIECHLE, *L.u.S.*: Kiechle, F. *Lakonien und Sparta.* Munich, 1963.

KNAACK: Knaack, G. Review of G. Turk, *De Hyla.* Breslau, 1895. In *Göttingische Gelehrte Anzeigen* 1896: 867–887.

KOCK, *C.A.F.*: T. Kock, ed. *Comicorum Atticorum Fragmenta.*

KRETSCHMER, *Einleitung*: Kretschmer, P. *Einleitung in die Geschichte der griechischen Sprache.* Göttingen, 1896.

LABARBE, "Koureion": Labarbe, J. "L'âge correspondant au sacrifice du *koureion* et les données historiques du sixième discours d'Isée." *Bull. Acad. roy. Belg. classe des lettres* 39 (1953): 358–394.

LACROIX: Lacroix, L. "La légende de Pelops et son iconographie." *B.C.H.* 100 (1976): 327–341.

LANGANEY: Langaney, A. *Le sexe et l'innovation.* Paris, 1979.

LAROCHE, "Toponymie": Laroche, E. "Etudes de toponymie anatolienne." *Revue Hittite et Asianique* 19 (1961): 57–98.

LASSERRE: Lasserre. F. "Notice" and "Notes." In Strabo, *Geographie.* Vol. 7, bk. 10. C.U.F. edition. Paris, 1971.

LEJEUNE, "Guerre": Lejeune, M. "La civilisation mycénienne et la guerre." In *P.G.G.A.*, pp. 31–51.

LÉVÊQUE, "Continuité": Lévêque, "Continuité et innovations dans la religion grecque de la première moitié du 1er millénaire." *P.d.P.* 1973, pt. 1: 23–50.

———, "Syncrétisme": Lévêque, "Le syncretisme creto-mycenien." In F. Dunand and P. Leveque, *Les syncrétismes dans les religions de l'Antiquité.* Leyde. 1975.

LÉVI-STRAUSS, *A.S.*: Lévi-Strauss, C. *Anthropologie structurale.* Paris, 1958.

LEVIN: Levin, S. "Love and the Hero of the Iliad." *T.A.P.A.* 80 (1949): 37–49.

LICHT: Licht, H., and P. Brandt. *Sexual Life in Ancient Greece.* Translated by J. Freese. Reprint. New York, 1953.

MAGRATH: Magrath, W. T. "The Athenian King List and Indo-European Trifunctionality." *Indo-European Studies* 3 (1975): 173–194.

MALTEN: Malten, L. "Das Pferd im Totenglauben." *J.D.A.I.* 29 (1914): 170-190.

MARROU, "Classes d'âge": Marrou, H.-I. "Les classes d'âge de la jeunesse spartiate." *R.E.A.* 48 (1946): 216–230.

———, *Education*: Marrou, H.-I. *History of Education in Antiquity.* Madison, 1982.

MAYER, *Gig. u. Tit.*: Mayer, M. *Die Giganten und Titanen in der antiken Sage und Kunst.* Berlin, 1887.

MEIER: Meier, M. H. E. *Histoire de l'amour grec dans l'Antiquité.* Leipzig, 1837. Translated from German and expanded by L.-R. de Pogey-Castries. Paris, 1930.

MELLINK: Mellink, M. J. *Hyakinthos*. Utrecht, 1943.

MICHELL: Michell, H. *Sparte et les Spartiates*. London, 1952. Translated from English by A. Coeuroy. Paris, 1953.

MILLAR and CARMICHAEL: Millar, C. M. H., and J. W. Carmichael. "The Growth of Telemachus." *Greece and Rome* 1 (1954): 58–64.

MOSCOVICI: Moscovici, S. *Society Against Nature*. Atlantic Highlands, N.J., 1976.

MÜLLER, *Dorier*: Müller, K. O. *Die Dorier*, 2 vols. 2d ed. Breslau, 1844.

MURR: Murr, J. *Die Pflanzenwelt in der griechischen Mythologie*. Innsbruck, 1890.

MYLONAS, *Mycenae*: Mylonas, G. E. *Ancient Mycenae, the Capital City of Agamemnon*. Princeton, 1957.

NILSSON, *G.F.*: Nilsson, M. P. *Griechische Feste von religiöser Bedeutung, mit Ausschluch der Attischen*. Leipzig, 1906.

————, *G.G.R.*: Nilsson, M. P. *A History of Greek Religion*. Westport, Conn., 1980.

————, *Mycenaean Origin*: Nilsson, M. P. *The Mycenaean Origin of the Greek Religion*. Cambridge, 1932.

OKA: Oka, M. "Telemachus in the *Odyssey*." *Journal of Classical Studies* 13 (1965): 33–50.

OLIVA: Oliva, P. *Sparta and Her Social Problems*. Amsterdam and Prague, 1971.

OLLIER: Ollier, F. *Le mirage spartiate. Etude sur l'idéalisation de Sparte dans l'Antiquité grecque, de l'origine aux Cyniques*. Paris, 1933.

————, *Commentaire*: Ollier, F. Translation of and commentary on Xenophon, *La Republique des Lacédémoniens*. Paris, 1933.

OVERBECK, *Gr. Plastik*: Overbeck, J. *Geschichte der griechischen Plastik*. Leipzig, 1893.

PARETI: Pareti, L. *Storia di Sparta arcaica*. Vol. 1. Florence, 1920.

PARKINSON: Parkinson, R. *Dreissig Jähre in der Südsee*. Stuttgart, 1907.

PÉLÉKIDIS: Pélékidis, C. *Histoire de l'éphébie attique, des origines à 31 avant Jésus-Christ*. Paris, 1962.

PERPILLOU: Perpillou, J.-L. *Les substantifs grecs en -eus*. Paris, 1973.

PICARD, *Luttes*: Picard, C. *Les luttes primitives d'Athènes et d'Eleusis*. In *Revue historique* 166 (1931): 1–76.

PICCIRELLI: Piccirelli, L. "Recerche sul culto di Hyakinthos." *Studi Classici e Orientali* 16 (1967): 99–116.

PRELLER-ROBERT: Preller, L. *Griechische Mythologie*. 4th ed. Berlin: C. Robert, 1894.

REINACH, *C.M.R.* or III: Reinach, S. *Cultes, mythes et religions*. 4 vols. Paris, 1905.

ROBERT, *Oidipus*: Robert, C. *Oidipus. Geschichte eines poetischen Stoffs im griechischen Altertum*. 2 vols. Berlin, 1915.

ROBINSON and FLUCK: Robinson, D., and E. Fluck. *A Study of the Greek Love-Names*. Baltimore, 1937.

RHODE, I: Rohde, E., *Psyche. Seelenkult und Unsterblichkeitsglaube der Griechen.* 3d ed. Tübingen and Leipzig, 1903. Translated by A. Reymond. Paris, 1928.

ROHEIM: Roheim, G. *The External Ones of the Dream, a Psychoanalytic Interpretation of Australian Myth and Ritual.* New York, 1969.

ROSCHER: Roscher, W. H., ed. *Ausführliches Lexikon der griechische und römische Mythologie.* 5 vols. Leipzig, 1884–90.

ROUX, *Delphes*: Roux, G. *Delphes, son oracle et ses dieux.* Paris, 1976.

ROUX, *Argonautes*: Roux, R. *Le problème des Argonautes.* Paris, 1948.

ROVERI: Roveri, A. "Istituzioni sacre della Grecia antiqua." *Enciclopedia Classica.* Vol. 3, pt. 2. Turin, 1959.

SAKELLARIOU, *Migration*: Sakellariou, M. *La migration grecque en Ionie.* Athens, 1958.

————, *Peuples*: Sakellariou, M. *Peuples préhelléniques d'origine indo-européenne.* Athens, 1977.

SCHNAPP: Schnapp, A. "Pratiche e Immagini di caccia nella Grecia antica." *Dialoghi di Archeologia.* New series, 1 (1979): 36–59.

————, *Les représentations de la chasse dans les textes littéraires et la céramique.* Thesis. Paris, 1973.

SCHRÖDER, *Gymnasium*: Schröder, F. R. "Hera." *Gymnasium* 63 (1956): 57–78.

SCHWARZ: Schwartz, G. "Iris und Ganymed auf attischen Vasenbildern." *J.Oe.A.I.* 51 (1976): 66–78.

SERGENT, "Frontières de l'Elide": Sergent, B. "Sur les frontières de l'Elide aux hautes époques." *R.E.A.* 82 (1979): 16–35.

————, "Liste de Kom el-Hetan": Sergent, B. "La liste de Kom el-Hetan et le Péloponnèse." *Minos* 16 (1977): 126–173.

————, "Mythologie et histoire": Sergent, B. "Mythologie et histoire en Grèce ancienne." *D.H.A.* 5 (1979): 59–101.

————, "Partage du Péloponèse": Sergent, B. "Le partage du Péloponèse entre les Héraklides." *R.H.R.* 190 (1977): 121–136; *R.H.R.* 191 (1978): 3–25.

————, "Représentation": Sergent, B. "La représentation spartiate de la royauté." *R.H.R.* 189 (1976): 3–52.

————, *Royauté*: Sergent, B. *Recherches sur la royauté mycénienne.* Thesis. Paris, 1975.

————, "Les trois fonctions": Sergent, B. "Les trois fonctions indo-européennes en Grèce ancienne: bilan critique." *Annales E.S.C.* 1979, pt. 6: 1155–1186.

SICHTERMANN: Sichtermann, H. *Ganymed: Mythus und Gestalt in der Antiken Kunst.* Berlin, 1952. And "Zeus und Ganymed in frühklassischen Zeit." *A.K.* 2 (1959): 10–15.

SNODGRASS: Snodgrass, A. M. *The Dark Age of Greece: An Archaeological Survey of the Eleventh to the Eighth Centuries B.C.* Edinburgh, 1971.

SYMONDS: Symonds, J. A. *Studies of the Greek Poets*. 3d ed. London, 1920.

TOD-WACE: Tod, M. N., and A. J. B. Wace. *A Catalogue of the Sparta Museum*. Oxford, 1906. Reprint. Rome, 1968.

TOYNBEE, *Problems*: Toynbee, A. J. *Some Problems of Greek History*. Oxford, 1969.

UNGER: Unger, G. F. "Der Isthmientag und die Hyakinthien." *Philologus* 37 (1877): 1–42.

VALLOIS, "Jeux Olympiques": Vallois, R. "Les origines des Jeux Olympiques. Mythes et réalité." *R.E.A.* 1926: 305–322; *R.E.A.* 1929: 114–133.

VAN GENNEP, *Rites*: Van Gennep, A. *Rights of Passage*. Translated by Monika B. Vizedon and Gabrielle L. Caffee, Chicago, 1961.

VERNANT, "Introduction": Vernant, J.-P. "La Guerre des cités." Introduction to *P.G.G.A.*, pp. 9–30.

———, *M.P.*: Vernant, J.-P. *Myth and Thought among the Greeks*. Boston, 1983.

———, *M.S.*: Vernant, J.-P. *Mythe et société en Grèce ancienne*. Paris, 1974.

———, *Mythe et tragédie*: Vernant, J.-P., with P. Vidal-Naquet. *Tragedy and Myth in Ancient Greece*. Translated by Janet Lloyd, Atlantic Highlands, N.J., 1981.

———, *Origines*: Vernant, J.-P. *The Origins of Greek Thought*. Ithaca, 1984.

———, *P.G.G.A.*: Vernant, J.-P. ed. *Problèmes de la guerre en Grèce ancienne*. Paris and the Hague, 1968.

VIAN, "Fonction guerrière": Vian, F. "La fonction guerrière dans la mythologie grecque." In *P.G.G.A.*, pp. 53–68.

———, *Géants*: Vian, F. *La guerre des Géants. Le mythe avant l'époque hellénistique*. Paris, 1952.

———, *Thèbes*: Vian, F. *Les origines de Thèbes. Cadmos et les Spartes*. Paris, 1963.

———, "Triade": Vian, F. "La triade des rois d'Orchomène: Etéoklès, Phlégyas, Minyas." *Hommages à Georges Dumézil*, pp. 216–260. Brussels, 1960.

———, "Typhée": Vian, F. "Le mythe de Typhée et le problème de ses origines orientales." In *Eléments orientaux dans la religion grecque ancienne*, pp. 17–37. Proceedings of the Colloque de Strasbourg, 22–24 May 1958. Paris, 1960.

VIDAL-NAQUET, "Chasse et sacrifice": Vidal-Naquet, P. "Chasse et sacrifice dans l'*Orestie* d'Eschyle." In Vernant, *Mythe et tragédie*, pp. 133–158.

———, "Chasseur noir": Vidal-Naquet, P. "Le chasseur noir et l'origine de l'éphébie athénienne." *Annales E.S.C.* 23 (1968): 947–964. Reprinted in *Chasseur noir*, pp. 151–175.

———, *Chasseur noir*: Vidal-Naquet, P. *Le chasseur noir. Formes de pensée et formes de société dans le monde grec*. Paris, 1981.

VOLLGRAFF: Vollgraff, W. "Inscriptions d'Argos." *B.C.H.* 33 (1909): 171–200, 445–466.

VÜRTHEIM: Vürtheim, J. G. "De Carneis." *Mnemosyne* 31 (1903): 234–60.

WEISER: Weiser, L. *Altgermanische Junglingsweihen und Männerbunde.* Baden, 1927.

WEST: West, M. L. "The Dictaean Hymn to the Kouros." *J.H.S.* 85 (1965): 148–159.

WESTERMARCK: Westermarck, E. *The Origin and Development of the Moral Ideas.* 2 vols. London, 1908.

WIDE: Wide, S. *Lakonische Kulte.* Leipzig, 1893.

WILAMOWITZ, *Eur. Her.*: von Wilamowitz-Moellendorf, U., ed. *Euripides, Herakles.* Berlin, 1889.

———, *Glaube*: von Wilamowitz-Moellendorf, U. *Der Glaube der Hellenen.* 2 vols. Berlin, 1931–32. Reprint. 1960.

———, *Gr. Tr.*: von Wilamowitz-Moellendorf, U. *Die griechische Tragoedien.* Berlin, 1899.

———, *Isyllos*: von Wilamowitz-Moellendorf, U. *Isyllos von Epidauros.* Berlin, 1886.

WILL, *Korinthiaka*: Will, E. *Korinthiaka. Recherches sur l'histoire et la civilisation de Corinthe des origines aux guerres médiques.* Paris, 1955.

WILLETTS, *Code*: Willetts, R. F. *The Law Code of Gortyn, Kadmos.* Suppl. 1. Berlin, 1967.

———, *Cults*: Willetts, R. F. *Cretan cults and festivals.* London, 1962.

———, *Society*: Willetts, R. F. *Aristocratic Society in Crete.* London, 1955.

WILLIAMS: Williams, F. E. *Papuans of the Trans-Fly.* Oxford, 1936. Reprint. Oxford, 1969.

WINDEKENS: Windekens, A. J. van. "Réflexions sur la nature et l'origine du dieu Hermès." *Rhein. Mus.* 104 (1901): 289–301.

WIRZ: Wirz, P. *Die Marind-anim von Holländisch-Sud-Neuguinea.* 2 vols. (parts 1–4). Hamburg, 1922–25.

WUILLEUMIER: Wuilleumier, P. *Tarente, des origines à la conquête romaine.* Paris, 1939. Reprint. 1968.

YALOURIS: Yalouris, N. "Trouvailles mycéniennes et prémycéniennes de la région du sanctuaire d'Olympie." *Atti Prim. Congresso Stud. Mic.*, Rome. 1 (1967): 176–182.

YOSHIDA, "Survivances": Yoshida, A. "Survivances de la tripartition fonctionnelle en Grèce." *R.H.R.* 166 (1964): 21–38.

———, 1965: Yoshida, A. "Sur quelques coupes de la fable grecque." *R.E.A.* 67 (1965): 31–41.

INDEX

Dionysus Antheus, 246
Dionysus Saotes, 182
Dioscorides, 89
Dioscuri, 146, 173, 174, 252, 255, 260
Diotimus, 154–55; *Heracleia,* 154
Dipolia, 20
Disoteria, 20
Dogons, 38
Dorylaus, 149
Dotis, 129
Dover, K. J., 53–54, 58, 154, 206, 207, 209
Dumézil, Georges, 19–20, 21, 22, 24, 106, 140–41; *Problème des Centaures,* 247

Echemenes, 210, 211
Echo, 83, 98
Egeria, 125
Eidothea, 197
Eilatos, 157
Eileithyia, 164
Elacataeon, 163
Elacatas, 163, 164, 165
Elacatia, 163, 164
Elatos, 161
Eleusis, 181
Eleuther, 75
Eleutherios, 183
Enarsphorus, 163
Endymion, 126, 259
Enmann, A., 92
Epaminondas, 144, 217, 226
Ephebes' gymnasium, 116–17
Ephorus, 14, 16, 17, 31, 35, 47, 57, 211; and Cretan pederasty, 26–27, 28, 30, 33, 34, 37, 64, 109; Strabo's text based on, 2, 7, 12, 13, 25
Epimenides, 30, 187
Epops, 82, 83
Eramai, 8
Erastēs, 8
Erato, 85, 86
Erechtheus, 92, 128, 147
Ergatai, 164
Ergatia, 164
Erinyes, 99
Eritharses, 113
Erōmenos, 8

Eros, 37
Erysichthon, 130, 131
Erythrae, 200
Eteocles, 129
Etymologicum Magnum, 254
Euaechme, 173–74, 175
Euanthes, 201
Euboea, 183
Euenus, 222
Euhippus, 173–74, 175
Eumelus, 108
Eumenides, 236
Eumolpus, 128, 130, 169, 204
Euphemus, 161, 162, 235, 236
Euphorion, 157, 159, 160, 161, 162, 260
Euripides, 18, 66, 95, 110, 133, 144, 147, 190; *Alcestis,* 103, 119; *Bacchae,* 233; *Chrysippus,* 71; *The Heraclidae,* 147–48; *Hippolytus,* 132, 133, 134; *Iphigenia among the Taurians,* 236; *Suppliants,* 127
Europa, 114, 115, 161, 197
Eurybatus, 243; myth of, 235–38
Eurydice, 110, 123
Eurymedon, 172
Eurystheus, 125, 139, 140, 147, 148, 149, 154, 164, 241, 242
Eurythoe, 76
Eurytus, 92, 130, 197
Eustatius, 147
Euxynthetus, 29
Evans, Arthur J., 19, 209
Eypo, 82, 83

Fates, 103
Femina, 11
Foley, M., 50
Foster parentage, 68, 116, 132
Frazer, J. G., 89, 253
Freud, Sigmund, 2

Gaea, 99, 236, 237
Galatea, 247
Ganymedes, 28, 257, 260, 267; and Zeus, 18, 35, 63, 68, 205–13 *passim,* 251, 261, 267
Gernet, Louis, 17–18, 175
Gerschel, Lucien, 30

PAUL D. SANSONE, O.F.M.

880917   24.95 (22.45)